D1617354

Progress in Self Psychology
Editor, Arnold Goldberg, M.D.

Progress in Self Psychology invites articles relevant to psychoanalytic self psychology to be submitted for publication. Send the original manuscript (double-spaced with references) and three copies to:

Arnold Goldberg, M.D.
122 South Michigan Avenue
Chicago, IL 60603

If the article is accepted, a diskette will be required as well. All submissions are refereed. Papers will not be returned if unacceptable.

BASIC IDEAS RECONSIDERED

Progress in Self Psychology
Volume 12

Arnold Goldberg
editor

THE ANALYTIC PRESS

1996   Hillsdale, NJ   London

©1996 by The Analytic Press
101 West Street
Hillsdale, NJ 07642

ISBN 0-88163-228-7
ISSN 0893-5483

Printed in the United States of America
10 9 8 7 6 5 4 3 2 1

This volume is dedicated to

RICHARD C. MAROHN, M.D.

November 12, 1934–November 19, 1995

Acknowledgment

We would like to thank Ms. Christine Susman, who provided secretarial and editorial assistance.

Contents

Contributors

Howard A. Bacal, M.D., F.R.C.P.(C), Training and Supervising Analyst, Institute of Contemporary Psychoanalysis, Los Angeles; Supervising Analyst, Institute for the Study of Subjectivity, New York; Former Director, Training and Supervising Analyst, Toronto Institute for Psychoanalysis.

Howard S. Baker, M.D., Senior Attending Psychiatrist, Institute of Pennsylvania Hospital, Philadelphia; Clinical Associate Professor of Psychiatry, University of Pennsylvania, Philadelphia.

Margaret N. Baker, Ph.D., Adjunct Assistant Professor, Institute for Graduate Clinical Psychology, Widener University, West Chester, PA; Consulting Psychologist, Institute of Pennsylvania Hospital, Philadelphia.

Beatrice Beebe, Ph.D., Associate Clinical Professor, Psychology and Psychiatry, College of Physicians and Surgeons, Columbia University, Faculty, New York University Postdoctoral Program in Psychotherapy and Psychoanalysis.

Janice L. Crawford, M.S.W., N.C. Psy. A., Faculty, The Training and Research Institute for Self Psychology, New York City; private practice.

Shelley R. Doctors, Ph.D., Invited Faculty and Supervising Analyst, Institute for the Psychoanalytic Study of Subjectivity; Faculty and Supervisor, National Institute for the Psychotherapies.

Mark J. Gehrie, Ph.D., Faculty, Training and Supervising Analyst, Institute for Psychoanalysis, Chicago.

George A. Hagman, L.C.S.W., Clinical Director, F. S. DuBois Center, Stamford, CT; Visiting Faculty, Training and Research Institute for Self Psychology, New York City.

Daniel Kriegman, Ph.D., Faculty, Massachusetts Institute for Psycho-
analysis; Editor-in-Chief, *The Journal of Self Psychology*; Founding
Board Member, The New England Center for Self Psychology.
Frank M. Lachmann, Ph.D., Core Faculty, Institute for the Psychoana-
lytic Study of Subjectivity, New York; Training and Supervising
Analyst, Postgraduate Center for Mental Health; coauthor with
Joseph Lichtenberg and James Fosshage, *Self and Motivational
Systems* (The Analytic Press, 1992) and *The Clinical Exchange:
Techniques Derived from Self and Motivational Systems* (The
Analytic Press, 1996).
Martin S. Livingston, Ph.D., Faculty, Postgraduate Center for Mental
Health; Co-Chair, Association for Psychoanalytic Self Psychology,
New York.
David S. MacIsaac, Ph.D., Founding Member, The New York Institute
for Psychoanalytic Self Psychology; private practice, Englewood, NJ.
Joseph Palombo, M.A., Founding Dean, Institute of Clinical Social
Work, Chicago; Faculty, Child and Adolescent Psychotherapy Pro-
gram, Institute for Psychoanalysis, Chicago; Associate Director, Neu-
robehavioral Center, Department of Pediatrics, Rush-Presbyterian-St.
Luke's Medical Center.
Susann Pangerl, Ph.D., Unitarian-Universalist Minister; Diplomate,
American Association of Pastoral Counselors, Member, Clinical,
Training, and Supervisory Staff, Center for Religion and Psychother-
apy of Chicago.
Lallene J. Rector, Ph.D., Associate Professor, Psychology of Religion,
Garrett-Evangelical Theological Seminary, Evanston, IL.
John H. Riker, Ph.D., Professor of Philosophy, Colorado College;
Author *Ethics and the Discovery of the Unconscious* (in press).
Crayton E. Rowe, Jr., M.S.W., B.C.D. Founding Member and Faculty,
The New York Institute for Psychoanalytic Self Psychology; Past
Chair and Founder, National Membership Committee on Psychoanal-
ysis in Clinical Social Work.
Estelle Shane, Ph.D., Copresident, Training and Supervising Analyst,
Institute of Contemporary Psychoanalysis; Training and Supervising
Analyst, Los Angeles Psychoanalytic Society and Institute, CA.
Morton Shane, M.D., Copresident, Training and Supervising Analyst,
Institute of Contemporary Psychoanalysis; Training and Supervising
Analyst, Los Angeles Psychoanalytic Society and Institute, CA.
Ruth B. Suth, M.A., L.C.S.W., Graduate and Guest Lecturer, Child and
Adolescent Psychotherapy Program, Chicago Institute for Psycho-
analysis; Private Practice, Wilmette, IL.
Peter G. Thomson, M.D., Training and Supervising Analyst and Former
Director, Toronto Institute of Psychoanalysis, Toronto, Ontario.

Introduction: Notes on the Integration, Reformulation, and Development of Kohut's Contributions

Crayton E. Rowe, Jr.

As self psychology gains acceptance in the United States and throughout the world (Ornstein, 1993), Kohut's fundamental contributions have been integrated into a growing number of theoretically disparate self psychology treatment models. For example, Kohut's concepts of selfobject and selfobject transference are integral to the theories of intersubjectivity (Atwood and Stolorow, 1984, 1993; Stolorow, Brandchaft, and Atwood, 1987; Stolorow and Atwood, 1992), motivational systems (Lichtenberg, 1989; Lichtenberg, Lachmann, and Fosshage, 1992), and the selfobject and object relations dual transference model (Stolorow and Lachmann, 1981, 1984/1985).

In addition, Kohut's formulations have generated considerable debate within self psychology, and reformulations of his fundamental constructs have been proposed. For example, Kohut's conceptualization of an individual having an "innermost design" (1977) that will unfold spontaneously in the treatment if required selfobject experiences are made available has been challenged (Stolorow, 1994)[1]; Kohut's view that empathic observation requires long-term empathic immersion in the patient's experience has been rejected as unrealistic (Stolorow, 1993, 1994); suggestions have been made to allow for an object concept to be included within the theory of self psychology along with the selfobject concept (Shane and Shane, 1988); a reformulation of the concept of selfobject has been proposed that is more in keeping with object relations theory (Bacal, 1990a, b); Kohut's belief that optimal frustration is central to the accretion of self structure has been questioned, and replacement concepts of internalization and structure formation processes have been offered (Bacal, 1985; Terman, 1988); and further, it has been conceptualized that internalization leads only to a rearrangement of structure rather than an accretion of structure (Wolf, 1989).

The continuous efforts to integrate and reformulate Kohut's conceptualizations attest to the profound influence Kohut's contributions are continuing to make in the development of self psychology theory.

However, the value of Kohut's contributions to the development of theory depends on how well his conceptualizations are understood and differentiated from other theories. I am referring here to the distinctions between theories constituting the specific dissimilarities that differentiate one theory from another.

In his final public address, Kohut (1981) stressed the need for careful discrimination and analysis of theory so that theoretical distinctions could be understood. He was concerned that the distinctions between his theories and Freud's were not sufficiently understood primarily because Freud's theories were not sufficiently understood:

> You know, I know my classical analysis so well; and that . . . because I do think that my colleagues don't. They don't even know anymore what I am arguing about. But they have made compromises in a vague way. I never do that anymore. I never think that way anymore. I believe all that. But nobody has ever faced up to the issue as the issue deserves. Freud was a genius. This is no way of treating Freud—to by-pass him [p. 529].

The problem of perceiving a concept's distinctions becomes more difficult when there is an effort at integrating it within another theoretical paradigm. The concept's distinctions become obscured since the

---

[1] Stolorow is in accord with Gill's (1994) objection to Kohut's conceptualization of an overall program of the self that will unfold spontaneously (within the context of developing selfobject transferences) if required selfobject experiences are made available. Gill's objection reflects the social-constructivist view (Hoffman, 1991).

concept is necessarily modified through its integration. Modifications of the same concept within disparate paradigms are necessarily diverse as each modification conforms to the premise of the individual paradigm. Therefore, one can conclude that the integration of the concepts of selfobject and selfobject transference in the self psychology treatment models referred to previously (intersubjectivity model, motivational systems model, and selfobject and object relations dual transference model) obscure, in different ways, the clinical distinctions intrinsic to these concepts—especially regarding how and to what extent selfobject transferences develop.

To be aware of the distinctions that are clouded through the integration of a particular concept, one has to have an awareness of the concept's distinctions before integration. For example, if we are to be aware of the distinctions that are obscured through the integration of the concept of selfobject transference in the preceding paradigms, we must be clear as to Kohut's understanding. Kohut gave us his final view in his posthumously published work of 1984. He reminded us that the focal point of treatment in self psychology was the development of the self-object transferences. As the selfobject transferences unfold, the analyst must be able to differentiate their various forms in order to understand the specific developmental needs of the patient. Kohut (1984) stated:

> The ability to differentiate between various types of selfobject transferences also gives us the opportunity to study in greater detail the developmental line characteristically associated with the archaic form of a particular self–selfobject relationship—from the archaic state that is revived at the beginning of the transference to the mature state which, as a result of the systematic and patiently pursued working-through process, may be attained at the end of successful analyses [p. 202].

A concept's distinctions are easily recognized when there is an effort to reformulate the concept. In reformulations the primary emphasis is on the delineation of distinctions in order to demonstrate the need for reformulation. For example, distinctions inherent in the concepts of selfobject and optimal frustration and proposed reformulations of those concepts have been widely debated and given considerable attention in the literature (see Bacal, 1985, 1988, 1990a, b; Terman, 1988).

Unlike a concept that is modified through integration, or through reformulation, a concept that evolves from its distinguishing characteristics retains its essential distinctions. It can be valued as a "true addition" to the concept, as it adds to the concept without challenging it (Goldberg, 1984/1985). For example, Wolf's (1976, 1980) introduction of ally–antagonist (adversarial) selfobject needs was a true addition to Kohut's concept of selfobject and selfobject transferences.

Limiting the awareness and exploration of distinctions between theories would be as unfortunate for the development of recently introduced self psychology paradigms as for the development of Kohut's fundamental constructs. The development of any concept depends on the development of its unique and differentiating characteristics.

We must pursue the distinctions evident in a particular theory within the context of what the theory determines as valid clinical data and valid methods of obtaining the data. This requires an awareness of the clinical process that led to formation of the theory. For example, if we are to develop the distinctions evident in Kohut's theoretical formulations, we must be aware that his discoveries were born out of the introspective empathic approach (1959, 1968a, b, 1971, 1977, 1981, 1984). Furthermore, we must be aware that Kohut believed it was only through a strict adherence to the experience-near mode of observation that the analyst could arrive at an awareness and an understanding of the unique complexities of the patient's mental life and especially the intricacies of the patient's selfobject needs. His discoveries (1977) took place over time and evolved from his "commitment to a methodology of the observer's long-term empathic immersion in the psychological field—in particular, with regard to clinical phenomena, of his long-term, empathic immersion in the transference" (pp. xxi–xxii). Kohut (1984) refined his definition in more operational terms: "The best definition of empathy— the analogue to my terse scientific definition of empathy as 'vicarious introspection'—is that it is the capacity to think and feel oneself into the inner life of another person" (p. 82). The development of Kohut's constructs, therefore, depends on a commitment to the experience-near mode of observation.

The distinctions intrinsic to Kohut's formulations have only begun to be explored. For instance, Kohut urged that the developmental lines of his discoveries of the three major selfobject needs—mirroring, idealizing, and twinship—be investigated. He thought that much of the work remains to be done, especially in the area of exploring the special needs of adolescents and the elderly as they face changing life circumstances. Kohut (1984) acknowledged that varieties of selfobject transferences are yet to be discovered: "there are still transferences—probably varieties of selfobject transferences—that have not yet been discovered and which, therefore, remain unanalyzed" (1984, p. 209).

The need for the discovery is indisputable if we are to become aware and understand the scope of developmental selfobject requirements. Only through discovery can we begin to analyze the heretofore unanalyzed selfobject needs of our patients.

However, discoveries of new forms of selfobject transferences have thus far been limited. With the exception of the introduction of the adversarial selfobject transference (Wolf, 1976, 1980), which has been largely neglected (Lichtenberg, 1990), there has been little in the literature that has illustrated new paradigms of selfobject transferences.[2] It can be suggested that this lack is a result of the resistance to in-depth exploration. Kohut warned that the experience-near mode of observation necessarily exacerbates the analyst's anxieties through lengthy periods of tolerating the unfamiliar and at times divergent directions of the patient's experience. Dread of helplessness and inactivity can solidify resistances to in-depth exploration (1959).[3] Perhaps it is this resistance that also explains the lack of attention in the literature to the development of the empathic mode of observation. It can be suggested that this lack is a serious omission, as discoveries of new forms of selfobject transferences are dependent on our ability to perceive new editions of selfobject needs with which we are familiar and those selfobject needs with which we are not familiar. We must be able to perceive the developmental aspects of these selfobject experiences in order to justify a new classification of these experiences as selfobject transferences (Kohut, 1984).[4]

Kohut (1984) was also clear that his discoveries were an expansion of analytic understanding rather than a deviation from traditional theory: "Self psychology does not advocate a change in the essence of analytic technique. The transferences are allowed to unfold and their analysis—the understanding of the transference reactions, their explanation in dynamic and genetic terms—occupies, now as before, the center of the analyst's attention" (p. 208). He added: "Self psychology is at one with the technical principle that interpretation in general, and the interpretation of transferences in particular, is the major instrumentality of therapeutic psychoanalysis" (p. 210).

The integration and reformulation of Kohut's contributions have been integral to the rapid evolution of self psychology theory. However, as theoretical positions proliferate and become more disparate, and distinctions are explored and developed, self psychology will be faced with the inevitable threats of divisiveness that have been characteristic of the growth of psychoanalysis in general. Divisiveness can be considered

---

[2] Wolf considered the vitalization-attunement experience, introduced by Stern (1985) as "vitality affects," a selfobject experience (Hunter, 1992).

[3] Kohut (1981), in his final extemporaneous address at the Fifth Conference on Self Psychology at Berkeley, California, expressed his concern about the persistent misinterpretation and devaluation of empathy as merely supportive.

[4] Dr. David MacIsaac and I (1989) have attempted to contribute to refining the experience-near mode of observation through developing a form of receptivity that we have termed "expanding attunement."

symptomatic of theoretical allegiances that disallow the acceptance of unique and differentiating distinctions between theories.[5]

Ironically, psychoanalysis seems more willing to accept divisiveness than its distinctions between its theories. Divisiveness surfaces as three distinct groups.

Goldberg sees three distinct divisions having developed in terms of how the analyst translates between psychoanalytic theories. Individuals can be classified as integrationists, compromisers, and anarchists. The integrationists attempt to bring divergent concepts together through translation; the compromisers believe that there can be an all-inclusive umbrella theory; and the anarchists sharpen differences for the purpose of emphasizing the incompatibility of different theories and denying any commonality of meaning (1984/1985).

Bergmann (1993) also recognizes three distinct groups that have developed within psychoanalysis as the result of an inability to find productive ways of communicating different views. He distinguishes the divisions in terms of how contributors to psychoanalytic theory are classified. He concludes that contributors can be viewed as three types: heretics, modifiers, and extenders. Heretics are considered to be outside psychoanalysis; modifiers are considered to contribute concepts that preserve Freud's concepts in that they evolve from his concepts; extenders expand psychoanalytic concepts without any modification.

Speaking to the development of psychoanalysis in general, Goldberg (1984/1985) provides a necessary direction for the growth of self psychology:

> The need is not for psychoanalysis to still the voices of dissent or discordance in the name of unity or familiarity or fidelity. We do not seem to lack for our cadre of orthodoxy. Rather, we need more, not less, bold and imaginative theories. Psychoanalysis suffers not from too much difference but rather from too little courage in staking out the unexplored for fear of being deposed and alienated [p. 133].

This volume of *Progress in Self Psychology* is another in a series of exciting collections of theoretical and clinical papers that clearly "stakes out the unexplored" and adds to self psychology's growing body of knowledge.

Riker's contribution examines Kohut's theory of the bipolar self independent of its clinical functions. He shows how Kohut's theory

---

[5]Divisiveness can be extreme. A familiar example is Freud's response to Adler's introduction of his theory of organ inferiority and masculine protest as a reformulation of the genesis of neuroses. Freud (1914) considered Adler's formulation to despoil the basic principles of psychoanalysis: "I must point out how all the psychological acquisitions of psycho-analysis have been thrown to the winds by Adler" (p. 56).

incorporates significant aspects of the self as elucidated in Western philosophical thought.

Kriegman contributes to our understanding of the empathic stance. Rather than solely focusing on maintaining a subjective position, he advocates a more natural evolutionary psychoanalytic model that includes an emphasis on deception, self deception, and distortion in human communication.

Bacal and Thompson wonder if self psychology demands too much of the analyst by requiring the renunciation of the analyst's selfobject needs. The authors argue that the analyst's selfobject needs are significantly affected by his or her selfobject experience in relation to the patient. The analyst's recognizing the legitimacy of his or her selfobject needs enhances the capacity to respond meaningfully. They wonder if analysts cannot sometimes give covert and overt expression to their aversive attitude when their selfobject needs are not met by the patient.

Gehrie's chapter considers the technical use of empathy with patients whose underlying structure is organized around adaptation to negative experiences. He presents clinical vignettes to illustrate innovative approaches at reaching the patient's seemingly inaccessible core experience.

Livingston contributes his understanding of a subtle form of impasse that can develop with the "nondifficult" patient. He presents eight consecutive sessions that highlight the working through of an impasse considered to be an intersubjective conjunction as differentiated from the familiar and stormy intersubjective disjunction.

MacIsaac's chapter highlights his concern that Kohut's view of the concept of optimal frustration is being devalued by some theorists. MacIsaac presents a case of a borderline woman whose treatment progressed primarily as a result of his understanding Kohut's meaning of this concept.

Shane and Shane review the literature regarding what is considered optimal in the clinical situation. They offer their concept of "optimal restraint" to guide therapists so that their responses are neither in excess or so withholding as to interfere with the treatment. Doctors recognize the importance of the Shanes' concept in that it preserves the clinical benefit of traditional analytic reserve without fixing technique within drive theory. Doctors emphasize that attention be paid to the intersubjective field in which the treatment takes place and suggest that analysts be prepared to understand what is being evoked in them in order to respond optimally.

Lachmann and Beebe show how concepts of self and mutual regulation, derived from a system approach to the study of infant-caregivers, can contribute to a theory of therapeutic action in adult treatment. They

describe the treatment of an adult suicidal patient to illustrate the contribution of mutual and self regulation theory to the analytic process.

Suth offers a clinical presentation of self psychological treatment of
a five-year-old vulnerable boy. The treatment includes collaborative
parental involvement. Shane discusses Suth's presentation and eluci-
dates the effectiveness of her treatment.

Baker and Baker present clinical material about attention deficit/
hyperactive disorder (AD/HD) in adults. In addition they offer a self
psychology–biopsychosocial schema that shows the interactive nature of
forces that interfere with the development and maintenance of a consolidated self. Palombo, in his discussion of the Bakers's chapter, highlights the importance of their contribution. Palombo points out that biological endowment has been a neglected area in self psychology and
agrees with the Bakers that it is important to distinguish between selfobject deficits and primary neuroregulatory deficits in patients with attention deficit/hyperactivity disorder.

Pangerl looks at the gender-related aspects of self psychology specific
to females. She delineates the patriarchal components of self-psychological theory as an effort to make possible a fuller appreciation of self
psychology's contributions to the psychological and cultural concerns of
feminism.

Rector addresses the significance of gendered representations of God
and the role of early selfobject experiences in an individual's preference
for a masculine or feminine God image. Rector urges us to take seriously the role of the gendered experience and its relation to the selfobject functions that religion provides for some patients.

This volume clearly shows that self psychology is on a promising trajectory and continues to fulfill its potential (Ornstein, 1993). We can
benefit more fully from its growing number of contributions by careful
analysis of the uniqueness of each. We must first recognize that fears
of accepting differences between theories pervade psychoanalysis
(Goldberg, 1984/1985) and can prevent the careful analysis needed to
perceive distinctions.

REFERENCES

Atwood, G. & Stolorow, R. (1984), *Structures of Subjectivity: Explorations in Psy-
choanalytic Phenomenology.* Hillsdale, NJ: The Analytic Press.
—— (1993), *Faces in a Cloud: Intersubjectivity in Personality Theory.* Northvale,
NJ: Aronson.
Bacal, H. (1985), Optimal responsiveness and the therapeutic process. In: *Progress in
Self Psychology, Vol. 1,* ed. A. Goldberg. New York: Guilford, pp. 202–227.

—— (1988), Reflections on "optimal frustration." In: *Learning from Kohut: Progress in Self Psychology, Vol. 4,* ed. A. Goldberg. Hillsdale, NJ: The Analytic Press, pp. 127–131.

—— (1990a), Does an object relations theory exist in self psychology? *Psychoanal. Inq.,* 10:197–220.

—— (1990b), The elements of a corrective selfobject experience. *Psychoanal. Inq.,* 10:347–372.

Bergmann, M. S. (1993), Reflections on the history of psychoanalysis. *J. Amer. Psychoanal. Assn.,* 41:929–955.

Freud, S. (1914), On the history of the psychoanalytic movement. *Standard Edition,* 14:7–66. London: Hogarth Press, 1957.

Gill, M. (1994), Heinz Kohut's self psychology. In: *A Decade of Progress: Progress in Self Psychology, Vol. 10,* ed. A. Goldberg. Hillsdale, NJ: The Analytic Press, pp. 197–211.

Goldberg, A. (1984/1985), Translation between psychoanalytic theories. *The Annual of Psychoanalysis,* 12/13:121–135. New York: International Universities Press.

Hoffman, I. Z. (1991), Discussion: Toward a social-constructivist view of the psychoanalytic situation. *Psychoanal. Dial.,* 1:74–105.

Hunter, V. (1992), An interview with Ernest Wolf. Part II: The analytic years to 1990. *Psychoanal. Rev.,* 79:481–507.

Kohut, H. (1959). Introspection, empathy, and psychoanalysis: An examination of the relationship between mode of observation and theory. In: *The Search for the Self, Vol. 1,* ed. P. Ornstein. New York: International Universities Press, 1978, pp. 205–232.

—— (1968a), Introspection and empathy: Further thoughts about their role in psychoanalysis. In: *The Search for the Self, Vol. 3,* ed. P. Ornstein. Madison, CT: International Universities Press, 1990, pp. 83–101.

—— (1968b), The psychoanalytic treatment of narcissistic personality disorders: Outline of a systematic approach In: *The Search for the Self, Vol. 1,* ed. P. Ornstein. New York: International Universities Press, 1978, pp. 477–509.

—— (1971), *The Analysis of the Self.* New York: International Universities Press.

—— (1977), *The Restoration of the Self.* New York: International Universities Press.

—— (1981), On empathy. In: *The Search for the Self, Vol. 4,* ed. P. Ornstein. Madison, CT: International Universities Press, 1991, pp. 525–535.

—— (1984), *How Does Analysis Cure?* ed. A. Goldberg & P. Stepansky. Chicago: The University of Chicago Press.

Lichtenberg, J. (1989), *Psychoanalysis and Motivation.* Hillsdale, NJ: The Analytic Press.

—— (1990), Rethinking the scope of the patient's transference and the therapist's counterresponsiveness. In: *The Realities of the Transference: Progress in Self Psychology, Vol. 6,* ed. A. Goldberg. Hillsdale, NJ: The Analytic Press, pp. 23–33.

—— Lachmann, F. & Fosshage, J. (1992), *Self and Motivational Systems: Toward a Theory of Psychoanalytic Technique.* Hillsdale, NJ: The Analytic Press.

Ornstein, P. (1993), Introduction: Is self psychology on a promising trajectory. In: *The Widening Scope of Self Psychology: Progress in Self Psychology, Vol. 9,* ed. A. Goldberg. Hillsdale, NJ: The Analytic Press, pp. 1–11.

Rowe, C. & MacIsaac, D. (1989), *Empathic Attunement: The "Technique" of Psychoanalytic Self Psychology.* Northvale, NJ: Aronson.

Shane, M. & Shane, E. (1988), Pathways to integration: Adding to the self psychology model. In: *Learning from Kohut: Progress in Self Psychology, Vol. 4,* ed. A. Goldberg. Hillsdale, NJ: The Analytic Press, pp. 71–78.

Stern, D. (1985). *The Interpersonal World of the Infant.* New York: Basic Books.

Stolorow, R. (1993), Thoughts on the nature and therapeutic action of psychoanalytic interpretation. In: *The Widening Scope of Self Psychology: Progress in Self Psychology, Vol. 9,* ed. A. Goldberg. Hillsdale, NJ: The Analytic Press, pp. 31–43.

—— (1994), Kohut, Gill, and the new psychoanalytic paradigm. In: *A Decade of Progress: Progress in Self Psychology, Vol. 10,* ed. A. Goldberg. Hillsdale, NJ: The Analytic Press, pp. 221–226.

—— & Atwood, G. (1992), *Contexts of Being: The Intersubjective Foundations of Psychological Life.* Hillsdale, NJ: The Analytic Press.

—— Brandchaft, B. & Atwood, G. (1987), *Psychoanalytic Treatment: An Intersubjective Approach.* Hillsdale, NJ: The Analytic Press.

—— & Lachmann, F. (1981), Two psychoanalyses or one? *Psychoanal. Rev.,* 68:307–319.

—— & —— (1984/1985), Transference: The future of an illusion. *The Annual of Psychoanalysis,* 12/13:19–37. New York: International Universities Press.

Terman, D. (1988), Optimum frustration: Structuralization and the therapeutic process. In: *Learning from Kohut: Progress in Self Psychology, Vol. 4,* ed. A. Goldberg. Hillsdale, NJ: The Analytic Press, pp. 113–125.

Wolf, E. S. (1976), Ambience and abstinence. *The Annual of Psychoanalysis,* New York: International Universities Press, 4:101–115.

—— (1980), On the developmental line of selfobject relations. In: *Advances in Self Psychology,* ed. A. Goldberg. New York: International Universities Press, pp. 117–130.

—— (1989). Therapeutic experiences. In: *Dimensions of Self Experience: Progress in Self Psychology, Vol. 5,* ed. A. Goldberg. Hillsdale, NJ: The Analytic Press, pp. 105–119.

I

Frustration
and
Responsiveness

Chapter 1

Optimal Frustration: An Endangered Concept

David S. MacIsaac

In recent years there has been a reexamination in the self psychology literature of the concept of optimal frustration. Although Kohut (1971, 1977, 1984) was insistent that optimal frustration is an essential aspect of the curative process, a number of authors (Bacal, 1985, 1988; Socarides and Stolorow, 1985; Terman, 1988; Bacal and Newman, 1990) have raised questions about its significance for cure and have recommended that the term be replaced by alternative constructs. The purpose of this chapter is to review these criticisms in light of the critical implications that such suggestions might hold for the theory and practice of self psychology.[1]

OPTIMAL FRUSTRATION: KOHUT'S VIEW

Though Kohut's concept of optimal frustration is well known, a brief review is necessary for the later discussion.

Although Kohut (1972) credits Bernfeld (1928) with first using the term, the idea of optimal frustration was used in classical analysis (Freud, 1946) in reference to the neutralization of drive energy and was later taken up by Kohut in reference to the internalization of selfobject functions. Through his experience-near empathic treatment stance, Kohut (1984) came to recognize that cure (i.e., "transmuting internalization") in

---

[1] I would like to express my thanks to Crayton E. Rowe, Jr. for his invaluable suggestions in the writing of this chapter.

psychoanalysis and the wholesome development of the self during child-hood occur via an initial two-step process.[2]

First, there must be a basic empathic attunement between the self and its selfobjects. In the therapeutic setting this attunement or bond is a secondary, by-product effect of the analyst's empathic intent of attempting to gain access to the inner life of his patient. It is not the result, as Kohut (1981a, b, 1984) frequently pointed out in his later writings, of an act of kindness or sympathy, or attempting to cure one's patients through love.

Second, manageable and minor nontraumatic failures of the empathic connectedness between the patient's self and the selfobject analyst must occur. Kohut termed these failures *optimal frustrations* and viewed them as inevitable occurrences in a therapeutic setting in which one human being attempts to grasp the inner life of another for the purpose of understanding and explaining.

Countless repetitions of this two-step sequence of basic attunement and optimal frustration over the course of a self-psychological analysis result in the internalization of impersonal functions associated with the selfobject analyst. In turn this leads to an increased resilience and capac-ity of the self to withstand the inevitable empathic failures both in and out of the analytic setting. This sequence prepares the self for an even-tual shift from early archaic self-selfobject bond to higher forms of self–selfobject relatedness normally associated with adult life.

From where do these frustrations spring? They may occur as the con-sequence of a number of factors, the most fundamental of which is the attitude (conscious or unconscious) of the analyst. Depending on the degree of resolution of the analyst's own self-disorder and his accompa-nying clinical stance, frustrations may range along a continuum from optimal to traumatic. At the same time real and concrete frustrations are part and parcel of the framework of treatment in such parameters as the analyst's abstinence, regular payment of fees, scheduled appointment times, the 45- or 50-minute hour, use of the couch, separations, and so on. However, the analyst's capacity to be attuned moment-to-moment to the experience of his patient and his ability to respond appropriately will determine whether the frustrations associated with these conditions are experienced as optimal or traumatic.

Kohut (1984) observed that even when the analyst's empathic com-munications are more or less correct, they still contain a modicum of frustration. This is so, Kohut argued, because 1) even when the analyst

---

2 This two-step process subsumes a three-step sequence that Kohut (1984) speaks of later as 1) reactivation of need, 2) nonresponse by the selfobject, and 3) reestablishment of a bond of empathy between self and selfobject.

successfully understands his patient, he is still not acting in accord with the patient's needs; 2) even if the analyst wished to meet the need, it would still not be possible since one "cannot find a non-traumatic relationship toward infantile needs" (Kohut, 1987, p. 92); 3) in treatment, as "formerly abandoned areas of development are again allowed to be reactivated in a setting that promises to be comparatively nontraumatic" (Kohut, 1987, p. 103), trauma associated with these emerging infantile needs is also reactivated; 4) and finally, an analyst's basically empathic communication is always optimally frustrating rather than optimally gratifying because ". . . through the analyst's more or less accurate understanding, an empathic bond is established (reestablished) between analyst and patient that substitutes for the de facto fulfillment of the patient's need" (Kohut, 1984, p. 103). Thus, Kohut (1987) is clear that "there is never any need—and by never, I mean never—there is never any need to be artificially traumatic. Simply to give the best you can give is traumatic enough, because you cannot fulfill the real needs" (p. 91).

It is important to note that Kohut (1984) postulated for future research the possibility that transmuting internalization can take place without the intermediate step of frustration. However, this postulate was not meant to do away with his longtime insistence that cure comes about through the two-step sequence outlined previously.

CRITICS OF OPTIMAL FRUSTRATION

A number of theorists within self psychology have been critical of the concept of optimal frustration and have suggested that it be replaced by alternative constructs that more accurately reflect how cure occurs.

Terman (1988) views the concept of optimal frustration as an outmoded holdover from drive theory, maintaining that it "has acquired the quality of moral purity, if not righteousness" (p. 114). He hypothesizes that internalization and structure formation have little to do with frustration. Like Terman, Socarides and Stolorow (1985) deemphasize optimal frustration as necessary for the development of structure. They state: "what is decisive is the responsiveness of the selfobject milieu to the child's depressive (and other) reactions. We are thus shifting the emphasis from 'optimal frustration' to the centrality of affect attunement" (p. 113, fn 3). Bacal (1985) considers optimal frustration as a method or approach with patients that has as its goal "not complying [with the needs of the patient] but trying just to understand and interpret" (p. 220). He classifies it as a form of manipulation, whereby the analyst makes "calculated errors thought to lead to manageable disruptions . . . and, thus, to transmuting internalization through the associated optimal frustration and its understanding" (p. 207). Thus, Bacal calls into question the fundamental significance of optimal frustration as necessary to psychological growth. He considers that this concept should be replaced by "optimal responsiveness," which he defines as "the responsivity of the analyst that is therapeutically most relevant at any particular moment in the context of a particular patient and his illness" (p. 202). In accord with his own thinking, Bacal (1988) welcomes Terman's (1988) replacement concept "dialogue of construction" as a process by which structure is formed through a repetition of dialogue that creates an enduring pattern. While Bacal recognizes empathy as the means by which the analyst tunes in to the patient's inner world, he characterizes optimal responsiveness as the analyst's "acts of communicating" his understanding. Thus, by his concept of optimal responsiveness, Bacal focuses on the analyst's "acts" or responses as the prime ingredient of analytic cure.

For Bacal (1988), frustration has no value in the treatment, especially when it is persistent: "When interpretations persistently fail to provide this experience [optimal responsiveness] for the patient . . . , then apart from the possibility that the interpretations may be wrong, the likelihood of traumatic frustration in the patient's early childhood must be considered . . ." (p. 130). In such an instance he suggests that an action be taken that may go beyond the normal parameters of treatment such as an adjustment of fee, changing appointments, and so on.

THE VALUE OF OPTIMAL FRUSTRATION—A CLINICAL VIGNETTE

I would now like to turn to a vignette that illustrates how my appreciation of the curative process via optimal frustration was integral to the psychological growth of my patient. The vignette also exemplifies how maintaining my empathic focus in the face of my patient's persistent frustrations and rage resulted in the development of the selfobject transferences and an expanded understanding that otherwise would not have been realized.

Introduction

Ms. B, a 27-year-old single woman, was referred by a colleague who had treated her for four years and felt he could no longer be helpful. He thought that this "borderline woman had insatiable demands," which made the treatment untenable for him. This had been her second treatment experience; she had previously been seen by another analyst shortly after she had dropped out of college owing to "intense anxiety and an inability to concentrate on her studies." In the interim she held down various clerical and secretarial jobs, but was consistently laid off because she was unable to complete assignments without demanding assistance from her fellow employees. Whenever demands were placed on her, she became highly anxious and frequently exploded in rage. She was described as being extremely anxious and "obsessed with rituals of cleaning." She was an only child and lived alone in her own apartment, supported by her wealthy parents. She had been evaluated psychiatrically on numerous occasions, but refused to take any medication because she felt it could be harmful to her physical health.

Ms. B was also described as having a number of strengths. She was personable, witty, and attractive, and maintained a regular routine of exercise at a local health club. She was highly intelligent and graduated from high school with honors. She enjoyed literature and writing, and had published a number of poems earlier in her school paper.

The Initial Session

When Ms. B called to set up an appointment, she announced in a faint voice that she had been directed to call and that I was to tell her when to come in. I felt I could have offered her any appointment time and she would have accepted, because I sensed that she had little or no regard for the importance of her own schedule. She immediately agreed to the first appointment I offered and quickly hung up.

When Ms. B entered my office, I sensed a sheepish and submissive quality. After I introduced myself, she stood motionless and silent, as if expecting me to direct her every move. After sitting, she remained silent. I wondered if she could share what she thought important for me to know. She looked into my eyes but made no effort to speak. I wondered if it was difficult for her to get started. Still looking into my eyes, she suddenly blurted out, "So what do you want me to talk about?" Without waiting for a reply, she mentioned how her other therapists always began the sessions by asking her questions. Then, with a flood of words she anxiously described the "horrible" feelings about initiating discussion: "I always hate when there is silence—it feels like an awful burden and pressure—that's when my thoughts start to go out of control and I feel like I just want to shut down my brain. . . ." Barely taking a breath, she spoke nonstop and said: "I resent you wanting me to speak. If I talk, I'll run over you with my words and become dominant."

Her words flowed in rapid fire and I sensed a building intensity as if she would explode with anxiety and frustration. I thought it important to communicate my awareness of her anxiety, but there now seemed no place for me to intervene without breaking her flow of intensity.

She described her feelings of hopelessness about treatment, especially since her former therapist admitted that he did not feel he could be
of further help and referred her to me. Then, just as suddenly as she had
begun, she broke off her flow of words and implored, "Do you feel you
can help me?"

Recognizing her intense concern and worry, I said, "I realize that this
is of deep concern to you, whether I can be of help."

I sensed an initial acceptance and then a sudden recoiling as she
snapped at me with anger: "I don't care about your concern—I want you
to answer my question—tell me, yes or no."

Staying with her experience, I said, "It sounds like nothing will suffice,
like you need some proof."

"You're right," she responded, "I need proof. If you can't prove it to
me right now, then what good are you? I need promises."

I sensed a sadness welling up as she appeared to be holding back
tears. I remarked, "I think you're feeling so very sad right now."

She nodded approvingly but abruptly fired back, "So what, if I am? I
still don't know if you can help me, but I guess that's just a stupid question. The other therapists told me they could help me, but they didn't—
they made promises, but they failed. Nothing works."

With increasing intensity, she continued: "My therapists have not
been smart enough because I still have my stupid problems. I thought
therapists are supposed to be smart—I've had dumb ones—they've failed.
How can I be sure you're smart enough and won't fail me like the others?" Looking around the room, she added, "You have a lot of books—
probably more books than the others had in their offices. You're not
going to find a case like me in those books. They're for normal people
and I'm not normal—I'm a sick person." Scowling at me, she queried:
"Do you think I'm sick? Do you think that therapy is for someone like
me? Or is it just for people who have jobs and can function in life? Can
you help me? Answer me!"

In the face of her angry demand, as I continued my immersion in her
experience, I came to an understanding of the depths of her frustration
and despair—like a psychic "black hole," where she was nothing but a
despicable wretch, a forsaken and forlorn "little girl," desperate for comfort but hopeless that it could ever be attained.

Attempting to capture this experience, I said, "Yes, it's hopeless to
feel you could ever get help, that therapy could ever be helpful to someone like you."

"You're damned right. I've been in therapy for so many years and it
hasn't helped. I'm worse now than before—at least before, I could do
things: go to school, have friends, think about a relationship. Now I'm

enslaved to my apartment, obsessed with cleaning and wishing I were dead."

Again, I sensed a certain sadness as her tone softened and she went on to tell of a painful compulsion that she called "hell cleaning," an every-other-weekend cleaning ritual of scrubbing the tiles in her bathroom for up to 10 or 12 hours. She described this experience as "being enslaved to a cruel taskmaster, and compelled to follow a rite of cleaning every tile in a prescribed sequence while scouring in a counterclockwise direction." She desperately wanted to free herself of this "painful" process, but felt terrified of ever giving it up. As she spoke uninterruptedly about "hell cleaning," and the contradictory fact that she could not get herself to vacuum or dust the rest of her apartment, I sensed that she was calmer, as if thoughts about this "hellish" process had some tranquilizing effect on her.

Then, just before the end of the session, as if she had an awareness of the time, she suddenly announced with resignation, "I know I have no choice. I have to come at least twice a week—I don't know if you have time—I especially don't know if you have time that fits with my volunteer job." She agreed reluctantly to two suggested times, as if she had been commanded, and then stood up to leave. Walking toward the door, she turned and said hesitatingly, "So, I guess you're not going to make any promises like my other therapists did, and you want me to speak—I don't know—this scares and angers me." She then walked quickly out the door.

Treatment Summary and History

Let me summarize briefly Ms. B's treatment before reporting a portion of a session in the third year, just prior to Ms. B's increasing her frequency to three sessions weekly. It is important to note that identifying data, without altering anything essential to the case, have been disguised to preserve confidentiality.

Ms. B's initial consultation occurred just before my summer break. During our second session she stated that I failed to understand her during our first session. When I explored what she meant, she said that I did not "give answers" or "direct the treatment" by asking leading questions. This disappointment and anger continued throughout the first year of treatment, even escalating in the second. Not infrequently during this period, she would shriek distressingly in the high-pitched and tormented tone of a very young child: "You're expecting too much of me. You think I'm normal just like your other patients—don't you understand that I'm sick, that I can't do this by myself?" Through my expanding attunement (Rowe and MacIsaac, 1989) to her shifting states of thinking and feeling, I came to understand the intolerable fragmentation anxiety associated with the expression of her independent thoughts and opinions. Lapses of silence during sessions were experienced as aloneness and terror. She thought that if she spoke, she should tell all her thoughts and would fail at accurately describing them. During her occasional moments of self-reflection in sessions, she would admit that she could only think about "meaningful issues away from" my office. This was reinforced in an occasional note left at my door or in messages recorded on my phone tape.

An obsession that plagued her and occupied many of the early sessions was what she had spoken of in the initial session as "hell cleaning." Though she complained bitterly of her "painful enslavement" to this "arduous and gruesome task," we gradually came to understand that there was an addictive aspect to it that protected her against the fear of "going crazy." She described the ritual as a trancelike state, in which she became mesmerized by the repetitive motion while being oblivious to the passage of time. She described herself as "snapping back" into consciousness and having no recollection of her activity.

Early History

In written notes that she would occasionally leave outside my office door, she wondered if her "hell cleaning" ritual was not connected to her memories of her mother, an intrusive and overprotective woman who "spent most of her days dusting and cleaning the house." Ms. B occasionally joked that her mother was "allergic to her," because she could not tolerate Ms. B's incessant talking, an aspect of their relationship that Ms. B felt went back as long as she could remember. She also described the mother as a highly anxious person who seemed panicked by the slightest problem. She recalls her hovering "like a black cloud over the home," constantly reminding her daughter not "to make a mess and to be careful" with anything she did.

She recalled being terrified of going to school and taking more than a year to adjust to preschool. When she did, she accelerated to the top of her class academically and became the teacher's pet in most grades.

Her father, a highly successful entrepreneur, treated her differently than her mother had treated her. He was calmer, less excitable, and enjoyed spending time with her. He frequently took her out for special treats, during which times she remembers his occasionally speaking about difficulties in his work. During these talks, she always recalled feeling overwhelmed by the thought of growing up and becoming an adult.

In high school she developed a small clique of friends that was considered by the other students as the "fringe element" in the school. She developed a relationship with a boy in junior year, which continued through her senior year. Though the boyfriend went off to college with her and they were even thinking of getting engaged, thoughts of marriage were upsetting to her. Eventually, in her sophomore year, the intensification of her obsessional thinking resulted in the breakup of her relationship and her dropping out of college.

Treatment Summary (Continued)

While her anger continued and even escalated through the second and into the early part of the third year of treatment, I sensed a significant change. Rather than being merely an expression of reactive helplessness, her anger took on a lively and almost humorous quality. For example, when I spoke, she ridiculed my "slow delivery" as an indication of my "mediocre intelligence." If I responded with more than a few brief sentences, she cut me off and told me that I'm "not making any sense." When she begrudgingly acknowledged that I may have understood her, she belittled my efforts as being "positive" and told me I was "just like Mr. Rogers." When I sat in silence and attempted to immerse myself in her experience, she would accuse me of "just sitting there like a dope." At the same time she despised herself for her anger and wondered why and how I tolerated her. When I said that I thought it was an important step ahead, and even a complement to our work that she was able to express her disappointment and anger openly, she smiled and admitted to feeling "delighted" that I "could take it" because it made her feel "intoxicated with power."

The vignette I'll share with you now is taken from a session in the middle of the third year of treatment when her anger had subsided and she was sharing in sessions more and more of the exhibitionistic aspects of her personality. As well, she had begun a paid part-time job, developed a few friends, and began writing poetry that she was sending to magazines and even local radio stations. Over the previous months she had contemplated giving up "hell cleaning."

A Vignette

Ms. B bounced into my office with a perkiness in her step and greeted me with a friendly smile and warm hello. She was smartly dressed and more fashionably groomed than usual. Rather than the sense of resignation and antagonism that generally characterized her initial moments in sessions, I sensed now a lightheartedness, as if she were excited to be there. Before she had removed her jacket and taken her seat, she began to speak: "My mother gave me a compliment today—she said I seemed stronger than I ever have. I questioned whether that were so, but it felt good to hear that, especially from my mother." She then added with a grin, "It must be my lucky day, because my boss also gave me a compliment—she claimed that I seemed more organized and that she was pleased with the way I was handling some very difficult clients on the phone. She point-blank said that she was impressed."

As Ms. B continued speaking affirmatively of her work, in particular, of how her abilities matched her responsibilities, she recalled past jobs and how she always felt overwhelmed by the demands. In a pleased tone, she affirmed that "for the first time in a job, I don't feel that way."

As she displayed her newfound strength, I sensed a sudden embarrassment as she spoke. "This can't be me talking—it feels like a different person." Then, as if speaking to herself, she muttered, "Maybe I should get back in my hole and start talking about the gutsy issues of hell cleaning, but I know what you'd say: I'm afraid of my strength and I want to go back to a familiar place. I've called you Mr. Rogers for saying things like that, but I think you're right—I am afraid."

Suddenly, I sensed in her a mild sadness as she uncharacteristically struggled to find words to express what was on her mind. Aware of her struggle, I responded, "It isn't easy for you." Immediately, I sensed her eyes reddening and noticed a tear trickle down her cheek. As if choking on her words, she spoke haltingly. "I don't want you to get the wrong idea, but I feel like I want to hug you. I feel so safe here and I don't want to leave—I even feel hopeful about my life."

She cried as she continued to express her idealization openly: "I feel so lucky that I found you and that you accepted me in the first place. In looking back on it, I'm so glad you could be strong and not give in to my demands. I also feel good that you could accept my frustration and anger—it was something that no one ever tolerated, especially my parents."

Suddenly her mood changed and she became more indignant as she reflected on her former treatments: "I feel like I wasted so much time, so many years—I don't understand why they gave in to me, why they even saw me in the first place. In a way they were no different than my parents, acquiescing to my tantrums. It's puzzling to me: if I can do it now, why couldn't I have done it then?"

Leaving my office at the end of the session, she kept repeating the same question as if speaking to herself under her breath.

CONCLUSION AND SUMMARY

It goes without saying that Ms. B's demanding that I allay her intense anxiety by giving answers, opinions, and promises may sound extreme,

but it is not uncommon in the treatment of a number of severe self disorders. Understanding Ms. B's need for direction and answers rather
than directly responding to her requests allowed for the analysis to proceed and for the further development of the selfobject transferences.

It might even be suggested that if I had assumed an attitude of gratifying her needs for answers in order to relieve the intensity of her frustration and anxiety, as her former therapists obviously did, I may have
bypassed very crucial understandings, and even worse, reinforced her
conviction that she was "a sick person" and incapable of helping herself.
In other words, meeting her demands by making promises, giving
answers, and offering direction may well have served as further proof of
her own helplessness and sense of incompetence.

To further clarify my point, I have attempted to show in my vignette
of Ms. B that responding with an act (i.e., agreeing to her demands)
would bypass a crucial understanding and perhaps destructively reinforce
her conviction of being "sick." On one hand, recognizing that frustration
is part and parcel of all analytic change frees the self-psychological analyst to maintain a primary focus on the patient's experience. On the
other hand, to view frustration as imposed upon the patient from without diverts the analyst's attention away from his primary focus on
empathic immersion and onto concerns about what the analyst can do
to relieve anxiety. I further understood that her demands did not represent some benign request for reassurance; rather, they embodied a validation of a core sense of her self as powerless and disabled vis-à-vis a
source of tyrannical might.

The views critical of the concept of optimal frustration clearly suggest
that the analytic situation is such that the psychological needs of the
patient must be met. They are a theoretical backdrop directing the self
psychologist's attention away from empathic immersion and toward the
offering of an optimally responsive act that alleviates the patient's frustration. They represent an attempt to meet the needs by giving something to the patient beyond a communication of understanding the
needs.

Furthermore, these views deemphasize the relevance and importance
of frustration and anxiety in the individual's emotional development.
They also deemphasize the importance of frustration and anxiety as an
integral part of the analytic process and thus direct the analyst to take
actions in order to keep the patient's frustration and anxiety to an optimally reduced level. As a result, the patient loses the opportunity to
come to an understanding of the full intensity of his or her frustrations
and anxieties, which reflect the depth and breadth of the earlier childhood trauma.

It naturally follows that limiting the patient's experience limits the depth of the analysis. The analyst's attention to maintaining a reduced level of frustration may communicate to the patient a lack of ability to tolerate frustration, aggression, and anxiety, and thereby unconsciously exacerbate the patient's fears of having any intense affects at all. By the analyst searching for some optimally responsive act rather than maintaining his focus on being immersed in the patient's experience, there is a very real danger that the patient will interpret the communication, as was true with Ms. B, as an indication that such intense states are dangerous and need to be avoided.

This focus on taking concrete actions to reduce the patient's frustrations rather than on a continued exploration makes valid those criticisms leveled against self psychology by traditional analysis, namely, that self psychology represents a "sanitizing of man" by not allowing for the expression of more intense affects such as "lust" and the "wish to kill." The attention of the analyst is shifted away from the self-psychological focus on the patient's experience and toward an object-relational mode of observing and responding. Furthermore, Bacal (1988) recommends that a patient whose intense frustration cannot be ameliorated by interpretation be offered "something that the analyst may regard as out of order; a change of demeanor or attitude, perhaps some action, such as the acceptance of a gift, an alteration of fees or appointment time" (p. 130). It might be suggested that this is just as manipulative as Bacal's own assertion that optimal frustration necessarily means the manipulation of the therapeutic environment in order to bring about cure.

Kohut (1984) defines optimal frustration as selfobject failures of "a nontraumatic degree" (p. 70). The definition makes it difficult to determine clinically when a frustration is traumatic and when it is nontraumatic. I would suggest an operational definition of the term, that is, optimal frustrations are those frustrations that are amenable to analysis. To offer an a priori response that ameliorates a patient's anxieties and intense affects before it has been determined whether they are analyzable abolishes an important analytic opportunity, one that offers the individual patient a chance to think through and discover certain strengths and abilities that he or she may feel convinced are not possible. For example, Ms. B lamented persistently early in our work, "You think I'm normal like your other patients—don't you understand that I'm sick, that I can't do this by myself?"

But how can the analyst know what is analyzable? We can only know the answer to this question by being attuned to the patient. Ultimately, it is the patient who teaches the analyst whether or not a frustration or intense affect is analyzable. We can never know before the fact. Of course, it is acknowledged that there are certain situations with particularly disturbed self disorders in which some parameter may be necessary. Such was the case of Kohut's severely depressed suicidal woman, to whom he extended his two fingers during one particular difficult period in her analysis. Kohut (1981a) was clear that he was not recommending such a response (even referring to it as a "doubtful maneuver"), but was only trying to show that there are times in treatment when a particularly disturbed individual may require more than understanding and explaining, and that such a parameter can flow naturally and appropriately from the analyst's ongoing empathic immersion. Yet, even in these instances, Kohut insisted that the analyst remain focused on the patient's experience in order to further understand the impact and meaning that such a parameter holds for the patient.

Finally, Kohut (1984) also speaks of certain severely disturbed "borderline" patients, not unlike Ms. B, who during the course of their treatment manifest such intense frustrations, alarming symptoms, and relentless attacks that the analyst is often left with little or no alternative except to maintain his experience-near focus while waiting out the storm. He believed that these extreme reactions are not always due to the "avoidable" empathic failures of the analyst, but may well be the result of "a necessary perception of misunderstanding" (p. 225, note 2) on the part of the analysand that recapitulates certain traumatic events of childhood.[3] Kohut suggests that the analyst who chooses to persist in the face of these hardships may be fortunate to observe a shift in his or her patient from a "borderline" condition to an analyzable narcissisitic personality disorder. However, he adds a critical sine qua non: "the analyst retains his analytic stance and, open-mindedly and non-defensively, attempts to resonate empathically with what the patient is experiencing" (p. 182). But to direct attention to the discovery of an optimally responsive act switches the analyst's focus from this critical self-psychological stance to an object-relational perspective, in which the focus is away from the patient's experience and toward the analyst as object initiating and doing.

In sum, Kohut maintained throughout his writings that optimal frustration is an experience-near construct, necessary for cure in psychoanalysis, that emerged from his empathic observations. It is not a technical approach, as suggested by some, that is imposed upon one's patients in

---

[3] Some might ask how, if at all, can an analyst distinguish a patient's frustrations due to incorrect analytic responsiveness in the present from those early childhood traumas of the past? As with the analyzability of frustrations, there is no a priori formula for sifting out one from the other because, more than likely, a patient's experience of frustration is an amalgam of both past and present. It is the analyst's expanding attunement to the ebbs and flows of the patient's experience in the moment and over time that will ultimately allow him to grasp the depth and breadth of the frustration, as well as to discover its origin and cause.

order to facilitate cure. Maintaining the latter position alters the term's meaning and shifts the analytic perspective from inside to outside, from self-psychological to object-relational, with critical implications for theory and practice.

REFERENCES

Bacal, H. (1985) Optimal responsiveness and the therapeutic process. In: *Progress in Self Psychology, Vol. 1*, ed. A. Goldberg. New York: Guilford, pp. 202–227.

—— (1988), Reflections on "optimum frustration." In: *Learning from Kohut, Progress in Self Psychology, Vol. 4*, ed. A. Goldberg. Hillsdale, NJ: The Analytic Press, pp. 127–131.

—— & Newman, K. (1990), *Theories of Object Relations: Bridges to Self Psychology*. New York: Columbia University Press.

Bernfeld, S. (1928), *Sisyphos, oder veber die Grenzen der Erziehung*. Vienna: Internationale Vereinigung für Psychoanalysis.

Freud, A. (1946), *The Ego and the Mechanisms of Defense*. New York: International Universities Press.

Kohut, H. (1971), *The Analysis of the Self*. New York: International Universities Press.

—— (1972), Letters of September 12th and September 23rd, 1972. In: *Search for the Self, Vol. 2*. New York: International Universities Press, pp. 867–870.

—— (1977), *The Restoration of the Self*. New York: International Universities Press.

—— (1981a), On empathy. In: *Search for the Self, Vol. 4*, ed. P. H. Ornstein. New York: International Universities Press, pp. 525–535.

—— (1981b), The semicircle of mental health. In: *Search for the Self, Vol. 4*, ed. P. H. Ornstein. New York: International Universities Press, pp. 537–567.

—— (1984), *How Does Analysis Cure?* ed. A. Goldberg & P. Stepansky. Chicago: The University of Chicago Press.

—— (1987), *The Kohut Seminars on Self Psychology and Psychotherapy with Adolescents and Young Adults*, ed. M. Elson. New York: Norton.

Rowe, C. & MacIsaac, D. (1989), *Empathic Attunement: The "Technique" of Psychoanalytic Self Psychology*. Northvale, NJ: Aronson.

Socarides, D. & Stolorow, R. (1985), Affects and selfobjects. *The Annual of Psychoanalysis*, 12/13:105–119. New York: International Universities Press.

Terman, D. M. (1988), Optimum frustration: Structuralization and the therapeutic process. In: *Learning from Kohut, Progress in Self Psychology, Vol. 4*, ed. A. Goldberg. Hillsdale, NJ: The Analytic Press, pp. 113–125.

Chapter 2

The Psychoanalyst's Selfobject Needs and the Effect of Their Frustration on the Treatment: A New View of Countertransference

Howard A. Bacal

Peter G. Thomson

We are aware of the multiple and complex definitions and conceptualizations of "countertransference" in the literature (see especially definitions and references in Rycroft, 1972; Moore and Fine, 1990) and we will not review them here. Historically, psychoanalysts have variously held two contradictory views on countertransference. One view is that it constitutes feelings on the part of the analyst that may interfere with the patient's therapy. The other is that it may be a valuable asset in the treatment process. Both these views of countertransference parallel, to a large extent, analysts' views of transference—that it may be an interference, a resistance, to the analysis and that it may serve as a major vehicle for the analytic process. Freud (1910) identified countertransference as an impediment to the effective treatment of the patient. This view persisted, for the most part, until 1950, when Heimann (1950) proferred a new definition and a novel perspective on countertransference. She regarded countertransference as comprising all the analyst's feelings toward the patient, and she argued that the analyst's emotional response to his patient provided him with one of his most useful tools for understanding the patient's unconscious. Sandler (1976) extended Heimann's idea to include the process whereby the analyst becomes alerted to important experiences within the patient by becoming aware of certain roles that the patient induces within the analyst. This process repeats significant early relationships for the patient.

Because of the difference in the role of the analyst from that of the patient in the treatment process, the psychology of the analyst has been relatively neglected. If we agree with Sullivan (1953) that *"everyone is much more simply human than otherwise"* (p. 32), then as therapists we must surely assume that we are made of the same psychological stuff as our patients. That is, we therapists, too, bring a relational history, a cumulative representation of our lived experience of interaction to the analytic situation. This puts us in a psychological position not unlike that of our patients, despite the difference in our roles.

Kohut, interestingly, took a similar view to that of Freud when he described the "narcissistic" countertransferences as interfering with the establishment of the narcissistic transferences. Kohut (1971) understood how the analyst tends to react in particular ways to these transferences: "The analyst's own narcissistic needs . . . may make it difficult for him to tolerate a situation in which he is reduced to the seemingly passive role of being a mirror of the patient's infantile narcissism, and he may, therefore, subtly or openly . . . interfere with the establishment or the maintenance of the mirror transference" (p. 272). And "the rejection of the patient's idealizing attitudes is usually motivated by a defensive fending off of painful narcissistic tensions . . . which are generated in the analyst when the repressed fantasies of his grandiose self become stimulated by the patient's idealization" (p. 262). Wolf (1979, 1980) and Kohler (1985) have elaborated on Kohut's views, using the new terminology of the "selfobject." The selfobject transferences refer to the need of the patient for self-restorative and self-sustaining responses from the analyst. Wolf (1979) coined the term "selfobject countertransferences" to denote the counterpart in the analyst of the selfobject transferences of the analysand, whether or not they are evoked by the analysand. That is, the analyst, too, has selfobject needs that are mobilized as a result of participating in the analytic process (see Wolf, 1980).

Kohut's introduction of the new language was more than a change in terminology. It underscored his view that so-called narcissistic phenomena reflect the frustration and distortion of a basic sort of psychological need—indeed, a *healthy* need of the self in a relational context. As Kindler (1991) has explicitly stated in his fine paper on the subject, every individual has at his core a need to be mirrored or affirmed. However, while the *analysand's* needs for selfobject responsiveness from the analyst have become increasingly accepted as psychologically legitimate, the *analyst's* selfobject needs in relation to the analysand, although they are understandable, have in practice continued to be regarded as largely undesirable. They are unfortunate reactions from which the analyst should attempt to decenter. In other words, we are still defining certain experiences of the analyst as "unhealthy." To put it plainly, the analyst should be ashamed of them. They constitute a problem that simply needs to be overcome. A large part of the problem is that analysts are, in effect, pretty good at disavowing their feelings when their selfobject needs are not met. We are not simply implying that "analysts are people, too" who have selfobject needs. We are, more importantly, also saying that because this is so it constitutes a very practical issue for the treatment of the patient. We have scarcely begun to explore the various ways in which the analyst's experience of his or her needs in relation to the patient and their satisfaction, frustration, or distortion affect the treatment process.

In this chapter, we will offer a new perspective on "countertransference." This perspective, in effect, supports the conceptual usefulness of restricting the usage of the term to refer to the interference with the analyst's therapeutic function. (This has, in fact, become the most common usage of the term.) We propose the view (see also Bacal, 1994) that the analyst's self is ordinarily sustained in his work by ongoing selfobject responses of the analysand, and we will argue that his or her analytic function may be substantially interfered with (i.e., countertransference reactions occur) when these selfobject needs are significantly frustrated. We will also suggest that the analyst's therapeutic function is enhanced as a result of his lessened requirement to protect himself or herself against the awareness of these needs. We will, further, suggest ways in which this goal may be attained—ways that centrally entail deactivating the sometimes disabling sense of shame that may accompany the awareness of our selfobject needs in relation to our patients.

We would affirm Wolf's view (1979) that, while we may have gained much from our personal analyses, none of us is entirely free from sensitivities, vulnerabilities, and longings that arise from personal and professional frustrations or injuries, both past and present. We plead for a measure of tolerance for the ubiquity of a wide range of inevitable shortcomings in the personalities of analysts. We do not of course condone the enactment by the analyst of selfobject needs or of any other needs in relation to the patient that are ethically unacceptable. When we speak of empathic failures or failures in optimal responsiveness, we are placing these against the background of the expectable performance of a committed therapist at the level of his or her experience and training. Having said this, we must acknowledge that all of us attempt to defend our-selves from the repetition of disruptive experiences and their disturbing affects—especially that of shame—with anyone, including with our patients.

Gunther (1976) emphasizes this perspective in his understanding of countertransference reactions. He sees them as enactments whose pur-pose is to restore the "narcissistic" equilibrium of the analyst that becomes disturbed in interactions with the analysand. They are symp-toms of the reassertion of the analyst's narcissistic needs. Wolf (1980) was the first to explicitly recognize the bidirectional nature of selfobject neediness in the analytic process and to recognize its value and its liabilities as it is experienced by the analyst. Kohler (1985), on the basis of the work of Beebe and Sloate, and Sander have described the com-plex interactions between the therapist's and the patient's selfobject needs as analogous to the interactions of the mother–child pair. Thom-son (1991, 1993) has extensively illustrated how selfobject disruption in the analyst in relation to the analysand provides a particular opportunity to study how this may have contributed to the derailment in the patient. Bacal (1994) has recently suggested that

> The therapist's experience of a selfobject relationship with the patient is not only pervasively operative in every therapeutic relationship but it constitutes a precondition for the therapist to respond in ways that will enable the patient to experience a selfobject relationship with him or her. Analysts regularly *expect* analysands to respond in a number of ways that are, in fact, self-sustaining or self-enhancing for the therapist [p. 28].

We submit that the complexity of these experiences requires concep-tualization that the term "countertransference" simply does not do justice to at all. We believe that certain processes operating in the analyst that affect the patient may be usefully conceptualized in terms of the meeting of selfobject needs or the frustration of selfobject needs. We concur with Wolf that the term "empathic resonance" usefully describes the situation when the analyst effectively undergoes a controlled regres-sion along with the patient in his efforts to remain attuned to him. How-ever, to regard this as an aspect of countertransference—a term that commonly designates an interference with the therapeutic process—is conceptually confusing. This limited regression is in the service of the therapeutic relationship. Our understanding of empathic resonance is similar to Balint's understanding of the harmoniously regressive archaic experience which he termed "primary love" or "primary object-love" (1937, 1968) as it occurs within the analytic dyad—an experience not

disjunctive[3] phenomena that affect the analyst's therapeutic function. These run "counter," if you like, to the selfobject "transference" needs of the analysand in the treatment.

It must be emphasized that the therapist's selfobject needs do differ from those of the patient insofar as they are represented through his or her therapeutic function. The most common selfobject need of the therapist is for mirroring of his function according to whatsoever way he conceives this function. If he conceives it as a caring attitude, he needs to be affirmed for this. If he conceives his function in terms of cognitive understanding, he needs affirmation for this. If, for example, he needs to idealize the patient, then he can feel wonderful if he perceives his patient as having special attributes. He may see his function as providing a holding, enlivening, reliably receptive ambience, for which he unconsciously needs affirmation. In the course of the analysis many of these needs are ordinarily met by the patient's attendance, his arriving and leaving on time, lying on the couch while he is there, staying awake, supplying associative material, listening to interpretations, paying a fee, picking up the tab for missed sessions, and so on—that is, conforming, more or less, to the routines of the analytic situation. In this situation, the analyst is usually no more aware that these routines may embody selfobject needs than he is of the air he breathes. To some extent, the analyst's training makes him take the meeting of these expectations for granted.

In his training of general practitioners for psychotherapeutic work, Balint (1964) referred to the "apostolic mission or function" of the doctor—"that every doctor has a vague, but almost unshakably firm, idea of how a patient ought to behave when ill. . . . It was . . . as if he had a sacred duty to convert to his faith all the ignorant and unbelieving among his patients." Balint added: "Although this idea is anything but explicit and concrete, it is immensely powerful, and influences . . . practically every detail of the doctor's work" (p. 216). We believe that these expectations derive not only from therapist's training—some may say, from his or her indoctrination—but also from the therapist's unmet selfobject needs that he brings to the patient in the therapy situation. Personal analysis may enable the therapist to engage some of these needs, but unless they are addressed more directly (as we shall discuss in a moment), they may remain largely unconscious and thus pose a poten-

---

[3] Countertransference reactions that involve the analyst's needs may also be conjunctive (or "collusive"). This may occur when the analyst tacitly—or even explicitly—encourages the patient to hope for the fulfillment—or enactment of—unmet needs of the analyst that correspond to those of the patient. In these instances (which are often unconsciously motivated), the analyst may sometimes find himself offering more than he can deliver. These reactions may thus also run counter to the therapeutic needs of the patient.

tial interference with the therapist's efficacy. Therapists' enhanced awareness of how their psychological needs and vulnerabilities have become organized into their professional working persona will enable them to become clearer about the limits to their capacity for optimal responsiveness to any particular patient.

Perhaps the therapist's predominant need is for affirmation of his capacity to understand and, in many instances, for his caring, humanistic motivation. We suspect that this need by therapists to be seen as decent, well-motivated human beings in their work is both pervasive and unacknowledged; yet it is difficult for analysts when they are thought to be anything but that by their patients. This need may reflect an inadequate working through of the "darker" or "nastier" sides of the analyst in his own analysis. Conversely, an analytic experience in which the dark side was all too vigorously attended to may repeat a trauma of the therapist's childhood. These experiences may leave the therapist with significant unmet needs that he or she brings into the consulting room. For some therapists, the meeting of such needs is at the center of their general raison d'être. The therapeutic work with their patients may serve to repair defects in self-structure that arose from a requirement to accede to the archaic selfobject needs of their caretakers.[4] The self-esteem and self-cohesion of these therapists will depend on their success in fulfilling the needs of their analysands (see Stolorow and Atwood, 1992).

When a patient becomes seriously disrupted, the analyst's selfobject needs may become significantly frustrated; in particular, the analyst may experience a loss of the sense of efficacy. He may also experience dysphoric affects such as anger, inadequacy, disappointment in himself, and shame.

CLINICAL ILLUSTRATION: TINA

A situation that illustrates a number of these issues arose with Tina, an accomplished and successful young architect. Tina had a mother who was continuingly and grossly out of tune with her affiliative-attachment needs, and who had been so, apparently, from Tina's early infancy. In her analysis, Tina railed bitterly, angrily, and despairingly against her mother's insensitivity, cruelty, and her near-total dismissal of the validity of her daughter's complaints. As she regressed in the transference, which was largely positive in an idealizing way, she began to experience the holiday breaks as quite intolerable. And on more than one occasion, she experienced herself dissociating and fragmenting during breaks in

---

[4] This requirement corresponds to the vertical split situation described by Kohut (1977) and to the false self reaction described by Winnicott (1960; see also Bacal and Newman, 1990).

ways that profoundly distressed her. However, she never appeared ill enough to justify hospitalization, nor was she at all interested in taking medication. The analyst responded by offering what he regarded as appropriate transference interpretations—essentially that she experienced him as repeating the neglect of her mother and deserting her as her mother and others had done in the past. Tina did not contest these interpretations, but they were of no help in relieving her painful symptoms.

As time went on, and each break produced the same horrendous distress, Tina began not only to rebuke the analyst for leaving on his holiday, but to imply that he should not be going, because of what it did to her. The analyst experienced a conscious resistance within himself to accepting the validity of his patient's request, that is, that the only way that he felt he could remedy the situation was never to take a holiday. He needed to feel that, despite her dissatisfaction, he was being a good therapist for Tina and he also needed to feel free to take a holiday. In other words, selfobject needs of the analyst that Tina had easily met all along and of which the analyst had been quite unaware, were now being significantly frustrated. It should be mentioned that Tina never appeared to want to go on holiday with the analyst—in which case he would have had *more* problems—and she was quite uninterested in phoning him as a substitute for his being with her.

The analyst eventually stopped attempting to explain (i.e., to interpret) the reasons for Tina's self-disruption during breaks, because he thought that she had gone off the deep end around this issue and that it was time to draw her attention to the "reality" of the situation—that it was quite unrealistic of her to expect him not to go on holiday, and that he would simply not entertain the idea seriously. This did not help either. The analyst was now torn between a sense of outrage and a sense of inadequacy, shame, and guilt. He was angry that the patient would deprive him of his right to something that was important and necessary to him, and that in doing so she was being outrageously excessive in her demands. He also felt inadequate as a therapist —nothing he could say was useful and his patient was, by her account, being made worse by the analysis and regarded him as a bad, cruel, and uncaring person. He liked and admired Tina, and generally felt good about his ongoing work with her. He did not, however, know what to do to remedy the situation as she experienced it. Tina left the analysis after four years but returned some months later for psychotherapy because she felt unable to hold onto a man. She consciously decided to avoid the regressive experience of analysis that would render her vulnerable to trauma at holiday breaks, but she referred, reproachfully, to the "failed" analysis—which failed, as she saw it, because of the analyst's inadequacies. Indeed, it would take several years more for the analyst to "get it," an achievement that, as Wolf (1980) has conveyed, would come from the growing strength and therefore decreasing vulnerability and neediness of the analyst's self. The analyst had to be able to accept that his responses were not good enough for the patient without experiencing a disabling sense of shame. Paradoxically, of course, this acceptance made him a better analyst for Tina.

It is useful to discover—to really discover—that one's selfobject need to be recognized by the patient as a good-enough therapist is common to all therapists, and that this need never completely disappears. This therapist's recognition and acceptance of the need enabled him to begin to provide Tina with what she *really* needed from him—the deep-going validation that she had been right all along, that he *was* insensitive to her needs and therefore was cruel to her. He placed his need for a holiday above her pain and he deserted her, like all the men in her life and like her mother, too. She was right—he didn't care about her all *that* much. She was, as she put it, "only" a patient, and he was "only" an analyst. She didn't need to experience his blame or his shame or his guilt. In taking his holiday, he had made the choice, at that moment, to put the needs of his self before those of Tina's. In other words, when she reproached him, all he had to do was to say "uh huh" and *mean* it, and she felt understood. Following this acknowledgment, Tina's reproaches to the analyst for his unresponsiveness to her suffering when he went on holidays did not recur.

When the selfobject needs and expectations of the analyst are met by the analysand, a situation of mutual regulation—a kind of harmony, as we have described it—prevails in the analytic ambience. At these times, the analyst may feel a variety of self-syntonic emotions, such as friendliness, concern, mild idealization, sympathy, compassion, and also sometimes anger or attraction of a regulatable degree toward the patient. However, when, for whatever reason, the analyst's needs are not met, he may experience the painful and even visceral sensations of disrupted self-states that can undermine his therapeutic function. These disruptions include distancing, disinterest, hostility and hatred, contempt, eroticism, prolonged boredom, sleepiness, or even falling asleep.

In the following example, the analyst experienced frustration of his need to feel that he had a function as a therapist. He was also frustrated in his need to experience himself as supplying care for the patient.

CLINICAL EXAMPLE: SARAH

For many months, Sarah, a young woman analysand, repeatedly asserted, often vehemently, that there was no relationship and that the

analysis was meaningless. Despite this she attended regularly. The analyst reacted to Sarah's assertion by interpreting it as a resistance to
transference. He repeatedly told her that she was avoiding her feelings
and needs regarding the therapist. The only effect of this was that the
patient reasserted, with even more passion and distress, that there was
no relationship. She became disillusioned with the analysis and indeed
with life itself. At one point, she cried, "Analysis is totally useless. Why
do you let me come? It's a big sadistic tease." One day, in great despair,
Sarah left a message on the analyst's answering machine telling him the
analysis was hopeless and she would not be returning. Galvanized into
action by fears of the patient's committing suicide, as she had attempted
to do several times in the past, the analyst contacted her and was able
to arrange an emergency double session. The analyst now began to
sense that he had not been attuned to his patient's aversive state, and
that he must set aside his preoccupation with defenses against transference. For the first hour or so, Sarah expressed her desperate and disillusioned state with great affective intensity. Then, perhaps sensing, via the
analyst's murmurs of assent, that he was more attuned, she became
calmer. She then spoke with much emotional pain of her father's
unavailability. She recalled climbing up onto his lap as a small child only
to experience him as "a hard wooden chair."

As the session drew to a close, she spoke of her former therapist in
the following words: "I did not meet his needs. He needed to do good.
He needed to have an impact." The therapist almost immediately recognized that these comments also referred to himself and fit well with his
attitude of the previous few months. He now recognized that his argu-
mentative interpretive activity, rationalized as theoretically sound, had
masked a frustrated selfobject need—a "countertransference reaction," if
you like. During that period he had had to avoid awareness of his need
to have a function, to be an "analytic somebody." He had thus failed to
attune himself to his patient's need to work through, in transference, a
repetition of her aversive experience of an unresponsive and unavailable
father.

In the vignette just described, the analyst attempted to satisfy his need
for efficacy[5] by repeated interpretations of his patient's need to deny her
transference feelings toward him. Interpretation has been accorded such
a high and unquestioned value in analytic practice that we have lost
sight of—or perhaps never saw—how intrinsic it is to the analyst's assertion of his role as an analyst. A little self-analysis will demonstrate that

---

[5] According to Wolf (1988), "*Efficacy need* is a person's need to experience the self as an
effective agent, that is, capable of eliciting a selfobject response" (p. 181).

most of us tend, at times, to step up our interpretive activity when we feel less effective with our analysand. We may then interpret simply to assure ourselves that we have a function. As training analysts, we often urge our students to make interpretations, especially transference interpretations. We believe that transference interpretations are not infrequently offered when the analyst feels unengaged with the patient. In one such instance, the analyst found himself drifting off during a patient's silence. He then experienced the urge to interpret that the patient was removing himself from the analyst and was thus making it difficult for the analyst to stay with him. Fortunately, the analyst was able to recognize that his own needs for stimulation and a sense of functioning were at odds with the patient's need to use him through silence, and that he would only experience the interpretation as the analyst's need for the patient to accommodate to him.

We are all familiar with the patient who continues to associate, apparently doing his own analysis, but who leaves the analyst out of his associations for long periods. Such a patient will not only tend to make the analyst sleepy (MacLaughlin, 1975; Dender, 1993) but will also tend to elicit transference interpretations, or interpretations about his or her resistance to transference. In our view, these interpretations are motivated unconsciously by a specific deprivation in mirroring: a depletion has occurred in the analyst's experience of being recognized, of being seen. The significance and utility of his existence as an analyst are simply not acknowledged. An ongoing selfobject need the analyst has generally come to count on his patient to meet is no longer being provided and the analyst feels useless and devitalized. The analyst then interprets in order to bring himself front and center. Although some patients may be able to shrug off such interpretations as simply incorrect, others may experience them as a disruptive transference repetition of the intrusive archaic selfobject needs of a significant caretaker.

CLINICAL ILLUSTRATION: TOM

Tom, a young psychologist in analysis, regularly talked on without pause and without any reference to the analyst. Tom clearly liked and admired his analyst, and the analyst quite liked Tom, who was upbeat and who struggled bravely and insightfully with the many problems in his personal relationships. The analyst, however, usually felt so bored and sleepy he could hardly stay awake. He rarely had the opportunity to make an interpretation; in any event, it did not appear necessary to do so, as Tom articulated everything the analyst regarded as relevant. In short, the analyst felt *unengaged* and *irrelevant* to Tom's therapeutic experience. However, Tom idealized the analyst's skills, and he would, from time to time, refer to "our relationship," which, he implied, he valued very much.

Whereas the analyst felt he needed to give *some* interpretations in order to be useful, the analysand admired the analyst's capacity (as the analysand experienced it) to appreciate his ability to understand himself. What no doubt helped the analyst to avoid interpretations (that is, confrontations) that the analysand was "resisting" the transference was that the patient was improving steadily, which provided him with a sense of satisfaction, if not a sense of efficacy. When he did, on rare occasions, offer such interpretations, the patient seemed to shrug them off: they were neither useful nor disruptive.

Late in his life, Winnicott (1971) came to the conclusion that he had often prevented or delayed deep change in his patients by his need to interpret. And Casement (1985) states: "I was often tempted to interpret just to reassure myself that I was still able to think and to function in the session, when things seemed chaotic, but I had to learn to refrain" (p. 177). We would add here that when the analyst reassures a patient, his underlying need is sometimes actually to reassure himself.

We have referred to the significance of shame in the therapist's experience of frustration and disruption of self-cohesion, and in particular to the difficulties in facing shame. Here is a vignette that illustrates this vividly.

Dr. S sought her analyst's help in connection with a distressing reaction she had to a psychotherapy patient who had been recurrently talking about discontinuing treatment. Dr. S had responded to her patient's talk of terminating his recently begun, once-weekly therapy sessions by telling him that, in her view, he should not only not quit but that he should come five times a week. Immediately after saying this, she felt suffused with an inexplicable sense of intense shame. There is no question that her shame was partially in reaction to her sudden awareness of what she had done. That is, asking her patient to do something that she realized he was quite unprepared to do made her feel foolish both to him and to herself—and to her analyst, when she reported it to him. She was also understandably reluctant at first to permit the analyst to include the vignette in this chapter, because, like most therapists, she did not quite believe that everyone, including her analyst, had had the same kinds of experience. There was more to understand, though.

Dr. S's patient had been suffering keenly as a result of the recent abandonment by his wife. His wife had begun an affair with her husband's boss and had moved in with him along with the patient's three children. The patient was trying now, with considerable difficulty, to live a new life on his own while continuing in his role as father on a part-time basis. Dr. S had been empathically resonating with his strongly disavowed—and intense—feelings of shame about his wife's abandonment. Dr. S had had similar feelings in comparable circumstances—some of which she had never completely owned. Dr. S was not new to experiences of abandonment. Prominent among them was the loss of her father—to whom she had believed she was special—who left home when she was a little girl. In addition, she was currently facing the painful possibility of losing her boyfriend. Her patient's talk of leaving stirred up disavowed feelings of shame associated with her experiences of abandonment. She could empathize with her patient and respond optimally to him as long as he did not do the same thing to her that others had done—and what his wife had done to him. When her patient announced his intention to leave her, she lost her empathic resonance with him because she had in part unconsciously apprehended him as *the* selfobject who must not desert her. The shame surfaced when she tried to get him to be with her even more frequently. She was, in effect, expressing her unconscious, unrequited love to her abandoning father, whose leaving she had been powerless to prevent.

Dr. S also came to see that her disavowed sense of shame, and that of her patient, was due to a feeling of inadequacy. Neither of them had felt able to maintain their regard for their idealized partners who had failed them (for the patient, this was his therapist, his wife, and his family; for the therapist, it was her patient, her boyfriend, and her father) and, in consequence, they were unable to retain their sense of self-respect. The commitment of her patient to the therapy unconsciously represented (that is, symbolized) for the therapist the partial but significant redressment of a lifelong disillusionment in an idealizing need and that of a mirroring need to be special again. The therapist had made herself vulnerable to shame because she needed to disavow her selfobject needs in relation to her patient. Had she been able to understand and accept them, she would likely have been able to offer her patient a considered therapeutic *response* instead of *reacting* to the "signal disruption" that his talk of leaving elicited.

This therapist's experience is not unique. Variations of her story about the significance and meaning of the relationship with her patient are common currency among therapists. We would claim that the patient's commitment to the treatment meets a universal idealizing selfobject need of therapists and a universal need of therapists to be mirrored as being effective and special to their patients.[6]

---

[6] The patient's commitment to the treatment likely also meets the need for attachment to a significant other—a need (that is in many ways similar to the need for selfobjects [see Bacal and Newman, 1990]).

Thus, the situation for the analyst is essentially the same as it is for the analysand: If the analyst cannot accept the psychological legitimacy of her selfobject needs in relation to the patient; she will be affected in the same kinds of ways as the patient, her needs will intensify and she may act them out, very likely in relation to the partner who has frustrated them—her patient. If we must protect ourselves from the shameful awareness of our needs in relation to our patients, we will not be able to resonate empathically or respond optimally to their comparable, disavowed needs. If, however, the analyst can accept the psychological legitimacy of these needs, it will significantly enhance his therapeutic function (see Bacal and Newman, 1990; Bacal, 1994). This is, in effect, what happened when Dr. S worked this through in this way with her analyst. In other words, when her sense of shame about these needs and expectations in relation to her patient decreased, her defenses against them also relaxed; as a result, she could then extend the same empathy and acceptance to both herself and her patient.[7]

We believe that it is only recently, in particular because of the work of Broucek (1991), Morrison (1989, 1992), and Wurmser (1981), that the ubiquity of shame in human experience is becoming recognized. The therapist is no less liable to experiences of shame and to those defenses against shame experience that Morrison has described. But these experiences also offer us the opportunity for fresh self-inquiry, self-understanding, and self-acceptance. There are a variety of ways of pursuing this. "More analysis" is often the prescription for such problems, and it can help. Formal consultation or supervision is another. These tasks can also be very effectively accomplished if the therapist's analyst is prepared to respond directly to the therapist's discussion of his or her therapeutic work during the analytic sessions. In this way, the analyst can offer his immediate understanding of his analysand's countertransference reactions as they relate to the frustration of her selfobject needs in the work with her patient. This, in effect, characterized the way that Dr. S's training analyst worked with her, a method of supervision that was regularly offered by Ferenczi, Balint, and others to trainees at the Budapest Institute of Psychoanalysis.[8]

---

[7] Gunther (1976) recommends that the analyst use "selective empathy" with himself as a means of monitoring his defenses and disturbances. Gunther's emphasis is on the expectable "narcissistic" difficulties that analysts will encounter when doing analytic work. We affirm his observations; our additional emphasis, however, is upon the ongoing selfobject functions that are ordinarily supplied by the analysand to the analyst, and the effects of their frustration.

[8] In Hungary, at the Budapest Psychoanalytic Institute, this was the usual form of supervision. When Balint emigrated to England from Hungary in the late 1930s, he offered this form of supervision to his trainee analysands at the British Institute of Psychoanalysis. He supervised the student's first training case during the student's own analytic hours. In this way, the student's countertrans-

Another effective approach is to seek out opportunities for open exchange with trusted colleagues. The exploring and sharing, in a collegial ambience, of experiences about the effects of frustration of our selfobject needs and disruptive states can be enormously useful. We regularly find that, as a result of these exchanges, we have less propensity to feel ashamed of our "failures"; at least, shameful feelings do not *inhibit* our self-inquiry. In effect, the discovery that these experiences are indeed universal appears to be especially helpful in enabling therapists to become freer to respond optimally to their patients. These discussions can be undertaken with especial effectiveness in groups of therapists—for instance, in the so-called Balint-type groups, whose ambience facilitates the forthright engagement of problematic intersubjective issues (or "countertransference" problems). In this situation, the discrepancy between the faulty therapist and the supposedly nonfaulty therapist is greatly diminished. In addition, the evolving bond of trust between members mitigates the shame of disclosing one's selfobject needs and the defenses against them. Concomitant with such a process, one's self undergoes significant strengthening.

There are some difficult or adversarial situations, however, that may particularly strain an analyst's capacity to maintain an empathic stance and benign bond with his patient. As one of us (H.B., in Bacal and Newman, 1990) has observed:

> [W]hen . . . certain of the analyst's selfobject needs surface and he perceives his patient as, so to say, "violating" his expectations or acting upon him beyond the threshold of his tolerance, [t]his may precipitate a reaction in the therapist that can trigger or exacerbate a disruption of the patient's sense of selfobject relatedness to him [p. 269].

Such situations, when the patient becomes disrupted and perhaps enraged, may reverberate back onto the analyst, resulting in further frustration of his psychologically legitimate needs for self-enhancing or self-restorative responses from his patient. Now the analyst may experience a spectrum of painful feelings such as rage, hatred, anxiety, profound discouragement, and loss of self-esteem. He also experiences the pressure of the requirement that he decenter from such feelings in order to remain in empathic contact with the patient. This, however, may be easier said than done, for it may seem to him that it demands that he totally disavow authentic aspects of his affective experience. We may ask whether self psychology demands too much of the analyst by

---

ference problems could be addressed with more immediateness, richness, and effectiveness than in the standard form of supervision, where the unconscious determinants of the student's countertransference can only be touched on by the supervisor. Dr. S was, in fact, worked with in this way.

requiring him to maintain the empathic stance at all times, which sometimes would seem to entail the complete renunciation of his or her self-object needs. We allow, and indeed often encourage children, parents, and patients to feel entitled to protest when their needs are not met. The long-suffering analyst tends to disallow himself such latitude. Moraitis (1993) has recently observed that

> [I]n order to achieve his objectives the analyst must forfeit his personal needs to the maximum degree possible, so that he can place himself or herself in the service of his patient and his science.
> I believe such demands are unrealistic and unwarranted. They place the analyst in the defensive position of claiming altruistic motives he usually questions in others and of disclaiming in himself the very needs he helps his patients to acknowledge and satisfy [p. 343].

Is it not the analyst's natural and perfectly human need to protest against the assault on his own sense of self? No doubt in the vast majority of instances such protest would not be expressed openly. But the right to give covert—and sometimes even overt—expression to his own aversive attitude may help protect the analyst from injury and, having acknowledged his legitimate needs, enable him to continue working with his patient.

For a long period in the analysis of a young woman, every interpretation the analyst made disrupted her. She angrily and contemptuously dismissed almost all his interventions. The analyst now, himself, became disrupted. He began to experience increasing degrees of mortification, shame, and disappointment in himself. He strove valiantly to restore both the patient's and his own self-esteem by searching for the "right" interpretation. This was all to no avail. Finally he withdrew in discouraged silence. As his own vitality and cohesion were undermined, so did this reverberate on the patient in a vicious circle. This analyst was unable to accord himself the right to protest, even inwardly, at the patient's failure to affirm him. It was only with the aid of a consultant that he was able to begin to tolerate her disillusionment. The problem of this analyst with this patient is one that might especially lend itself to the kind of group discussion and support that we have suggested.

Winnicott (1947) recognizes that the analyst will, at times, hate the patient, especially the regressed patient (p. 195). He regards it as important that the analyst acknowledge this hate to himself and tolerate both the patient's hate and his ingratitude. Winnicott is, in effect, implying a significant selfobject need on the part of the analyst that is being deeply frustrated by the patient. In our experience, if the analyst accommodates to the analysand on a continuous basis in order to avoid the patient's experiencing intolerable trauma in the transference,[9] the hate engendered in the analyst by the prolonged frustration of his selfobject needs will inevitably interfere at times with the analyst's therapeutic function.

We recognize that not all analysts find adversarial situations difficult or disaffirming. In fact, some analysts feel mirrored or stimulated by the cut and thrust of an aversive encounter, as do some patients. The different personalities and theoretical approaches of analysts indicate great variation in their selfobject needs and expectations. The number of permutations and combinations in mutual selfobject needs, and frustrations of such needs, in the psychoanalytic situation must be infinite.

Stolorow and Atwood (1992) emphasize that sustained empathic inquiry must include the therapist's continual reflection on his ongoing subjective processes (i.e., as part of the intersubjective field). We believe it should be possible for an analyst to become practiced in monitoring his self states as they are affected by those of the patient and by the effects of external factors on his life.

We have argued that the analyst's self states are significantly affected by his selfobject experience in relation to the patient. In other words, what enables the analyst to carry out his therapeutic task—what, so to speak, keeps the analyst going—centrally includes responses on the part of the analysand that provide the analyst with selfobject experience.[10] The recognition that it is psychologically legitimate for the therapist to have these needs and that their frustration contributes to countertransference reactions will not only alter our conceptualizations of the therapeutic process but will also enhance our capacity to respond optimally to our patients.

REFERENCES

Bacal, H. A. (1985), Optimal responsiveness and the therapeutic process. In: *Progress in Self Psychology, Vol. 1,* ed. A. Goldberg. New York: Guilford, pp. 202–226.
—— (1994), The selfobject relationship in psychoanalytic treatment. In: *A Decade of Progress, Progress in Self Psychology, Vol. 10,* ed. A. Goldberg. Hillsdale, NJ: The Analytic Press, pp. 21–30.
—— & Newman, K. M. (1990), *Theories of Object Relations: Bridges to Self Psychology.* New York: Columbia University Press.

---

[9] We are referring here to trauma that tends to occur when the analysand regresses to pathognomonic, genetically related disruptions in the transference—what Balint called "the basic fault" (Balint, 1968; Bacal and Newman, 1990).

[10] Lessem and Orange (1992) suggest that the mutuality of selfobject experience is associated with an increasingly solid bond of seeker and healer. That is, the therapeutic process is enhanced by the patient and analyst both experiencing the other as providing selfobject functions.

Balint, M. (1937), Early developmental states of the ego: Primary object-love. In: *Primary Love and Psycho-Analytic Technique,* new and enlarged ed. London: Tavistock, 1965.

—— (1964), *The Doctor, His Patient & The Illness,* 2nd ed. London: Pitman.

—— (1968), *The Basic Fault.* London: Tavistock.

Basch, M. (1992), *Practicing Psychotherapy.* New York: Basic Books.

Broucek, F. J. (1991), *Shame and the Self.* New York: Guilford.

Casement, P. (1985), *Learning from the Patient.* New York: Guilford.

Estrella, C. (1993), Optimal responsiveness: An exploration of the subjective and intersubjective experiences of psychotherapists. Unpublished. Ph.D. dissertation, California Institute for Clinical Social Work.

Dender, J. M. (1993), The phenomena of sleepiness in the analyst. Presented at the 16th Annual Conference on the Psychology of the Self, Toronto, Oct. 31.

Freud, S. (1910), The future prospects of psychoanalytic therapy. *Standard Edition,* 11:139–151. London: Hogarth Press, 1957.

Gunther, M. S. (1976), The endangered self: A contribution to the understanding of narcissistic determinants of countertransference. *The Annual of Psychoanalysis,* 4:201–224. New York: International Universities Press.

Heimann, P. (1950). On countertransference. *Internat. J. Psycho -Anal.,* 31:81–84.

Kindler, A. (1991), Mirror transference and the need for confirmation. Presented to the Toronto Psychoanalytic Society, Oct. 9.

Kohler, L. (1984/1985), On selfobject countertransference. *The Annual of Psychoanalysis,* 12/13:39–56. Madison, CT: International Universities Press.

Kohut, H. (1971), *The Analysis of the Self.* New York: International Universities Press.

—— (1977), *The Restoration of the Self.* New York: International Universities Press.

Lessem, P. & Orange, D. Emotional bonds: The therapeutic action of psychoanalysis revisited. Unpublished.

Lichtenberg, J. D. (1989), *Psychoanalysis and Motivation.* Hillsdale, NJ: The Analytic Press.

McLaughlin, J. T. (1975), The sleepy analyst: Some observations on states of consciousness in the analyst at work. *J. Amer. Psychoanal. Assn.,* 23:363–382.

Moore, B. & Fine, B. (1990), *Psychoanalytic Terms and Concepts.* Binghamton, NY: The American Psychoanalytic Association & Yale University Press.

Moraitis, G. (1993), The analyst's quest for self-consciousness. *Psychoanal. Inq.,* 13:333–347.

Morrison, A. (1989), *Shame: The Underside of Narcissism.* Hillsdale, NJ: The Analytic Press.

—— (1994), The breadth and boundaries of a self-psychological immersion in shame: A one-and-a-half person perspective. *Psychoanal. Dial.,* 4:19–35.

Rycroft, C. (1972), *A Critical Dictionary of Psychoanalysis.* New York: Penguin.

Sandler, J. (1976), Countertransference and role-responsiveness. *Internat. Rev. Psycho-Anal.,* 3:43–47.

Stolorow, R. D. & Atwood, G. E. (1992), *Contexts of Being: The Intersubjective Foundations of Psychological Life.* Hillsdale, NJ: The Analytic Press.

Sullivan, H. S. (1953), *The Interpersonal Theory of Psychiatry.* New York: Norton Library. William Alanson White Psychiatric Foundation.

Thomson, P. G. (1991), Countertransference in an intersubjective perspective: An experiment. In: *The Evolution of Self Psychology: Progress in Self Psychology, Vol. 7,* ed A. Goldberg. Hillsdale, NJ: The Analytic Press, pp. 7–92.

—— (1993), The influence of the analyst's narcissistic vulnerability on his work. *Psychoanal. Inq.*, 13:348–364.

Winnicott, D. W. (1947), Hate in the countertransference. In: *Collected Papers of D. W. Winnicott*. London: Tavistock, 1958, pp. 194–203.

—— (1960), Ego distortion in terms of true and false self. In: *The Maturational Processes and the Facilitating Environment*. London: Hogarth Press, 1965, pp. 140–152.

—— (1971), *Playing and Reality*. London: Tavistock, pp. 101–102.

Wolf, E. S. (1979), Transferences and countertransferences in the analysis of disorders of the self. *Contemp. Psychoanal.*, 15:577–594.

—— (1980), Empathy and countertransference. In: *The Future of Psychoanalysis*, ed. A. Goldberg. New York: International Universities Press, pp. 309–326.

—— (1988), *Treating the Self*. New York: Guilford.

Wurmser, L. (1981), *The Mask of Shame*. Baltimore: Johns Hopkins Press.

Chapter 3

Self Psychology in Search of the Optimal: A Consideration of Optimal Responsiveness, Optimal Provision, Optimal Gratification, and Optimal Restraint in the Clinical Situation

Morton Shane

Estelle Shane

Eleven years ago Howard Bacal presented a paper at the Sixth Annual Conference on the Psychology of the Self that proved to be seminal for self psychology and was entitled "Optimal Responsiveness and the Therapeutic Process" (1985). With this paper, and the introduction of a new concept, optimal responsiveness, as well as a new way of viewing the analyst's participation in the therapeutic process, a conversation was begun among us that is still going on. Charles Spezzano (1993) has written, based upon his own application to psychoanalysis of Richard Rorty's (1989) work, that new psychoanalytic concepts appear when we want to discuss certain clinical problems with each other, but we perceive ourselves to be unable to discuss them adequately in the language and conceptual framework familiar and available to us. This has been the history of psychoanalysis from its beginnings. To paraphrase Spezzano, the evolution of psychoanalytic theory is an ongoing conversation, and the exchanges that make up this psychoanalytic conversation are yielding ever more useful clinical concepts. So, here *we* are now, in *this* presentation, entering into the conversation about the optimal in the clinician's response. We will focus on guidelines that may help direct us in our search for the appropriate and the useful in the therapeutic moment. We do so with full understanding that any contribution we may make will lead at best to no more than a temporary solution to the clinical problem at hand, or a temporary rest in the dialogue.

The chief participants in this conversation about the optimal in psychoanalysis have included, over time, Sigmund Freud (1911–1915), Anna Freud (1965), Kohut (1971, 1977, 1984), Wolf (1976, 1989), Stolorow, Brandchaft, and Atwood (1987), Bacal (1985), Terman (1988), and, most recently, Lindon (1994). In this chapter, we will focus mainly on the latter three (i.e., Bacal, Terman, and Lindon), who themselves have referenced and amply discussed the important contributions of the others, and we will begin with our own assessment of where the field rests at the present time, and where the conversation has stopped so far.

The impact of Bacal's challenging 1983 presentation was that of calling into question Kohut's generative contribution concerning the role of optimal frustration via transmuting internalization in fostering the structuring and restructuring of the self. As optimal frustration was so central to Kohut's thesis on how analysis cures, the challenge to it had to be made with care and with great persuasiveness, and Bacal was eminently successful in achieving these requirements. In effect, what Bacal accomplished was to demonstrate that Kohut's covert tie to classical analysis hampered his capacity to break free of some hidden assumptions of classical theory. Kohut's accurate observation that clinical work with self-disordered patients is punctuated by disruptions requiring repair, and that following such repair the patient seems improved, was confounded with this sense that it was the frustration itself, requiring that the patient assume functions heretofore supplied by the analyst, that was responsible for the improvement and growth of structure. In contrast, Bacal reasoned that just because structure building *followed* optimal frustration and its repair, this did not mean that there was an inevitable cause-and-effect relationship between moderate frustration and structure building. Bacal argued that what created new structure was the patient's sense of being understood that followed the disruption attendant on the frustration and its repair. Optimal responsiveness, leading to a resumption of harmony in the relationship, is therapeutic not because understanding of the disruption is therapeutic, but

because understanding in itself is therapeutic, that is, leads to psychological growth.

The valorization of frustration had been linked in classical theory to
beneficial results because the Freudian model of secondary-process
thinking and structure building was related to and depended on the frustration of primary-process drive discharge and gratification (Rapaport,
1960). Although Kohut was able to drop the drive model, he could
never relinquish the idea that frustration in itself was beneficial, viewing
it as adding to the establishment of what he had originally termed the
"narcissistic equilibrium" of the patient, and later, harmony, strength,
and cohesiveness of the patient's self.

Bacal was able to persuade many to believe otherwise, leading to the
introduction into our clinical vocabulary of the term and concept
"optimal responsiveness" and, as well, to a set of new questions
regarding what it means to be "responsive," and especially what is
meant by "optimal." Noting that Kohut himself had posed the question
about what is optimal in optimal frustration, but had never arrived at a
satisfactory answer, Bacal, describing "responsiveness" as the therapist's
act of communicating his understanding of the patient to the patient,
then defines the "optimal" as that response which for that particular
patient will be most suited to the patient's developmental capacity and
selfobject needs for human relatedness. Further, optimal responsiveness
was presented by Bacal as the umbrella term that would subsume optimal frustration, gratification, and provision. Bacal noted that whereas
frustration and gratification are both inevitable in the clinical relationship,
neither serves as an appropriate treatment goal for the analyst; the analyst should neither seek to deliberately frustrate, however optimally, nor
seek to deliberately gratify. Rather, the proper goal in the clinical situation is that the analyst, having understood his or her patient, should then
communicate that understanding through an optimal response.

Bacal offers to the analyst two guidelines toward the optimal
response. The first derives from Kohut's concept of a developmental line
of empathy, an advance from understanding to interpretation to be
offered by the analyst in response to a progression the analyst has
observed in the patient from an earlier, more archaic form of capacity to
feel the analyst's empathy, in which a literal holding environment or an
experience of merger is required with the analyst, to a more evolved
form of capacity to feel the analyst's empathy, where a more
metaphoric holding environment provided through verbal understanding
or explanation is now adequate to serve the patient's selfobject needs.
Kohut had illustrated this progression by speaking of the young child's
needing bodily contact, and then the child's developing to a capacity
wherein words alone could achieve the same result. This was translated

into the clinical realm by Kohut in his famous and final demonstration of empathy with a severely disturbed patient to whom he offered his hand, (or, more, accurately, a restrained two fingers), and also in the distinction he made between the understanding phase of interpretation and the explaining phase. Thus the developmental line of empathy serves as the first guideline offered by Bacal for optimal responsiveness. The second guideline he offers toward optimal responsiveness also derives from Kohut's writings—the state of self–selfobject relatedness along a continuum of disruption and repair. When the patient is in a disrupted state, and the self–selfobject relationship is at an impasse, a different sort of response is called for from the analyst than when the selfobject tie has either been restituted or is perceived as smoothly ongoing.

With this comprehensive, indeed groundbreaking, statement, it is interesting to note that the conversation about the optimal did not rest there. Three years after Bacal's paper was presented, Terman appeared at the Eighth Annual Conference on the Psychology of the Self (1986) to address the audience on "Optimal Frustration: Structuralization and the Therapeutic Process." Terman's paper proved to be a useful addition to Bacal's original thesis, providing more than just supporting evidence for it. Terman's own opposition to Kohut's concept of optimal frustration derives primarily from two sources. The first source is evidence from his psychoanalytic practice, which to him clearly did not conform to Kohut's theory of structure building via optimal frustration and transmuting internalization, but instead convinced him that in the clinical situation, understanding of the old and creation of the new had *nothing* to do with the experience of *frustration*; rather, it was the experience of *satisfaction* that opened new pathways for the patient and remade old ones. The second source for Terman's opposition was drawn by him from *developmental* studies, the findings from which preclude the concept that structures can arise or develop from *absence* in the dyad, or *interruption* of the dyad, as would seem to be inherent in a frustration model of development. On the contrary, findings from developmental studies emphasize that structuralization of the mind grows only out of the presence of human relationships, not apart from them.

Terman cites the developmentalist Kenneth Kaye, who stresses the two-way process of creating and structuring the infant's mind, the parent continuously drawing the child forward in the dyad, in the zone of proximal development, eventually toward a full partnership. Terman also refers to Daniel Stern to demonstrate that it is the repetition and participation of the caretaker in the child's activities, not the absence of the caretaker, that lays down governing patterns. To quote Terman (1988), "The shaping, molding, and structuring of internal states . . . occurs by way of the vicissitudes of attunement" (p. 125), not by way of frustration. Terman's point again is that frustration does not build structure, and he refers to Socarides and Stolorow, who contend that it is the *intactness* of the selfobject tie that permits the resumption of development, not its disruption following frustration.

Supportive of Bacal's position, then, Terman actually goes beyond him with an important addition to our understanding to how structure is formed, both in development and in the clinical situation. Terman argues that the concept of frustration leading to structure has distracted us from the variety of transactions between caretaker and child and between analyst and patient; that these transactions, taken together, create patterns adaptive or maladaptive; and that it is the repetition of the pattern itself that ultimately builds structure. Anticipating the Darwinian neurophysiologist Gerald Edelman (1992), as well as Goldberg (1991), Modell (1993), and Trevarthan (1994), Terman (1988) asserts here that "the doing is the making," the dialogue of construction between parent and child and between therapist and patient, *is* the structure; there is no need to posit a two-part process wherein one first experiences and then internalizes to build enduring function; rather, the structured schema is created by the transaction itself, in real time, as the transaction occurs. And it is "repetition, not absence or interruption, [that] creates the enduring pattern" (p. 125).

Thus Terman uses experimental findings from infant and child observation to support his own clinical experience, and although he is well aware that such developmental findings cannot be depended on to *prove* analytic theory, he obviously believes that such findings *can* be used to bolster, shape, and delimit theory, providing an important external coherence (Strenger, 1991) and confirmation from related disciplines, and we certainly agree with this approach.

At that same conference, Bacal responded to Terman's paper, finding himself in essential concurrence with him. Bacal specifically refers to a point Terman makes that interpretation serves to make the patient feel understood, being "tantamount to the provision of what was missing in the patient's past." Bacal adds that a good interpretation is nevertheless but one component of the analyst's optimal responsiveness, and perhaps not even the most therapeutic one. There are noninterpretive responses, responses that are out of the ordinary, that the analyst *may* or may *not* be *willing* or *able* to provide. Bacal notes that the patient says, "Be who I need you to be; don't just interpret it," and if the analyst cannot find a way to be that, the patient may have to accept the limitations of analysis, at least with that analyst. Bacal emphasizes that noninterpretive responsiveness may be just what the patient needs, and although most analysts do know this, they hesitate to discuss it or to write about it freely.

Thus we see how, in Bacal's remarks, an invitation can be heard to continue the conversation about the optimal. When in 1993 Lindon addressed the Sixteenth Annual Conference on the Psychology of the Self, he entered the dialogue with his own paper entitled "Gratification and Provision in Psychoanalysis: Should We Get Rid of the Rule of abstinence?" asserting that we should get rid of the rule of abstinence and that we should replace it with the concept of optimal provision. Bacal's invitation, then, to discuss openly, without fear, noninterpretive optimal responsiveness was addressed by Lindon's clinically rich and openly presented paper containing illustrations of both interpretive and noninterpretive interventions, though Lindon himself was acting independently, unaware of Bacal's and Terman's earlier contributions.

Lindon's particular emphasis is on the rule of abstinence, which he contends is both pantheoretical and universally obstructionistic to the unfolding of the analytic process. He asserts that the analyst, rather than having a withholding, frustrating stance designed to enhance the patient's verbalization and ultimate insight through interpretation, should instead tailor his or her response to the patient's requirements. To perceived developmental *needs* on the part of the patient, the analyst should respond with optimal *provision*; to perceived urgent *desires* on the part of the patient, the analyst should respond with optimal *gratification*. Although gratification and provision exist in every analytic relationship, these concepts cannot be encompassed by a "rule," such as had existed in the rule of abstinence, but must be approached instead by what is optimal for the particular patient. This inevitably leads back to the central question, What is optimal in optimal provision? "Optimal provision," Lindon (1994) tells us, "could be defined as any provision which, by meeting a mobilized developmental longing, facilitates the uncovering, illuminating, and transforming of the subjective experiences of the patient" (p. 559), a definition informed by Stolorow, and Atwood's (1984) own definition of psychoanalysis, namely, a process that aims at uncovering, illuminating, and transforming the patient's organizing principles. By offering many clinical illustrations, Lindon provides a sense of what he means by "optimal" and certainly what he means by "provision." Countertransference enactments are recounted, Lindon warning that provision may become subverted to addiction in a process of mutual enactment that obstructs the *analytic* process.

At this point we would like to enter into the conversation more directly, hoping to further an understanding of the optimal in the therapeutic dyad. We are persuaded by Bacal that optimal responsiveness, defined by him as the responsivity of the analyst that is therapeutically most relevant at any particular moment in the context of a particular patient and his or her pathology, does accurately identify the therapeutic goal of the clinician, that the clinician does not seek to frustrate, nor even to gratify, but to respond in such a fashion as to communicate to the patient that he or she has been understood, in both direct (interpretive) and indirect (noninterpretive) ways. We believe that the capacity for optimal responsiveness comes through empathy and affect attunement, but the guiding principle is informed by one's particular theory of development and pathology as it applies to a specific patient. From our own perspective, the other familiar terms traditionally used to guide the therapist's intervention are subsumed *under* optimal responsiveness, including Lindon's optimal provision (the response to the patient's *need*) and optimal gratification (the response to the patient's *desire*).

We would, along with Lindon, eliminate the rule of abstinence, but we would in fact go further, replacing the term altogether, since it connotes an absence, or shutting down of response. Still, we believe there is some need for reserve, so we would offer the term "optimal restraint" as supplying that function, that is, a response within the therapeutic dyad that is neither in excess of what is needed or desired by the patient, nor so withholding or so unspontaneous that it serves to derail the process. As with provision, restraint should be tailored, insofar as possible, to the clinical moment with the particular patient, ideally negotiated and coconstructed by both participants. As for optimal frustration, we are in agreement with the tenor of the conversation thus far that the concept of optimal frustration is a relic of the past, that while the patient may at times be frustrated, this is not an appropriate or desirable treatment goal for the therapist to have. We feel this altered view of the process has profound meaning for how all analyses will be understood in the future, allowing us not only to *proceed* differently, but to *reflect* differently on the analyses we have already completed.

We would like to devote the remainder of our presentation to a further consideration of guidelines toward optimal responsivity in the analytic situation. We will begin with a brief discussion of our own perspective on clinical self-psychological theory as our view of clinical theory introduces one important guideline toward the optimal.

As we have stated elsewhere (1992), self psychology as a single homogenous entity does not exist; there are now many self psychologies. We ourselves integrate current self-psychological theory with intersubjectivity, in an effort to modify the direction of self psychology toward a more truly relational developmental perspective. We strive to establish an ambiance of safety so that the patient may gradually risk exposing his or her conscious and preconscious private world. Eventually, defenses against uncovering what is feared, sequestered, and repressed are interpreted in their present here-and-now manifestation, in the transference, and in their genetic roots. The whole process, the messenger and the message (Schlesinger, 1988), is viewed by us as constituting the therapeutic action, in a contemporary mode of corrective emotional experience. Although we retain as singularly important the idea of self-object relatedness, equating it more or less with Stern's core self in relation to a self-regulating other, we don't believe that the selfobject concept is sufficient to explain all types of relatedness either in development or in the clinical situation, and we don't find either that the concept of mature, as distinct from archaic, selfobject relatedness answers our concern. We find it essential to postulate as well another dimension of relatedness, an intersubjective relatedness, that encompasses a subjective self in relation to an intersubjective other wherein each subject in the dyad can appreciate the other as a person in his or her own right, each possessing a separate and distinct mind and set of motives, intentions, and emotions, not all of them positive, leading in the direction of a mutuality and intimacy between two subjectivities. In Stern's (1994) terms, it is the interactive state of "I know that you know that I know" and "I feel that you feel that I feel," and most importantly, we would add, "I care to know and feel all about us, about you, about me, and about our 'we-ness'" (Emde, 1988).

Although we appreciate and borrow freely from the contributions of Stolorow, Brandchaft, and Atwood to self psychology, in particular their concept of intersubjectivity as defining the mutual influence of each person upon the other in the intersubjective matrix between them, as well as their concept of unconscious (sequestered) organizing principles in both patient and analyst, requiring the analyst's articulation and interpretation, our difference with them is that we view the concept of intersubjectivity in a less global fashion, reserving the capacity to interact in an intersubjective fashion to a relationship wherein *each* member in the dyad is concerned with the otherness, the subjectivity of the other. By maintaining this distinction, we can better conceptualize and delineate the quality of selfobject relatedness from the more mature capacity for a self–other relatedness wherein the other is appreciated as a person in his or her own right.

We conceptualize, then, only the dimension of experience that corresponds to the subjective self and the intersubjective other as truly intersubjective, in that in such a case, each person in the dyad is vitally interested in the subjectivity of the other. In contrast, the patient who is relating to his or her analyst in the selfobject dimension is not relating to his or her analyst as a subjective entity, but, in selfobject terms, is relating to the analyst as a provider of functions, or experiences a requisite for self-sustenance, with little or no involvement in the other's complex inner world and little or no capacity for, or interest in, mutuality or inter-subjective intimacy. In the clinical situation, the selfobject dimension of relatedness is distinctly one-sided; the analysis, ideally, fully concerned with the intrapsychic world of the patient via empathy, as well as being concerned with his or her own intrapsychic world, and the intersubjec-tivity between himself and his patient, whereas the patient uses the rela-tionship in a more one-sided way, via selfobject functions. We want to clarify that this more focused view of intersubjectivity inherent in our clinical theory is not meant to detract from what Stolorow, Brandchaft, and Atwood have told us about the significant impact of each member of the dyad on the subjective experience of the other; this important insight remains valid whether that other, the analyst, is experienced by the patient in the intersubjective or in the selfobject dimension.

One pathway to optimal responsiveness, then, stems from the thera-pist's attention to which dimension of relatedness is in the foreground at any point in the analysis. For example, a young woman who suffered from a development impairment wherein she could, in effect, only relate to others as archaic selfobjects complained bitterly to her analyst one day about a good friend's slighting her by canceling a small dinner the woman had been planning to celebrate the patient's birthday. The patient had been depending on the dinner to ameliorate her sense of being alone, and was now faced with the prospect of being deserted on her birthday. The depth of her pain, genuine and understandable, was the center of her focus, and it was only in passing that she noted to her analyst the reason for the cancellation, that the friend was pregnant, having struggled for years to achieve this, and was now at risk of losing her child and was ordered by her physician to remain at bed rest. The patient could talk about this situation and note her own reluctance to commiserate with her friend's grief, which she understood intellectually, but not emotionally. She said, "I tell her everything about myself, and I always expect her to feel for me, but I cannot and I am not interested in, hearing about or feeling for her." The patient, then, was able on her own to see the irony of the situation, the lack of symmetry in the rela-tionships she establishes. Her analyst responded to her with an affirma-tion of her feelings but without any attempt to interpret the patient's dis-comfort with her own perception of this imbalance. The analyst did not confront her with her developmental incapacity, interpret its origins, or in any way bring it into the transference, to the analyst's own experi-ences of being similarly unresponded to and unappreciated by this patient; in other words, a garden variety self-psychological response was offered by the analyst, informed by knowledge of this patient's archaic selfobject neediness.

Our point is that optimal responsiveness for this patient would require taking into consideration the dimension of relatedness currently at the forefront of her experience. In contrast, in another analytic dyad, a depressed female patient whose parents have been unhappy with one another, and distant and controlling with her, comments to her male analyst, who is in supervision with one of us, that she knows he is subtly but distinctly interested in her, both as a person, and more pertinently, as a sexually desirable woman. She also tells him that she feels he is unhappy in his own personal life, and that she knows she adds with her presence in his life some essential vitality and interest to his existence. As it happens, the patient's perceptions are absolutely correct on all counts, including her assertions about her analyst's sexual interest in her, and at times, even his sexual excitement. Moreover, the patient tells her analyst that she feels sorry for him, that she wishes to comfort him, knows that he really desires her comfort, and would like a romantic involvement with her, but that both understand that such an affair is out of the question.

On his side, the analyst knows that she knows all of this, he appreciates her for it, feels a poignancy in the intimacy of their relationship, and is able to use all of this to respond in a respectful, insightful way that does not deny her reality, and yet shows optimal restraint. This analyst could have interpreted his patient's sense of his own unhappiness as transference, a displacement from her own parent's troubled marriage, but chooses more authentically and more optimally to stay with her in the here and now, despite his own discomfort at being so exposed, cognizant of this patient's capacity to relate on a fully intersubjective level and resonate accurately with his self state. Aware that he is hewing a fine line between optimal and nonoptimal, even dangerous, responsivity, he proceeds nevertheless to explore her experience of him, never denying her reality and perceptiveness, and knowing that such risks constitute the occupational hazard of all well-functioning, self-attuned, self-reflective analysts. This analyst was appreciative also of this patient's selfobject needs which indeed have come to the fore many times; he was appreciative that his patient's capacity for reading his subjectivity was derived from the necessity throughout her childhood of being aware of and alert to her parent's fluctuating and sometimes dangerous moods. Nevertheless, he did not mistake this particular instance of intersubjective mutuality for a simple, unconscious genetic recreation, nor for a need on her part for a one-sided provision of self-regulating functions. It is our contention, then, that both dimensions of relatedness must be kept in mind as guidelines to the quality of optimal responsivity, as well as what is subsumed under this umbrella term (viz., optimal provision, gratification, and restraint).

Another guideline in our search for the optimal is attention to a comprehensive organization of motivational systems, such as the one first Lichtenberg (1989) and now Lichtenberg, Lachmann, and Fosshage (1992) delineate. By detecting in a given patient precisely what motive is most prevalent in the therapeutic moment, we can come closer to identifying the "main meaning," to use Lawrence Friedman's (1996) apt phrase, and with that understanding, respond most optimally. For example, an anorexic bulimic patient who has severe problems in regulating her physiological need states, particularly her eating and defecating, works together with her analyst in a way that highlights the patient's physiological disregulation. The analyst does not translate her patient's difficulty into classical dynamic motivational formulations such as forbidden oedipal wishes to bear a child, or oral aggressive wishes to destroy a hated mother within, trends that could certainly be found, if one seeks them, sifting through what the patient brings in. Nor does the analyst address the problem in the attachment realm, though this longing, too, can be discerned quite easily in the patient's association. Rather, the analyst goes directly to the patient's urgent inability to deal with the psychological effects of her chronic eating and bowel disregulation, which inability is analyzed both within present and past disturbed relationships, especially the relationship with her mother, her thin and beautiful mother who always felt that the patient was too fat.

The analyst will deliberately inquire as to how and what the patient eats, both in her periods of bulimia and in her periods of anorexia. She actually shares with her patient information about what she herself eats, and how she herself attempts to maintain her own weight and health. The analyst continues to focus on this motivational system irrespective of its more or less obvious connections to other motivational systems more salient in the analytic literature. She abides her own discomfort at not acting like a *real* analyst, because she has detected that the main meaning in this patient's disturbed relatedness is encompassed in this motivational-functional system. She therefore relates to the patient directly in this dimension, in order to respond optimally, using provision, in Lindon's sense (i.e., dietary direction, shared nutritional needs, and the like) and, again in Lindon's sense, gratification (i.e., self-revelation of her own private battle in the same arena so as to provide a sense that the patient is not alone in the difficulty, but shares it with her much-admired, idealized analyst). By recognizing multiple motivational systems, then, the therapist has a greater chance of responding most precisely to the patient's predicament.

An example follows wherein the main meaning for the patient is found in the attachment-motivational system. This foreground need was confounded because for the analyst, a confused state of feeling sexual stimulation, and then guilt and shame over it, interfered for a time with his capacity to respond optimally. Some years ago a woman patient was in the middle of an analysis that had gone on for five years when she developed an eye pathology that led over the next year to marked diminution in her vision, and ultimately blindness. Understandably distressed, the patient in time requested that the analyst hold her hand while she was lying on the couch, at least at the beginning of each hour, and that upon leaving, she be allowed to stroke his arm for some moments, and at times to feel his face. These requests appeared quite understandable in view of the patient's need to augment the perception of her analyst and her vital attachment to him through touch, but the analyst, who was overly rigorous in regard to allowing any physical contact with patients, or to put it more simply, was uptight, found himself, while without question acceding to his patient's request, in a state of discomfort; he unavoidably and involuntarily experienced his interaction with his patient, when either holding her hand or being stroked by her, as sexually charged. This dissonance within himself had to be resolved as quickly as possible in order to allow him to be optimally responsive to his patient, to be, that is, attuned and available to his patient's need for special provision in the attachment sphere, which is where *she* was.

As he came to be able to respond more authentically to her touch, with a less divided internal state, the analyst was then also able to reflect upon his exceeding rigor, his need to do the right thing and be the proper analyst, and he was able as well to look back on previous experiences with patients in which he might have been more optimally responsive in this same way. The change in him was facilitated in part by an appreciation of the fact that the attachment-motivational system was separate from, not derivative of, the sensual-sexual system as he had originally been taught. Were the main meaning of the patient's desire for physical contact within the sensual-sexual sphere, then the analyst, to respond optimally, might still have acceded to this blind patient's request, but he would have pursued the inquiry into its main meaning for the patient in a different direction. Thus, detecting as closely as possible the salient motive in the clinical moment facilitates an understanding of the most helpful way to be with and respond to a given patient.

As a final example of the use of motivational systems to aid in the achievement of optimal responsiveness, we will provide an instance derived from the assertive-exploratory mode. The analyst greets her patient in the waiting room and is struck by the beauty of the patient's jacket, which is lying on the chair next to where the patient was sitting. The analyst spontaneously remarks about it, commenting on the lushness of color, and they enter the office together talking of other things.

At the end of the session, which was filled with the patient's emotion concerning her relationship with her inadequately responsive mother and who had died when the patient was 21, the patient and analyst get up together. The patient lifts her jacket from the couch and quite suddenly extends her arm, saying, "Here. You admire this, I really don't, and I want you to have it." The analyst, nonplussed, completely taken off guard, and striving to remain an analyst with an appropriate degree of optimal restraint, after first spontaneously reaching out to take it from the patient's hand, and noting, without wanting to, the pure pleasure of its expensive silken feel, again just as spontaneously returns it to her patient, saying, "I simply can't just take your jacket; let's talk about it tomorrow."

The next day the patient returns furious, ready and fully energized to explore the encounter with her analyst. She jumps right in with the following statement: "How can you be so stupid and unfeeling? You of all people know how hard it is for me to feel I have anything of worth to offer. You know how hard it is for me to take a chance and do something risky and experimental. You know how hard it is for me to assert myself at all. And yet you humiliate me by rebuffing my offer of something which belongs to me, and which you like. I can only think it is because it is *mine* that it is distasteful to you, and I feel ashamed, and angry with *you* that you caused me to feel this way." At this point, the analyst feels remorseful, confused, disturbed, and humiliated herself. Now she is *truly* uncertain as to what to do, and uncertain also about what she should have done the day before. Groping and slouching toward the optimal, she responds by telling her patient that the patient's offer was only made, after all, in response to the analyst herself having admired it, that it was not something the patient would otherwise have intended to give her, and it wasn't as if it were a gift she had brought in with the full expectation of presenting it. She also tells the patient that she feels remorse for how she had handled the situation up till now, that certainly she had no intention of squelching the patient's experimental mood, and that, in fact, the analyst's response was based on her own awkwardness, her own sense of being thrown off balance. By these statements the analyst had intended to support the patient's new and tentative effort to assert herself.

And the analyst's remarks did seem to repair the moderate impasse, for the next day the patient, exhibiting a new resourcefulness and a fine sensitivity and irony, ceremoniously presented her analyst with the jacket in an elaborately gift-wrapped box. The analyst this time acted with more grace, both to the gift and to the joyful and humorous spirit with which it was offered. Over the weeks that followed, the incident was considered in terms of the many meanings, conscious and unconscious, of this mutual enactment for both parties. The ongoing analysis of the event is not relevant to our discussion here, except to say that it left the pair somehow more closely connected and more at ease with one another.

We will turn now to a consideration of guidelines toward the optimal response inherent in specific diagnostic categories as recognized by various self-psychological contributors. The work of Basch (1988) concerns the clinician's determination as to how affect is subjectively perceived and integrated, or not integrated, in a given patient. The manner in which affect is perceived and integrated is conceptualized by Basch as contributing to the development of different pathological states; in his system, the pathological state itself serves as a guideline to the therapist's most appropriate and useful response. For example, Basch has identified pathological self-states resulting from an initial failure of the affective bond between the infant or very young child and its caregivers, wherein the normal mutual regulation and self-regulation of affect is interfered with, requiring from the clinician a specific type of responsiveness, namely, one that enhances the patient's capacity to be soothed and regulated, as well as to self-soothe and self-regulate. For example, a patient who has had a history of maternal deprivation begins treatment with her therapist by coming in so late to each scheduled session that only five or ten minutes remain. The therapist responds initially by just accepting her lateness, and using what is left of their time together for attempting to deal with her anxiety, which increases predictably during the session—increasing, that is, as the session progresses. This pattern leads the therapist to deduce that the patient's lateness is a function of the degree to which being with him causes her unbearable stimulation, so that she, either consciously or unconsciously, titrates the time with him and thereby self-regulates her anxiety within the therapeutic matrix. The strategy of not interpreting the lateness, or even questioning it, works, because the patient feels increasingly comfortable with her therapist and can then allow herself to spend more of the allotted time with him, arriving less late as the therapy progresses. This exemplifies the need, with patients who have suffered from a significant failure in the affective bond, for the therapist to attend first and foremost to that patient's need for soothing and regulation.

Basch has also identified self states that result from failures of the caregiver to attune to and name for the child particular affect states, leaving the individual unable to identify feelings and emotions, and requiring of the clinician that he or she empathically sort out and name these feelings and emotions for and with the patient as the optimal response. Basch asserts that such pathological self states are not usefully addressed through affirmation, *that* specific response should be reserved for the patient who recognizes his or her affect states, but feels shame in relation to them.

Whereas Basch particularizes in this way individuals who suffer from pathological affect states and the response from the therapist that is most optimal, Stolorow and his colleagues write more inclusively about affect integration, which entails conditions wherein affect is rendered inaccessible to the individual, offering to the therapist an approach encompassing close attention to and empathy with the patient's feeling states as they manifest and shift in the transference.

And for another brief example of the use of diagnostic categories as guidelines toward the optimal, Goldberg (1995) offers a comprehensive approach to the treatment of perversions. His understanding of the pathology involved leads him to address an interpretive mending of the vertical split viewed by him as etiologically significant in these narcissistic behavior disorders. Thus, the guideline to the optimal response offered by Goldberg is to actively *interpret* aspects of the vertical split, especially within the transference.

We will turn now to a final guideline toward the optimal, which is to be found in an important contribution by Beebe and Lachmann (1994) entitled "The Three Principles of Salience" and which concerns how structure is developed, or how an infant learns in the normal parent–child relationship. The three principles of salience describe interaction structures in the first year of life, and include the familiar concept of disruption and repair, and the concept of heightened affective moments. But the most salient of these three avenues toward structure building observed in the infant–caregiver dyad is that of ongoing regulations, a concept developed by Beebe and Lachmann, which serves as the most overarching of these three principle. The ongoing regulations construct captures the characteristic patterns of repeated interactions, the patterns of mutual regulation and self-regulation that the infant comes to recognize and expect. This going-on-being in the infant–caregiver dyad is characterized not by dramatic moments, either disruptive or epiphenomenal, but by the quiet, uneventful experiences of well-being in the relationship that have largely escaped attention because of their background quality. It's interersting in this context that in an earlier presentation of this chapter, a fourth principle of salience was noted, that of the familiar frustration-gratification sequence, but the authors ultimately decided that these experiences were secondary to the other three principles noted here. This conclusion, drawn from the arena of infant and child observation, confirms the clinical sense of all the contributors to the conversation about optimal responsiveness considered here: frustration is not a useful guide for the clinician as a method of enhancing development progression and structure building.

We believe that a conclusion can be drawn from this convergence of clinical and observational data; not only is the clinical importance of frustration as a vehicle for meliorative change diminished, as we have just said, but more than this, the significance of continuity in the analytic dyad is confirmed. Being safe and in-sync with one's caregivers, whether in childhood or in analysis, is important both for normal development and for therapeutic change. It would seem that if these findings from the clinical situation and the laboratory are taken seriously, one will see more reports in the literature than currently exist wherein analysis is described with less attention to disruptions that frustrate and dismay the patient, but which *do* make the analyst feel that he or she is truly doing analysis. If our theory doesn't focus especially on frustration and impasse, perhaps our clinical work, both as experienced and as reported, will take on a different look. We think of analyses we ourselves have conducted that are characterized by a minimum of disruption and impasse, and that have seemed to us, at moments of uncertainty and self-doubt, for that very reason, to be inadequate, incomplete, and insufficiently deep, even though the therapeutic results appear to be as good, or even better, than analyses that look like the picture a theory of optimal frustration would seem to dictate.

For example, a patient in the field, finishing seven years of a successful training analysis—successful, that is, by any measure of symptomatic and character improvement and conflict resolution—tells his analyst that he cannot help but feel that something must have been missing, that both he and the analyst must have overlooked deeply buried conflicts of aggression, murder, envy, and the like. The patient would be concerned about this from time to time *during* the analysis, too, whenever he would compare his own analytic experience with certain of his contemporaries, and especially, when he would be taught by analysts who had a particular dramatic flair for the "deep"; the analyst himself, in response, could not help but wonder whether this might have some validity. But try as they may, the pair could do no more than work together in a general atmosphere of calm, cooperation, and friendly feeling, despite occasional misunderstandings and disruptions. Then there is another analytic pair who are currently completing eight years of analysis wherein the work is characterized throughout by a similar continuity, smooth developmental progression, and articulation of an increasingly illuminated life narrative. In this instance the patient doesn't have any doubts about the value and depth of her analysis, but then, the patient is not in the field. The analyst, however, does worry at times that something must have been missed or overlooked—it seems on the whole to be too simple, too easy, and too pleasant an experience to be *real* analysis, that is, an analysis pockmarked by frustration, disruption, and strife.

We wonder if the result of this entire contemporary psychoanalytic conversation about the optimal response might be to relax self psychologists even further, in concert with Kohut's observations about the relative ease with which the self psychologist does his or her work (1984). But we would like to close on a note of some discomfort: The notion of a pursuit of the *optimal* is itself, perhaps, too *optimistic* (the words share the same Latin root), and possibly somewhat dangerous for that reason. Though optimism is essential, it carries with it the hidden and mistaken confidence that one should seek for perfection, that one can actually discover the just-right response for every patient in every situation.

REFERENCES

Bacal, H. (1985), Optimal responsiveness and the therapeutic process. In: *Progress in Self Psychology, Vol. 1,* ed. A Goldberg. New York: Guilford, pp. 202–226.

Basch, M. (1988), *Understanding Psychotherapy: The Science Behind the Art.* New York: Basic Books.

Beebe, B. & Lachmann, F. M. (1994), Representation and internalization in infancy: Three principles of salience. *Psychoanal. Psychol.,* 11:127–166.

Edelman, G. M. (1992), *Bright Air, Brilliant Fire: On the Matter of Mind.* New York: Basic Books.

Emde, R. N. (1988a), Development terminable and interminable. 1. Innate and motivational factors from infancy. *Internat. J. Psycho-Anal.,* 69:23–42.

——— (1988b), Development terminable and interminable. 2. Recent psychoanalytic theory and therapeutic considerations. *Internat. J. Psycho-Anal.,* 69:283–296.

Friedman, L. (1996), Main meaning and motivation. *Psychoanal. Inq.,* 15:437–460.

Freud, A. (1965), *Normality and Pathology in Childhood.* New York: International Universities Press.

Freud, S. (1911–1915), Papers on technique. *Standard Edition,* 12:89–171. London: Hogarth Press, 1958.

Goldberg, A. (1991), *The Prisonhouse of Psychoanalysis.* Hillsdale, NJ: The Analytic Press.

——— (1995), *The Problem of Perversion: A View from Self Psychology.* New Haven, CT: Yale University Press.

Kohut, H. (1971), *The Analysis of the Self.* New York: International Universities Press.

——— (1977), *The Restoration of the Self.* New York: International Universities Press.

——— (1984), *How Does Analysis Cure?* ed. A. Goldberg & P. Stepansky. Chicago: University of Chicago Press.

Lichtenberg, J. (1989), *Psychoanalysis and Motivation.* Hillsdale, NJ: The Analytic Press.

——— Lachmann, F. M. & Fosshage, J. L. (1992), *Self and Motivational Systems.* Hillsdale, NJ: The Analytic Press.

Lindon, J. A. (1994), Gratification and provision in psychoanalysis: Should we get rid of the rule of abstinence? *Psychoanal. Dial.,* 4:549–582.

Modell, A. H. (1993), *The Private Self.* Cambridge MA: Harvard University Press.

Rapaport, D. (1960), The structure of psychoanalytic theory. *Psychological Issues,* Monogr. 6. New York: International Universities Press.

Rorty, R. (1989), *Contingency, Irony, and Solidarity.* Cambridge, MA: Harvard University Press.

Schlesinger, H. (1988), A historical overview. In: *How Does Treatment Help?* ed. A. Rothstein. Madison, CT: International Universities Press, pp. 7–27.

Shane, M. & Shane, E. (1992), One self psychology or many? *J. Amer. Psychoanal. Assn.*

Spezzano, C. (1993), *Affect in Psychoanalysis: A Clinical Synthesis.* Hillsdale, NJ: The Analytic Press.

Stern, D. (1994), The Maternal Constellation. Presented at Cape Cod, MA.

Stolorow, R., Brandchaft, B. & Atwood, G. (1987), *Psychoanalytic Treatment: An Intersubjective Approach.* Hillsdale, NJ: The Analytic Press.

Strenger, C. (1991), *Between Hermeneutics and Science.* New York: International Universities Press.

Terman, D. M. (1988), Optimum frustration: Structuralization and the therapeutic process. In: *Progress in Self Psychology, Vol. 4,* ed. A. Goldberg. Hillsdale, NJ: The Analytic Press, pp. 113–126.

Trevarthan, C. (1994), Intersubjectivity in parent–infant interaction. Presented at the Institute of Contemporary Psychoanalysis, Los Angeles.

Wolf, E. (1976), Ambience and abstinence. *The Annual of Psychoanalysis,* 4:101–115. New York: International Universities Press.

—— (1989), *Treating the Self.* New York: Guilford.

Chapter 4

Notes on the Contribution of the Analyst's Self-Awareness to Optimal Responsiveness

Shelley R. Doctors

While the subject matter of responsiveness, provision, gratification and restraint—what the analyst does—is located in the psychoanalytic situation, moment to moment clinical decisions are critically related to the larger question—why she does what she does and how beneficial change occurs. What is the optimal way to respond so that change will occur? Morton and Estelle Shane's useful review of the optimal responsiveness literature thus bridges two levels of discourse. One level refers to that which is "observable" or empathically accessible in the clinical situation. The other is "inferential" and refers to mental processes presumed to mediate the clinical events. Although for heuristic purposes we can describe these levels, they are not easily separable in practice, as what the analyst does ought to be shaped by her understanding about what produces change.

In reviewing the contributions of Bacal (1985), Terman (1988), and Lindon (1994), the Shanes focus largely on the clinical level of discourse, addressing themselves to clinical moments when the analyst must decide how to respond. Their ecumenical approach utilizes complementary theories of development and pathology to guide the practitioner's responsiveness (Basch, 1988; Lichtenberg, 1989; Goldberg, 1995). All such technical suggestions imply assumptions on another level about how change proceeds. The Shanes do not undertake to fully resolve the question of *how* the analysts' actions contribute to the formation and transformation of psychic structure in the patient. They (Shane and Shane, 1994) quote Terman (1988), "The doing is the making," in advancing their idea that "the dialogue of construction . . . is the structure" (p. 6). They also cite the important work of Beebe and Lachmann (1994) in emphasizing the contribution of on-going regulations to the development of psychic structure.

Beebe and Lachmann's on-going collaborative work is at the cutting edge of attempts to utilize infant research to clarify foundational psychoanalytic concepts about how experiences become structuralized. The concept of structure in psychoanalysis, however, is currently in flux, if not disarray (see Shapiro, 1988, for a review). After reviewing 21 papers on the topic of psychic structure, Schafer (1988) commented on the "shift toward minimalism in theoretical formulation," linking this theoretical shift to "cultural changes favoring emphasis on process as against entity, subjective experience, individualistic theory construction and rejection of sharp demarcation of the boundary between observer and the observed" (p. 295). There remain different ways of thinking about what structure is, how it develops, and how it is transformed. Unfortunately, we can't wait for our theories to catch up to our clinical needs in order to address those needs.

What is the optimal way to respond so that change will occur? This is the question that caused Bacal (1985) to follow in Kohut's footsteps in privileging his empathic-introspective knowledge of the lived clinical moment. All the self-psychological responses to Kohut's concept of optimal frustration (Kohut, 1971, 1977, 1984) inevitably come up against the unresolved problem of how experience is structuralized, which is, however, beyond the scope of the Shanes' review and, certainly, beyond the scope of this discussion.

My particular focus will be on the contribution of the analyst's capacity for comfortable self-reflection in the construction of analytic responsiveness, provision, and restraint. In other words, I will accent the introspective aspect of our methodology (Kohut, 1959) to show that it is a component of the well-functioning, optimally responsive analyst. I will also suggest that the Shanes' new idea of optimal restraint preserves the clinical benefit deriving from traditional analytic reserve without further wedding our technique to drive theory.

Many self psychologists have argued against the idea that frustration, in and of itself, is helpful (Bacal, 1985; Terman, 1988; Lindon, 1994; Shane and Shane, 1994; Basch, 1995). Each of these critics has sought to account for healthy structure building in the realm of constructive experiences. Combining Bacal's ideas (1985) with Terman's (1988), one might say it is *satisfying* experience, the experience of being understood, that is therapeutic. Optimal responsiveness has come to mean communicating understanding to the patient in a form which is appropriate to the patient (Bacal, 1985) and, hence, usable by him or her. Understanding may be communicated in words or actions, for *all* lived experience is the raw material of structure. The specific transference meaning of being understood will eventually become clarified and available to be interpreted (Gill, 1982; Stolorow, 1994).

Frustrations create structures, too. The patterned expectancies which function to anticipate and avoid frustration are themselves structures. These structures, which arise in consequence of selfobject tie disruption, can often be transformed through the disruption-repair cycle work that Kohut described.[1] Whereas the content of such work focuses on the injuries sustained, I believe it is the *process itself* that is the locus of clinical benefit. An already injured person secondarily longs for understanding of his or her painful reaction, while fearing or expecting further disruption. Therapeutic action derives, not from the experience of frustration itself, but from the meaning the patient makes of the analyst's responsivity to his frustration (Stolorow, 1994) and the way in which this reorganizes previously structured expectations. Through disruption-repair cycles, an expectation of repair and of having a partner in the process may become structuralized (F. Lachmann, 1994, personal communication).

Some theory is pertinent to understanding the Shanes' new idea of "optimal restraint." Ideas about frustration and abstinence have common roots in drive theory. Once one steps away from a theory of instinctual drives as central to psychological life, one can also step away from the technical prescriptions instituted to manage the drives (see also Basch, 1995). From *that* vantage point, what has been called abstinence on the part of the analyst becomes an obsolete concept. However, another rationale for a stance of this type (Atwood and Stolorow, 1984) relates to a principle of academic gestalt psychology. An indistinct or ambiguously perceived object is likely to be "organized" (phenomenologically) along the lines of the configurations which structure a person's own subjective world. The wisdom, therefore, of the analyst, *in general*, talking less than the patient, offering less personal information, and so on, is not entirely antiquated. Such analytic behavior may be helpful in the overarching task of discerning, engaging, and transforming the structures that characterize the patient's self-organization. The Shanes' term, "optimal restraint," properly preserves this piece of analytic wisdom. It is

---

[1] Brandchaft's work on pathological structures of accommodation (1994) reveals constituents of these structures that sometimes render them refractory to disruption-repair cycle intervention.

a valuable, necessary part of this set of concepts. Although it is no longer considered automatically "wrong" for the analyst to say or do noninterpretive things (and may be *just right*), the *effects* of her activity on the treatment require continued analytic scrutiny.

I'm going to restrict my comments now to a consideration of two concepts that are embedded in all the Shanes' examples. In the language of the other contributions to this area they would be called (1) the "optimally functioning analyst," and (2) the "optimally functioning analytic dyad." Both of these ideas have been previously discussed without being so labeled by many psychoanalytic theorists. I have reservations about the use of the word *optimal*, which may activate a fear that in our performance we fall short of some elusive, external standard of perfection.[2] I prefer a self-reflexive standard similar to that implied by Aristotle's definition of the good: that which functions in accordance with its own design.[3] Henceforth, I will use the phrase "well-functioning" to connote the Aristotelian standard. The well-functioning analyst refers to the noble ideal of bringing oneself into an internal alignment so as to function in harmony with who one is. The well-functioning analytic dyad, therefore, is one which functions to maximize the unique set of potentialities within it for beneficial transformation.

In defining the well-functioning analyst, I will be amending Atwood and Stolorow's (1984) contribution to the topic of frustration and responsiveness. They state: "We suggest that the rules of abstinence, neutrality, and anonymity can be subordinated to a more general and inclusive therapeutic principle that the analyst's actions in the therapeutic situation should as much as possible be determined by his understanding of the nature, origins, and functions of the configurations currently structuring the patient's subjective experience" (p. 45). I suggest that a corollary of that dictum is pertinent to our discussion of responsiveness. That is, the analyst's actions in the therapeutic situation should, additionally, as much as possible be influenced by his or her understanding of the nature, origins, and functions of the configurations currently structuring his or her own subjective experience.

The extent and reliability of one's introspective capacities can be affected by a range of activities—personal analysis, supervision, study groups, and the experience of doing the work itself. Broadly speaking, we are looking at how the analyst gets "centered" (Doctors, 1994b) and

---

[2] Both Stolorow and Orange have independently advanced (personal communications) Winnicott's term "good enough" (Winnicott, 1951) for just this reason.

[3] I assume that Aristotle is the source of King's (1945) definition of normal ("The normal is to be defined as that which functions in accordance with its [structural] design"). Kohut (1984) drew on King's definition of normal.

how the analyst comes to "comfortably inhabit his or her own experience" (Doctors, 1994a). To consider the instance of personal analysis, we no longer believe in the fully analyzed person, if that is taken (in the old sense) to mean that everything that was once unconscious is now conscious. Rather, in seeking to engage, illuminate, and transform the structures of experience, we aim for "optimal flexibility."[4] A young analyst in a study group in New York said, "I get it. It's making the invariant variant!" At its best, analysis has always been a superb vehicle wherein one could gain intimate, detailed knowledge of the nature, origins, and functions of the configurations that structure one's own experience. I am emphasizing the relationship in which this takes place. It is *particularly* when self-knowledge is acquired in a largely harmonious atmosphere that one gains *comfortable* access to the inner world. In accenting the atmosphere characterizing the process, I am suggesting that it becomes structuralized and a constituent of the degree of comfort one later has in self-exploration. Self-awareness and self-assurance go hand-in-hand. One "knows the territory," so to speak, gains a facility at recognizing the configurations being evoked, and, by dint of repeated *safe* experience, thereby increases one's tolerance for "visiting" those "places."

It is in this manner that the analyst's capacity to "decenter" (Atwood and Stolorow, 1984) and "self-right" (Tolpin, 1986) are enhanced. In supervision and study groups, as well as in analysis, if safety characterizes the atmosphere, it will interact with cognitive processes to enhance capacities for comfortable self-awareness. The well-functioning analyst is characterized by a suppleness, an ability to move around within her experience that enables her to respond rather than react to the patient. Wholehearted participation[5] in doing the work itself develops the analyst's "optimal flexibility."

The well-functioning analyst is beautifully exemplified in the Shanes' case examples. We see the empathic–introspective modality in action. The Shanes lead us through instances in which the analyst's empathic grasp of the patient's state guides the analyst. They regularly include instances of introspection that contribute to the analyst's responsiveness.

Both examples illustrating what the Shanes call "selfobject relatedness" and "intersubjective relatedness" reveal analysts able to tolerate many forms of personal discomfort while giving *priority* to the unfolding of their patient's experience. In the example of the woman who couldn't feel for her friend's problems, the analyst could recognize versions of the

---

[4] This is closely related but not identical to Atwood and Stolorow's (1984) concept of "optimal structuralization."

[5] The notion of wholeheartedness as a description of the analyst's engagement was developed by Gotthold (1992).

reported experience that had occurred in the treatment. The analyst knew what it had felt like to be in relation to that patient when she was functioning in this mode.[6] However, the analyst also judged that the patient was not "ready" to deal with the effects of her own behavior and didn't, therefore, attempt to move the dialogue toward it. In regard to the woman who correctly recognized much that was painful and "private" in the analyst, I believe it was crucial that the analyst was sufficiently in touch with himself and "at home" with his painful issues to avoid reacting to the patient in a defensive, distant, and controlling way. Such a response would have repeated the configuration of childhood experience (e.g., "People who are unhappy are too preoccupied to attend to me, hence I must attend to them").

Although comfortable self-reflectiveness is necessary in *all* the work, this capacity is of paramount importance in the area of provision described by Lindon. I, too, see our goal as facilitating "the uncovering, illuminating, and transforming of the subjective experience of the patient" (Lindon, 1994, p. 559), but often one understands only retrospectively the responsiveness that facilitates as opposed to that which obstructs. When decisions have to be made without sufficient understanding of their meaning for the patient, it is most helpful if the analyst has comfortable access to the meanings the provision has for himself. This was precisely the situation Bacal faced in the case he cited in his original paper (Bacal, 1985). He sensed and said that he thought the fee reduction requested by the patient might have other unexplored meanings. I am drawing attention to Bacal's self-knowledge, which allowed him to know *what* he could do in that treatment. There may well be other analysts who could not do that, or other patients with whom fee reduction would be less feasible for Bacal. Bacal (1985) has stated: "If . . . the analyst . . . feels he cannot respond to the archaic selfobject demand, no shame should attach to his refusal" (p. 224). I believe each analyst must know what he or she can manage and not offer something he or she will later resent.

I am in complete agreement with the Shanes' conclusion that "the significance of on-going mutual and self-regulations in the dyad is confirmed" (Shane and Shane, 1994, p. 23). I wish there were time to develop the implications of the dyadic nature of the treatment situation in which this all takes place. I believe that there is always and only an "analytic couple" (Bacal, 1985) and, to paraphrase Ornstein (1988), what is "characteristic . . . [for a particular] dyad and for no other" (p. 156). This is an idea that flows naturally from the selfobject concept and

---

[6] This is the experience of the patient that Fosshage (1995) has termed "the other-centered listening perspective."

gives rise to a host of implications we are only beginning to consider. (For an excellent review of the relation between infant research and the psychoanalytic process, see Beebe and Lachmann, 1988a, 1988b, 1994; Beebe, Jaffe, and Lachmann, 1992; Lachmann and Beebe, 1992.)

A well-functioning dyad maximizes the potentialities within it to discern, engage, and transform the constricting and self-defeating structures of the patient's experience. Simultaneously, the dyad aims to maximize the potentialities within it to create new, self-enhancing structures. The analyst's capacities for introspection emerge as a significant factor influencing the viability of the dyad because it is the analyst's "structures" that generate responsiveness to the patient.

When we broaden our perspective from a focus on the patient to a focus on the dyad, the view of analyzability changes. From a dyadic systems view (one example of which is intersubjectivity),[7] each dyad is unique and there are a range of different, successful analyses conceivable for any one person. The question expands beyond "what the patient needs" or even "what the analyst is capable of" to the question of goodness-of-fit in the dyad. Thus, analyzability shifts from a property of a single personality to a property of the dyad. I do not mean to convey that the die is irremediably cast at the outset. The analyst's self-reflection, flexibility, and personal expansion can be crucial in salvaging a well-functioning analytic dyad from the midst of a faltering one. (See Stolorow, Atwood, and Trop [1989] for a discussion of varying degrees of "decentering" experienced by a group of analysts over a range of cases.) What this all means is that each individual is potentially analyzable by *someone,* but now, no longer by *anyone* (Stolorow, 1990; Doctors, 1992). We have always intuitively known this and attempted to create good "matches" in referrals made and cases accepted.

Each analytic couple faces the challenge of utilizing the unique opportunities created by the intersection of their particular personalities to maximize beneficial structural change. Although the primary focus of this beneficial change is the patient, the task of doing this work often produces beneficial change in the analyst as well. Despite affectively searing moments, a feeling of harmony often characterizes the atmosphere when the dyad is functioning well. I would suggest that the sense of well-being enjoyed by the woman patient whose analysis progressed smoothly (Shane and Shane, 1994) may be an indicator of a well-functioning analytic dyad. It seemed a shame that both the male patient

---

[7] To review the contributions of intersubjectivity in the broader sense, see Atwood and Stolorow, 1984; Stolorow, Brandchaft, and Atwood, 1987; Stolorow and Atwood, 1992; Stolorow, Atwood, and Brandchaft, 1994.

who had been trained as a therapist and his analyst were too sophisticated theoretically to allow themselves to thoroughly enjoy one of the fruits of their joint labors.

To conclude, the Shanes have produced a timely overview of responsiveness, provision, gratification, and restraint along with an array of suggestions for gauging the patient's state. Emphasizing the intersubjective field in which treatment takes place, I add the proviso that the analyst be as prepared as possible to understand what is being evoked in him or her so as to be "optimally responsive."

REFERENCES

Atwood, G. & Stolorow, R. (1984), *Structures of Subjectivity: Explorations in Psychoanalytic Phenomenology*. Hillsdale, NJ: The Analytic Press.

Bacal, H. (1985), Optimal responsiveness and the therapeutic process. In: *Progress in Self Psychology, Vol. 1*, ed. A. Goldberg. New York: Guilford, pp. 202–226.

Basch, M. (1988), *Understanding Psychotherapy*. New York: Basic Books.

———— (1995), Kohut's contribution. *Psychoanal. Dial.*, 5:367–373.

Beebe, B., Jaffe, J. & Lachmann, F. (1992), A dyadic systems view of communication. In: *Relational Perspectives in Psychoanalysis*, ed. N. Skolnick & S. Warshaw. Hillsdale, NJ: The Analytic Press, pp. 61–82.

———— & Lachmann, F. (1988a), Mother-infant mutual influence and the precursors of psychic structure. In: *Frontiers in Self Psychology, Progress in Self Psychology Vol. 3*, ed. A. Goldberg. Hillsdale, NJ: The Analytic Press, pp. 3–25.

———— & ———— (1988b), The contribution of mother–infant mutual influence to the origins of self and object representations. *Psychoanal. Psychol.*, 5:305–337.

———— & ———— (1994), Representation and internalization in infancy: Three principles of salience. *Psychoanal. Psychol.*, 11:127–165.

Brandchaft, B. (1994), Structures of pathologic accommodation and change in analysis. Unpublished manuscript delivered at Association for Psychoanalytic Self Psychology's Bernard Brandchaft Day Conference, March.

Doctors, S. (1992), Discussion of the relational self: A new perspective for understanding women's development by Judith Jordan, Ph.D. *Contemp. Psychoanal. Rev.*, 7:72–82.

———— (1994a), Further thoughts on the "unbearable embeddedness of being." Discussion for Panel: Realities lost and found: Trauma, dissociation and psychic reality, Division of Psychoanalysis (39), A.P.A., Spring Meeting, Washington, DC.

———— (1994b), Finding the center. Keynote address at graduation. National Institute for the Psychotherapies, New York, June 10.

Fosshage, J. (1995), Countertransference as the analyst's experience of the patient: The influence of listening perspectives. *Psychoanal. Psychother.*, 12:375–391.

Gill, M. (1982), *Analysis of Transference, Vol. 1*. Madison, CT: International Universities Press.

Goldberg, A. (1995), *The Problem of Perversion*. New Haven, CT: Yale University Press.

Gotthold, J. (1992), The Curative Fantasy. Presented at 15th Annual Self Psychology Conference, Los Angeles, CA.

King, C. (1945), The meaning of normal. *Yale J. Biology & Med.,* 17:493–501.

Kohut, H. (1959), Introspection, empathy and psychoanalysis: An examination of the relationship between mode of observation and theory. *J. Amer. Psychoanal. Assn.,* 7:459–483.

——— (1971), *The Analysis of the Self.* New York: International Universities Press.

——— (1977), *The Restoration of the Self.* New York: International Universities Press.

——— (1984), *How Does Analysis Cure?* ed. A. Goldberg & P. Stepansky. Chicago: University of Chicago Press.

Lachmann, F. & Beebe, B. (1992), Reformulations of early development and transference: Implications for psychic structure formation. In: *Interface of Psychoanalysis and Psychology,* ed. J. Barron, M. Eagle & D. Wolitzky. Washington, DC: The American Psychological Association, pp. 133–153.

Lichtenberg, J. (1989), *Psychoanalysis and Motivation.* Hillsdale, NJ: The Analytic Press.

Lindon, J. (1994), Gratification and provision in psychoanalysis: Should we get rid of "the rule of abstinence"? *Psychoanal. Dial.,* 4:549–582.

Ornstein, A. (1988), Optimal responsiveness and the theory of cure. In: *Learning from Kohut, Progress in Self Psychology, Vol. 4,* ed. A. Goldberg. Hillsdale, NJ: The Analytic Press, pp. 155–160.

Schafer, R. (1988), Discussion of panel presentations on psychic structure. In: The concept of structure in psychoanalysis. *J. Amer. Psychoanal. Assn. Suppl.,* 36:295–312.

Shane, M. & Shane, E. (1994), Self psychology in search of the optimal: A consideration of optimal responsiveness: Optimal provision; optimal gratification; and optimal restraint in the clinical situation. Presented at Conference on the Psychology of the Self, Chicago, October.

Shapiro, T., ed. (1988), The concept of structure in psychoanalysis. *J. Amer. Psychoanal. Assn. Suppl.,* 36:3–385.

Stolorow, R. (1990), Converting psychotherapy to psychoanalysis: A critique of the underlying assumptions. *Psychoanal. Inq.,* 10:119–130.

——— (1994), The nature of therapeutic action of psychoanalytic interpretation. In: *The Intersubjective Perspective.* Northvale, NJ: Aronson.

——— & Atwood, G. (1992), *Contexts of Being: The Intersubjective Foundations of Psychological Life.* Hillsdale, NJ: The Analytic Press.

——— Atwood, G. & Brandchaft, B. (1994), *The Intersubjective Perspective.* Northvale, NJ: Aronson.

——— Atwood, G. & Trop, J. (1989), Impasses in psychoanalytic therapy: A royal road. *Contemp. Psychoanal.,* 25:554–573.

——— Brandchaft, B. & Atwood, G. (1987), *Psychoanalytic Treatment: An Intersubjective Approach.* Hillsdale, NJ: The Analytic Press.

Terman, D. (1988), Optimum frustration: Structuralization and the therapeutic process. In: *Learning from Kohut, Progress in Self Psychology, Vol. 4.* Hillsdale, NJ: The Analytic Press, pp. 113–125.

Tolpin, M. (1986), The self and its selfobjects: A different baby. In: *Progress in Self Psychology, Vol. 2,* ed. A. Goldberg. Hillsdale, NJ: The Analytic Press, pp. 115–128.

Winnicott, D. (1951), Transitional objects and transitional phenomena. In: *Through Paediatrics to Psycho-Analysis.* London: Hogarth Press, 1975, pp. 229–242.

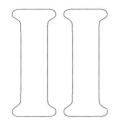

Philosophical Issues

Chapter 5

The Philosophical Importance of Kohut's Bipolar Theory of the Self

John H. Riker

Although Kohut's bipolar theory of the self has received voluminous critical attention as a clinical hypothesis that illuminates a particular set of psychological disorders and has been subjected to some philosophical reflection (see especially Detrick and Detrick, 1990), it has not received a full critical examination as a theory of the self independently of its clinical functions. What follows is an attempt to show how Kohut's theory of the self intersects with a number of the most important theories of the self in Western thought, relates to their vocabularies, incorporates a number of their profoundest insights, and helps solve some of the tradition's most vexing problems while leaving some others unexplored.

Grandiosity and idealization constitute the two poles of what Kohut terms the bipolar nuclear self. The bipolar self has two sources of primary motivation: desires and ideals. The desires (needs) of the grandiose pole say "This is what I want"; the idealized pole asserts "This is what you ought to become." In other words, humans have as part of their natural constituencies both "desire-based motivation" and "authoritative motivation" (Scheffler, 1992). There is a tension between these two poles, for grandiosity gives the sense that as a particular being I am absolutely adequate and entitled to have my needs met, whereas the idealized pole stands in opposition to the self-satisfaction of grandiosity by holding up an ideal of what I might become, but am not.

This tension is mediated, according to Kohut, by the particular idiosyncratic talents and abilities the person has that can ground ambitions and be used to realize the ideal. The particular talents and abilities give definiteness to the ideal and transform a vague general notion of what a good human being is into a particular ideal for what I as an individual self can achieve. This concretizing of the ideal allows the self-assertive ambitions to focus on definite ends. When the energy and liveliness of the grandiose pole align with a particular bent of character and set of skills in pursuit of an ideal for which they are particularly suited, then a fully integral nuclear self is born. "This tension arc is the dynamic essence of the complete, nondefective self" (Kohut, 1984, pp. 4–5).

As simple as this theory may seem—and Kohut rarely expands on it except for its clinical ramifications—it has profound consequences for philosophical and moral theories of the self. To see these consequences, it will be necessary to examine each of the poles of the self in turn and then the nuclear self as a whole.

THE GRANDIOSE POLE: KOHUT, FREUD, THE SOPHISTS, AND NIETZSCHE

The most archaic ground of the self is, for Kohut, a kind of primal energy that can transform itself into ambition and desire, but retains a certain indefinable and unspecifiable élan or sheer life force. As such, the grandiose pole seems very much like Freud's libido—the driving energy of life, which in his later writings became like Eros in Plato's *Symposium* (Freud, 1921). But the differences are telling. The grandiose pole is not primarily sexual but a general reservoir of energy available for any number of ends, including sexual ones under appropriate conditions and stimuli. On one hand, Freud's libido seems to be a blind biological force unconnected to a self or person that persists after its object regardless of whether it is repressed or not. It is indefatigible and undefeatable. On the other hand, Kohut's grandiose energy is intrinsically tied to a self-valuation. As such it is fragile and can survive and persist as a life-force only if it receives proper mirroring and nourishment. This is not a blind natural energy but a tenuous human function that contains both a reservoir of primal energy *and* a primal valuation of the worth of that energy determined by selfobject responses to it. When it is not positively mirrored, an internal void appears in place of a primal liveliness and the energy partially converts into narcissistic rage.

There are a number of philosophical predecessors of Kohut who claim that the grandiose pole or its equivalent—individual desire and ambition—is the very core of the self. The first of these theoreticians were the Sophists, who appear as Socrates's enemies in Plato's dialogues. The fifth century b.c.e. was a time of radical change in Athens; the old morality of acting according to one's proper position in society was breaking down as new economic and political structures came into being. With the breakdown of social convention, the question of what should ground human activity arose with ferocious intensity. The Sophists' answer was that humans should live from individual desire. The best life was to expand one's desires to the fullest and gain enough power or craftiness to satisfy them, regardless of whether the desires were considered right or wrong by the moral code. Here I think we can see the identification of the self with the grandiose pole of Kohut, for the self is conceived of as a set of primary individual desires.

Socrates countered the Sophists by saying that life must be based on what is good—on a universal ideal of excellence—rather than desire, for desire creates immense chaos in both the psyche and the state. Here we see Socrates championing the idealized pole of the self (about which I will have more to say shortly); he understood the enormous tension in Athens to be a conflict between which of the two poles of the self should be emphasized once humans have been released from their imprisonment in social role structures. The Sophists thought Socrates was negating individual vitality by claiming that all humans should attempt to realize a universal moral ideal, whereas Socrates thought a life devoted solely to the satisfaction of individual desires meaningless, chaotic, and one that reduced humans to the level of the beasts.

Although some philosphers since the Sophists sided with their locating the self in individual desire and ambition (most notably, Hobbes), most followed the Platonic and Christian traditions of conceiving the essence of individuals as the realization of a universal ideal (a Platonic form, God's will, the Stoic sage, etc.). It was not until the later part of the nineteenth century, with the philosophy of Nietzsche, that a full, compelling statement of the self as sheer particular energy striving to attain power and grandiosity appeared.

For Nietzsche, all life is at base a zest for life itself. At the core of human beings is a driving, forceful will-to-power which seeks to be free, act spontaneously, and create values unconstrained by convention or social pressure. Humans at their most profound level are sheer points of energy attempting to assert their particular individualities in a world of forces that often stand opposed to this assertion. The best life is the active assertion and triumph of one's particularity in the world.

Like Freud and the Sophists, Nietzsche proclaims that there is an ultimate dichotomy between the natural and the social, the individual and the moral. For all of these thinkers the chief enemy of natural individual self-assertion and vitality is the morality of society. Nietzsche's *Genealogy of Morals* (1887) attempts to show how morality arose as a conspiracy of the weak or slave class to crush the spontaneous activity of the nobles. The constrictions of social morality make a human "like a wild beast hurling itself against the bars of its cage" (p. 218). Whereas Freud refuses to give up the necessity of morality, Nietzsche attempts to lure those who are vital enough to read his works into a world "beyond good and evil" (1886), a world in which they as individuals will create the values by which they live rather than being boxed into the narrow cage of Christian middle-class mediocrity.

Nietzsche both captures and mobilizes the zest of the grandiose pole. No philosopher excites students more than Nietzsche, for he is the arch nonconformist in philosophy, the thinker whose style and thought breaks boundaries and frees philosophic discourse from stifling conventions. Reading him is akin to seeing great painters, musicians, dancers, or others who reinvigorate our need to spontaneously express our concrete particularity by so deeply expressing their own.

However, as close as Kohut and Nietzsche are in proclaiming the archaic priority of particular grandiose energy, two profound differences separate them. First, Kohut identifies the natural enemy of spontaneous life energy not as society or moral convention, but as a lack of empathic responsiveness on the part of a child's earliest selfobjects. Thus, Kohut's analysis allows for the possibility of a person's being both individually vital and moral—a possibility that not only seems required by evolution if we are to be social beings who also have their own individual goods (Slavin and Kriegman, 1992), but one that has been actualized countless times by myriads of people the world over. The identification of a lack of responsiveness in selfobjects, rather than morality, as the crucial factor in the destruction of individual vitality is also important because it opens up the possibility for a responsible, psychoanalytically based social and political theory. Society cannot do without morality, but it can alter its child-rearing practices.

The second crucial way in which Kohut differs from Nietzsche is that for Nietzsche grandiose energy is the singular core of the individual, whereas for Kohut it is part of a bipolar self and is balanced by an ideal. Without this balance, there can be no theory of development, no reason for the grandiose energy to be anything other than infantile self-assertion. All grandiose energy can do by itself is to celebrate itself in play and creation, the activities of childhood. Indeed, Nietzsche (1885) claims that the highest metamorphosis of the spirit is to be a child. Ideals are important for Nietzsche in that they act both as obstacles for the self to overcome and as expressions of its creative powers, but they do not represent essential possibilities for the self, the realization of which gives joy.

THE IDEALIZED POLE: KOHUT, FREUD, AND PLATO

Kohut does not specify clearly what he means by ideals and how they operate in the psyche aside from providing a soothing function. However, ideals typically have the function of acting as lures for development, spurs to achievement. An ideal represents a vision of what we might be and, as such, is an impetus to achieve a state beyond what we presently are.

Just as Kohut's grandiose pole appears to be both like and unlike Freud's libido, so the idealized pole is both like and unlike the superego. Like the superego, it is built from identifications with parents and incorporates the values of the parents. It is used to limit and direct the ambitions of the grandiose pole. But Kohut's idealized pole is genuinely teleological—it lures the individual to development rather than imposing a harsh and punishing constraint on libido, except when it is injured. Freud has some sympathy with a positive ego ideal in his middle works, in which the ego ideal is seen as replacing the early state of narcissism and we momentarily reestablish the perfection of that stage when we achieve it. However, with the development of his structural psychology in *The Ego and the Id* (1923), the ego ideal is almost completely replaced by the repressive, guilt-producing superego. In his attempt to have a model of the psyche that fit the nineteenth-century notion of what a rigorous scientific system should be, Freud could not allow for the possibility of teleological causation. Only force and impact can move things.

Having a teleological idealized pole as part of the basic structure of the self is critically important for ethics and morality, for it means that "oughts" and ideals are natural to humans rather than being foreign obstacles imposed by society. Of course, not all problems of ethics are solved with the discovery of the natural basis for ideals. That there is an idealized pole of the archaic self says nothing about what the content of the ideal should be; it does not answer questions about what makes some ideals superior to others, or what makes one ideal moral and another (such as that of Nazism) hideous. However, it does say that we have a natural need and desire to live with and for ideals, and the absence of this motivation constitutes a pathology. Without such a psychological ground, ethics would have to be seen as a foreign element in psychological life.

In claiming that humans can be teleologically moved by an ideal as part of their most archaic nature, Kohut joins forces with Socrates, Plato, and most of the Western philosophical tradition. Socrates agreed with the Sophists that the traditional way of living human life according to set social roles and codes had to be overcome, for such a life denied the possibility for both human autonomy and rationality—our two most distinctive and profound traits. When humans are forced to follow set social roles, they are neither free to determine their own lives nor do they need to use reason, as their values and life courses are fundamentally set. But whereas the Sophists wished to replace social roles with individual desire as the basis for activity, Socrates saw desire to be as arbitrary as social roles and far more chaotic and destructive. Thus, his problem was to find a basis for human behavior that was grounded in the autonomous functioning of the individual and could serve to give stability to both the individual and society. He discovered this by seeing that all individuals participated in universal structures of meaning and value. While individual humans might be unique, they have as their common essence that they are all human. Although the world abounds in a myriad of goods, each one has the essence of being good.

When individuals identify themselves with these universal essences and act from their common humanity and goodness rather than from particular desires for individualized goods, then a great sense of well-being comes over them, for in this identification their lives gain meaning beyond senseless desires that come and go. Also, the fear of death is alleviated, for although one dies, the essence of who one is (humanity) does not. Ideals give a core stability to the personality that can nourish it in dark and desperate times. As Socrates says at his trial, "Nothing can harm a good man either in life or after death" (Plato, *Apology*, 41d). Since good persons are fully identified with the ideal of goodness, which is unchanging, they need fear nothing, for nothing could move them from the ideal.

For Socrates, Plato, and almost the entirety of the Western ethical tradition, the great enemy of the ethically ideal life has been seen as personal desires and appetites. This opposition has often been formulated in terms of a mind—body split in which the mind or soul has rational powers or is close to God, whereas the body participates in animal life and drags us down to the level of the beasts. Hence, this theory demands a rigorous asceticism that Nietzsche found to be destructive of individual vitality and spontaneity.

Kohut differs from the Platonic tradition in three important ways. First, the great enemy of ideals in life is not for Kohut desire, but the lack of a caring selfobject willing to provide a nurturing safe environment. The elimination of individual desire is both impossible and hideous, yet it lies at the core of our moral tradition. A more viable social theory would affirm the fundamental worth of individual desire, especially when it is organized by ideals. It is not desire that is destructive of society, but narcissistic rage and split-off drives that develop when the nuclear self is injured due to inadequate selfobject relations.

Second, for Kohut the idealized pole is not an abstract universal ideal, but an imago closely tied both to one's particular grandiose energies and one's peculiar bent of character and talents. Identification with an abstract universal ideal without relation to the particularity of who one is creates what Horney, Winnicott, and Masterson call a false self. It is an ideal that constantly makes one feel guilty for not being able to realize it, for we are concrete individuals that can never be fully ideal. This guilt produces depression and anxiety, which makes all of life, regardless of what is in fact achieved, unrewarding and unsatisfying. Kohut's carefully integrated self-ideal avoids this problem. Yet such an emphasis on the individualized ideal raises a question of how and whether such an ideal can transform itself into a moral ideal—an ideal by which humans can respect and care for one another because we are all humans. Kohut's idealized pole recognizes a psychological necessity; Plato's universal ideal recognizes a moral one.

Third, unlike Plato and the mainstream moral tradition, for whom ideals represent the core of the self, Kohut sees the idealized pole as only part of the bipolar self. Life is not simply becoming an ideal, for it then loses all of its lusty vitality; nor is it simply desire, for then it would simply be infantile. Although Freud also recognizes a bipolar source of motivation, his libidinal id and moral superego seem always to be in conflict, driving humans to seek a state of respite through regression, repression, and renunciation. But for Kohut there can be a productive and joyous dialectical development between the grandiose and idealized poles of the self, with the ideal luring ambitious energy into more complex and mature forms of attainment.

THE DIALECTICS OF THE NUCLEAR SELF: KOHUT, HEGEL, AND SARTRE

The grandiose pole represents the personal desire for self-gratification emphasized by the Sophists and interpreted by Nietzsche as the dynamic, driving will-to-power that seeks to free itself of all obstacles. The idealized pole represents the ethical universal championed by Socrates, Plato, and the moral tradition. Both positions saw a part of the basic truth of the self and both mistook their part for the whole truth of human nature. On one hand, the Sophists' overemphasis on grandiose desire without an ideal leads to immature, nondevelopmental patterns of gratification. On the other hand, Socrates' overemphasis on the ethical ideal can negate the particular vitality of the individual, leading to guilt, depression, and the substitution of an ideal self for a real one. It is only when both poles are fully operative that optimal growth and maturity can occur. The ideal lures us into more complex states of existence, and the grandiose positive self-representation prevents us from falling into depression and guilt for not yet being the ideal.

Of all the philosophers it was Hegel in his *Phenomenology of the Spirit* (1841) who saw most clearly that personal development consisted of a sustained dialectical struggle between oppositions within the self. The *Phenomenology* is probably the most difficult book in all of philosophy to read, for in it Hegel tries to elucidate human life as a number of dialectical oppositions—subject and object, particular and universal, individual and social—that operate at psychological, social, historical, and metaphysical levels.

The most crucial dialectical opposition for Hegel is that between subject and object. The goal of all subjects is to attain complete freedom and self-knowledge. What limits this pursuit are objects; they stand in opposition to us because they are not fully knowable or controllable by us. An object wouldn't oppose us if we found it to be the same as us, that is, insofar as we found that it mirrored and affirmed our very existence in its existence. Hence, our task with objects is to overcome their opposition to us by consuming them in desire, dominating them, or appropriating them into ourselves as knowledge. Insofar as objects remain unknown, uncontrolled, or dominant over us, we cannot experience the world as a home or achieve our goal of full autonomy and knowledge.

All ordinary attempts to overcome the opposition of objects to the subject end in failure. Objects can never be fully known; their particularity and materiality are surds that stand forever beyond knowability. We can consume objects in desire, but once we do, then either desire dies (and with it ourselves, for in this mode we fully identify with desire) or the object no longer exists in such a way that it can affirm us. We cannot prove our worth through the domination of others (the master–slave relation), for the slave cannot really affirm the lord, as he is so devalued by the lord as to not be worth anything. The lord, who has enslaved others in order to achieve freedom and power, in turn becomes entirely dependent on them (hence, unfree), while they, in their knowledge of labor, can gain a sense of independence and power that the lord cannot (however, they are still politically in bondage). Hence, humans seem doomed to live in a world that does not mirror or affirm the subject and its goals of freedom, knowledge, and being at home.

The dialectic of the universal and particular can be put more succinctly, since we have already seen it functioning in the analysis of the grandiose and idealized poles of the self. We experience the world and ourselves as composed of particulars. I never empirically experience "humanity," just Derek, Ethan, and Sophia. I do not write on "deskness" but this particular desk here and now. However, when I attempt to know what the world is and who I am, I always find universals. Who am I? A philosopher, teacher, and husband—all universals that can be and are shared by numerous people; there is nothing particular about them. Particularity is robust with life, teaming with variety and color, profound in its felt intensities. But it is blind, for it does not and cannot know itself. When humans engage the world through knowing it, they can have meaning and understanding, but life is lost as particularity is transformed into an abstract set of universals. When we live as particulars, life is robust with individual desire, sensation, and feeling; when we live in our humanity, we live according to universal laws and ideals that can apply to all and give life meaning. It seems that humans are caught between either unconsciously and unknowingly living the concreteness of who we are in all its vitality or rising to the level of critical conscious awareness, in which case we lose our vital particularity.

The third dialectical opposition is between the individual and the social. The individual who is devoid of culture is abstract and empty, but one who is fully a part of his culture is reduced to a mere set of social functions and loses his individuality. Society is a set of roles, functions, and variables; it is unconcerned about what particular individuals fill its slots so long as someone does. Individuals come and go; institutions and their functions remain. People taught philosophy before me at Colorado College and will teach it after I retire; if I were not teaching it, someone else would be. The reduction of individuals to variables in a role structure makes us want to assert the irreducible individuality that each one of us is. But what is individuality without one's culture? What would one be without language, music, art, schools, history, and so on? Nothing. As social, we are mere cultural variables without individuality; as individuals without culture, we are empty of content—mere abstractions. How can we be both social and individual?

Hegel's elucidation of these core oppositions created a profound new base from which theories of self had to work, and the philosophies of a number of great thinkers since him—including those of Nietzsche, Freud, Sartre, and Lacan—are based on them. Hegel's own solution to these oppositions was to propose that humans can attain a stage of reason that knows that everything is ultimately a part of God. God, or Absolute Spirit, has split itself into dialectical oppositions in order to develop into a fully conscious, all-knowing, completely developed, and completely realized being, and thus all oppositions can be fully resolved, for all subjects and objects, universals and particulars, and individuals and historical cultures are part of the developing nature of God.

As the nineteenth century developed, Hegel's grand metaphysics and ultimate belief in the absolute power of reason became fully undermined by growing doubts that the oppositions he had so brilliantly elaborated could be rationally and politically resolved. Kierkegaard (1843) claimed that only a heroic leap of faith into the absurd could make one fully whole, both universal and particular. It could be done with an absolute relation to the Absolute, but this could neither be understood nor spoken. Nietzsche (1889) broke the Gordian knot of the dialectical oppositions by declaring that one side of them was fully bankrupt and a sham: free spirits will choose subjectivity, particularity, and individuality over the oppression of ethical ideals, restraining objects, and cultural impositions. Freud found the oppositions so powerful as to drive the psyche into a fierce diremption within itself, with part of the opposition (individual desire) having to go into the unconscious while a universal moral code and cultural forms dominated consciousness.

Another response to Hegel was Sartre's existentialism (1943). For Sartre, we can neither free ourselves from dialectical oppositions nor resolve them. Human beings are inherently split, for their core is a consciousness that is pure activity with no identity ("nothingness" or "being-for-itself"). Yet, what this consciousness most seeks is precisely to have an identity ("being-in-itself"). All attempts of consciousness to assume an identity must fail, for consciousness is just that which cannot be defined by any structure. A conscious being can always say "I am now this (a professor), but I could be something else—I am free." Since consciousness can assume any identity, none necessarily define it.

Humans then have a choice of living authentically or living in bad faith. Living authentically means remaining within the paradox of both having and not having an identity. We form ourselves, but are always beyond the form, always free to change. Bad faith is the attempt either to reduce oneself to an identity and deny one's freedom to change or to deny that one has chosen an identity and is, in fact, something in particular at a given time. Given the human need for an identity and the inability to reduce oneself to an identity, the essential human emotion is anguish and our most authentic state is nausea.

Kohut (1977) also says that human life is tragic, but his tragedy is very different from that of Sartre. The tragedy of life for Kohut is that we begin life as gods, basking in unlimited narcissistic power and glory, and slowly must come to terms with the facts that we are mortal and limited. Also, because we have genuine essential selves, there are the tragic possibilities that we might not realize them or that the realization of them requires us to die or deeply suffer. Rather than the tragedy of the split self, this is a tragedy that only whole selves can fully experience, accept, and incorporate. Both Sartre and the psychoanalytic thinker closest to him, Lacan, would strongly object to Kohut's theory, saying that Kohut is once again trying to foist on humans the illusion that we can be whole, an illusion that makes us neurotic, obsessive, and unhappy.

We can now see how Kohut's theory of self differs so radically from the mainstream European tradition that has developed since Hegel. Kohut shares with this tradition the understanding of a dialectical opposition at the core of the archaic self, but for Nietzsche, Freud, and Sartre, this opposition cannot be mediated or overcome, and therefore we must declare that human life is unremittingly conflictual and doomed to repressive forces, nausea, subterfuge, and suffering or we must celebrate the nonunified, multicentered self. Both alternatives are problematical. It is difficult to accept conflictual suffering as our necessary lot, and it is dangerous to accept that selves are normally multicentered, for such a position leaves unclear the distinction between healthy functioning and fragmented pathological functioning.

Given the dialectical oppositions, how can Kohut have such a positive outlook on the possibility of wholeness in life? How can the particular spontaneous dynamic energy ever be happily structured into ideal general patterns and objective conceptions of itself? How can the individual with its unique desires ever enter the social world without some kind of repression or crushing of life forces?

The core difference between Kohut and these other thinkers is that, for him, the self is a set of selfobject functions. These functions are at first performed by others (objects) and then later performed by the self, another person, a nonperson, or a combination of all three, depending on one's developmental stage, history, and contingent circumstances. When they are first performed by an object, that object is not outside the boundaries of the self affecting it. Rather, since it is performing a crucial function of the self, it is experienced as part of the self. As Kohut has said, his is not an object relations theory (Goldberg, 1990), for the primary objects of early childhood are not exterior to the child's psyche, but part of it. Once the child is able to successfully internalize the selfobject responses to it, then it can more or less perform these functions itself, although as Kohut often said, we never fully outgrow our need for selfobjects and positive responses from them.

Goldberg (1990) captures what it means for the self to be composed of selfobject relationships:

> Selfobjects are not experiences. They are not distinct and separate beings. These two ideas insist on the boundary between individuals and demand that we maintain what is internal in opposition to what is external. Selfobjects are the others that allow one to achieve and maintain an individual integrity. They are what makes us what we are, our very composition. But the individual is not thereby reduced to these selfobjects, since there is an "ownness" inhering in the individual that goes beyond, and is logically distinct from, these relations. Individual integrity and internal relatedness are not incompatible. They are joined together to form the self [p. 126].

In the selfobject function, then, the opposition between subject and object is destroyed at a base level. What is the subject? It is partially the functioning of objects. What are objects? They are capable of functioning as part of the subject. How can there be an ultimate subject–object opposition when subjects are objects and objects subjects?

There is one case in which a dialectical opposition does arise in the self, and that is when others do not properly affirm and empathically mirror the infant. Kohut and Hegel are in agreement that if objects are not empathically mirroring and affirming of the self, then they stand in opposition to it and cause a horrifying split in the subject. "What leads to the human self's destruction, however, is its exposure to the coldness, the indifference of the nonhuman, the nonempathically responding world" (Kohut, 1984, p. 18). Hegel's demand that the entire universe perform the function of mirroring the self can be read as a recalling of this early primordial narcissistic need. If narcissistic needs are met in childhood, then we can slowly grow out of them and accept the world as other than us and often opposed to us without losing either our selves or our happiness. The split, deeply conflicted self that Freud, Sartre, and Lacan find to be ontologically basic is, for Kohut, not the fate of all human selves, but the result of early devastating injuries. The difference here is crucial, for it separates Kohut from postmodern theory, which denies the possibility of grand narratives, especially the grandest of them all: the narrative of an essential unified self.

Kohut also softens the other dialectical oppositions. The universal–particular opposition becomes the opposition of the idealized pole and the grandiose pole, with the idealized pole luring the grandiose energies into development. It can do this without massive conflict because the tension arc of individual propensities, talents, and proclivities mediates between the two poles, adjusting the ideal toward the idiosyncratic person and adjusting the primal energies toward the ideal. The individual–social opposition is also alleviated when we realize that the individual is constructed on the basis of its internalization of social objects. This is not to say that there are no energies that wish to assert their individual vitality in opposition to the social structure and moral code. Such a denial would negate the great insights of Nietzsche and the Sophists. Selfobjects are not simply absorbed or internalized, but transformed. "The 'foreign protein' of the selfobject and of the selfobject's functions, whether in childhood or during analysis, becomes split up after being ingested; its constituents are then reassembled to form the self in accordance with those individual patterns that characterize the growing child's (or analysand's) specific psychic 'protein'" (Kohut, 1984, p. 160).

In short, Hegel, Kierkegaard, Freud, and Sartre see human beings as faced with dialectical oppositions so powerful that we either must make some utterly heroic effort to overcome them (Hegel's jump to Absolute Reason, Kierkegaard's leap of faith) or come to terms with the fact that human life is torn by unsolvable conflicts and the best we can hope for is to replace neurotic suffering with authentic suffering (Freud and Sartre). With the notion of the self as a set of selfobject functions, Kohut softens these dialectical oppositions to make the joyous development of a whole self possible. Certainly, development involves suffering, for it demands we abandon one solidified self-position in order to attain another, but when this occurs in situations of "optimal frustration" the pain of loss is balanced by the joy of achievement and discovery.

Which theory is superior? Are humans really confronted with hard, unsolvable contradictions at the core of the self, or are these oppositions such that, in a good enough environment, they can be mediated in a wholesome developmental process? I offer two reasons, aside from Kohut's persuasive clinical observations, for why Kohut might have a more viable theory. First, Kohut can account for both the happy person and the tortured, split person. However, Freud, Sartre, and Lacan must claim that the happy, whole person is only an appearance, an illusion. Underneath the facade of wholeness and the sense of being fully at ease with oneself are raging conflicts and emptinesses. It certainly seems as though there are genuinely happy, joyful human beings not seriously torn by conflicts; to have to call them "illusions" out of fidelity to a theory indicates that something is wrong with the theory. Indeed, one of the greatest (and least read) thinkers of the twentieth century, Alfred North Whitehead, said that the worth of a theory was dependent on how little it had to call illusion (Whitehead, 1927).

Second, Kohut's theory intersects with, supports, and gains support from two of the most vital movements in self theory in the last quarter century: evolutionary theory and feminism. Contemporary evolutionary theory has made great strides in understanding the social behavior of animals and calls for a view of the human individual as one who both has concerns for others and asserts his or her own individual needs that can conflict with those of others (Slavin and Kriegman, 1992). Kohut's bipolar self contains both of these aspects of the self. Also, in ecological theories of the self, human beings are seen as intrinsically related to their natural and social environments, rather than as atomic, independent units. Kohut's theory of selfobjects is deeply consonant with this kind of theory and, indeed, has been used as a basis for an ecological theory of the self (Riker, 1991).

In softening the dialectical oppositions and asserting the primacy of an inextricable web of subject and object, particular and universal, society and individuality, Kohut is very close to the dominant theory of the self coming from recent feminist thinkers. Attempting to conceive of the self from a woman's perspective, theorists such as Carol Gilligan (1982), Jean Baker Miller (1976), and scholars at the Stone Center at Wellesley (Gilligan, 1988) have constructed a relational concept of the self. The relational self does not have rigid ego boundaries, does not hold autonomy to be the highest value, and does not attempt to solve ethical issues by appeal to abstract general moral laws. Rather, the relational self is inextricably interwoven with particular other persons in such a way that its identity is inconceivable without reference to its connections with these others. In Kohut's terms, selfobject relations occur throughout life.

CONCLUSIONS, IMPLICATIONS, AND DEVELOPMENTS

As we have seen, Kohut's theory of the bipolar self incorporates a number of the most important aspects of the self discovered and elucidated in the history of philosophy. It contains the vitality of the spontaneous, creative, energetic self that Nietzsche championed along with the grounding relation to ideals that Socrates and Plato saw must be part of any stable and developing human being. It recognizes the oppositions that Hegel found to be at the base of human existence but understands them in such a way that their resolutions are possible without extreme existential anguish or heroism. It is consonant with the relational theories of self currently being developed in ecological philosophy and feminism.

However, before calling everyone to a banquet to celebrate Kohut's glorious achievement, we need to understand that it does force us to abandon a number of cherished ethical notions and that it is not a complete theory of the self, for it lacks a concept of the mature self. I will end this piece by merely stating how Kohut's theory demands a reorientation toward our basic moral categories and making a few suggestions as to what is needed to have a full theory of the self.

If human beings have nuclear selves, then we must relinquish our notion that we are free to become whatever we want to be. We have our individual natures and cannot escape them. They are our fates. Freedom is not openness of possibility for the self, as it is traditionally conceived of in liberal philosophy. We are not free to realize a general ideal of human excellence. Rather, freedom must be reconceived as the freedom to realize the particular self that one is.

A second implication of Kohut's theory of the self as composed of selfobject relations is that we must relinquish the notion of complete autonomy as definitive of adulthood. As self psychologist Ernest Wolf (1988) says:

The observation that the self cannot exist for long in a psychological vacuum is a finding that is not easily accepted. The very emergence and
maintenance of the self as a psychological structure depends on the continuing presence of an evoking-sustaining-responding matrix of selfobject
experiences. The discovery heralds the end of another cherished illusion
of Western man, namely the illusory goal of independence, self-sufficiency, and free autonomy [p. 28].

For Kohut (1984), "a move from dependence (symbiosis) to independence (autonomy) in the psychological sphere is no more possible, let
alone desirable, than a corresponding move from a life dependent on
oxygen to a life independent of it in the biological sphere" (p. 47). The
difference between an infant's selfobject relations and a mature adult's is
not between dependence and independence, but between being totally
dependent on others to provide the needed responses and being able to
provide oneself with the needed selfobject responses, whether this
means relying on intimate friends, nourishing oneself with a good book
or piece of music, or getting therapy.

A third implication is that not everyone has the full possibility of being
a moral agent, another high value of liberal philosophy. If moral agents
are those people who can take into account the needs of others and
empathize with them, then deeply injured selves suffering from narcissistic disorders are unable to be full moral agents. They are not to be
blamed for not being moral, for they are not responsible for the selfobject failures that occurred in early childhood and could not be otherwise
than they are without the aid of intense psychotherapy.

Finally, although Kohut's theory is a powerful and enlightening way
of viewing the archaic ground of the self, it is not a full theory of the self,
for it lacks an examination of what constitutes an adult configuration of
the self. Kohut (1965) does give a number of qualities of the healthy,
mature person such as humor, creativity, and wisdom, but this does not
constitute a theory of adult self-structure. For instance, although Kohut
has shown that the self needs ideals to function, he has not examined
why or whether some ideals are better than others. However, the ideals
that can sustain the child or the adolescent are hardly adequate for the
adult. What are the marks of an adult ideal? The child's ideal is closely
tied to itself, but adult ideals must take into account one's presence in a
community of adults. That is, they should be moral ideals. But how and
why should a person give up a narcissistic ideal for a moral one?

I do not fault Kohut for not addressing these issues, as they are primarily topics for social psychologists and ethicists. Kohut was a psychoanalyst committed to exploring the roots of profound psychic disorders.
These occur in early childhood with a faulty construction of the nuclear
self. People can have failures in choosing satisfying narratives, and the

development of the higher critical faculties can be impoverished, conventional, and annoyingly inconsistent. However, although bad narrative choices and nonoptimal development of the ego capacities can lead to unhappiness, boredom, and unfulfilled lives, they rarely lead to neuroses or narcissistic personality disorders. They are the province of the ethicist, not the psychotherapist. Not all unhappiness comes from early psychological injuries; sometimes it comes from poor choices, neglected education, inopportune circumstances, and misfortune. Kohut's bipolar theory of the self is a sound basis for a full theory of self; now it is up to others to expound on how its possibilities can be fully realized in mature adult life.

REFERENCES

Detrick, D. W. & Detrick S. P., eds. (1989), *Self-Psychology: Comparison and Contrasts.* Hillsdale, NJ: The Analytic Press.

Freud, S. (1921), Group psychology and the analysis of the ego. *Standard Edition,* 18:90–92. London: Hogarth Press, 1955.

Gilligan, C. (1981), *In a Different Voice.* Cambridge, MA: Harvard University Press.

—— Ward, J. V. & Taylor, J. M. (1988), *Mapping the Moral Domain.* Cambridge, MA: Harvard University Press.

Goldberg, A. (1990), *The Prisonhouse of Psychoanalysis.* New York: International Universities Press.

Hegel, G. W. F. (1841), *The Phenomenology of Mind,* trans. J. B. Baillie. London: George Allen & Unwin, 1949.

Kierkegaard, S. (1843), *Fear and Trembling,* trans. H. V. & E. H. Hong. Princeton: Princeton University Press, 1983.

Kohut, H. (1965), Forms and transformations of narcissism. *J. Amer. Psychoanal. Assn.,* 14:243–272.

—— (1977), *The Restoration of the Self.* New York: International Universities Press.

—— (1984), *How Does Analysis Cure?* ed. A. Goldberg & P. Stepansky. Chicago: University of Chicago Press.

Miller, J. B. (1976) *Toward a New Psychology of Women.* Boston: Beacon Press.

Nietzsche, F. (1885), *Thus Spoke Zarathustra,* trans. W. Kaufmann. New York: Penguin Books, 1978.

—— (1886), *Beyond Good and Evil,* trans. R. Hollingdale. New York: Penguin Books, 1990.

—— (1887), *The Genealogy of Morals,* trans. F. Golffing. New York: Doubleday, 1956.

—— (1889), *The Will to Power,* trans. W. Kaufmann & R. Hollingdale. New York: Random House, 1968.

Plato. *Collected Dialogues,* ed. E. Hamilton & H. Cairns. New York: Pantheon Books, 1961.

Riker, J. (1991), *Human Excellence and an Ecological Conception of the Psyche.* Albany, NY: SUNY Press.

Sartre, J-P. (1943), *Being and Nothingness,* trans. H. Barnes. New York: Philosophical Library, 1956.

Scheffler, S. (1992), *Human Morality*. New York: Oxford University Press.
Slavin, M. & Kriegman, D. (1992), *The Adaptive Design of the Human Psyche*. New York: Guilford.
Whitehead, A. N. (1927), *Process and Reality*. New York: Macmillan.
Wolf, E. (1988), *Treating the Self*. New York: Guilford.

Chapter 6

On the Existential/ Subjectivism– Scientific/Objectivism Dialectic in Self Psychology: A View from Evolutionary Biology

Daniel Kriegman

From the very beginning of the history of human ideas, there has been an ongoing debate about the validity of perception and communication. Does what we see—and what we say we see—bear any resemblance to the way the world actually is? If so, how much? In the seventeenth century, Francis Bacon (1620) began a line of thinking that ultimately led to modern science with its objectivist epistemology. His suspicions about humans as accurate observers were pronounced: "Man's sense is falsely asserted to be the standard of things: on the contrary, all the perceptions, both of the senses and the mind, bear reference to man and not to the universe; and the human mind resembles those uneven mirrors which impart their own properties to different objects . . . and distort and disfigure them" (*Novum Organum*, i, 41). Empirical tests become essential when the human mind is considered to be such a source of distortion.

Two and a half centuries later, within a culture completely dominated by the epistemology of Western science, Freud began his training as a neurologist. It is not surprising that the issue of the accuracy of human perception and communication ultimately became a major psychoanalytic theme. The ego's capacity to accurately know what is real has long been considered a sign of healthy functioning. The "distortions" inherent in transferential relating have often been considered the sine qua non of transference itself: if the patient's experience of the analyst is colored (distorted) by the past, then we are dealing with transference; if not, we are dealing with the "real" relationship (Greenson, 1971). For example, in a recent article describing a psychoanalytic perspective on couples and marital therapy, Finkelstein (1988) quotes Merton Gill (1986, personal communication) as saying: "It may be all very well to speak about a perspectival view and multiple plausible assessments of reality, but it still makes an important difference as to whether the patient's spouse would generally be considered nonsupportive or whether this is a significant 'distortion' on the patient's part as seen by most external observers" (p. 910).

Finkelstein (1988) then notes that:

> Schafer (1985) describes how analysts . . . do not always work within the confines of psychic reality. . . . He says, "The analyst requires some ground to stand on in order to make analytic sense of what is being reported in the analysand's associations." The analyst does this on the basis of "versions of common human situations and cause-effect relations that . . . meet the criteria of narrative good fit" (pp. 544–545). Thus, the analyst shifts in his focus of listening between the psychic reality of the analysand and what the analyst believes is "actually" happening in the patient's life [pp. 910–911].

Finkelstein goes on to argue for the advantages of bringing marital therapy to psychoanalysis: "There is . . . no assurance that an analytic patient will ever provide information that will allow the analyst to unravel some of these 'distortions.' The marital therapist, by contrast, is in a position quickly to observe the 'actual' interactions of his patients and to identify their 'distorted' views of each other as they appear to an external observer" (p. 911).

In reacting to this quite ingrained and widespread psychoanalytic view of the patient's distortions and because of his concern that the analyst, in judging the patient's experience, was leaving the field-defining empathic stance, Kohut (1982, 1984) pleaded with analysts to try to remain within the patient's subjective experience. Others (Atwood and Stolorow, 1984; Stolorow, Brandchaft, and Atwood, 1987; Stolorow and Atwood, 1989) have attempted to take this position to its extreme. Based on their interpretation of the work of the philosophers Husserl, Heidegger, and Sartre, they propose an existential phenomenology in which reality is seen as a subjective construction (Atwood and Stolorow, 1984). As the world can only be known through our experience of it, reality only exists in subjectivities. The universe has no external, independent existence apart from our subjective experience of it. Thus, the most fundamental ground of reality is subjective experience itself.[1] In attempting to be consistent with this view, they ultimately call for a separation of psychoanalysis from the natural sciences.[2]

---

[1] Note that both Stolorow and Atwood (personal communications, 1995) appear to have moved from this earlier position and both feel they can embrace Orange's (1995a) moderate realism. In Orange's epistemology, grounded in the pragmatism of the American philosophers Charles Sanders Peirce and William James, certain aspects of experience are made (construed, organized) by the perceiver whereas others are given (brute, unavoidable), "like a forty-mile-an-hour wind that smacks us in the face." In the pragmatic perspectivalism that James developed from Peirce's pragmatism, what is "true" is what *works* for the individual. In James's sense, this "pragmatism" embraces a basic human empiricism compatible with the viewpoint of this chapter; but James goes beyond empirical knowledge of the world. For James, anything that works in making life easier or more enjoyable is reasonable to believe: if religious myths "work," in this sense, for example, then it can be as reasonable to believe in them as an alternative theory that may lead to more accurate predictions. Thus, pragmatic perspectivalism is somewhat compatible with yet ultimately incompatible with the epistemological stance suggested in this paper. Note that this very distinction between James's view and my own (i.e., James's attempt to reconcile science and religion using Peirce's conception of pragmatism) was "the origin of Peirce's decision to disassociate himself from the doctrine by rebaptizing his own view 'pragmaticism,' a term which he described as 'ugly enough to be safe from kidnappers'" (White, 1955, p. 158).

Despite their current willingness to embrace Orange's moderate realism, the earlier work of Atwood and Stolorow laid out the epistemological issue more starkly and, for this chapter, the inconsistencies and problems in their stance are clearer in that work (also see Carveth, 1995). As Orange (1995b) notes, there are numerous statements in the works of Stolorow and Atwood that are quite consistent with the epistemological stance taken in this chapter. But rather than suggest that this means I have misunderstood the intersubjectivists, this is exactly my point: by the very nature of the extreme perspectivalist position they suggest, they end up being inconsistent and continually slip into a more objectivist epistemology. Stolorow (personal communication, 1995) made it clear that he and Atwood are not proposing a general epistemology. For example, he noted that he would not want someone to drive a car using the epistemology they propose for psychoanalysis. But is it possible to have one epistemology for psychoanalysis and another for the rest of one's life? As will be seen, this is a tricky stance that many analysts cannot maintain. Ultimately, I am proposing a single epistemological stance for psychoanalysis (the *introspective* science of complex mental states observed via empathy and introspection), natural science (the *extrospective* sciences), and daily life (common sense and experience).

[2] Atwood and Stolorow (1984) and Stolorow and Atwood (1994) certainly use the term "science" and define psychoanalysis as an interpretive science. However, their "science" is interpretive (hermeneutic) in that they are defining criteria for determining meaning in a single case. Although I find myself agreeing with the criteria they set out for tests of validity (again, meaning in the particular case) and how such tests must by the nature of the process differ from tests in the natural sciences where the subject matter is "external," I think they end up using the word *science* in a totally different manner from what most people understand it to mean. In their conception, because meanings arise in a specific intersubjective field we cannot expect independent verifiability

Recently, Stolorow (1995) lamented this as a misreading of intersubjectivity theory: "None of us claims that objective reality does not exist" (p. xvi). Yet I will not only suggest that such a claim is implied in their writing (also see Carveth, 1995), I will, in a sense, go further and (somewhat paradoxically) suggest that there is nothing outside of subjective experience about which to speak. However, I will end up in a framework that—unlike intersubjectivity theory as it has been developed thus far—is more compatible with natural science (with prediction, causation, and intersubjective verifiability), that can include objectivity, and that actually necessitates some acknowledgment that distortion is an important human, intersubjective phenomenon. At this point, let's just look briefly at the ways in which the challenge to—if not the outright rejection of—objective reality is implied in the work of the intersubjectivists.

---

by other observers—as in the natural sciences. But the natural sciences don't require *simultaneous* independent verification; the independent observer must simply carry out a similar process in their own setting. Note that the process must be *similar*, not *identical* (exact sameness would be impossible). In fact, verification of scientific theories is often enhanced when a theory can explain a number of similar but not necessarily identical events occurring in similar but not identical contexts. Contrast Stolorow and Atwood's (1994) distinction between psychoanalysis and the natural sciences—they claim that only in the latter do we find the "doctrine of replication"—to Kohut's (1977, p. 141; 1980, p. 515) plea to analysts to suspend their disbelief and test the ideas contained within self psychology with their own patients—to see for themselves if replication is possible (in similar but not identical situations).

In addition, Stolorow and Atwood (1994) and Atwoood and Stolorow (1984) call for a psychoanalytic phenomenology that is based on structuralism, which they contrast with causal analysis: "causal thinking leads to the use of *prediction* as a criterion for assessing the adequacy of an explanation" (p. 23). Without prediction, why would anyone go to an analyst? There is implicit, causal/predictive thinking involved, that is, the immersion in an analytic relationship (cause) will lead to a productive change (prediction). Testing causes (the different analytic interventions prescribed by self psychology) and examining their outcome (how well they lead to the predicted result) is exactly what Kohut called for: a test of the theory of self psychology by application and observation to assess whether it worked. We all do this all the time; it is the way we learn what works and what doesn't work clinically. By rejecting the utility of the concepts of causation and prediction, Stolorow and Atwood have parted with many self psychologists who believe that ultimately the criteria of natural science (e.g., causation, prediction, and independent verification) can be applied to psychoanalysis to test ideas and clinical interventions. This is generally accepted even though few analysts find that such tests are most meaningful in controlled, statistical studies. Rather, we function as scientists—using causation, prediction, and independent verification to determine the value of our ideas (validity)—when we apply *Stolorow and Atwood's* own criteria for determining validity in each independent clinical interaction. We can function as "scientists" (as the term is generally understood) on *a case by case basis* while simultaneously believing that a statistical analysis of controlled studies of behavior (i.e., academic psychology's methodology as contrasted with the psychoanalytic method) comes as close to capturing the essence of the essential subjective experience of being human as a chemical analysis of pigments comes to capturing the experience that one may have when viewing a great painting (see Kohut, 1977).

In their attempt to explicate their position on this issue, Stolorow and Atwood (1992) claim that "we encounter a reification . . . involving the experience of the world as real and existing separately from the self. What psychological purpose can be ascribed to the reifying of the experience that there is an enduring world distinct from the self?" (p. 11).[3] As Atwood and Stolorow (1984) note, the philosophical underpinnings of such notions can be found in Husserl's phenomenology: "Whereas traditional sciences take the existence of the world for granted as a 'pregiven' reality, transcendental phenomenology suspends or 'brackets' assumptions regarding the nature of objective reality . . . [using] a mental operation by which the phenomenologist frees himself from presuppositions and moves into a perspective from which what had previously been taken as real presents itself purely as a field of appearances" (p. 9). In Husserl's terms, this enables the philosopher to break free from the strongest and most universal internal bondage: the pregivenness of the world.

Such statements certainly seem to me (despite Stolorow's disclaimer) to challenge the notion that a reality separate from the self exists, that there is "an enduring world distinct from the self" to use his terms. Furthermore, I believe that such notions are related to the intersubjectivists' attempt to take the definition of the psychoanalytic field as limited by empathy and introspection and "push to its limits Kohut's (1959) proposition" (Stolorow et al., 1987, p. 5). In this push, they reject any use within psychoanalytic investigation by the analyst of knowledge gained from extrospective modes of data gathering. In contrast, following Wolf (1983), Shane and Shane (1986), and Basch (1986)—all of whose work the intersubjectivists specifically reject in this regard—I hope to show how such knowledge can, at times, aid the analyst in maintaining and even deepening the empathic stance (also see Slavin and Kriegman, 1992). It is in the rejection of any role for extrospective knowledge and objectivity (within psychoanalytic investigation) that the intersubjectivists reveal a tendency toward an extreme relativistic stance in which Stolorow (1995) can claim that "the concepts of objectivity and distor-

---

[3] Unfortunately (because it makes the argument more complex as the following was probably formulated to avoid the very criticism being made), Stolorow and Atwood go on to speak of a subjective *sense* of a reality separate from the self, a sense of reality that is sustained by the intersubjective field. This becomes reified when the deep insecurities of modern life (psychological aloneness) make it too frightening for a person to see that his or her sense of reality is being sustained by a particular intersubjective field. The contradictions in this attempt to acknowledge a *sense* of reality while maintaining an extreme subjectivist view are taken up in footnote number 21 to a following discussion of psychosis and delusions.

tion have no place within the theoretical lexicon of psychoanalysis" (p. xvi).

Although Atwood and Stolorow (1984) are careful not to fall into the extremes of existential phenomenology,[4] there appears to be a tendency throughout their work to use such concepts to challenge *any* notion of the analyst's "objectivity"; certainly they create a taboo against holding *any* notion of patients' "distortions." Although I am in wholehearted agreement with their *aim*—the prevention of the elevation of the analyst's reality to a position of dominance to which the patient must acquiesce—this chapter explores the possibility that there may be better *methods* to guard against the abuses that concern the intersubjectivists (a concern shared by almost all self psychologists), and that such methods may actually deepen our understanding of intersubjective experience. The view I will be developing is actually highly consistent with existential phenomenology[5] while simultaneously being far more compatible with natural science.

Science has been based on the notion that there is something more objectively real than subjective experience and that the true nature of the world can be more closely approximated through careful observation, data accumulation, and theory development. Such a position takes the material world as given and assumes that we can approach a more accurate representation of an a priori (i.e., existing prior to our perception of it, or "pregiven") material world through observation, experimentation, and theory development. Despite the many critiques of objectivist science—especially as it is used by psychology—as an anachronism that has been overthrown by the Heisenberg uncertainty principle, the theory of relativity, chaos theory, and postmodernist critiques of scientific objectivity, it is clear that the notion of a reality existing independent of biased, subjective observation—a reality that can only be approximated by careful repeated observation—still holds sway as the underlying philosophical paradigm for science.[6]

---

[4] For example they recognize that Husserl's radical autonomy (of the transcendental ego) from the world of appearances has solipsistic contradictions, and they see Sartre's radical notions of freedom in which consciousness is not determined by anything other than itself as incompatible with both considerable human experience and with our understanding that even the experience of freedom has genetic origins the vicissitudes of which affect its development.

[5] It is actually *more* consistent with existential phenomenology as it much more fully (but not completely) embraces Husserl's, Heidegger's, and Sartre's concerns about how others can define oneself and alienate one from oneself. Their struggle with interpersonal conflict has to be removed before the intersubjectivists can make use of their notions of how the world of experience is created by the experiencer (see Atwood and Stolorow, 1984; Slavin and Kriegman, 1992).

[6] Consider, for example, Sucharov (1992) and Holt (1989). I believe that Sucharov's attempt to apply the uncertainty principle to self psychology—which leads to his call to make permanent Kohut's temporary expedient of adopting a complementarity approach to psychoanalysis—is a mis-

AN EVOLUTIONARY VIEW OF THE EMPATHIC STANCE

Although Kohut was unable to follow the intersubjectivists into their separation of psychoanalysis from the *Zeitgeist* of science (see Kohut, 1980), I will argue that it is precisely this *rejection of the objectivist view* that enables the intersubjectivists to maintain a stance of exquisitely empathic inquiry. It should become clearer as we proceed that the rejection of objectivity helps the analyst maintain consistent empathy because the empathic stance is not a simple technical maneuver; rather, it is a profoundly *unnatural* stance (Kriegman and Slavin, 1990; Slavin and Kriegman, 1992). Whereas *empathy* is entirely natural, a consistent, unremitting empathic *stance* (or *sustained* empathic inquiry) vis-à-vis another's subjective experience cannot be found in the natural world—not even in the often idyllically pictured mother–infant relationship. As evolved animals, humans—like all other living creatures—have been designed (shaped) by evolution (natural selection) to maximize their success. Though parental success overlaps greatly with the success of their children, a parent's interests are never exactly the same as the interests of *one* child (Trivers, 1974). Nowhere in nature will you find an organism that generally gives up its own interests and adopts those of another. As has been argued (Kriegman and Slavin, 1990; Slavin and Kriegman, 1992), conflicts of interest are omnipresent. This "evolutionary" perspective is not a reversion to the dog-eat-dog, Hobbesian, or classical Freudian views. The evolutionary perspective supports innate, mutualistic motivations just as well as it does selfish ones (Kriegman, 1988, 1990).

However, it is important to acknowledge that, even in the analytic setting, conflict is always present. No analyst can achieve a consistent

---

application of an extremely experience-distant theory to the science of complex mental states that can only be known through vicarious introspection (this is examined further in footnote 17). In contrast, consider Holt's analysis in which he describes a process of giving up naive realism for relativism and then ultimately replacing that by critical realism. Naive realism is the belief that the observer does not affect the observed. Relativism is the belief that there is no reality outside of subjective observation. And critical realism is the awareness that beyond numerous relativistic perspectives—and the inevitable effects of the observer on the observed—there exists a reality that can be transformed by certain rules to yield the different perspectives. Far from saying that everything is relative, Einstein's theory of relativity provided the transformational rules that allow us to view the essence of the universe as *invariant* but show how each observer will see a different picture! Holt's analysis and conceptualization of critical realism (as I understand it) is quite close to the viewpoint presented in this chapter.

empathic immersion in another's experience.[7] The design of our psyche mitigates against it. Even a largely consistent empathic stance is very hard to achieve. In a recent discussion of Evelyne Schwaber's persistent struggle to come to share her patient's point of view, Lawrence Friedman (1992) states:

> Dr. Schwaber shows us something that we might not see as clearly in Kohut: it is not just empathy that is powerful, but the wish and effort to empathize. Dr. Schwaber puts the spotlight on what is in the shadow of Kohut's theory: the negative aspect of empathizing is as important as the positive; the empathizer's willingness to give up his own investment. . . . The analyst is frustrating her own natural thinking style in order to . . . come close to the patient. Recognizing the magnitude of the sacrifice, the patient can probably feel the analyst's urge toward closeness almost physically. Ordinarily, only an unusually dedicated love would produce such a self-sacrificing devotion. . . . Most analysts want to know their patients well. But they are not all equally willing to discomfort themselves in the process, and not all theories encourage such discomfort.

I suggest that Friedman has accurately captured some of the enormous meaning hidden within the struggle to maintain an empathic stance and that Kohut and the self psychologists have, indeed, left the meaning of this struggle in the shadows. That is, for many self psychologists, the empathic stance is largely a technical maneuver. In self-psy-

---

[7] Anna Ornstein (personal communication, 1994) argues that we must remember that empathy is value neutral and thus there is no need to see a conflict with one's own self-interest when one maintains an empathic stance: the empathizer can be acting out of self-interest and not in the interests of the one whose experience is being empathically understood. However, this is not *therapeutic* use of empathy. In the clinical setting, we find empathy used for the *patient's* interests to be part of the curative process. Empathy aimed at understanding the patient in the pursuit of the *therapist's* interests is not only not therapeutic, it is often unethical and destructive. It is the persistent employment of clinically useful empathy—an unremitting empathic stance used almost solely for the best interests of the other—that is unnatural.

Furthermore, there are numerous moments in analysis—possibly more than those moments in which this is not so—in which the natural inclination of the analyst's mind will be to take an entirely unempathic stance that does not attempt to see the patient as subject (see P. Ornstein's [1979] definition of the empathic stance) and rather sees the patient as object, or in which the analyst is pursuing thoughts related to himself or herself and is relatively unaware of the patient. Although some of these moments may be productively understood as countertransference reactions, frequently the analyst will naturally be pulled away from an empathic stance in the pursuit of thoughts unrelated or even inimical to the patient: we therapists have our own problems, interests, and agendas and we simply do not stop thinking about them when the patient enters the consulting room. The need to pull oneself out of such moments to reenter the clinically useful empathic stance (i.e., the empathic stance that is being used for the pursuit of the patient's interests) is a struggle. This will be discussed further as we look at Friedman's (1992) response to Schwaber's attempts to maintain a viewpoint entirely within the patient's subjectivity.

chological clinical discussions, the failure to maintain an empathic stance is almost always attributed to some unanalyzed aspect of the analyst's pathological narcissism.[8] A full appreciation of the enormous cost to anyone of maintaining an empathic stance—and thus the reason for many empathic failures—is largely absent from self psychology.[9]

THE INTERSUBJECTIVIST SOLUTION TO THE "PROBLEM OF EMPATHY"

In their struggle to remain true to their patient's experience and in their determination not to slip into confrontations that elevate the therapist's "reality"—often, as they have demonstrated, at the cost of the patient's well-being—the intersubjectivists appear to turn to existential phenome-

---

[8] Though more recent writings (e.g., Stolorow and Atwood, 1992) acknowledge the *inherent* difficulty in maintaining an empathic stance, they do not appear to identify the source of this difficulty. Without the notion of inherent *conflict* between individuals, they have no source for the fact that "seeing himself and the world consistently through the eyes of another can pose serious threats to the analyst's personal reality and sense of self" (p. 93). Why is adopting another's view so difficult? Why is it so threatening? Though their clinical discussions (Stolorow and Atwood, 1992) now acknowledge how a particular patient's ways of organizing the world can be problematic for a specific analyst with needs and vulnerabilities threatened by such organizing principles (i.e., they are emphasizing the complex interplay between the two parties), there still is a sense that an analyst whose vulnerabilities have been sufficiently analyzed will not have such a conflict. There is no conception of *inherent conflict* between individuals with a concomitant *built-in tendency* on the part of all parties to hold to one's own views and protect them from the influence of others—a conception that can be readily found in the phenomenological and existential authors that they use as their philosophical foundation *only after they remove* this inherent conflict between people (Atwood and Stolorow, 1984). Thus, the *inherency* and *inevitability* of conflict in the analytic setting is given no foundation despite an attempt to acknowledge some difficulty in maintaining an empathic stance.

[9] Anna Ornstein (personal communication, 1994) claims that she and Paul Ornstein have indeed struggled with and described some of the difficulty in maintaining an empathic stance. She says that one must first differentiate the *developmentally* naturally mutualistic relationship between mother and child and the *clinical* situation in which an individual who has been traumatized is trying to find an empathic resonance. It is far more difficult to empathically "hold" a traumatized child who is now an adult than it is to hold an infant. However, as important as this distinction may be—and I believe it does indeed account for some of the most difficult problems in attaining an empathic tie with many patients—it still does not address the inevitable conflict in human relations that is not based on pathology (prior trauma). Even in good-enough parenting relationships, there is significant conflict based on inherently divergent aims between parent and child (Trivers, 1974) that exist prior to traumatic empathic failure. In fact, much, if not most, traumatic empathic failure—which can have exactly the effect that Anna Ornstein describes—may have its roots in inherent conflicts of interest that exist prior to empathic failure (see Slavin and Kriegman, 1992). It is this inherent conflict—that, despite enormous overlapping interests, there are also quite problematic (conflict-causing), inherently divergent aims separating parent and child—that has been missing from self psychology.

nal philosophy. Their philosophical solution works like this: If in our analytic work we utilize an epistemology in which there is no world existing separately from the self (or from subjectivity), then we are simply dealing with the intersection of subjectivities creating an intersubjective field in which the analysand's subjectivity must be granted the same epistemological validity as the analyst's subjectivity, which includes the analyst's psychoanalytic theory and interpretive understanding. These two subjectivities are merely two variations of existential phenomenal constructions of reality. No more "objective" reality exists against which one can compare these two constructions and therefore neither is to be given higher epistemological status, for neither can be considered more objective than the other. Neither can appeal to science, psychological theory, prior experience, or any other ground to claim that their views, conceptions, and perceptions have any claim to "accuracy"; neither can claim that the other's view is "distorted" (see Stolorow, 1995, p. xvi).

This stance eliminates the ground necessary for many clinical con-frontations—most of which are, in fact, of dubious value and often are quite harmful—and it provides a framework for a far-reaching empathic acceptance of the patient's subjective experience. In this view, problem-atic conflict results from the failure of the therapist to decenter from his or her reality to join with the patient on the meeting ground created in the intersubjective field. In clinical discussions, the failure to sufficiently decenter is almost always laid at the door of the therapist's pathology.

Some illustrations may enable me to elaborate this position to clarify some of my terms and the point of view being critiqued. As I noted, the view I am taking in this chapter actually embraces much of the essence of subjectivist, existential phenomenology. However, it will also become clear that there are crucial differences between an approach that leads to rejection of a scientific worldview (the intersubjectivist position), and the subjectivist stance I utilize that can incorporate scientific empiricism along with its related concepts of objectivity, validity, distortion, causa-tion, prediction, and intersubjective verifiability. In this latter (more mod-erate) subjectivist stance, we can retain a conception of an objective reality that is part of each person's subjective experience (see Stolorow and Atwood, 1992) while simultaneously it is subjectively known that reality exists in some form that is independent of subjective experience (see Holt, 1989, and footnote 6).

A CLOSER LOOK AT THE EXISTENTIAL, SUBJECTIVIST PERSPECTIVE

It appears quite correct to say that the only world that we can know to exist is the world of our experience. What—if anything—exists outside of our experience can only be described metaphorically and can never be known (see also Kohut, 1983, p. 391). In a sense, this can be taken to indicate that psychic reality is the only reality; internal representations are "more real" (are the *actual* content of experience) than the hypothetical "real objects" (that can never be experienced and are *assumed* to exist).[10] For example, if I were to hold up a red rose, we would all

---

[10] What is also fascinating is the degree to which those who created the dominant, Western, empirical system of knowledge shared this view of the limits of knowledge (Kors, 1993). Empiricism—scientific testing of ideas about the world—is often incorrectly placed in opposition to subjectivism, the belief that the only knowable world is the world of subjective experience. However, for those individuals most responsible for taking up the mantle of Bacon's call for an inductive science and for bringing the empirical/scientific method to a position of prominence in Western thought (Locke, Berkeley, and Hume), there was no opposition between empiricism and the subjectivist limitation of knowledge. For the British empiricists (and Voltaire following Locke), there is nothing knowable outside of human experience. All we can talk about is what we experience and how different aspects of our experience relate to one another. Our knowledge of the world is absolutely bounded by what we can experience; there are no exceptions. (Experience is defined as being *both* sense impressions and mental reflection—the experience of mind operating—upon those impressions; thus abstract ideas can be part of knowledge.) Yet, rather than lead the empiricists to eschew notions of objectivity, this very notion led them to emphasize the importance of carefully observing, comparing, analyzing, and measuring the *data* of *subjective* experience along with our subjective *ideas* about how our world of experiences is structured. An ultimate reality, the world beyond experience that gives rise to experiences, was assumed by Locke to exist but—by the very nature of the experiential/subjectivist limits on what can be known—we can have no knowledge of its nature other than our experiences. Locke was quite emphatic: All we can say about such ultimate reality is "I don't know." Bishop Berkeley believed that true religion gives us some knowledge of the ultimate (external) reality that gives rise to our internal experiences; the external reality must be the mind of God in which all that is exists. Hume went further then either Locke or Berkeley. In Hume's skepticism, since all we can know are our experiences, what exists beyond them (what "gives rise" to them) is completely unintelligible. For Hume, it is meaningless to talk about that of which we can have no knowledge whatsoever. Meaningless statements are best left unsaid. For many reasons beyond the scope of this chapter, I believe that a revised and updated version of Locke's position is most consistent with both common sense and modern science: our experiences arise through our interactions with something not directly knowable that exists beyond our experience.

Using an empiricist epistemology, we can speak about the content of our subjective experiences and our expectations for subjective experience in the future with a higher or lesser degree of certainty depending on our knowledge, but even here we can only talk probabilistically—future experience can disconfirm or modify what we thought we knew. This is consistent with the view taken in this chapter, which embraces the subjectivist notion that the only world we can know (i.e., speak meaningfully about) is the world of subjective experience. However, the view being presented here fully embraces scientific empiricism as essential to the accumulation of knowledge about the world of our experience. Without trying to squeeze human experience into the methods of academic psychology (i.e., attempting to strictly apply numerical measurement to our observations), the scientific method can be applied to psychoanalysis on a case-by-case basis (also see footnote 2). It is my understanding that Kohut was making a call for this type of *empirical* observation and

agree that it is red. That is, we all would use the word *red* to refer to the sensation of color that we experience when we look at it. But we know that human nervous systems vary. It is quite likely that some people may have the experience that another may know as "red-orange," "orange," or even—if they are color blind—what another may experience as "green" when they look at the rose. But, because we all call the rose "red" whenever we *experience* that particular hue (that particular wavelength of light), we all agree that the rose is red. But where and what is the "red"? Is it in the rose? It would seem that the redness of the rose—and by logical extension, all its other features—must be *a subjectively created experience existing in the mind of the beholder* (see Basch, 1988).

This is an essentially phenomenological subjectivist view in which reality is, in fact, a creation of the psyche; a subjective experiential construction of reality is all we can know to exist. A cogent description of this existential subjectivist position was provided by Watts (1966) who also proposed some insights into the resistance to its acceptance. Watts examined the phenomenon we call a rainbow. A rainbow requires three elements for it to exist: the sun, moisture in the atmosphere, and an observer. All three must be present and they must be in a certain angular relationship for the rainbow to be manifested.

> Diaphanous as it may be, a rainbow is no subjective hallucination. It can be verified by any number of observers, though each will see it in a slightly different position. . . . The point is, then, that an observer in the proper position is as necessary for the manifestation of a rainbow as the other two components, the sun and the moisture. Of course, one could say that *if* the sun and a body of moisture were in the right relationship, say, over the ocean, any observer on a ship that sailed into line with them *would* see a rainbow. But one could also say that if an observer and the sun were correctly aligned there would be a rainbow *if* there were moisture in the air! [p. 92].

---

testing of his theory when he asked analysts to try out his ideas and see if *their* experience in the analytic setting did or did not fit with his self-psychological formulations.

Note that empiricism—with the erroneously associated notion that in empiricist perspectives the perceiver must be considered a passive spectator—has also been placed in opposition to constructivism in which the perceiver actively constructs the experience of the world (Rabin, 1995). Contrast this view of the supposed passivity of perception in empiricist epistemology with Kant's *Critique of Pure Reason* in which the same empiricist limits on what an be known are fully integrated with the notion that the human mind *structures* experience according to certain human perceptual characteristics. The *empiricist* limits on knowledge are fully consistent with (and the call for empirically grounded inductive science is significantly based upon) the notion that we *construct*, color, and shape what we experience (see the quote from Francis Bacon at the beginning of this chapter).

Somehow we feel that, if we have sun and moisture over the ocean *without an observer*, the rainbow still exists. But if we have the observer and sun both within a potentially proper, rainbow producing angular relationship *without moisture in the air* then there is no rainbow. In this latter condition the elimination of

> a good, solid "external reality," seems to make it an indisputable fact that, under such conditions, there is no rainbow. The reason is that it supports our . . . mythology to assert that things exist on their own, whether there is an observer or not. It supports the fantasy that man is not really involved in the world, that he makes no real difference to it, and that he can observe reality . . . without [influencing or creating] it . . .
>
> Perhaps we can accept this reasoning without too much struggle when it concerns things like rainbows . . . whose reality status was never too high [to begin with]. But what if it dawns on us that our perception of rocks, mountains and stars is a situation of just the same kind? . . . We [are] simply . . . saying only that creatures with brains are an *integral* feature of the pattern which also includes the solid earth and the stars, and that without this integral feature . . . the whole cosmos would be as unmanifested as a rainbow without droplets in the sky, or without an observer. [This notion] makes us feel insecure because it unsettles a familiar image of the world in which rocks, above all, are symbols of hard, unshakable reality, and the Eternal Rock a metaphor for God himself. [This] mythology . . . had reduced man to an utterly unimportant little germ in an unimaginably vast and enduring universe. It is just too much of a shock, too fast a switch, to recognize that this little germ with its fabulous brain is evoking the whole thing, including the nebulae millions of light-years away [pp. 92–93].

THE LIMITS OF EXISTENTIAL SUBJECTIVISM

Such an existentialist, subjectivist view does not force us to the absurd conclusion that before there were life forms there was no universe. The point is that we know there is a universe consisting of atoms, protons, electrons, electromagnetic forces, and so on. But these are only metaphors we use to enable our psyches to have some intuitive sense of the essence of the universe that is *not knowable*, that lies beyond experience, for even the greatest scientists cannot begin to say what the underlying essence is of the phenomena we refer to with words such as protons, quarks, neutrons, atoms, photons, the strong and the weak nuclear forces.[11] Although we use *models* in which the underlying fabric

---

[11] Gleick (1992) notes how modern physicists are increasingly giving up "visualization." Earlier physical models were based on metaphorical models we could sense (see) in our minds as they have counterparts in the real world (e.g., the model of an atom with little ball electrons rapidly circling a core, each electron at a different energy level). Such models have given way to ones in

of the universe is composed of these basic particles, forces, and arrangements of matter, all we can actually know is the *human* experience that comes into being (is known) when the human nervous system interacts with the unknown essence of the world, an unknown essence that even skeptical scientists take on "faith" to exist; for what scientist would argue against the notion that something not knowable exists, something that we are merely struggling to envision using metaphors, models, or hypothetical constructs like protons, electrons, atoms, and so on.

This view supports aspects of existential subjectivism, but it simultaneously suggests the existence of *something* beyond experience, even if that something can never be directly experienced and can only be described metaphorically or with mathematical scientific models. Although one may embrace even extreme subjectivism as containing profound truths, it is clear that something exists beyond our subjectivities.

There is a story of an ant on a leaf that was being drawn underwater by a whirlpool. "Help," cried the ant, "the world is drowning." Maybe so, if we are referring to the ant's subjective experience of the world. But clearly there is something that goes on existing beyond our deaths. The ant's narcissistic grandiosity is echoed by our own horror and essential incomprehension of death. Yet we know that the world does not disappear when we go to sleep, enter unconsciousness, or die. It is true that the only world we can know is the world of subjective experience, but we must simultaneously embrace the notion of *something* (even if it

---

which, for example, an electron is not in any one position but simultaneously in all positions possible at different levels of probability! What can that mean? What can that refer to in our experience? It works in the sense that plugging the probabilities into the equations yields better predictions. But anyone who has read Hawking's *A Brief History of Time* quickly gets the sense that we are talking about fundamentally incomprehensible (i.e., unvisualizable) phenomena. His (1988) description of modern physics is replete with notions as unintelligible as the following:

> In this approach a particle does not have just a single history, as it would in classical theory. Instead, it is supposed to follow every possible path in space-time, and with each of these histories there are associated a couple of numbers. . . . The probability that the particle passes through some particular point is found by adding. . . . When one actually tries to perform these sums, however, one runs into severe technical problems. The only way around these is the following peculiar prescription: One must add up the waves for particle histories that are not in the "real" time that you and I experience but take place in what is called imaginary time. Imaginary time . . . is in fact a well-defined mathematical concept. . . . That is to say, for the purposes of the calculation one must measure time using imaginary numbers, rather than real ones. This has an interesting effect on space-time: the distinction between time and space disappears completely [p. 134].

is not directly knowable) that exists beyond experience—a world that does exist *separate from the self*. Further, the evolutionary biological perspective in suggesting an intuitive, innate knowledge of the existence of an "objective" reality that stands apart from subjective experience poses a profound challenge to the existential phenomenalist position.

SUBJECTIVITY AND OBJECTIVITY FROM AN EVOLUTIONARY PERSPECTIVE

Both altruistic and selfish motives are essential for maximizing one's inclusive fitness, but from the evolutionary perspective each individual is trying to influence others in a manner that benefits the individual's own unique, inclusive fitness (Slavin 1985, 1990; Kriegman and Slavin, 1989; Slavin and Kriegman, 1990, 1992). Maximizing inclusive fitness is the only goal underlying all life forms, structures, motivations, and behavioral tendencies.[12]

Because the self-interest of two individuals is never the same, conflict—indeed, problem-causing conflict—is an inherent feature of the relational world. As such, subjective views of the world will also be in inherent conflict (Slavin and Kriegman, 1992, 1996). In this perspective, subjectivities are not attempts to form accurate views of the world. Rather, subjective worldviews are biased attempts to formulate a sense of reality (a sense of what is real) that is most consistent with our own personal interests, agendas, and goals. To a significant degree, an individual's goals are furthered by *accurate* perception that enables effective action. But there are also significant ways in which *distorted* (biased) perception can be highly adaptive. Consider one common example that is striking in the contrast between Freud and Kohut. Freud (1914) described some of the distortions inherent in parents' attitudes toward their children:

> Overvaluation . . . dominates, as we all know, their emotional attitude. Thus they are under a compulsion to ascribe every perfection to the child—which sober observation would find no occasion to do—and to conceal and forget all his shortcomings. (Incidentally, the denial of sexuality in children is connected with this.) . . . Illness, death, renunciation of enjoyment, restrictions on his own will, shall not touch him; the laws of nature and of society shall be abrogated in his favour; he shall once more really be the centre and core of creation—"His Majesty the Baby," as we once fancied ourselves . . . Parental love, which is so moving and at bottom so childish, is nothing but the parents' narcissism born again [p. 91].

---

[12] The limitations and criticisms of this adaptationist perspective (e.g., Gould, 1980), specifically in regard to psychoanalysis, are discussed elsewhere (Kriegman and Slavin, 1989; Slavin and Kriegman, 1992).

Kohut, in contrast, does not question the fact that parents distort, but completely reverses the pejorative tone found in Freud. The distortions are adaptive and healthy, or in Kohut's term, "normal" (see Kriegman, 1988, 1990). Consider his discussion (1984) of overstimulation by doting parents and

> the functionally analogous overvaluation of analysands by their analysts. We have in general been taught to look upon these attitudes as misguided, as manifestations of the fact that our sober judgment has been led astray by our emotions. And analysts in particular have interpreted their tendency to think more highly of their patients . . . than others who know them . . . as variants of countertransference . . . that must be mastered and eventually dissolved by self-analysis . . . into the dynamics . . . of such distorted judgments. . . . [H]owever, there is another dimension to this attitude that pertains to both parents . . . and analysts. . . . [T]his overvaluating attitude . . . is "normal" [in] that it expresses the fact that, as parents and therapists, we are indeed functioning in accordance with our design and that an analyst who consciously eradicates this attitude . . . is . . . misguided [p. 190].

Distortions, even loving ones such as these that, as Kohut suggests, are necessary for healthy development often lead to conflict between individuals. I remember one initially funny interaction between two otherwise quite sophisticated and level-headed colleagues who got into an increasingly serious argument as to whose one-and-a-half-year-old daughter was more beautiful.

Worldviews, beliefs, and overall subjectivities are designed to enhance the inclusive fitness of those holding such views. In this perspective—completely independent from whatever additional problems are introduced by narcissistic pathology—subjectivities inevitably clash. Communication, then, is not an attempt merely to impart information. In a biased relational world, we have *competing* subjectivities. It is not a matter of indifference what the subjective experience of another is to each individual. People distort, deceive, and self-deceive. Unlike the tendency in self psychology to see such biased perception and deception as a result of empathic failure, I believe it has been shown that such tendencies toward distortion and deception operate without empathic failure and may, in fact, generate problematic empathic failures rather than simply result from them (Kriegman and Slavin, 1990; Slavin and Kriegman, 1992). In fact, deception and the ability to counter deception by more accurate perception are major features of the biological world. If humans, like all existing organisms, have evolved to maximize their interests, then we must consider the possibility that biased perception, deception, and self-deception may be working to promote those interests.

As an important aside, note that in this view of distortion and biased perception, I am not retreating to the view shared by ego psychologists, Kleinian object relations theorists, and some interpersonalists—that the *therapist* has a clearer view of reality than the patient, who distorts. Rather, although we can acknowledge that the patient's view of reality may be less self-reflective owing to a lack of prior analytic experience, both the therapist's and the patient's views of reality are constantly colored by an innate tendency to form perceptions biased toward one's own interests. Furthermore, in addition to this *adaptive* tendency to engage in biased perception (on the part of *both* patient and analyst), because the psyche is a self-enhancing, fitness-optimizing "organ," the *patient* is almost certain to have more direct access to signals and affects representing the patient's true interests than the therapist is—even though the therapist may have ideas and insights that at times can help to illuminate the patient's interests better than the patient's conscious, verbalized thoughts. Thus, in the view I am presenting of inherent bias and distortion—in *contrast* to more classical views—the patient is more likely to accurately sense his or her own self-interest, true aims, goals, and objectives. This evolutionary, adaptive view resonates strongly with Kohut's (1984) oft-quoted statement: "that many times when I believed I was right and my patients were wrong, it turned out . . . that *my* rightness was superficial whereas *their* rightness was profound" (pp. 93–94).[13]

Before I return to the general discussion of the evolutionary view of inherent bias, another digression appears necessary to discuss the post-modernist attacks on truth, science, and objectivity. I introduce this brief discussion by noting that I share the intersubjectivists' concern that the notions of objectivity and distortion can (and often have) led to abusive attempts to get patients to reshape their experiential world in order to bring it into accordance with the analyst's subjectivity. Yet I believe that the best protection against such abuses lies not in denying what we know to be true (that people "distort"), but in a fuller realization of how self-interested and biased *all* perspectives are likely to be (see Slavin and Kriegman, 1992). It is probably no coincidence that a concern over the abuse of power and authority in psychoanalysis leads the intersubjectivists to reject objectivity just as similar concerns about the abuse of power in society (e.g., racism and sexism) leads postmodern critics of the use of language and science to reject *representationalism*—the view that there is an intrinsic relationship between words and world (Gergen,

---

[13] This emphasis differentiates the self-psychological from other analytic attitudes toward a patient's distortions. For a fuller elaboration of this perspective that clearly includes the notion of distortion, see Kohut, 1984, p. 182, 182n.

1994). In this view, there are no facts, just interpretations (see Foucault, 1979).

Postmodern challenges to a scientific worldview are steeped in extremist cultural relativism and an extreme relational view of language in which "truth" or "reality" are merely social constructions in a particular culture at a particular time. In such a view, for example, Gergen (1991) following Rorty[14] (1979), "The conception that knowledge represents external reality becomes merely optional" (Smith, 1994, p. 408). Gergen (1994), a postmodernist, unabashedly summarizes the postmodern attack on representationalism thusly: "Whatever is the case makes no requirements on our descriptions or theories, and our modes of writing and talking have no necessary consequences for action" (p. 412). Yet, as Smith (1994) notes, we can take the "constructionist, contextualist, and yes feminist critiques very seriously . . . [and yet not conclude that truth claims can be reduced to] rhetoric and politics, even when we become more alert to the role of rhetoric and politics in our would-be scientific discourse" (p. 409). That is, we can try to account for the effects of the observer on the observed, for the observer's biased agendas, and for the effect of the observer's cultural and personal assumptions (prereflective unconscious organizing principles) without rejecting the notions that reality exists and that words can refer to something beyond social convention. The earth never was at the center of the universe with the heavens revolving around it daily. It was never flat and no one sailed over the edge no matter what people believed and what the Church said.

In fact, the distorting tendencies that concern the postmodernist are seen in the evolutionary view to be universal (though politically correct postmodernists cannot make universal claims). Furthermore, if words, ideas, and concepts do not simply reflect reality (and here I am in full agreement with the postmodernists) but rather have social, political, and cultural assumptions and implications interwoven within them,[15] then it

---

[14] Rorty, in turn, seems to be expanding on the position of Derrida (1978).

[15] Hegel placed ideas in a historical context: our beliefs cannot be seen as simple, correspondence reflections of a reality that exists independent of our observation. Rather, beliefs are shaped by the larger cultural context in which they take form. Marx then took Hegel's notion of how, as a culture changes, new ideas develop in an inevitable dialectic with older, culturally embedded ideas, and he systematically showed how the dominant ideas at any time support the interests of those currently in power. Following Marx, the postmodernists developed the trend toward deconstructing ideas so that the underlying assumptions and values of a set of beliefs can be analyzed to reveal just whose interests are being served. As can be seen from the current discussion, these philosophical developments can be highly consistent with an evolutionary perspective on conflict, bias, and belief despite the fact that evolutionary biology, in general—and sociobiology especially—is often associated with reactionary politics.

is of vital importance to have an innate empirical suspiciousness built into our psyches, an "I'm from Missouri; show me!" kind of attitude. The paradox is that the valid social realities that motivate the postmodernist attack on naive realism (see footnote 6) underscore the importance of scientific empiricism![16]

Socrates attacked the sophists' use of extreme relativism to support a self-serving, "might makes right" view of morality: In a world where truth was relative, there was nothing wrong with those in power determining truth to be that which was in accord with their interests. Of course, this is, in fact, the way history proceeds. "Terrorist revolutionaries" become "founding fathers" if they win and are executed as "murderers" if they lose. It is both ironic and simultaneously illustrative to note that the use of epistemological stances is now reversed. The naked assertion that "might makes right" would not win many elections in the modern world. Therefore, those in power today needed to find an alternative way to justify their privileged position. They have thus developed complicated objectivist arguments supporting their claim that they are the proper ones to rule and that the manner in which they currently wield power is both appropriate and necessary. They are opposed in this use of objectivism by those who (in their own attempt to gain greater power and influence) argue for a relativistic conception of truth that shows how supposed objective truths are really biases supporting the interests of the powerful. This reversal illustrates how flexible conceptions can be when they are placed in the service of the human tendency to use ideas to promote one's self-interest.

In a similar way, evolutionary biology itself can be (and has been) used in a reactionary manner supporting the interests of those in power. It can also be used, however, to reveal the deceptive and self-deceptive ways in which those in power hide their pursuit of self-interest behind a whole range of notions, e.g., freedom, national interest, truth, caring concern, fairness, love of God, economic necessity, and so on. The evolutionary perspective, itself, predicts this flexible use of beliefs: the human tendency to create and hold to concepts, philosophies, and belief systems is derived from the benefit they provide to the self-interest of those holding them. This is the selective pressure (adaptive advantage) that shaped the tendency to develop and promulgate world views and perspectives on reality.

[16] If one wants to safeguard the central importance of the empathic perception of our patients' subjective experience and protect patients from the abuses that arise from dogmatic adherence to particular psychoanalytic theories, rather than eschewing scientific empiricism, consider the following prescription:

The doctrine of those who have denied that certainty could be attained at all, has some agreement with my way of proceeding at the first setting out; but they end in being infinitely separated and opposed. For the holders of that doctrine assert simply that nothing can be known; I also assert that not much can be known in nature by the [use of opinion and dogma] (37). In general, let every student of nature take this as a rule: that whatever his mind seizes and dwells upon with peculiar satisfaction is to be held in suspicion, and that so much the more care is to be taken in dealing with such questions to keep the understanding even and clear (58). The understanding must not be allowed to jump and fly from particulars to remote axioms . . . It must not be supplied with wings but rather hung with weights to keep it from leaping and flying (104). One method of delivery alone remains to us . . . we must lead men to the particulars themselves . . . while men on their side must force themselves for awhile to lay their notions by and begin to familiarize themselves with facts (36). [Such men must]

I now end these digressions and return to the more general discussion of inherently biased worldviews. Because, frequently, those around us are not merely imparting information, but are trying to influence our subjective experience of the world to be consistent with a subjective view that is in *their* best interest, in the course of evolution there must have been strong selective pressures to develop a protection against such influence. I would suggest that an important part of the foundation of such a protection is the awareness that around us exist not accurate views of the world, but rather subjective biases that include some valid information and a good deal of bias. This suggests that *built into the human psyche* is a conception of *validity* (i.e., objective reality) as well as subjectivity (that is, *potentially biased* conceptions of reality). Thus, existential phenomenology aside, natural selection may have designed an organism that has an innate belief in the existence of a reality separate and distinct from the biased subjectivities that are sensed surrounding each individual.

Human brains are designed for a "midworld," not the macro- or microworlds. When we attempt to understand the macroworld (infinite space or the number of stars and galaxies in the universe, infinite mass and time halting at the speed of light) or the microworld (what an electron is "made" of, or the forces that bind the atom) our midworld models break down. There was no evolutionary need (selective pressure) to design a brain that functioned to comprehend the large-scale architecture of the galaxies or the submicroscopic world of the atom. Thus, our psyches are structured to function in a midworld while we are simultaneously aware of phenomena beyond our midworld experience in both the macro- and microworlds. We then use midworld metaphors (creating models) to aid us in attempting to grasp the nature of the unknowable (i.e., that which we are unable to know directly) macro- and microworlds.[17]

---

resolutely compel themselves to sweep away all theories and common notions, and to apply the understanding, thus made fair and even, to a fresh examination of particulars (107) [Francis Bacon (1620), *Novum Organum: First Book of Aphorisms*].

Those familiar with Kohut's struggle with classical psychoanalysis may find in Bacon's prescription a formula similar to Kohut's plea to analysts to look afresh at the data before them in order to build an experience-near theory that does justice to that data.

[17] This distinction between the midworld of our experience and the macro- and microworlds also explains why Sucharov's (1992) application of complementarity is so inappropriate for psychoanalysis (see footnote 6). In complementarity, two incompatible theories are used alternately to understand different aspects of a phenomenon. In physics, this has occurred in interpreting experiments investigating the nature of light. Certain experiments are best understood, and the results accurately predicted, when light is considered to be composed of particles (photons), each

Similarly, the design of the psyche enables us to sense the existence of something not knowable, of reality that cannot be *directly* known; all we can know of this ultimately unknowable reality is our own subjective experience of it and the subjective experiences of others as they are presented to us. Thus there is a sense of something "ultimately real" that is felt as existing independent both from others' biases and from our own potentially misleading beliefs, wishes, and motives. The psyche is designed with an intuitive awareness of the fact that our subjective sense

---

with a discrete mass. Other experiments cannot be predicted or explained using this model, and for these the wave model of oscillating, nondiscrete, undulating quantities of energy leads to accurate predictions and better explanations. There has been no way to integrate these models, and light is considered to be best understood by sometimes using a wave model and at other times using a particle model, depending on which works better in the particular situation. This is a *pragmatic* nonintegration of two models, yielding a dual model that has, somewhat facetiously, been referred to as the "wavicle" model of light. This pragmatic oscillation between two theories is justified in our study of light because our midworld models break down when we try to apply them consistently to the microscopic world. Thus, when looking at any particular micro- or macroworld phenomenon, we simply pick the most adequate of our inadequate midworld models if we want to try to "visualize" a particular aspect of the phenomenon.

In his early development of self psychology, Kohut used a similar strategy oscillating between the classical model to explain some phenomena (oedipal neuroses) and the new psychology of the self to explain others (narcissistic disorders). As a *temporary* expedient, borrowing the strategy of complementarity from physics made some sense. But, as in the case with theories of light, this was due to a *failure*, an unavailability of a larger, cohesive, internally consistent picture of the human psyche. As time passed, Kohut developed just such an overarching theory and that is what self psychology has become. This development toward greater cohesiveness in psychological theory over time makes sense just as it makes sense that our probing deeper into the micro- and macroworlds leads to further breakdowns in our ability to visualize and thus increases our use of makeshift midworld models. That is, unlike the attempt in physics to understand the nature of light (a microworld phenomenon), our psyches were designed precisely to comprehend the psychoanalytic midworld phenomena—human experience, meaning, and action—that we are examining. Oscillation between two inadequate models (even if necessary in physics) should *not* be used to suggest a valid method—except as a temporary expedient while developing a more overarching theory—for using our midworld-designed minds to comprehend the very midworld phenomena they were designed to understand.

It is interesting to note that, in his attempt to formulate a religious refutation of this view, George Berkeley (1710) showed a clear understanding of this relationship between the "natural" (a century and a half later to become "evolved") design of the psyche and those aspects of the world that are beyond the midworld in which we must function:

> It is said the faculties we have are . . . designed by nature for the support . . . of life, and not to penetrate into the inward essence and constitution of things. Besides, the mind of man being finite, when it treats of things which partake of infinity it is not to be wondered at if it run into absurdities and contradictions, out of which it is impossible it should ever extricate itself [*Treatise Concerning the Principles of Human Knowledge*, Introduction, 2].

of reality is a working model of something that can never be known—something fundamentally unknowable existing beyond subjective awareness. We naturally sense that our subjective map or model of reality is buffeted by the biased realities presented by others and by our own wishes and fantasies, both of which experience teaches us to mistrust to some degree. Our experience has shown that what others present and what we have believed and wish to believe can lead to our making highly fallible subjective models of the world. Thus, we have an innate sense of both something "true" and of biased realities (our own and others). This is so even though—just as we cannot directly know the macro- or microworlds directly, only our midworld models of them—we don't have the ability to formulate a model of the unknown true without using the contents of subjective experience.

THE HUMAN AS NATURAL SCIENTIST

We can go one step further. Even though our psyches are not simply designed for accurate perception and are rather designed to formulate worldviews that are most consistent with our individual agendas, there are many ways in which these agendas require a significant degree of accurate perception (i.e., of reliably useful knowledge of how the world is actually structured). We can even conclude that science itself has been "built into" the psyche. To reach this conclusion we must define science in a very specific way. Clearly, the elaborate scientific methods, technologies, statistical analyses, and culture of science with its particular concepts and politics—all of which have come to characterize "science"—have *not* been structured into the human psyche. However, if we define science in a very simple way—as experimentation and observation designed to achieve attitudes and understandings about the world that lead to accurate prediction and control of events in the world—then humans can be seen to be natural scientists.

In fact, a thorough understanding of aspects of the environment and the ability to reliably predict how the environment will behave appears to be the very capacity for which natural selection has "designed" the human brain. This is noted most clearly when one observes a small child, or even an infant, exploring a new object. Over and over they repeat the same actions as if to see if they will get the same results. Then they vary these actions to see what new result will occur. Once they have tried all the actions they are capable of, and achieved all the novel results, they move on to some new focus of attention. The next time they encounter the original object, there is a sense of knowing the structure of the object, how that object will behave, and how their actions will affect it. Children are natural empiricists.

But even more important than empirical exploration of the inanimate world are the testing and probing of the human surround. In this perspective, people in general (and our patients, especially) should be seen as "social scientists" (Harold Sampson, personal communication, 1995; also see footnote 20). It is now widely held among evolutionary biologists and anthropologists that human intelligence evolved not primarily for manipulation, understanding, and control of material aspects of the physical world, but rather for understanding, predicting, and attempting to control *human* behavior and its impact on us. There was little or no complex technology with which to control the inanimate world over the four million years or more of our evolution as a species. Yet during this time the human brain exploded in size. Rather than being technology focused, our brains appear to be complex "social computers" that allow us to predict, and attempt to influence the behavior of the most important objects in our environment, other humans. The ability to observe and predict the behavior of others was essential for the survival of our ancestors.[18] Thus, *social* evolutionary pressures shaped the rapid devel-

---

[18] This is probably the selective pressure that led to the evolution of our empathic capacity. An in-depth sense of another's experience gives us a foundation for predicting the other's behavior (What will they do? Are they reliable?) and sensing both how and when to try to influence others. Our psyches appear to be complicated social computers designed to comprehend complex mental states. What an ironic mistake it is for many academic and behavioral psychologists and biopsychiatrists to attempt to "turn off" this marvelous device! Academic psychologists claiming that only their approach safeguards objectivity eschew the attempt to perceive complex mental states through empathy/introspection and try to replace it with complicated, numerical, statistical analyses of isolated bits of behavior (see footnotes 2 and 10). Some behaviorists continue to insist that human experience is an epiphenomenon that can be ignored in the study of actions (behavior). From an evolutionary-psychoanalytic viewpoint, intentionally ignoring the data obtainable only through the use of the most sophisticated and exquisite perceptual device ever produced seems like a highly misguided strategy.

Modern biopsychiatrists not only increasingly question the usefulness of engaging in a long-term empathic exploration of the meaning of another's experience, they can go much further and— sometimes without considering the value or meaning of such experience in an individual's life— attempt to chemically "adjust" experience by shutting troublesome parts of it down or by "turning up the volume" on other parts (Kriegman, in press). While research is called for to determine if the following anecdote reflects a larger reality, a recent experience suggested to me that the "better living through chemistry" philosophy may already be more than an approach to the treatment of others; it may be far along in the process of becoming a belief system—a way of life. After having my blood drawn and answering detailed questions regarding my medical history (as part of an application for life insurance), the interviewer/phlebotomist told me I was the *first* of the psychiatrists or psychologists he had interviewed (out of approximately 20) who was not taking an antidepressant and/or Ritalin. He said he was repeatedly surprised to find that many were using both simultaneously!

With the negative press psychoanalysis has received in recent years in the mainstream media, with the anti-analytic trend in academic psychology, with the short-term behavioral approaches that are increasingly popular with managed care, and with biopsychiatry and its alliance with the psy-

opment and enlargement of the human brain (Trivers, 1971, 1985; Kriegman, 1988, 1990; Kriegman and Slavin, 1989).

In the process of navigating through a biased social world, the human psyche intrinsically uses—as a *tool* for managing biased communication—the innate anticipation[19] of a world we can discover that has predictable responses, relatively reliable rules for certain interactions, and its own structure—a world or reality that is independent of 1) our subjective fantasies, wishes, and beliefs, and 2) the fantasies, wishes, beliefs, and communications of others. There was a need (selective pressure) for the development of such a tool by psyches that evolved to function within a predictable world governed by reliable "laws of nature," yet presented to us, in large part, through the biased views of others. As the infant explores new objects, it inevitably experiences certain frustrations and rapidly learns that its wishes do not influence the outcome, only certain actions do. In a world we can explore and discover, there are realities stubbornly independent of what goes on within us. A child must struggle to come to terms with the difference between one's wishes, fantasies, and needs—even powerfully felt needs—and the realities of the world. "No matter how much you wish it were true doesn't make it true." "Just saying it's so doesn't make it so." Simultaneously, a child attempts to learn to distinguish between what is communicated by others about the world from how the world is actually structured. As we know from clinical experience, these maturational accomplishments are never fully achieved.

IMPLICATIONS FOR PSYCHOANALYSIS: THE CLINICAL COST/BENEFITS OF THE SUBJECTIVIST STANCE

Elsewhere it has been shown that maintaining a nearly unwavering empathic stance, that is, joining in the patient's subjective experience,

---

chopharmaceutical industry (also increasingly supported by managed care), psychoanalysis is becoming the only remaining major approach to emphasize the empathic mode of data gathering. Though there are many reasons for this trend, the upshot is that what may be our most impressive evolutionary achievement—our empathic capacity—is being increasingly ignored.

[19] By "innate anticipation," I am implying that the small child *turns* to explore and understand the world with a biologically built-in expectation that it can discover and comprehend the structure of its environment in a manner similar to the way the newborn infant *turns* its head with an innate expectation that it will find a breast (or other source of milk) when a stimulating object touches its cheek. There appear to be many innate programs for learning—with "innate anticipations" or "built-in expectations"—that have been structured into the human psyche. One major example can be found in the work of Chomsky (1972) who has shown how the remarkably rapid acquisition of a *specific* language can occur only if there is an innate, preexisting understanding of those *universal* aspects of the "deep structure" of the way sounds, words, and sentences relate to meanings in all languages. (See Slavin and Kriegman, 1992, for a fuller discussion of the notion of innate knowledge.)

and accepting that such subjective experiences have essential validity, is an a priori condition for effective treatment (Kohut, 1982, 1984; Ornstein, 1979; Ornstein and Ornstein, 1980; Stolorow, Brandchaft, and Atwood, 1987; Kriegman and Slavin, 1989; Slavin and Kriegman, 1992).[20] It has been suggested (Slavin and Kriegman, 1992) that the intersubjectivists, by taking an extreme relativistic or perspectivalist point of view, are enabled to take a remarkably unwavering stance in accepting a patient's internal subjective experience. However, they do so at a cost. The price that must be paid is an inconsistency in the analyst's own internal experience, as Friedman's (1992) comments about the discomfort of the empathic stance suggest. We naturally believe that sometimes our patients' beliefs are grossly biased and at times "distorted." The extreme subjectivist position entails an inconsistency that cannot be maintained by many clinicians, and therefore we find that many analysts, in remaining true to their *natural* "scientific" attitude, reject extreme "perspectivalism." Let's look a bit closer at the cost of empathy.

Part of the cost in maintaining the extreme subjectivist position is the denial of the *natural* human sense of an objective world that can be discovered, understood, and predicted (i.e., an objective world that is independent of any specific subjectivity). A related cost is internal inconsis-

---

[20] In fact, this view of inherent bias, distortion (deception and self-deception), and interpersonal conflict forms the foundation for a view of the empathic stance as *the* essential ingredient in psychoanalytic treatment (Slavin and Kriegman, 1992). However, the meaning of an empathy-based relationship is understood to be quite different from that commonly found in self psychology: the experience of being consistently understood takes on different meaning in a theory that assumes the psyche is designed to function in a world of conflicting and biased viewpoints in which sustained empathic inquiry would be a most unusual phenomenon. This may also explain why Weiss and Sampson (1986) place so much emphasis on the patient's need to *test* the analyst—operating essentially as a scientist both consciously and unconsciously (Harold Sampson, personal communication, 1995)—to determine if it is *safe* to proceed in their treatment.

In self psychology, there is a tendency to see something akin to the therapist's sustained empathic stance as a natural, developmentally expectable part of human experience. Part of what Friedman (1992) seems to have been aiming at when he said that self psychology leaves part of the meaning of empathy in the shadows is the sense that the empathic other is primarily *allying* himself or herself with the patient's deepest interests despite a natural tendency *not* to do so (the natural tendency being to primarily pursue his or her own interests instead). The meaning of the empathic stance in this view is that it is a tangible, dramatic alliance with the patient's interests (as represented by the patient's point of view or bias) in a world of conflicting interests. Slavin and Kriegman (1992, 1996) describe a process of negotiation in the clinical setting that requires change on the part of both patient and analyst as part of a therapeutic relationship between two people designed to function in a world of competing interests. It is striking that Goldberg (1984) arrives at a similar notion (of negotiated mutual change) as his solution to the tension between realism and relativism. Such a view—along with Kohut's emphasis on empathy and introspection—may enable us to protect the patient from the abuse of being forced to accommodate to the analyst's reality, without needing to reject the notions of objectivity and distortion in human communication.

tency in theory construction. For example, the intersubjectivists (Stolorow, Brandchaft, and Atwood, 1987; Stolorow and Atwood, 1992) talk about psychotic delusions having truth encoded within them. But how can one speak of a delusion (or the truth encoded in it) if no more objective reality exists about which one can be deluded? The intersubjectivist might reply that he or she does not necessarily accept a patient's subjectivity as true. Truth is a concept derived from an objectivist epistemology that the intersubjectivists reject for psychoanalysis (Atwood and Stolorow, 1984; Stolorow and Atwood, 1989).[21] However, on what ground can one subjectivity label the other subjectivity "deluded" and only containing *encoded* truth? Why not conclude that the analyst's subjectivity is deluded and needs to be altered to come into line with what was formerly called the patient's "delusions"? Without the notion of "distortion," which (along with objectivity) Stolorow (1995) has claimed has "no place within the theoretical lexicon of psychoanalysis" (p. xvi), what can the term "delusion" refer to? (See also Goldberg, 1990, p. 24.)

Stolorow and Atwood (1992) aptly point out that trying to show patients how their experience of reality is distorted is often experienced as a profound assaultive threat to the patient's self. In some cases, this can be hidden from the clinician (and the patient) by a compliant patient who hides the threat and develops a false self accommodation to the therapist's worldview. However, most clinicians, who have also been patients, know from their experience on either side of the couch that these are not the only possibilities. Not infrequently a therapist's suggestion that reality is different from the patient's experience is not only not experienced as an assault or threat to the self, but is experienced as a relief or an alternative that allows for new configurations of experience and possibilities for action.

Despite repeated explorations of the discrepancy between his self perception and how others saw him, and despite numerous reconstruc-

---

[21] As noted in footnote 3, Stolorow and Atwood (1992) now speak of a subjective sense of what is real. However, their attempt to acknowledge this essential aspect of human experience without abandoning a thoroughly subjectivist view of reality is fraught with contradiction: 1) "I subjectively experience aspects of my subjectivity as objectively real"; 2) but, "I subjectively have developed and experience a philosophical way of viewing the world in which there is nothing objectively real beyond any subjectivity"; so 3) "I simultaneously hold two completely incompatible subjective beliefs." The intersubjectivist holds to a belief in the objective reality of the world and simultaneously holds that such a belief is a reification of what is really just a subjective experience (Stolorow and Atwood, 1992, p. 11). They then oscillate back and forth between these two views: when attempting to *talk to* a patient (especially a psychotic one), they take the latter stance. When *talking about* a psychotic patient, they take the former stance. This is a tricky maneuver that flies in the face of most therapists' own experiences and thus is not possible for many clinicians.

tive interpretations of the sources of his devaluing self conception, the patient remained unable to consider alternative views of himself as possessing any competence or value. In one dramatic, provocative confrontation, the therapist forcefully told this high functioning, senior vice president of a major New England bank that his extremely negative self image was an indication of "psychotic thinking." After an initial look of surprise, the patient visibly brightened as he was actually able to consider the possibility that his habitual self image was sadly way off the mark. The therapist essentially *mirrored* his competence back to him (functioned as a mirroring selfobject) even though, at the moment, the patient's subjective experience contained no such image to mirror. The therapist presented a truly alien way of viewing the patient—an alternative way of affectively organizing the patient's experience that could not be found in his unconscious organizing principles.

In addition, note that no patient wants to sense that we experience his or her reality as just as good as any other. Just consider the sexually abused patient who, after asking if the therapist believes in the reality of the patient's memories, is told—either directly or implicitly—that what actually happened is not as important as what the patient believes happened. When patients need their reality affirmed, supported, or joined with, they want to sense that the therapist truly believes in the *objective realness* of their experience. Thus, in more than one way, patients frequently need to sense that the therapist believes in the objectively real.

There is a fundamental inconsistency in a clinical theory that rests on a nonjudgmental, nonobjectivist epistemology and then provides clinical descriptions of the patient's subjectivity slowly becoming more like the analyst's subjectivity through interactions in the intersubjective field. While Stolorow et al. may object that this is *not* their goal, one goal that they must surely have in treating a patient with delusions would be for the patient to discover the truth *encoded* in the delusion and eventually to hold onto that truth *without the delusion.* "Anna's relinquishment of her delusions . . . could occur only because the subjective truth encoded in those delusions had been fully acknowledged and understood within the therapeutic dialogue" (Stolorow et al., 1987, p. 167). In this process, presumably the patient's subjectivity is altered to come more in line with the analyst's subjectivity that originally recognized the patient's subjective experience as delusional and containing *encoded* truth; that is, the patient's subjectivity is altered to come more in line with a subjectivity that includes the analyst's developmental theory, a theory of an unconscious—such as the intersubjectivists' dynamic unconscious in which certain aspects of the *patient's* experience have been barred from consciousness whereas the analyst remains aware that such experiences must exist in the patient's dynamic unconscious—and numerous other insights that the analyst hopes to impart to the patient. If all that exists are subjectivities with no lesser or greater validity (i.e., no lesser or greater claim to being a more objective match to the "real" world) why give any epistemic superiority to the analyst's subjective world, theories, interpretations, and reconstructions over the patient's "delusions"?

As noted at the beginning, this whole discussion is actually an ancient debate. Consider the interchange between the ideas of Protagoras: "Man is the measure of all things: of the things that are, that they are; and of those things that are not, that they are not" and Socrates: "Protagoras, admitting as he does that everybody's opinion is true, must acknowledge the truth of his opponent's belief about his own belief where they think he is wrong. . . . If no one is entitled to say what another thinks is true or false, where is the wisdom of Protagoras to justify his setting up to teach others, and to be handsomely paid for it? And where is our need to go and sit at his feet, when each of us is himself the measure of his own wisdom?"

Note that the point I am making is not "the fear of anarchy in the analytic relationship" (Stolorow, Atwood, and Brandchaft, 1994) in which one worries that role confusion is the outcome of the rejection of objectivist epistemology. I see no sign whatsoever of role confusion or a dangerous diminution in the authority of the analyst in any of the cases presented by the intersubjectivists. Rather, the point is that they are logically inconsistent when they claim to reject objectivist epistemology and then proceed to use it. It is such explicitly stated or intuitively sensed inconsistencies that make the extreme perspectivalist stance of the intersubjectivists unacceptable to many analysts, despite the fact that the clinical work based on their existential intersubjectivism appears to be brilliantly perceptive and effective. It is my contention that intersubjectivity theory provides a way to join with the patient's experience in a necessary and thorough manner that maximizes therapeutic effectiveness, yet is based on a philosophical intellectualization—with problematic inconsistencies—that many analysts cannot utilize.

TOWARD A SUBJECTIVIST, EMPIRICAL (EXPERIENTIAL) DEFINITION OF OBJECTIVITY FOR PSYCHOANALYSIS

Although I believe one must accept the subjectivist view that the true nature of the world is always an unknown and can only be apprehended through our subjective perceptions, we can still define an "objective reality" that stands in contrast to "subjective realities." *Objective* reality can be defined as that group of *subjectively* perceived features of the universe—along with the *subjectively* apprehended rules of interaction, transformation, and relationship between these features—that maximizes reliable and accurate predictions and explanations of *subjectively* experienced events.[22] Even if it can only be known through specific subjective experiences of it, such an "objective reality" stands in marked contrast to subjective beliefs that fail these standard scientific, empirical tests—beliefs such as astrology, psychotic denial of a child's death, belief in a medium's ability to communicate with the dead, the notion that the earth is flat and at the center of the universe, phrenology, and Scientology and other cultic beliefs (Kriegman and Solomon, 1985a, b).

Just as Stolorow et al. (1987) described, my patient could not relinquish her delusion (that she killed her mother by eating her, as the hallucinated, persecutory voices insisted) until the truth encoded within the delusion was fully acknowledged (see Slavin and Kriegman, 1992, pp. 171–172). Yet I knew from the first day I heard this delusion that 1) despite the encoded truth it may (and did) contain, it was a *distortion* (she was an infant when her mother died during childbirth), and 2) one goal of treatment was for her to be free of such an ugly belief. Sometimes I do know my patient is wrong just as I can be wrong as a therapist and erroneously interpret something to mean what it does not. Note that, for the intersubjectivists, the *therapist's* notions can be erroneous (Stolorow and Atwood, 1992, p. 106). It is precisely their concern about the tendency of gross failures of attunement to retraumatize patients that makes me want to join with them in identifying the therapist's erroneous (distorted) interpretations. When it comes to looking at what the *therapist* does, it seems even harder for the intersubjectivists to remain consistent with the claim that "distortion" has no place in the lexicon of psychoanalysis.

In the clinical setting, aspects of this more objective reality can be seen in contrast to *beliefs* about the analyst and about the analyst's feelings and attitudes that are a manifestation of transference and are not based on accurate perception (Goldberg, 1990). Science—and, I suggest, the structure of the human brain as well—is based on the empirical exploration of the world in an attempt to form an accurate (i.e., more objective) subjectivity. Despite Kohut's (1984) emphasis on opening a path of empathy between the self and selfobjects as the essence of a psychoanalytic "cure," analysts almost universally continue to see certain increases in the accuracy of a patient's subjectivity—the concordance between one's subjectively held views of the world and the

---

[22] Objective reality can also be defined in more intersubjective terms as those features of experience and principles of organizing subjective experience that lead to reliable predictions about future subjective experience.

way the world is actually structured[23]—as signs of increasingly healthy functioning.[24]

In addition, the clinician is frequently confronted by a patient's urgent request for aid in determining what is, in fact, real. We are not simply asked for validation (mirroring) of our patients' experiences. Often, very confused patients trying to cope with complex relational realities—especially those attempting to obtain an accurate view of themselves—intuitively sense that there is a more objective view than their conflicting internal self-images and their conflicting and confusing views of others. Frequently, our patients—sensing that beyond their own subjective experience must lie a more accurate view of the world—are actually asking for aid in developing a clearer, more objective picture of themselves in the context of their relational world.

Aspects of the ability to differentiate the notions of objective and subjective reality underlie our differentiating fantasy from reality. Such ideas about the distinction of objective and subjective reality are nonclinical, nontheoretical, essential, universal, and basic human notions that have been structured into the human psyche over millions of years. It is part of the essential human experience that others who are biased in favor of their own self-interest can be wrong, and can even be "crazy." These notions can be found in all cultures and all languages at all times. They are an inherent and inevitable part of almost all subjectivities, and the propensity for creating and holding such notions has been built into the human psyche. Just as the newborn infant's eyes will

---

[23] Such phrases as "the way the world is actually structured" are not meant to imply knowledge of the world *beyond* experience. Rather than employing a version of a correspondence theory of truth, I use such phrases to refer to subjective experience and subjective organizing principles that maximize our ability to reliably predict future subjective experience. Since the only world we can speak of is the world of subjective experience, when one talks about the "real nature of the world," one is speaking of those subjectively held perceptions and notions that make the most sense of past experience and most reliably predict future experience.

[24] As noted previously, certain biased (distorted) perceptions are also indications of normal, healthy functioning. Kohut (1984) was certainly right to question Freud's "truth morality" and the ways in which it colors our goals and theories. Over 100 years ago, the American pragmatist, Charles Sanders Peirce, noted that natural selection could have formed the basis for both accurate perception, logic, and reason as well as distorted perception and beliefs:

> Logicality in regard to practical matters (if this be understood . . . as consisting in a wise union of security with fruitfulness of reasoning) is the most useful quality an animal can possess, and might therefore result from the action of natural selection; but outside of these [practical matters] it is probably of more advantage to the animal to have his mind filled with pleasing and encouraging visions, independently of their truth; and thus, upon unpractical subjects, natural selection might occasion a fallacious tendency of thought [From "The fixation of belief," *Popular Science Monthly*, 1877].

follow the path of a ball that has traveled behind a screen—indicating that a built-in anticipation of the principles of inertia have been structured into the human psyche—the human psyche has been structured to ensure the universal awareness of bias and the notion that other subjectivities can be "delusional" or simply wrong. The built-in, distinct notions of subjectivity and objectivity are an integral part of the foundation for those human activities that we now call science. It is this foundation that I am calling the inherent empiricism built into the human psyche.[25]

CONCLUSIONS

It is possible to accept the primacy of subjective experience as the only source of knowledge of the world while retaining the capacity to evaluate subjectivities on the basis of their accuracy. That is, beliefs, understandings, and explanations can be evaluated by their ability to organize and explain our subjective experience in useful ways that lead to accurate prediction and control of our world. In this view, subjectivities can include intersubjectively verifiable scientific models with their focus on causal relationships and prediction as well as notions of objectivity (accuracy) and distortion (bias).

---

[25] It should be noted that there is an inherent opposition between the notion of innate (built-in) dispositions and knowledge, and the extreme subjectivist view of reality. Plato and Socrates believed in innate knowledge and—as can be seen in the quotations preceding—they also fought against the Sophists' notion of subjectivist philosophy. There appears to be a relation between the belief in innate knowledge and objectivity. If knowledge can be built in, it must be in response to some reliable features of the universe that are independent of specific viewpoints and individual experience. If all knowledge is constructed and the universe is created in the act of perception, then there cannot be any a priori knowledge. Thus the extreme subjectivist and interpersonalist positions (e.g., Mitchell, 1988) tend to eliminate any conceptualization of innate knowledge or inner predispositions: everything other than the need to organize experience (the intersubjectivists) or to maintain relationships (the interpersonalists) is constructed through experience.

As an interesting aside, consider Locke's "blank slate," empirical scientism. In the Lockean view, there is no preexisting knowledge and the metaphor of the blank slate is often used to contrast nature and nurture; the blank slate is the ultimate nurture theory. In this view, there is nothing inherent in the human psyche at birth; all human psychological phenomena are derived from experience. However, Locke appears to have believed in innate, a priori knowledge! Though he would not have called it such, it is clear from his religious notion of "divine providence" that the human mind is designed (has preexisting, divinely planned structures similar in some ways to Kant's notion of a priori concepts that structure experience) to apprehend and understand the world in which we live. Having no category for understanding how an "innate anticipation" of the structure of the world could be built into the human psyche (writing two centuries before the theory of evolution), Locke attributed the uncanny ways in which the human mind appears to readily understand and organize experience to divine providence rather than innate knowledge of the way the world is structured (see the discussion of innate knowledge of the structure of language in footnote 19).

In developing a clinical theory and approach, we must never lose sight of the fact that the only knowable reality is the subjective experience that comes into being when our psyches interact with the unknowable essence of our world. Although this unknowable essence can be metaphorically described using scientific models and constructs, it is clinically essential to retain the primacy of subjective experience.[26] This is part of what Kohut (1971, 1977, 1982, 1984) meant when he focused on the importance of experience-near theory for psychoanalysis. Though Kohut never addressed the issue in the terms being utilized here, he emphasized that the only meaningful psychological reality is composed of the experiences that can be grasped through vicarious introspection or empathy, and that these are the field-defining "tools" of the empathic scientific investigator/psychoanalyst (Kohut, 1959, 1982).

Yet Kohut did not deny the usefulness of experience-distant theory. Even though he ultimately rejected the classical psychoanalytic paradigm that he referred to as an experience-distant theory, he did not reject it *because* it was experience-distant. He rejected the experience-distant *classical* theory because it contained a *distorted* view of the human psyche—a view of human psychological experience that was inconsistent with the empirical data obtained through vicarious introspection. Kohut realized that only an emphasis on experience-near theorizing could correct and guard against the distortions of human experience that were theory-bound within the classical perspective. He never rejected the need for experience-distant theory and realized that *every* advance in self-psychological theory added a layer of more experience-distant theory (i.e., scientific models or metaphors that are used to organize the data obtained through empathic immersion in another's subjective experience).

Although an extreme existential subjectivist position provides the purest safeguard for experience-near, empathic observation, it does so at a cost too great for many analysts to pay. It has been shown that an evolutionary psychoanalytic model that includes an emphasis on deception, self-deception, and distortion in human communication—and thus implicitly indicates that some communications and subjective experiences can be more accurately in sync with reality—actually can enable the analyst to *deepen* the empathic stance (Slavin and Kriegman, 1992,

---

[26] This is like Goldberg's (1984) view in which the paramount importance of *relativism* within a *real world* is recognized. That is, real actual events do or do not occur (e.g., incest), and the reality of such events clearly matters. However, we can still only deal with psychic reality, which is relative, as each person may experience and react to the world in dramatically different ways. In my wording, the paramount *relativism* is represented by the "primacy of subjective experience," which is the experience of the real world, that is the experience of "the unknowable—but metaphorically and subjectively (experientially) describable—essence."

1996). This evolutionary framework also provides a firm foundation —which is not based on an extreme philosophical stance unavailable to most analysts—for the clinical primacy of the empathic stance. Rather, in this latter view the emphasis on the clinical importance of empathically sharing the subjective experience of the patient is grounded in our only *scientific theory of creation* (Trivers, 1985), the theory of evolution.

REFERENCES

Atwood, G. & Stolorow, R. (1984), *Structures of Subjectivity: Explorations in Psychoanalytic Phenomenology.* Hillsdale, NJ: The Analytic Press.

Basch, M. F. (1986), Clinical theory and metapsychology: Incompatible or complementary? *Psychoanal. Rev.,* 73:261–271.

——— (1988), *Understanding Psychotherapy: The Science Behind the Art.* New York: Basic Books.

Chomsky, N. (1972), *Language and Mind.* San Diego: Harcourt Brace.

Derrida, J. (1978), Structure sign and play in the discourse of the human sciences. In: *Writing and Difference,* ed. A. Bass. Chicago: University of Chicago Press, pp. 278–300.

Finkelstein, L. (1988), Psychoanalysis, marital therapy, and object-relations theory. *J. Amer. Psychoanal. Assn.,* 36:905–931.

Foucault, M. (1979), *Discipline and Punish: The Birth of the Prison.* Townsend, WA: Bay Press.

Freud, S. (1914), On narcissism: An introduction. *Standard Edition,* 14:67–102. London: Hogarth Press, 1957.

Friedman, L. (1992), Discussion of Evelyne Schwaber's paper, "Psychoanalytic theory and its relation to clinical work." Scientific Meeting of the Psychoanalytic Society of New England, East, October 24.

Gergen, K. J. (1991), *The Saturated Self.* New York: Basic Books.

——— (1994), Exploring the postmodern: Perils or potentials? *Amer. Psychol.,* 49:412–416.

Gleick, J. (1992), *Genius.* New York: Pantheon.

Goldberg, A. (1984), The tension between realism and relativism in psychoanalysis. *Psychoanal. & Contemp. Sci.,* 7:367–386.

——— (1990), *The Prisonhouse of Psychoanalysis.* Hillsdale, NJ: The Analytic Press.

Gould, S. J. (1980), *The Panda's Thumb.* New York: Norton.

Greenson, R. (1971), The "real" relationship between the patient and the psychoanalyst. In: *Explorations in Psychoanalysis.* New York: International Universities Press.

Hawking, S. W. (1988), *A Brief History of Time.* New York: Bantam.

Holt, R. R. (1989), *Freud Reappraised.* New York: Guilford.

Kohut, H. (1959), Introspection, empathy, and psychoanalysis. *J. Amer. Psychoanal. Assn.,* 7:459–483.

——— (1971), *The Analysis of the Self.* New York: International Universities Press.

——— (1977), *The Restoration of the Self.* New York: International Universities Press.

——— (1980), Reflections on advances in self psychology. In: *Advances in Self Psychology,* ed. A. Goldberg. New York: International Universities Press, pp. 473–554.

———— (1982), Introspection, empathy and the semicircle of mental health. *Internat. J. Psycho-Anal.*, 63:395–407.

———— (1983), Selected problems of self-psychological theory. In: *Reflections on Self Psychology*, ed. J. D. Lichtenberg & S. Kaplan. Hillsdale, NJ: The Analytic Press, pp. 387–416.

———— (1984), *How Does Analysis Cure?* ed. A. Goldberg & P. Stepansky. Chicago: The University of Chicago Press.

Kors, A. (1993), *The Origin of the Modern Mind.* Springfield, VA: The Teaching Co.

Kriegman, D. (1988), Self psychology from the perspective of evolutionary biology: Toward a biological foundation for self psychology. In: *Frontiers in Self Psychology, Progress in Self Psychology Vol. 3*, ed. A. Goldberg. Hillsdale, NJ: The Analytic Press, pp. 253–274.

———— (1990), Compassion and altruism in psychoanalytic theory: An evolutionary analysis of self psychology. *J. Amer. Acad. Psychoanal.*, 18:342–367.

———— (in press), The effectiveness of medication: The *Consumers Report* Study, Vol. 51, No. 10.

———— & Slavin, M. (1989), The myth of the repetition compulsion and the negative therapeutic reaction: An evolutionary biological analysis. In: *Dimensions of Self Experience: Progress in Self Psychology, Vol. 5*, ed. A. Goldberg. Hillsdale, NJ: The Analytic Press, pp. 209–253.

———— & ———— (1990), On the resistance to self psychology: Clues from evolutionary biology. In: *The Realities of Transference, Progress in Self Psychology, Vol. 6*, ed. A. Goldberg. Hillsdale, NJ: The Analytic Press, pp. 217–250.

———— & Solomon, L. (1985a), Cult groups and the narcissistic personality: The offer to heal defects in the self. *Internat. J. Group Psychother.*, 35:239–261.

———— & ———— (1985b), Psychotherapy and the "new religions": Are they the same? *Cultic Studies J.*, 2(1):2–16.

Mitchell, S. (1988), *Relational Concepts in Psychoanalysis: An Integration.* Cambridge: Harvard University Press.

Orange, D. (1995a), *Emotional Understanding: Studies in Psychoanalytic Epistemology.* New York: Guilford.

———— (1995b), Discussion of Daniel Kriegman's paper, "On the existential/subjectivism–scientific/objectivism dialectic in self psychology: A view from evolutionary biology." Eighteenth Annual Conference on the Psychology of the Self, San Francisco, October 22.

Ornstein, P. (1979), Remarks on the central position of empathy in psychoanalysis. *Bull. Assn. Psychoanal. Med.*, 18:95–108.

———— & Ornstein, A. (1980), Formulating interpretations in clinical psychoanalysis. *Internat. J. Psycho-Anal.*, 61:203–211.

Rabin, H. M. (1995), The liberating effect on the analyst of the paradigm shift in psychoanalysis. *Psychoanal. Psychol.*, 12:467–482.

Rorty, R. (1979), *Philosophy and the Mirror of Nature.* Princeton, NJ: Princeton University Press.

Schafer, R. (1985), The interpretation of psychic reality, developmental influences, and unconscious communication. *J. Amer. Psychoanal. Assn.*, 33:537–554.

Shane, M. & Shane, E. (1986), Self-change and development in the analysis of an adolescent patient. In: *Progress in Self Psychology, Vol. 2*, ed. A. Goldberg. New York: Guilford, pp. 142–160.

Slavin, M. (1985), The origins of psychic conflict and the adaptive function of repression: An evolutionary biological view. Psychoanal. & Contemp. Thought, 8:407–440.

—— (1990), The biology of parent–offspring conflict and the dual meaning of repression in psychoanalysis. J. Amer. Acad. Psychoanal., 18:307–341.

—— & Kriegman, D. (1990), Toward a new paradigm for psychoanalysis: An evolutionary biological perspective on the classical-relational dialectic. Psychoanal. Psychol., 7(Suppl.):5–31.

—— & —— (1992), The Adaptive Design of the Human Psyche: Psychoanalysis, Evolutionary Biology, and the Therapeutic Process. New York: Guilford.

—— & —— (1996), Why the analyst needs to change: Toward a theory of conflict, deception, and mutual influence in the therapeutic process. Submitted for publication.

Smith, M. B. (1994), Selfhood at risk: Postmodern perils and the perils of postmodernism. Amer. Psychol., 49:405–411.

Stolorow, R. (1995), Introduction: Tensions between loyalism and expansionism in self psychology. In: The Impact of New Ideas: Progress in Self Psychology, Vol. 11, ed. A. Goldberg. Hillsdale, NJ: The Analytic Press, pp. xi–xvii.

—— & Atwood, G. (1989), The unconscious and unconscious fantasy: An intersubjective developmental perspective. Psychoanal. Inq., 9:364–374.

—— & —— (1992), Contexts of Being. Hillsdale, NJ: The Analytic Press.

—— & —— (1994), Toward a science of human experience. In: The Intersubjective Perspective, ed. R. Stolorow, G. Atwood & B. Brandchaft. Northvale, NJ: Aronson, pp. 15–30.

—— —— & Brandchaft, B. (1994), Epilogue. In: The Intersubjective Perspective, ed. R. Stolorow, G. Atwood & B. Brandchaft. Northvale, NJ: Aronson, pp. 203–209.

—— Brandchaft, B. & Atwood, G. (1987), Psychoanalytic Treatment: An Intersubjective Approach. Hillsdale, NJ: The Analytic Press.

—— & Lachmann, F. (1984), Transference: The future of an illusion. The Annual of Psychoanalysis, 12/13:19–37. Madison, CT: International Universities Press.

Sucharov, M. S. (1992), Quantum physics and self psychology: Toward a new epistemology. In: New Therapeutic Visions: Progress in Self Psychology, Vol. 8, ed. A. Goldberg. Hillsdale, NJ: The Analytic Press, pp. 199–214.

Trivers, R. (1971), The evolution of reciprocal altruism. Quart. Rev. Biol., 46:35–57.

—— (1974), Parent–offspring conflict. Amer. Zool., 14:249–264.

—— (1985), Social Evolution. Menlo Park, NJ: Benjamin Cummings.

Watts, A. (1966), The Book: On the Taboo Against Knowing Who You Are. New York: Vintage Books.

Weiss, J. & Sampson, H. (1986), The Psychoanalytic Process: Theory, Clinical Observation, and Empirical Research. New York: Guilford.

White, M. (1955), The Age of Analysis: 20th Century Philosophers. New York: New American Library.

Wolf, E. (1983), Aspects of neutrality. Psychoanal. Inq., 3:675–689.

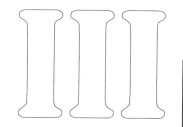

Clinical

The Contribution of Self- and Mutual Regulation to Therapeutic Action: A Case Illustration

Frank M. Lachmann

Beatrice Beebe

Empirical infant research can expand our understanding of therapeutic action in adult treatment (Beebe and Lachmann, 1994; Lachmann and Beebe, 1992a, 1996a). The concepts of self- and mutual regulation, derived from a systems approach to the study of infant–caregiver interaction, permit a more detailed view of patient–analyst interaction and the processes of analytic change. A case is used to illustrate the origins and transformations of a patient's psychopathology. In this case, chronically mismatched interactive regulations led to premature, drastic self-regulations. We trace the interactive processes of therapeutic action.

We have previously offered three organizing principles derived from infant research to describe how interactions are regulated, represented, and begin to be internalized in the first year of life (Beebe and Lachmann, 1994; Lachmann and Beebe, 1996a). These principles are "ongoing regulations," "disruption and repair" of ongoing regulations, and "heightened affective moments." They constitute hypotheses about how social interactions become patterned and salient. Although infant research has been construed as relevant to adult treatment in many ways (Emde, 1988; Horner, 1985; Osofsky, 1992; Sander, 1985; Seligman, 1994; Soref, 1992; Stern, 1985, 1995), in this chapter we focus on the principle we consider to be overarching, ongoing self- and mutual regulations. Through metaphor and analogy, we apply this perspective to analyst–patient interaction, verbal and nonverbal, in one case.

We use a theory of the interactive organization of experience that is based on a dyadic systems view (Beebe, Jaffe, and Lachmann, 1992; Lachmann and Beebe, 1996b; Samaroff, 1983; Sander, 1977, 1983). In this perspective, organization is an emergent property of the dyadic system and a property of the individual. Thus this view integrates the simultaneous influences of mutual and self-regulation. Mutual regulation refers to a model in which both partners actively contribute to the regulation of the exchange, although not necessarily in equal measure or in like manner. Self-regulation refers to self-comfort and the capacity to regulate one's states of arousal and organize one's behavior in predictable ways (Beebe and Lachmann, 1994).

The necessity for integrating both self- and mutual regulation in early development argues for their integration in a psychoanalytic theory of adult treatment as well (Beebe and Lachmann, 1996a; Lachmann and Beebe, 1989, 1992a). Mother and infant, and analyst and patient, jointly construct patterns of social relatedness. These patterns guide the management of attention, participation in dialogue, and affect sharing. Each partner influences the process through his or her own self-regulatory range and style, and through specific contributions to the pattern of interaction (Lachmann and Beebe, 1996a).

The organization of experience is the property of the interactive system and of the individual (Sander, 1977, 1985). Experience is organized as predictable; coordinated rhythms, tempos, sequences, affective intensities, postures, greetings, and separations unfold. At the same time, self-regulatory styles emerge. Characteristic and expected adaptive and nonadaptive patterns of mutual and self-regulation are thus constructed (Beebe, Jaffe, and Lachmann, 1993; Beebe and Lachmann, 1994; Tronick, 1989).

This model of development derived from infant research cannot, of course, be directly translated into the adult psychoanalytic situation. In adults, the capacity for symbolization and the subjective elaboration of experience in the form of fantasies, wishes, and defenses further modifies the organization and representation of interactive patterns. However, what makes this model appealing for adult treatment is that it makes no assumptions about the dynamic content of adult experience. It focuses entirely on the process of interactive regulation (Lachmann and Beebe, 1996a).

The person's capacity to respond and be socially engaged depends not only on the nature of the partner's input, and on the nature of the person's responsivity, but also on the person's regulation of his internal state (Beebe and Lachmann, 1994). State is used broadly to refer to affect, arousal, and its symbolic elaboration. From infancy on, people differ in the crucial capacity to modulate arousal, shift state, and tolerate and use stimulation to organize behavior in predictable ways (Als and Brazelton, 1981; Korner and Grobstein, in 1977).

Specific failures in self-regulation affect the quality of mutual regulation. For example, infants with specific self-regulatory difficulties may place undue burdens on the responsivity of their partners. Whether derived from variations in individual endowment or failures in mutual regulation, difficulties in self-regulation affect the quality of engagement.

Likewise, specific failures in mutual regulation compromise self-regulation. For example, as in the case to be discussed, affect regulation (Socarides and Stolorow, 1984/85), anxiety, tension, and aloneness (Alder and Buie, 1979) may then be relegated to solitary measures, without a sense of support. Expectations of being abandoned when one is vulnerable may arise. Rather than an expanding self-reliance and self-suffiency, aversions, anxieties about relationships, or self-protective depersonalization may ensue (Beebe and Lachmann, 1994).

Our integration is not designed to supplant dynamic formulations. Instead, it can provide the analyst a more differentiated view of the regulation of interactions and the organization of experience that goes beyond interpretation. Numerous well-established psychoanalytic concepts already cover some of the same terrain as self- and mutual regulation. For example, ongoing regulations have been subsumed within discussions of patterns of transference and countertransference (Lachmann and Beebe, 1992b), the "holding environment" (Winnicott, 1965), and the "background of safety" (Sandler, 1960).

In the treatment of the case to follow, we emphasize the analyst's and patient's mutually regulated interactions of affect, mood, arousal, and rhythm. Nonverbal interactions at the microlevel of rhythm matching, modulation of vocal contour, pausing, postural matching, and gaze regulation are usually not given adequate recognition in the treatment process (Beebe, 1993). We describe their powerful moment-by-moment impact on the joint construction of the psychoanalytic relationship, and we track the alterations in the self-regulatory ranges of both patient and analyst.

Attention to self- and mutual regulation helps the analyst contact "difficult-to-reach" patients where the critical cues go far beyond the usual verbal exchange. This perspective also explicates the interactive construction of selfobject experiences.

We are not proposing a new technique, nor are we arguing for decreased attention to dynamic issues in treatment. Instead, we reverse the figure-ground perspective customarily used in describing analytic treatment. We place the mutually regulated nonverbal exchanges into the foreground and dynamic conceptualizations into the background.

The nonverbal interactions on which we focus have been included among noninterpretive analytic behaviors (e.g., Freud, 1909; Ferenczi, 1929; Lindon, 1994). These interventions have been made when words were considered inadequate to retain a therapeutic connection with certain patients. However, we hold that nonverbal interactions, like noninterpretive actions, do constitute interpretations, although not packaged in the customary form. Their intent is to provide a primary contribution to the patient's expectation of mutuality and being understood. They provide access to a patient who is in a state not accessible to more usual forms of therapeutic dialogue.

CLINICAL ILLUSTRATION

Karen (treated by F. L.) began psychoanalytic therapy after her first suicide attempt. When her then-boyfriend flirted with another woman, she took all the pills in her medicine cabinet. Like an automaton, she watched her actions "from a bird's eye view from a corner of the room." This detached, depersonalized state felt to her as though she were "behind a pane of glass."

At times Karen would become aware that she had lost several hours and would find herself in a different part of town, with no memory of how she got there. In one of these states, toward the end of her first year of therapy, Karen made a second, similar suicide attempt.

Karen is in her sixth year of treatment on a three-session-per-week basis. When she began therapy, she was 27 years old. Her life had been declining since her graduation from high school. At that time her parents literally dragged her from her room to deposit her at an out-of-town college. She succeeded in remaining there for four years, excelling in some of her courses, and at the same time barely passing others. After graduation, she gained admission to a drama school in England and studied there for a year.

Upon her return to the United States, Karen continued to study acting and attempted to find work as an actress. She suffered from a severe sleep disturbance. Unable to sleep during the night, she tended to fall asleep in the early morning hours. When awake, she could not mobilize herself. She thus missed many auditions, missed call-backs when she did have a successful audition, and failed to appear for acting jobs when she did get hired.

Karen found it difficult to speak to me. She felt she had nothing to say and began sessions by asking, somewhat mechanically, "What shall we talk about?" Initially, I responded by summarizing previous sessions, for example: "We spoke about how messy and dingy your apartment is." She might then speak about an apparently unrelated topic, for example, encounters with various acquaintances. I thought these experiences left her with feelings of abandonment, disappointment, a sense of exploitation, or regret about her withdrawn manner.

Privately I came to understand Karen's opening question as an attempt to orient herself and determine whether or not a connection could be established with me. I believed that waiting for her to begin, or throwing her question back, would have failed to recognize her tentative attempt to reach out to me. Overtly Karen hardly acknowledged my presence, although she did ask, "What shall 'we' talk about?"

Gradually I came to appreciate that Karen dreaded conversing with me. She anticipated that she would have difficult feelings she would have to regulate on her own. This expectation suggests an imbalance between mutual and self-regulation in her development. With the expectation of chronic misregulation, a preoccupation with self-regulation and the management of negative affect ensues (Gianino and Tronick, 1988; Tronick, 1989). For Karen, despite her preoccupation with self-regulation, the nature of her self-regulatory efforts were severely impaired. Her sleep disturbance, listless state, and lack of "desire" were evidence of this impaired regulation of affect and arousal.

What self-regulatory range did Karen bring to treatment? A narrow range of tolerable affect, arousal, and engagement; an immobile face; a tendency to space out; and massive efforts to dampen down her reactivity to all stimulation. In sessions she looked out of my office window as she sat in her chair with her coat on. When she did look at me, it was a sideways glance. Interactions with Karen were dominated by her withdrawal.

Slowly Karen began to reveal her experiences in her family. From the age of five on, she was awakened during the night by her parents' fights. She could hear their shouts through the walls of her bedroom. Her mother would accuse her father of staying out at night with other women and her father would, at times, be physically abusive toward her mother. The fights terrified her, especially after her mother asked her who she would want to go with if she and her father separated. She remembered not wanting to go with either one. They never did separate.

Karen was born shortly after her parents' graduation from high school. Neither parent hid from Karen that their future plans were scuttled by their marriage and her birth. In reaction Karen began to pray at night. By the time she was seven, she had made a deal with God. If He would stop her parents from fighting, she would give up her life. From that time forward she was preoccupied with suicide and suffered from severe, persistent sleep disturbances.

In high school, Karen frequently cut classes because she could not tolerate the noise made by other students. Sometimes she would get as far as the classroom door, stand outside, and be unable to enter. She would then go home and spend the day studying alone. She did appear for examinations, on which she did very well. During afternoons and evenings she worked as a cashier at a local shopping mall. In fact, she worked continuously until the end of her high school years. Since then and until her treatment was well under way, she had not held a job.

By the age of 17, Karen had formed an intimate sustaining relationship with a fellow student, Brian. He was her best friend and confidant. When he unexpectedly died of a brain tumor, she was despondent. Her parents insisted that she get over her loss quickly. They could not recognize that Karen had lost the one person to whom she felt close and whom she trusted. She retreated to her room, felt "without desires," and was increasingly aimless. This was not the first time she experienced these states. On previous occasions they were more or less transient. At this point they crystallized as a recurring dominant state.

When Karen began therapy, 10 years later, these states were still prominent and affected the nature of our interaction. Though we sat facing each other, Karen looked away from me. Her face was immobile. Her voice had no contouring. She kept her coat on. Even when I spoke to her she did not look at me. Her self-constriction powerfully affected me. I felt reluctant to jar her precariously maintained presentation.

I responded to her constriction by partially constricting myself. I allowed myself to be influenced by her rhythm. I narrowed my own expansiveness to more closely match the limits imposed by her own narrow affective range. I did look at her continuously, but I kept my voice even and soft. In my initial comments I remained within the limits of the concrete details that she offered. I thus altered the regulation of my own arousal, keeping it low and limiting my customary expansiveness. She was effective in communicating her distress and I was able to respond by providing her with a range of stimulation that more closely matched the limited level of arousal she could tolerate. However, as I restricted my own expressiveness, at times I became fidgity and squirmy. She seemed oblivious to my moments of discomfort.

Gradually her tolerance for affective arousal increased and I could become more expansive. She was able to talk about affectively more difficult material. Her voice remained soft but with more contouring. She spoke about social relationships and acting auditions that raised the specter of competition. But she felt that she had no right to live. She withdrew from these situations lest she draw attention to herself. Initially these explorations had little effect on her life. Our dialogue, however, did increase the affective range that she could tolerate in the sessions.

During the first two years of the treatment, Karen moved from descriptions of her environment, the inanimate world, to descriptions of interpersonal relationships and explorations of her subjective states. At the same time I also shifted from summaries of the previous sessions to elaborations of her feelings and reactions. Sometimes anticipating her formulaic opening, "What shall we talk about?" I began sessions by asking her how she was feeling. Sometimes, before verbally responding, her right upper lip would twitch and constrict briefly, or her leg would jiggle rapidly. I came to understand these signals as an indication that she was tense and had been feeling moody, depressed, or without energy since our last meeting. We focussed on her specific reactions and tried to find a context for them. I detailed nuances of feelings and moods such as annoyance, rebuff, eagerness, enthusiasm, or disappointment. I told her that it seemed to me that she experienced many emotions as though they were annoying intrusions. After some time, I was able to add descriptions of Karen as "considering," "hoping," "planning," or "expecting." That is, I distinguished among categories of affect and time, and acknowledged her authorship of her experience. I kept apace with Karen's gradually more personalized communications. The extent of her visible discomfort waxed and waned. However, she did appear more comfortable about accessing, revealing, and understanding her subjective life in both its reactive and proactive aspects.

Although I was not unaware of restricting and monitoring my responses to Karen, I was not following a premeditated plan of nonverbal treatment. Qualities of nonverbal communication, such as vocal rhythm, pitch, contour, and the level of arousal are usually out of awareness, but we are able to bring them into focussed attention. It was mostly in retrospect that I became aware of the salient role played by these nonverbal, mutually regulated interactions and their effect on Karen's and my self-regulation. I assumed that through these interactions, Karen felt some sense of validation leading to the tentative engagement of a selfobject tie.

To enable Karen to maintain the fragile developing selfobject tie, I did not make explicit the possibility that Karen refound aspects of her experience with Brian in the therapeutic relationship. To do so could have increased her self-consciousness and her propensity toward overstimulating anxiety. She would have needed to protect herself against a repetition of another attachment and loss-abandonment sequence.

Instead, I recognized Karen's affective reactions and her dread of retraumatization in her current relationships. We translated her associations, symptoms, nightmares, enactments, and hallucinations into more direct statements about herself and her experience. We discussed the vagueness that characterized much of her life as indicating what she was afraid to perceive, feel, believe, wish, imagine, or remember. My comments were directed toward recognizing her attempts at self-definition. In this way her previous, almost exclusive reliance on drastic self-regulation through withdrawal, depersonalization, and derealization began to shift. Her sense of agency increased. For example, as her dread of retraumatization in new situations diminished, she showed a wider variation of facial expressions. Occasionally she smiled. Furthermore, she registered for, attended, and participated, in some classes.

In the course of the first two years of treatment, Karen recalled her parents' fights and was increasingly able to describe other painful events. However, until we explored them, these memories had been retained as unconnected experiences. They correlated with Karen's sense of fragmentation. In making connections among these memories, her feelings, and their current relevance, I continually depicted Karen as living and having lived a life with temporal, affective, and cognitive dimensions. I described the events to her, with some slightly increased affective elaborations. Increasingly, she could tolerate my amplification of her affect.

These memories spanned the fifth to eighth years of her life. In the earliest event we pieced together, Karen was required to mail a letter for her mother at the post office. Karen recalled feeling abject terror at having to walk past some derelicts to mail the letter.

Karen recalled that she could not leave her mother's side. Nor could she explain to her mother why she was so afraid. Her mother encouraged her to mail the letter by telling her how big and grown up she was. We came to understand that walking alone past the derelicts meant to Karen that she would be showing her mother that she was "growing up." She would then be telling her mother that she was able to fend for herself. Based on the fights Karen had overheard, I said that her fear of revealing her "growth" grew out of her belief that her mother wanted to "dump" her and, in fact, could not wait to do so. Showing independence would result in imminent loss of support. Karen responded with silent tears. She rarely responded to such reconstructions directly. However, new recollections subsequently did emerge.

Another memory concerned a visit to a department store where Karen had one of her first asthmatic attacks. She tried to tell her mother that she could barely breathe. She could not keep up with her as they rushed from one department to another. Her mother told her that the shopping was important. Karen should not complain so much.

Karen recalled the department store visit as we were exploring how she neglected her health, especially her teeth, skin, and allergies. I commented that through her body and frequent upper respiratory illnesses, her complaints were given voice. There she retained an eloquent record of her feelings. The twitch of her upper lip and her foot jiggles also constituted such a silent record of her moods and feelings.

Karen had come to consider her physical state as unimportant. She could now imagine that she must have felt hurt by her mother's dismissive and neglectful behavior. She had been anxious about her breathing difficulty, but most of all, fearful of evoking her mother's disapproval by complaining. Her solution in the department store had been to redouble her efforts to stay close to her mother, attempt to dampen her own arousal, and hope that the ordeal would soon be over.

The third memory involved Karen's sleep difficulty, which continued even after the parental fights ceased. To cure her sleep difficulty she was confined to her room. While exploring this symptom, Karen reported that she was currently feeling a sudden urge to travel to Iceland. She then recalled that she had attempted to deal with her sleep problem by putting herself to sleep in an empty bathtub. There she could fall asleep because "it was quiet." But, most important, the "whiteness" and the hardness of the tub felt so good. It afforded her a sense of security and protection. However, when her parents discovered her, she was sent to her room immediately after supper so that she could try to get to sleep early.

Obediently Karen remained in her room. She watched the outside world from behind her window. She felt excluded and frustrated and began to draw on the walls of her room. These creative, exploratory, assertive efforts were quickly punished. She was given a bottle of cleaning fluid and told to undo the damage. Later, however, she was presented with a paint set, but she felt too resentful toward her parents to use it. The paint box was never opened. Some years later, in a similar vein, she was given a chemistry set because she showed some interest and ability in her science classes. However, aside from being presented with the paints and chemicals, no one in her family took any interest in her. No one inquired about the two sets. Neither was ever used. Karen acknowledged that she would have liked to use the paint and chemistry sets but could not bring herself to do so.

Karen clung to her room until she was dragged by her parents to college. Her room was her refuge and she felt protected in it, even though alone. Her banishment and "voluntary confinement" to her room paralleled my sense of her inaccessibility in the therapeutic relationship. I made this connection with the expectation that Karen's inaccessibility could be explained and thereby diminished more directly. She thereupon dreamed of a "barren countryside." In association she recalled hallucinatory experiences. When she was confined to her room and would look out of her window she sometimes saw cars go by without drivers. We discussed the "barren countryside" dream, a self-state dream, as conveying her sense of barrenness. We connected it to the "aimlessness" depicted in her hallucination. I told her that she depicted herself as living in a world in which no one was at the wheel. Perhaps she longed for someone in her family to take an interest in her and assume some control. I also inquired whether she might be feeling this way currently in her treatment. Such heavy-handed transference queries never yielded much. On further reflection, however, I felt that my expectations of her exceeded a level of functioning that she could tolerate. Through her dream and her recollection of the hallucinations, she was reminding me of her still-depleted state, her barrenness. She was letting me know that I should not rush ahead of her (as her mother had in the department store) and lose sight of the severity of her difficulties. Her dread of being dumped at the first signs of "growth" still prevailed.

The three memories of being at the post office, in the department store, and confined to her room constitute a series of model scenes (Lachmann and Lichtenberg, 1992; Lichtenberg, Lachmann, and Fosshage, 1992). Each one shaped segments of our interactions, though the "confinement" theme dominated the others.

The model scene of standing in her room and looking out at life through her window gathered together a number of previous salient issues and shaped subsequent experience. In her room, she was protected from the injurious expectation of her family and the "noise" and potential exploitativeness of her peers. In her room she did not need to fear that she might "blow others away" or become an object of envy. She also avoided the danger of feeling helpless, frustrated, and out of control. Through her continuous self-sacrifice, she maintained a firm grip on her parents' tie to her and her claim on them.

The mother–daughter relationship, encapsulated by the model scenes, depicted patterns of mutual regulation that tilted Karen toward solitary self-regulation. At first she did attempt to regulate heightened, painful affect states, such as her terror at the post office and in the department store, by trying to elicit her mother's participation. She pleaded with her mother at the post office and clung to her in the department store. Feeling ignored, she expected that independent steps would lead to abandonment. Therefore, heroic efforts at self-regulation were undertaken. In essence, drastic self-regulation attempts substituted for a balanced integration between self- and mutual regulation (Tronick, 1989).

By the time Karen was confined to her room, she had come to tolerate her aloneness and restrict her activity. Her efforts to engage her family had all but ceased. Her physical symptoms and hallucinations increased her withdrawal. She felt ineffective in engaging her parents and confined herself to altering and influencing her physical and subjective states. Drawing on her walls served as a desperate signal for attention. But her refusal to touch the paint and chemistry sets suggested that her withdrawal contained a significant degree of self-sacrifice and defiance. Karen could not risk putting herself in the position of expecting recognition from her parents and being disappointed. To avoid this danger she kept her creative and intellectual interests to herself. She lived out her grim, unconscious belief (Weiss and Sampson, 1986) that she had "no right to a life" (Modell, 1984). Her suicidal preoccupation, her neglect of her physical well-being, her propensity to disregard physical illness, her social withdrawal and minimum functioning in life, and her retreat from attention no matter how much she desired it all converged in her conviction that her parents' life (and hence the world) would have been better off had she not been born.

Her relationship with Brian in late adolescence provided a notable exception to these convictions. Through her relationship with him, Karen had retained some hope for a reciprocal connection and sensual and sexual responsivity. A significant sector of her life had been left relatively intact. However, overall her development remained constricted.

Karen developed physical symptoms in lieu of accusations and complaints, withdrew from people, and found solace in the "bathtub." The "bathtub" differed as a solution from the others in that she created her own protected environment. Her confinement to her room thus became an enforced exclusion from her family. Yet it provided some protection against the overstimulating parental quarrels and their obliviousness to her needs.

During the treatment the self-protective aspects of Karen's bathtub experience appeared transformed as a visit to Iceland. Karen began to acknowledge the talents that were unrecognized by her family. Her creativity remained sequestered in her private world with considerable ambivalence. For example, she studied acting but did not perform.

Convinced that she had been a burden to her parents and the source of their difficulties, Karen considered her solitary confinement to be justified. In refusing to make use of the resources that her parents gave her, she found a self-defeating but nevertheless modest triumph. In the confines of her imagination, creative elaborations of her experience continued in silence and in private. These could be accessed in the course of her treatment and became the imagery of her poetry.

Karen had written poems at various times in her life. During her second year of treatment she turned to writing poetry in a more determined way. A poem she brought to a session was dedicated to the memory of Brian. In it she depicted her loneliness and her alienation from her family. She ended with a plea to Brian: "Run after me but never let me go."

To "use" therapy, for which her parents paid, meant to Karen that she had to surrender her defiance and capitulate to them. She had not used the paint box, the chemistry set, or the acting classes. Why surrender now? It became clear then, why, during the first two years of treatment, she continued to indicate that she had made no progress and that she was as depressed as ever. Based on Karen's failure to work and earn money, her parents echoed her feeling that she had not made any progress in therapy. I asked Karen what would happen if her parents were to stop their financial support of her. She said, "I would probably be dead, now." It was as though Karen was giving her parents another chance to decide, Do you want me to live or not? Since the financial support included payment for her treatment, I also understood her remark to allude to her need for therapy and its importance to her.

During the first two years of treatment, Karen usually came to the sessions encased in the room in which she was isolated by herself and her family. She either stayed in her room literally by not coming to sessions, or figuratively through her communicative difficulties. Often sessions felt to me as though we were meeting for the first time. She never made any reference to what had gone on in a previous session, so I did. She did appear to be moved by some of my affect-laden descriptions of her experience. When she was moved, tears would roll down her cheeks. She could not usually say why she was crying.

During these first two years of treatment, Karen missed at least one of her three weekly appointments and arrived late for the other two. Missing sessions or arriving late increased her sense of failure. When I gently inquired about this pattern, she told me that it was an achievement that she could get herself to the sessions as often as she did.

During these first two years I referred Karen to a psychopharmacologist but she did not take the medication with any regularity. Fortunately, the unused medication was not at hand when she made her second suicide attempt. During the first two years, Karen also had two abortions to which she reacted with increased depression. Twice during the second year of her treatment, I met with Karen and her parents but they could not grasp the severity of Karen's difficulties. I felt that she was still a high suicide risk.

After the second suicide attempt, waiting to see whether or not Karen would arrive for her appointments became very anxiety arousing for me. I felt that without some more active intervention on my part, her depersonalized state and the suicidal potential would continue. I needed more reliable and intensive contact with her. I needed to feel less worried, and that I had a chance of reaching her.

Thus, at the beginning of her third year of treatment, I decided to telephone Karen about two hours before every appointment. I reminded her of the time of our meeting and told her that I looked forward to seeing her. Within about three to four months, Karen no longer missed sessions.

Karen had engaged me sufficiently that I had begun to feel desperate. When I had decided to call her, I was not conscious of her plea in the poem "Run after me but never let me go." However, I was evidently responding to it. In retrospect, my enactment exactly matched the presymbolic quality of many of Karen's communications. We may ask whether her long-standing, continuously reinforced conviction that she was fundamentally unwanted would have budged in the face of verbal interventions and explanations alone. Could attuned understanding have better facilitated the therapeutic process? Were my calls an extension of empathic immersion in her subjectivity? Or was I requiring Karen to connect with me on my terms and at her expense?

Though valid, these questions imply that my self-regulation and my role in the mutual regulation could have been reduced or eliminated. Although a dramatic departure from customary analytic work, the telephone calls emerged out of a mutual regulation in which my capacity to tolerate anxiety had reached a limit. Furthermore, my enactment concretely made the following interpretation to Karen: You are wanted. We hold that this enactment was a critical part of the regulatory process and therapeutic action in this case.

Despite Karen's detachment, her responsivity to some of my comments did evoke an intense engagement on my part. Her dramatic response to my calls about coming regularly to sessions indicated how profoundly she could be influenced by me. Her response exactly matched what I needed to feel, so that the treatment—and she—had a chance. Not only was her sense of efficacy promoted as I altered and restricted my responsivity, but my sense of efficacy was promoted as she expanded her responsivity. Thus a complex and intricately matched mutual regulation took place.

By the end of the third year, the gradually firming selfobject tie made suicide less likely and diminished her depression. She had to admit that she had not felt so well in many years. She even volunteered that she did not think she could ever make another suicide attempt.

During the first year of my calls, if she were still asleep, her answering machine would pick up and I would leave a message. As Karen became less depressed and felt more energetic, she often left her house before my call. She would then come to the sessions without a reminder and would receive my message only upon arriving at her home in the evening. On several occasions I asked how she felt about my telephone calls. She told me that it was "OK" for me to call. I understood her "OK" as her only way of saying that she wants the calls. She could not acknowledge that she needed them. With her "OK" she gave me permission to call as if also reassuring me that I was not intruding. In this response it is apparent that Karen was still quite detached and protected herself in the privacy of her room.

By the beginning of the fourth year of treatment, Karen appeared more alive and accessible. The gradual establishment of a relatively reliable selfobject tie shifted Karen's self-regulatory capacities toward greater tolerance for affect and arousal. Although she remained rather constricted, she gained increasing access to her own experience and her own history. Past and current impressions gained expression in her writing.

In this fourth year Karen wanted to talk to her mother about the recent death of an acquaintance. It was an event that bore certain similarities to the death of Brian. Her mother suggested that they meet at a bar that had music to talk about this death. Karen then telephoned me. She had felt guilty about her actions at the last meeting with this acquaintance and she was not also disappointed and furious with her mother for fending her off. Thus, in spite of her continuing state of detachment, she was able to use our tie to restore herself in this crisis.

In her fifth year of treatment, Karen's interest and talent as a writer enabled her to enroll in a graduate program, attend classes, and submit assignments. Through her visit to Iceland she succeeded in having some poetry published. Though she still sought relationships with charismatic men who were unstable and irresponsible, she was no longer so compliant and dependent. She practiced "safe sex."

Karen's conviction that she would cause fewer problems for her family by shutting herself away remained a dominant theme. In fact, it received continuous confirmation when she visited her parents. They did not seem to be aware of her widening range of affect and capacity. She was told by them not to come into the living room when they were entertaining friends because her depressing and uncommunicative manner put a pall on the company.

Karen is emerging as an adventuresome, foolhardy, overly trusting, resourceful, funny, and still somewhat self-sabotaging person. In her own succinct way she summarized her gain in her treatment: "I used to not be able to talk to people. Now I can talk to people."

DISCUSSION

Karen's lifelong experiences of rebuff led to a premature reliance on drastic and restricting self-regulatory measures such as avoidance, depersonalization, derealization, and dampening of her own affect. Designed to avoid retraumatization, these measures only partially protected her.

She maintained a precarious balance between self-expression and self-annihilation.

In Karen's development, sounds had become shattering noises obstructing emotional contact. Vision had become a remote sense. She felt as though she were looking at herself and her experiences from a distance. Breathing, sleeping, and spatial orientation were impaired. Sensual-affective experiences were overarousing, emerged as physical symptoms and disruptive imagery such as hallucinations and nightmares. Unable to regulate affect states on her own, she avoided emotionally arousing and thus potentially disruptive experiences.

The relationship with Brian revived Karen's expectations of being affectively validated and part of a dyad. It rekindled her expectation that she could trust her feelings, be included in someone's internal life, and form a bond. We assume that the tie to Brian reengaged an earlier, precarious selfobject tie to her parents. With the death of Brian, Karen was traumatized (Lachmann and Beebe, 1996b). Not only did she lose the only person to whom she felt connected, but her parents also failed to validate her profound devastation. Thus, selfobject ties were irreparably disrupted.

The treatment of Karen illustrates the role of mutual and self-regulation in the therapeutic establishment of the selfobject tie. Karen's fears of retraumatization were investigated, and her feelings were labeled, differentiated, and affirmed. As with Brian, she feared that attachment would lead to loss. Furthermore, her restricted self-regulatory range interfered with her ability to tolerate the excitement and hope generated by the expectation of being accepted, understood, and included in a bond. These difficulties pervaded her friendships, classes, and work possibilities as well as her treatment.

Karen's immobile face, flat voice, sitting with her coat on, not looking, and having nothing to say required extraordinary measures. To reach her, the therapist had to restrict the range of affect and activity so that Karen's level of arousal remained tolerable to her. Speaking in a soft and even voice, and slowing the rhythm, increased Karen's tolerance for arousal. She began to talk about her life with a voice and face that were more alive. The therapist was able to expand the level of his own arousal and address her fears of retraumatization. In turn, Karen was less withdrawn. Fragments of her history emerged, from which three model scenes could be constructed. This increasing coherence led to Karen's ability to report a dream and a hallucinatory association of "cars without drivers." The therapist could then interpret her inaccessibility and her world where no one was at the wheel.

Although Karen was able to acknowledge that she would be dead without this therapy, her two abortions, extensive depersonalizations, second suicide attempt, frequent latenesses, and continuous missed appointments led the therapist to make a dramatic intervention by telephoning her before every appointment. The fact that Karen was able to respond equally dramatically by coming regularly enabled the therapist to feel that he could continue to work with her. Karen was able to experience her own influence on the therapist's activity, and she could experience her therapist influencing her level of arousal. For both patient and therapist, self-regulation was altered through these mutual regulations. Thus, extensive work on Karen's depersonalized state and efforts to reregulate both of us had set the stage sufficiently well that the telephone calls could make a dramatic impact.

We have focused on the nonverbal dimension in order to illustrate the contribution of mutual and self-regulation to therapeutic action. When the treatment began, solitary self-regulation was Karen's main method of survival, and it was failing. The treatment attempted to open up her self-regulation so that it could be included in a dialogue. Instead of viewing analyst and patient as two isolated entities, each sending the other discrete communications, we have illustrated a view of the treatment relationship as a system (Beebe et al., 1993). This theory of interaction specifies how each person is affected both by his or her own behavior (self-regulation) and by the behavior of the partner (interactive regulation) on a continuous moment-by-moment basis (Beebe, 1993; Beebe and Lachmann, 1988, 1994).

REFERENCES

Adler, G. & Buie, D. (1979), Aloneness and borderline psychopathology: The possible relevance of child developmental issues. *Internat. J. Psycho-Anal.*, 60:83–96.

Als, H. & Brazelton, T. B. (1981), A new model for assessing the behavioral organization in preterm and fullterm infants. *J Amer. Acad. Child Psychiat.*, 20:239–263.

Beebe, B. (1993), A dyadic systems view of communication: Contributions from infant research to adult treatment. Presented at the 16th Annual Conference of the Psychology of the Self, Toronto.

—— Jaffe, J. & Lachmann, F. M. (1993), A dyadic systems view of communication. In: *Relational Views of Psychoanalysis*, ed. N. Skolnick & S. Warshaw. Hillsdale NJ: The Analytic Press, pp. 61–81.

—— & Lachmann, F. M. (1988), The contributions of mother–infant mutual influence to the origins of self and object representations. *Psychoanal. Psychol.*, 5:305–337.

—— & —— (1994), Representation and internalization in infancy: Three principles of salience. *Psychoanal. Psychol.*, 11:127–165.

Emde, R. (1988), The prerepresentational self and its affective core. *The Psychoanalytic Study of the Child*, 36:165–192. New Haven, CT: Yale University Press.

Ferenczi, S. (1929), The principle of relaxation and neocatharsis. In: *Final Contributions to the Problems and Methods of Psychoanalysis*. New York: Basic Books, 1955, pp. 126–142.

Freud, S. (1909), Notes upon a case of obsessional neurosis, *Standard Edition*, 10:153–318. London: Hogarth Press, 1955.

Gianino, A. & Tronick, E. (1988), The mutual regulation model: The infant's self and interactive regulation and coping and defensive sapacities. In: *Stress and Coping*, ed. T. Field, P. McCabe & N. Schneiderman. Hillsdale, NJ: Lawrence Erlbaum Associates, pp. 47–58.

Horner, A. (1985), The psychic life of the young infant: Review and critique of the psychoanalytic concepts of symbiosis and infantile omnipotence. *Amer. J. Orthopsychiat.*, 55:324–344.

Korner, A. & Grobstein, R. (1977), Individual differences at birth. In: *Infant Psychiatry*, ed. A. Rexford, L. Sander & T. Shapiro. New Haven, CT: Yale University Press, pp. 66–78.

Lachmann, F. M. & Beebe, B. (1989), Oneness fantasies revisited. *Psychoanal. Psychol.*, 6:137–149.

——— & ——— (1992a), Reformulations of early development and transference: Implications for psychic structure. In: *The Interface of Psychoanalysis and Psychology*, ed. D. Wolitzky, M. Eagle & J. Barron Washington, D.C.: American Psychological Association, pp. 133–153.

——— & ——— (1992b), Representational and selfobject transferences: A developmental perspective. In: *Progress in Self Psychology, Vol. 8, New Therapeutic Visions*, ed. A. Goldberg. Hillsdale, NJ: The Analytic Press, pp. 3–15.

——— & ——— (1996a), Three principles of salience in the patient–analyst interaction. *Psychoanal. Psychol.*, 13.

——— & ——— (1996b), Trauma, interpretation, and self-state transformation. In preparation.

——— & Lichtenberg, J. D. (1992), Model scenes: Implications for psychoanalytic treatment. *J. Amer. Psychoanal. Assn.*, 40:117–137.

Lichtenberg, J. D., Lachmann, F. M. & Fosshage, J. (1992), *Self and Motivational Systems*. Hillsdale, NJ: The Analytic Press.

Lindon, J. (1994), Gratification and provision in psychoanalysis: Should we get rid of the rule of abstinence? *Psychoanal. Dial.*, 4:549–582.

Modell, A. (1984), *Psychoanalysis in a New Context*. New York: International Universities Press.

Osofsky, J. (1992), Affective development and early relationships: Clinical implications. In: *Interface Between Psychoanalysis and Psychology*, ed. J. Barron, M. Eagle & D. Wolitzky. Washington, DC: American Psychological Assn. Press, pp. 233–244.

Samaroff, A. (1993), Developmental systems: Contexts and evolution. In: *Mussen's Handbook of Child Psychology, Vol. 1*, ed. J. Kessen. New York: Wiley, pp. 237–294.

Sander, L. (1977), The regulation of exchange in the infant–caretaker system and some aspects of the context–content relationship. In: *Interaction, Conversation, and the Development of Language*, ed. M. Lewis & L. Rosenblum. New York: Basic Books, pp. 133–156.

——— (1983), Polarity paradox, and the organizing process in development. In: *Frontiers of Infant Psychiatry*, ed. J. D. Call, E. Galenson & R. Tyson. New York: Basic Books, pp. 315–327.

——— (1985), Toward a logic of organization in psycho-biological development. In: *Biologic Response Cycles: Clinical Implications*, ed. H. Klar & L. Siever. Washington, DC: American Psychiatric Press, pp. 20–36.

Sandler, J. (1960), The background of safety. *Internat. J. Psycho-Anal.*, 41:352–356.

Seligman, S. (1994), Applying psychoanalysis in an unconventional context: Adapting infant–parent psychotherapy to a changing population. *The Psychoanalytic Study of the Child*, 49:481–500. New Haven, CT: Yale University Press.

Socarides, D. & Stolorow, R. (1984/1985), Affects and selfobjects. *The Annual of Psychoanalysis*, 12/13:105–120. New York: International Universities Press.

Soref, A. (1992), The self, in and out of relatedness. *The Annual of Psychoanalysis*, 20:25–48. New York: International Universities Press.

Stern, D. (1985), *The Interpersonal World of the Infant*. New York: Basic Books.

—— (1995), *The Motherhood Constellation*. New York: Basic Books.

Tronick, E. (1989), Emotions and emotional communication in infants. *Amer. Psychol.*, 44(2):112–119.

Weiss, J. & Sampson, H. (1986), *The Psychoanalytic Process*. New York: Guilford.

Winnicott, D. W. (1965), *The Maturational Processes and the Facilitating Environment*. New York: International Universities Press.

Chapter 8

Countertransference and Curative Process with "Nondifficult" Patients

Martin S. Livingston

"Difficult" patients have received a great deal of attention in the psychoanalytic literature. It has been "difficult" patients, like Kohut's (1968, 1971) Miss F, who have stretched the limits of existing clinical and theoretical knowledge resulting in new conceptualizations, such as those of self psychology and intersubjectivity. Brandchaft and Stolorow, in their article entitled "The Difficult Patient" (1988), point out that "the therapist's ability to deepen his reflective self-awareness when faced with difficult patients can enable him to recognize and decenter from recurrent patterns in himself that, in general, limit his ability to comprehend his patient's experiences of him from within their own subjective frames of reference" (p. 93).

In the case of "difficult patients," what is often experienced by both analyst and patient as so difficult (what most often produces the stormy impasses we associate with such patients) is the occurrence of what Stolorow and Atwood (1992) refer to as intersubjective disjunction. At these times, the patient's experience of the situation (and especially of the analyst) is sharply at odds with that of the analyst. This is particularly uncomfortable when the patient attributes qualities to the analyst that are disowned and thus become an onslaught on the analyst's sense of his own identity. If the analyst, in order to preserve what Stolorow and Atwood refer to as his own "organizing principles," treats the patient's view as a distortion, then he invalidates the patient's experience, thus provoking an understandable rage.

In these instances of intersubjective disjunction, in contrast to utilizing the object-relational concept of projective identification (which often leads to attributing the analyst's subjective experience to an interactional communication from the patient), the core of a self-psychological approach suggested by Lichtenberg, Lachmann, and Fosshage (1992) is "that the analyst accept and then explore the patient's attributions." They refer to this "as wearing the attribution as if it were a suit of clothes, a costume, or a role that is assigned to the analyst." The analyst's ability to contain the often uncomfortable or even painful inner experiences stimulated during this process provides a nurturing selfobject function for the patient. In addition, this containment allows the analyst to become more reflectively self-aware of his own contributions to the intersubjective interplay. The analyst's task in such situations is often a difficult one.

On the other hand, some patients are very skillful at not placing this uncomfortable demand on the analyst. These treatment situations represent the other side of the coin from the stormy situations we understand in terms of intersubjective disjunction. The situation is one of intersubjective conjunction (Stolorow and Atwood, 1992). The patient, in these cases, experiences the therapy setting, and particularly the analyst, only in a manner that coincides with the analyst's self-experience. I refer to such patients as "nondifficult" in the sense that in working with them, there are no threats to the analyst's identity, organizing principles, or sanity. Working with these patients proceeds without stormy empathic ruptures and without the patient's experiencing the therapist as a failing selfobject. The work proceeds, but ever so slowly and without a clear sense of vitality. Clearly, we cannot think of such treatment, and the patients involved, as "easy" unless we settle for a very minimal result for years of effort.

The thesis of the present chapter is that the analyst's use of his own subjectivity (his countertransferential responsiveness) is just as inherently connected to the curative process in the treatment of patients who do not provoke uncomfortable reactions in the analyst as it is in the treatment of the difficult patients described previously. These patients do not display "negative transferential responses" and neither therapist nor patient experiences a sense of impasse. These cases are not brought into supervision in a desperate call for help. In fact, they are not often mentioned in supervision or written about at all.

It is generally recognized that the analyst's use of his own subjective experience of both the patient and the interaction in sessions must serve as "a central guide for inquiry and intervention" (Fosshage, 1993) with all his patients. However, it seems important to underscore the importance of a "self supervisory" process that sharpens the analyst's reflective self-awareness, especially with these "nondifficult" patients. The very nondifficulty along with a lack of vitality in the sessions should serve as a warning sign calling for such a process.

I wrote this chapter as an illustration of such a "self supervisory" process and its particular relevance with a "nondifficult" patient. My plan was to take detailed notes that would include my subjective experiences in an attempt to deepen my understanding of what was taking place, sharpen my own self-awareness, and revitalize a treatment process that felt stuck. In addition, the clinical material demonstrates how a shift in thinking can provide the courage to see a patient in a different light, which in turn provides a productive impact on the curative process.

Two shifts are illustrated. One shift took place during the project as a consequence of my self-supervision. The other shift actually took place during the previous years in which I was immersed in self-psychology and intersubjectivity. In an earlier treatment with the same patient, I was guided by a more classical approach in which I focussed on the patient's resistances as intrapsychic phenomena. In the current analysis, after a five-year interruption, I saw these same "resistances" as the patient's need to protect herself from further selfobject failure and retraumatization. As a self psychologist stressing empathic immersion into the inner world of the patient, I am always interested in my impact on my patient's mental state. However, at this moment in time, my conceptual emphasis in undertaking the current project centers on an intersubjective view of the sessions because the concepts of intersubjective conjunction and disjunction are in the foreground of my organization of the material. It is confusing to try to delineate the intersubjective from the self-psychological aspects of the actual treatment process. It is clearly informed by both.

Mrs. A is the mother of three grown children, who represent her most alive sense of self. The aliveness displayed so well in her children and in her discussion of them is controlled and diminished in the rest of her life. Her body is overweight and has become a manifestation of her passivity. Her smile and an occasional glimmer in her eyes or excitement in her voice are strongly suggestive of the seed of an attractive and alive self that is largely hidden from view. She is the first of two adopted daughters followed by a natural-born son. Her father was extremely volatile, easily angered, and disapproving. Her mother was described as tense and insecure, seeking constant reassurance that "everything is under control." The overall feeling of the patient's experiences in the family was a desperation to fit in and to hide anything that might suggest she did not belong. In short, Mrs. A's childhood was a massive accommodation to the needs of her parents and the seeds of selfhood were well hidden. It was the perfect background to develop a "nondifficult" patient.

Although I did not conceptualize the earlier treatment in self-psychological terms at the time, what transpired was largely a gradual unfolding of an idealizing transference that provided a nurturing selfobject experience. A strong empathic bond was sustained with very little sense of rupture and repair. Interpretive work remained on the level of "understanding" and rarely moved to Kohut's (1984) second level of "explanation." Partly because I was still working from a classical theoretical model with which I had become disenchanted but not ready to replace, I do not recall much interpretive clarity in this early work. Furthermore, it seemed important to allow a lengthy period of sustained empathic responsiveness and to allow the patient to progress at her own pace. She seemed very appreciative and insistent on this, and became very anxious at any attempts to explore her perceptions of me in any depth. In other words, I think that a prolonged and uninterpreted idealizing transference was unfolding that provided an essential nurturing experience and perhaps also failed to sustain a position of empathic inquiry into our relationship. Treatment was interrupted when the patient's acting out resulted in a serious financial disaster of which she was intensely ashamed. Her withdrawal took place over only a few weeks without plan or discussion and contact was totally broken off. She returned to treatment five years later on a four-times-a-week basis after her father's death left her financially comfortable. The sessions that will be presented took place four months after her return.

MONDAY 6/6

The atmosphere in this session is, as usual, friendly and warm while lacking any sense of aliveness as the patient talks about a situation at work where her boss, who is about to be let go by the board, is trying to make the patient her ally. My mind wanders, and then my attention returns as the patient, after a long silence, reports that she is "doing something to herself." In response to my encouragement, she relates that she is "numbing herself" so as not to feel anything or think anything. I (with my lapse of attention in mind) inquire if she has any awareness of what triggered her doing this to herself. She is visibly embarrassed and remains quiet.

My thoughts turn inward and I am aware that I am very comfortable with this patient. I feel no pressure to be anything more than a warm accepting listener or sometimes just a presence in the room as she sits in silence for varying amounts of time. I am never impatient or frustrated with her and in general do not feel any need to push her. I am comfortable staying with her slow, steady pace and trusting of a gradual unfolding process. Yet I am aware that my attention varies greatly in intensity and at this moment I question my complacency (still with interest rather than any sense of anxiety). I decide to wonder aloud if her numbing herself might be related to a subtle sense she might have of fluctuations in my attentiveness or in her own sense of connectedness.

The beginning of a shift is evident here. As soon as I decided to embark on this self-supervision I began to reflect on my own fluctuations of attention. I understood these fluctuations differently years ago; then I saw them as either indications that I was picking up the patient's resistance or as irrelevant mood changes in me. Now I have several self-psychological concepts to help me. I am alert to the possibility that her response might have been triggered by experiencing my lapse as a self-object failure. I also have a different understanding of resistance now. I sense the possibility that her defensive numbing might well be a protection against experiencing a painful loss of my attunement rather than seeing my lapse as a response to her numbness. In this moment I move closer to an empathic stance and also suggest a tentative "explanation" for her response. This seems to lead her into a more introspective and deeper therapeutic process.

She says she has a sense of when she began to close off. She hesitates to express it further and then briefly reassures me that it is in response to her own inner thoughts and not to any action of mine. We both acknowledge with interest that this represents a clear pattern (an invariant organizing principle). Blame is never attributed to me as a nurturant figure, but is often internalized instead. I tentatively offer an interpretation at this point. I suggest that perhaps her reluctance to see my contribution to her distress is related to a fear of losing her sense of being connected to me.

At this point the session flows easily. Mrs. A reports that the trigger for her numbing herself was her awareness of a wish to be more connected. She is excited with this awareness and says that both the numbing and the trigger were clearer this time than they ever were before. Then she relates an awareness of a fantasy she often has in sessions. There are a thousand people staring in silence, waiting for her to say the right thing. She wants very much to satisfy them, but feels totally inadequate and has no idea what they want.

After the session, I ponder my attitude toward Mrs. A. Is my comfortable acceptance of her pace a nurturant acceptance, the provision of a needed selfobject experience, or could it also, in part, interfere with the inquiring part of sustained empathic inquiry? And, how does my experience of the absence of demands in the relationship relate to the thousand people staring?

TUESDAY 6/7

As the session begins, I am struck by the contrast between my self-state in response to Mrs. A and my experience with the patient in the session just before. In the preceding session, that patient was distrustful and blaming. She felt she could not be vulnerable with me because I had my own ideas and beliefs that would interfere with responding to her and her needs. I felt on unsure ground, as if nothing I could say would be received as empathic or on target. At one point, I formulated the thought that the patient's experience of me was that who I was as a person interfered with her process. I voiced something tentatively in that direction; and as I said the words out loud, I felt peaceful. It became okay with me to have her see me as not good enough. The session then proceeded more easily with the patient realizing that she needed me to be different than who I am but could not verbalize it clearly.

As the session with Mrs. A unfolds I find myself still thinking about the contrast between my experience with the previous patient and my subjective state as I listen to Mrs. A. I become aware that the self-supervisory work I have been doing with Mrs. A helped me to decenter in a very uncomfortable session. As "difficult" patients do, the other patient was confronting me with a role about which I was not happy. My discomfort was clearly related to an intersubjective disjunction. The very overtness of the disjunction allowed me to become self-reflective and then return to a deeper grasp of the patient's experience and to a more peaceful acceptance of the situation.

As the session with Mrs. A continues I breathe a sigh of relief. The atmosphere in the room is not charged. My thoughts return to my interest in the intersubjective context in the present moment. My attention is focused and my self-state is comfortable. My presence as a nurturing selfobject is accepted and appreciated. In experiencing these contrasts I begin to wonder if some version of the difficult previous session lies beneath the surface of my relationship with Mrs. A. I am aware that I am far from eager for such an experience.

Mrs. A is silent as I go through this thought process inwardly. Now, as I am more clearly focused on her, she begins by relating that the long silence is her way of "getting a grip on herself." When she thinks about the last few sessions she feels as if she is "a pinball machine with a ball rolling around inside and hitting things—ringing buzzers and setting things off."

I begin to explore this rich imagery with her, but quickly find my thoughts returning to my previous more "difficult" patient. When I realize this I also notice that Mrs. A has become silent again. I inquire as to what she is experiencing as I think to myself that my wandering has perhaps triggered a feeling of abandonment and thus a "numbing" of herself. She flashes a lively smile and relates that she is clearly "doing it." She is aware of the trigger and is very reluctant to speak of it. "It is just totally against the rules."

Once expressed, the prohibition softens and she proceeds to tell me about her experience of these moments. It is different from my expectation that I am to be blamed—that my inattention was experienced as abandonment or evidence of my lacks. On the contrary, her clear experience is that she felt momentarily scared and was afraid that if she explored, or even expressed, her fear, it might be met with disapproval or disdain. To prevent this, she numbed herself and, as she experienced it, "made me disappear" by ignoring me.

She is afraid I will think her imagery is silly. I choose to disclose that I too experienced a "disappearing" at those moments. It feels a bit risky to let her know that I was, in fact, failing to sustain my end of our connection at those moments. She could experience it as a selfobject failure and abandonment, because after all, at some level, I feel that it is. On the contrary, she seems enlivened by my disclosure. Apparently, it validates her affective imagery. She becomes more open and tells me how afraid she is to expose these thoughts.

Later in the session it appears to me that although she is afraid of and attempting to limit my disapproval at those moments, what is actually limited by her behavior is the exposure of her pain and fears to my responsiveness. She is quiet momentarily—digesting what we have arrived at. Then she reports a sense that her head is being "stuffed." Her association to this experience is that it is "like when you need to cry and you can't." This leads to a recounting of many childhood experiences with "croup" and "stuffed sinus problems."

As the session ends, I go back to underline that what I heard as most important was her sense of taking total responsibility for her parents' or my lapses and that it seemed "against the rules" for her to see others as responsible. Mrs. A very thoughtfully mumbles something about how big they all were and then relates that it was really a collusion. "They never wanted to hear anything else. It would have made them uncomfortable." As she leaves the session she comments with some degree of excitement, "It was like a deal." As I say good-bye I gently add, "It doesn't sound like a good deal. Let's talk some more about it."

At this point the nature of the "nondifficult" impasse is coming into focus. The "deal" crystalizes what Brandchaft (1994) refers to as "structures of pathological accommodation." Mrs. A has developed a deeply learned pattern of accommodating to the needs of her selfobjects in order to maintain her connection to them along with the borrowed cohesiveness it provides. She diminishes and controls all expression of her own wants and feelings because these would have made her parents uncomfortable. So it becomes quite understandable that intersubjective disjunction poses a major threat of abandonment in the analysis and thus keeps her from opening herself to the growth process. What was still not clear to me at this point was my contribution to this impasse.

THURSDAY 6/9

The session begins with a lengthy description of the day's events at work. The boss's mother has died and Mrs. A has the chore of notifying a long list of friends and acquaintances. I decide to listen quietly, not sensing any affect or involvement in myself or the patient.

After what seems to me a long time, the report is halted and there is an awkward pause. In response to my inquiry into her experience of the early part of the session, she smiles, mildly embarrassed, and explains that she "doesn't know how to keep from doing what happened last time." We share some awareness that today's reporting is a related behavior. I remind her that what we need to do is to observe and explore what goes on between us, not necessarily to prevent anything.

After another long silence, during which I manage to sustain a good degree of quiet attentiveness, she smiles again and relates her discomfort whenever she experiences my paying attention to her. "It is as if I want it very much and at the same time I don't want it." Now she hears voices she experiences as "not her own," which she carefully distinguishes from a hallucination. "I hear a child's voice," she continues. "A child mimicking an adult. You know, like repeating a tone that she has heard an adult using. It says, 'Leave me alone—stop pestering me.' Then it becomes a little girl's voice, clearly frightened and pleading to be left alone. Finally, it sounds like a warning." She looks up at me with a frightened expression on her face and explains, "This is a crazy place—a place I don't go." As the session ends she asks, "If I let the voices speak, will they ever go away?" I try to be reassuring through my manner and nonverbal encouragement. I restrict my verbal response to an empathic reflection of knowing how scary it is to explore this place, at the same time choosing not to reassure her anxiety directly about the voices because I feel that to do so at this point will dilute the unfolding process. I am uneasy about the possibility that my lack of such reassurance might be experienced as a break in empathy. However, in the following session it appears that my response was experienced as empathically attuned in grasping her fears. As we shall see, Mrs. A seems encouraged by my understanding and goes on to reveal her fragmentation fears and her need for connectedness.

FRIDAY 6/10

This session, quite unlike the previous one, begins with a sense of aliveness and immediacy. "I am nuts," she says. "Ready to explode. I think I
have always had this fear. Now I'm so aware of it. I'm afraid I will fall
apart and be all in pieces. I won't be able to put myself together and
then you will leave before I can. I'll be all alone and apart. It is much
too scary when I am alone. I have to get a grip on myself—to keep
together."

    For an instant, I am inwardly frightened by the intense poignancy of
the patient's expression. Her frequently hospitalized psychotic sister
flashes into my mind and I want to call time out for a diagnostic conference with myself. I have images of presenting this case after the patient
falls apart and being asked how on earth I thought she was a candidate
for analytic treatment four times a week.

    I try to contain this process within myself, without communicating any
fear on my part, and note that it is probably not unrelated to her fear of
creating discomfort and rejection if she opens up. I reflect how painful
and frightening the thought of being left at the end of a session (while in
midprocess) can be. She relates a fantasy she has had of asking me to
promise that I won't leave her while she is in pieces. She explains that
when she is calm she knows that I wouldn't, but that when she is scared
it is hard to hold onto that. She adds, "Even though you have never
rejected me all these years, I haven't shown you this crazy place yet—so
it doesn't count."

    The session continues to flow although the patient is still frightened.
She describes how she sits poised to protect herself—to regain her grip
at any moment. We also explore some of the patterns of her life and
she is impressed by how much she does to avoid these feelings. There is
a great deal of sadness as she becomes aware of the cost of these protective devices in lost contact and intimacy.

    The focus sharpens onto our relationship and her need to keep me at
just the right distance—not too near, yet not too far away. "It is as if I
look up every now and then to be sure I haven't pushed you to where
you will be unreachable. It is like I want to be sure you are on the shelf,
but your attentiveness can't get too close because then I would feel all
this crazy stuff coming out."

    The session ends with Mrs. A becoming frightened that I will see her
as manipulative and pulling my strings. When I inquire into the meaning
of the word *manipulative*, she explains with a disdainful expression that
it relates to a dishonest controlling and that she would hate to be seen
that way. I respond that I see she feels very vulnerable in exposing her
need to control the distance between us and that her exploration of

these needs is certainly an honest expression (rather than a disguised manipulation).

As the session ends, she asks shyly if "all this is really okay." In contrast to the way I chose to respond yesterday, today I respond simply and directly to her request for reassurance. Perhaps this is, in part, being sensitive to how she might experience the fact that this is Friday (and thus just before the weekend interruption) and also in part a response to my sense of how much anxiety would facilitate the process or halt it. Then again, perhaps I just needed to make the simple human response at this time. As we part, I tell her with an enthusiastic warmth, "Yes, it is very okay—in fact exciting."

MONDAY 6/13

Interestingly, I find myself wanting to write about this session in the past tense (as most case material is presented), rather than in the "as it is happening" (present tense) style I used in presenting the previous sessions. I think that this reflects a shift in the intersubjective (transference/countertransference) atmosphere. At this point in the process, some things have changed. I think the patient has developed an increased capacity to reflect upon both her inner process and what she is experiencing with me. At the same time, as a result of my self-supervisory reflection on this material and my own subjective responses I was beginning to be able to decenter more completely than I had previously been able to do with this patient. I could see once again, with this patient too, that the subjective meaning of my responses (of who I am) may be different for the patient than for me. Decentering, of course, means focusing on the meaning things have for the patient. In the manner of a working-through process, analysts need to learn this lesson over and over again. The aim of reflective self- awareness in the analyst is to enable him to return to an empathic immersion in the patient's experience.

In today's session, I felt deeply confident in the work we were doing and the unfolding process. However, I remember myself as speaking frequently and I don't recall any specific interpretive activity. I think my comments were simply encouraging and empathic. It has become easier for me to sustain an attentive and inquiring focus. Perhaps my decision to write in the past tense reflects a momentary shift in the balance of my being a participant observer toward the observer side. I did not feel experience-distant. I felt very in tune in an experience-near way, yet more observer than participant.

Mrs. A also seemed to take a more observing or reflecting stance —perhaps in response to my stance or at least in a coordinated dance with mine. She began the session, after a rather brief pause, with a report that she had been thinking about the places she is not supposed to go and that she feels a trust and willingness to go into them. She explained, and I concurred, that it was not possible to just decide to do it intentionally, but that when it comes up she will be more on the side of going into the crazy feelings and sharing them with me than she had ever felt before.

She then proceeded to relate some thoughts and associations to her awareness of making a "deal" not to bring up anything that might make me uncomfortable in return for being able to keep me at just the right distance. After we shared a chuckle over her need to reassure me that it was about her father and not really about me, she began to explore the genetic roots of the "deal" in a way that was both clearer and emotionally more connected than ever before. She went back and forth between observations of her experience with me and her role in not upsetting each family member from early childhood through recent years.

Her father had a violent temper. She described him as "turning blue with disgust" if anyone said the wrong thing and recalled (with terror) his threat to "send her back to the Indians" (since she was adopted, she experienced this as both a real danger and an assault on her identity)—a statement that she was uncivilized and different from the rest of the family.

Her sister, Jane, was unstable and easily upset. She was frequently overtly delusional and eventually went through several hospitalizations. It was Mrs. A's role to understand and support her—certainly not to express anything that would provoke a fragmentation and psychotic withdrawal. Mother shared in the attempt to provide safety for Jane. She gave emotionally to Jane in a way she never did to the patient. Then, when she was drained, she turned to Mrs. A whose role was to help her get back a sense of order. To this day, mother begins phone conversations to Mrs. A with the phrase "Hello, is everything under control?"

Later in the session, Mrs. A connected her mother's need for her to "fix things" with her own sense of having to draw a line in the sand "and not let anyone get too close." "It is as if mother gets too close, she will suck something away from me and I won't have it anymore."

At one point she reflected on how much of her life had followed from her view that it is not safe to let anyone too close. She saw that she was holding to a view that organized all her experiences and that the view was, at least in part, erroneous. She experienced some sadness at this thought and then shifted to explaining that she had to draw that line or else she wouldn't have had any sense of herself. I reflected that it was quite understandable that she needed to hold to her way of viewing people in order to protect herself, and it was sad that it blocked her from some of the closeness she so much wanted. As the session ended she exclaimed with a sense of pain that until now she "couldn't even think about this organizing principle, it just operated."

TUESDAY 6/14

On Tuesday the session began with Mrs. A expressing a fear that I would become bored and give up on her. I asked if she had any sense that I was behaving in a way that might trigger that fear. I was finishing my lunch as she came in and wondered aloud if that might have been a trigger. She assured me that it was not anything I had done and talked briefly about how important her sense that I had never given up on her was to her ability to keep coming even when she felt hopeless and discouraged.

I inquired, "If not me right now, whom did you experience as giving up on you?" She spoke with a lot of quiet emotion of her sense that her birth mother had given her up and her fear that it was because of something about her. Even more poignant was her sense that in recent years, searches by birth mothers have become much easier (in contrast to a child's search for her parents). "Even years later, she could have tried to find me. It is as if she has given up again."

She then talked about how important not giving up was to her. It forms a strong core of who she is. She also talked at length about her sense that her father gave up on her and that when he threatened to "send her back to the Indians," it seemed to her a result of her wanting so much. She related, sadly, how she has erased so much of herself, hoping that he would approve of her. She was surprised that when he died, she felt a loss, even though she never felt he had given her very much.

Toward the end of the session, I offered my first interpretive comment in the past two sessions. I commented that perhaps her sense of loss at her father's death was related to the finality—that she had never given up her hope that if she "erased parts of herself" he would someday respond with the love and approval she yearned for, and now it was never to be. I affirmed that her quality of never giving up was a strength that in many ways helped her survive and feel a sense of cohesion in herself. Then I added that perhaps it also kept her in a "bad deal" whereby she sacrificed parts of herself and experienced others as failing to keep their end of the bargain, leaving her yearning and unfulfilled.

She was obviously moved as we sat quietly for a while. Then she related that she had begun to feel overwhelmed and was trying to understand it all. I said that sometimes it might be more important to just experience her feelings and there was no need to understand and keep it "under control" or even to put in words the sadness I could already see on her face. She cried quietly for a while, and as she was leaving she rested her head on my shoulder in a very peaceful embrace.

The peaceful embrace at the end of this session is clearly an important and controversial intervention. I experienced it as a natural response to the patient's reaching out. Mrs. A seemed to need a sense of connectedness with me and an encouraging support for her courage in beginning to open up areas that threatened to overwhelm her. What did this mean to the patient? It has become apparent, after several months of exploration of her experience of me once the impasse under discussion was loosened, that my responsiveness and emotional connection with her leads to considerable conflict. On one hand she has begun to experience it as an invitation to open up and to resume an intense developmental process. On the other hand, it represents a grave danger of retraumatization. She feels closeness as prohibited and threatening. It stirs overwhelming regressive needs. Physical touch runs the risk of increasing this conflict. At the same time, it can provide a sense of connectedness and safety to face overwhelming feelings. Closeness and distance in psychotherapy, and the pursuit of the optimal in responsiveness as well as in restraint, are the subject of many papers (e.g., Bacal, 1985; Livingston, 1991; Lindon, 1994; Shane and Shane, 1994). The issue of touch in analysis and what it means to each patient must be considered in the light of this work.

For the moment, let us consider Mrs. A's response. As we shall see in the next session, she begins to explore, more directly than she ever has done, some of her need to control closeness and distance with me and how that relates to our "deal." The material reflects some sense of danger—perhaps triggered in part by the physical contact. At the same time, the session is enlivened, we are both spontaneous, and the "deal" is explored. Perhaps the process was enhanced by the supportive contact and by the interpretive activity I reported. I do not think we can clearly separate the two. Also, my shift toward a willingness to "wear the attributes" is clearly in the atmosphere at this point. That shift, in my opinion, is the key to lifting the impasse.

THURSDAY 6/16

Mrs. A begins by relating that she has become aware that the tension beginning shortly before every session has more content than she has been reporting. "I feel a pressure," she relates, "a questioning of what am I going to do with you. I think about ways to distract you or to occupy you. It's like I am a lion tamer and you are the lion on a box. I have my whip and a chair and I have to watch you very carefully." She pauses briefly and I encourage her to go on. "I'm not allowed to say these things. If I do, or do anything at all to make you uncomfortable, then you will pounce. You will be on top of me—pinning me down and biting."

The rest of the session centers around how hard it is for her to see me this way—yet becoming increasingly conscious that she holds both views at the same time. She knows that she trusts me more than she has ever trusted anyone, yet she also fears that I will pounce upon her if she breaks the deal and fails to keep me comfortable.

I tell her the story of a man who keeps snapping his fingers. When he is asked why he does this, he explains that it keeps the lions away. When his friend exclaims that there are no lions within thousands of miles his smug reply is, "See, it works!" We laugh together as the session ends and talk briefly about how our "deal" is gradually and tentatively being challenged for the first time.

FRIDAY 6/17

"A sated lion is no danger to anyone." Mrs. A begins with a saying that has stuck in her mind since she read it in a novel last night. We both acknowledge the truth in the saying and leave its connection to the intersubjective context unverbalized for the moment.

"I feel a clear physical tension in my body," she reports. "I am ready to fight you." She stops to let me know how confusing and crazy it feels to express these experiences. We talk briefly about her fear that I will feel blamed for her fears and about her difficulty in clarifying my contribution to the experience. I decide that my repeated attempts at inviting her to talk about what I might be doing to trigger her fear seems counterproductive at this point.

My attempts at encouraging her to explore my role in perpetuating our "deal" seem unproductive as well. In fact, asking her to express what is not in her awareness at the moment is itself an empathic break and seems to increase her sense of craziness. I acknowledge, in an attempt to repair the break, that my requests seem to make her more uncomfortable. She responds by again assuring me that the feelings are within her; at the same time she does seem relieved by my comment. She then speculates, "The lion could be in me too. I erase parts of me that could be dangerous. I keep a grip on things."

It occurs to me that there is a meaningful connection here. What she is touching on is that she is afraid of her *own* wanting and hunger as well as the other person's. There is probably little clarity of separate self and object in this experience. I choose my response here with some thoughtfulness, keeping in mind the saying about the sated lion with which she began the session. I comment, "What I hear you saying is that it is the hunger which feels dangerous." Her reply is spontaneous and includes a touch of play. "Sure, if I'm the meal." Then she quiets down and expresses an awareness that her response raised some fear right in this moment.

I sense that this moment presents an opportunity to return to my temporarily suspended attempt to invite her to include my presence and responses as contributing to what I now see clearly as an impasse that has kept Mrs. A from attributing any qualities to me that might create an intersubjective disjunction—that is to say, in her language, she is not allowed to view me in any way that does not coincide with my view of myself. It is a soft and gentle impasse, the impasse of the "nondifficult patient," but it is, nevertheless, an impasse.

With a sense that we have been working through this impasse over several sessions and with a very quieted excitement, I inquire at this point if she "has ever seen me as hungry in some way." I sense that this material is within her awareness. There is a long pause during which I wait hopefully. My patience is rewarded as she—very timidly, at first—explains, "It isn't really hungry—at least that's not the word. The word is different, but it has all the feelings we are talking about as hunger." Then, with some growing sense of the validity of her experience, she says directly to me, "Your interest scares me. You look at me with intensity and interest. I want it and it is very scary."

I remain attentively silent as I realize that what I feel as one of my best qualities, my intense empathic listening stance, can in some way pose a danger to her emerging sense of self. This is a bittersweet moment for me. It is painful to hear that what I see as nurturing and wonderful can also be connected to something "bad." Memories flash through my mind like wildfire. I see myself as a little boy being interested in an aunt's beautiful inner thigh and feeling confused about what was all right. I remember some patients (as well as friends) who were uncomfortable with what they called my "overintensity." I somehow learned to channel that intense listening and wish for contact into my therapeutic stance, and I know that it is an important aspect of curative process with many people. So in this moment, I feel excited at the effect of my willingness to sustain an attitude of empathic inquiry and reflect on the organizing principles that have contributed to what had been a slow, draining quality in the work with Mrs. A. I feel excited and optimistic that my self-supervision is freeing up the logjam and that there is room for an increased spontaneity and some intersubjective disjunction. I also feel a bit confused and hurt.

I contain my own process pretty well and simply continue to listen attentively. This appears to be a good enough response as it enables

Mrs. A to go on to explore her experience of my interest. She feels ashamed and confused. She is afraid that she is encouraging the interest—after all, she does want it. She continues, "Maybe I will encourage it and it will be a misinterpretation. Then I'll feel humiliated. I want it and I don't want it. I'm confused about whether it is wrong for me. Is it shameful? It isn't clear whether these feelings relate to something that happened. I know I was always uncomfortable with my parent's friends who 'really loved me.' Their interest scared me. I didn't understand it. I told my mother I didn't want to go to visit them and she told me I was silly or that of course I wanted to see them. It colors my whole life. It certainly colors how I feel in therapy."

As she was leaving she asked if tomorrow was my birthday as she had thought. I acknowledged that it was, and she wished me a happy birthday. I said with a smile that it was nice that she remembered.

A half hour later she left a phone message on my machine. Tearfully she said that she "realized that not all interest has to be bad." Then she cheered up and, as if it was an unimportant incident, said, "I'm really glad that you were pleased that I remembered your birthday."

I felt good in response to the message. I understood it on two levels. Having finally let me know that my interest scared her, she is beginning to feel nurtured by it. In addition, her obviously significant experience of my pleasure at her remembering my birthday even after 5 years sounded to me like an affirmation that her interest in me is not shameful or bad but in fact is received as pleasurable.

In conclusion, I would like to underscore that the impasse of the "nondifficult" patient often centers, as it did with Mrs. A, around a need to maintain intersubjective conjunction. To understand more fully the patient's subjective experiences, the analyst must deepen his own reflective self-awareness. In the self-supervisory process presented I was clearly guided by several self-psychological and intersubjective concepts. These pointed up my discomfort in "wearing the attributes" Mrs. A needed to express and helped me to digest the validity of her perceptions of me and the subjective meanings my words and actions had for her. However, the key to really decentering and focusing on the patient's experience was a willingness first to go deeper into my own subjectivity and see how it interfered with the process. The patient's analysis took off as the analyst's self-analysis took off.

SUMMARY

"Difficult" patients, and the stormy transference/countertransference impasses they often trigger, have been the focus of a great number of

———— (1971), *The Analysis of the Self*. New York: International Universities Press.

———— (1984), *How Does Analysis Cure?* ed. A. Goldberg & P. Stepansky. Chicago: University of Chicago Press.

Lichtenberg, J., Lachmann, F. & Fosshage, J. (1992), *Self and Motivational Systems: Toward a Theory of Psychoanalytic Technique*. Hillsdale, NJ: The Analytic Press.

Lindon, J. (1994), Gratification and provision in psychoanalysis: Should we get rid of "the rule of abstinence"? *Psychoanal. Dial.*, 4: 549–582.

Livingston, M. (1991), *Near and Far: Closeness and Distance in Psychotherapy*. New York: Rivercross.

Shane, E. & Shane, M. (1994), In pursuit of the optimal in optimal frustration, optimal responsiveness, and optimal provision. Presented at the 17th Annual Conference on the Psychology of the Self, Chicago.

Stolorow, R. & Atwood, G. (1992), *Contexts of Being: The Intersubjective Foundations of Psychological Life*. Hillsdale, NJ: The Analytic Press.

Chapter 9

Empathy in Broader Perspective: A Technical Approach to the Consequences of the Negative Selfobject in Early Character Formation

Mark J. Gehrie

From the time of his earliest forays into the psychology of the self, Heinz Kohut (1959, 1966, 1971) emphasized the signal importance of empathy, "the mode by which one gathers psychological data about other people" (1966, p. 261), as the primary mode of access into the experiential world of the patient. His emphasis on this concept has had a reverberating effect throughout the analytic world and has been recognized by most analysts as a critical foundation for virtually every analytic intervention, although exactly how it is defined (beyond "vicarious introspection") has varied considerably, along with the specifics of its application and conception of its effects. Kohut's (1977) commitment to "long-term empathic immersion" (p. xxii) was a commitment to a methodology he considered not only essential for the pursuit of analytic goals, but a sine qua non of the analytic enterprise—one that vastly expands the analyst's capacity for understanding the range of the patient's experience, and communicating that understanding to the patient.

Throughout his work, Kohut went to some lengths to clarify that empathy was not a magical tool, and must not be used as a definer of the nature of the analytic transaction. He noted (1980) that "when we speak of scientific empathy as a mode of observation and as the definer of a scientific field of investigation, we are pointing to a value neutral *process* . . . or, as I prefer to say, to an *operation*. In other words, whatever term we choose, we must clearly distinguish empathy from the result to which the empathic operation leads" (p. 485). He added (1984): "we must beware of mythologizing empathy, this irreplaceable but by no means infallible depth psychological tool. Empathy is not God's gift bestowed only on an elect few" (p. 83).

Here empathy is affirmed as an "irreplaceable tool" for data gathering, and therefore as a guide to intervention, but explicitly not as a form of intervention per se. To reiterate, empathy informs interventions but does not *define* their nature or content. Kohut (1982) was specific about differentiating the levels of epistemology versus emotionality in discussing empathy: "We must differentiate between two levels: (a) empathy as an information-gathering activity, and (b) empathy as a powerful emotional bond between people" (p. 397). And again, quite directly: "In this sense empathy is never by itself supportive or therapeutic. It is, however, a necessary precondition to being successfully supportive and therapeutic" (p. 397). By implication, the nature of the way that the analyst communicates his understanding may vary enormously. Clinically, exactly what constitutes an "empathic" grasp of any given experience or situation varies with the range of possible experience, and may often refer to levels of experience which are not readily convertible to the usual means of (symbolic) verbal communication.

This, in turn, raises the possibility that under certain circumstances, an empathically informed response may take a shape or form that may not be immediately recognizable (to the objective observer) as most apparently "in tune with" or "responsive" to the manifest content of the patient's communication. It may not be possible, in other words, to predetermine a particular form of response as decidedly the "most empathic"; what in the end achieves that status must await the particulars of the unearthing of the patient's level of experience in focus at the moment. The nature of the response should be framed in the terms of that level if it is to have a chance of being utilized by the patient in a meaningful way. Particular forms of response, therefore (e.g., those characterized by the "mirroring" validation or affirmation of a patient's subjective experience), are appropriate to certain circumstances and not necessarily to others. Kohut (1982) was also specific about this: "I did not write about empathy as associated with any specific emotion such as, in particular, compassion or affection" (p. 396). When misapplied, such an approach may inadvertently become the independent rather than dependent variable in the analytic transaction.

In line with these considerations, it seems apparent that the across-the-board use of concepts such as "empathic attunement" or "optimal responsiveness" as behavioral guides for intervention and chief organizers for psychoanalytic technique in self psychology may in many instances fail to address several related contingencies. Among these contingencies are the following: 1) the emergence of hostility in the transference may not always be the product of an iatrogenically induced narcissistic injury ("empathic break"); 2) early developmental traumata may be mistaken for iatrogenic regressions belonging to the "here and now"; and 3) the use of some standardized, presumably "empathic" approach may elicit or determine specific phenomena that become observable in an on-going analytic interchange (as does any technique relied on with unswerving singularity) and may interfere with the emergence and recognition of other factors.

In reference to the first issue noted previously, as suggested by the case of Mr. K (Brandchaft, 1992) and in my discussion of Ornstein's (1993) case of a different Mr. K (Gehrie, 1993a), the analyst's responses were not in any meaningful way "unempathic" despite the clear breakdowns in the selfobject transferences. Ornstein (1993) reports that Mr. K required "explicit appreciation . . . unrestrained, explicit admiration . . . [even] outright jubilation" (pp. 149, 151) from the analyst in order to avoid an experience of disruption based on his "inner rage." Despite such efforts on Ornstein's part, "there was no carryover from one such apparently successful session to the next. It was as if in each session trust had to be built up again from the beginning" (p. 151). The loss of cohesiveness of the patient's self-experience could not, in other words, be reliably assigned in these instances to the analyst's failure to provide optimal selfobject functions. Under these conditions, the argument that their empathy was inadequate is tantamount to forcing the data into a theoretical framework in order to maintain the all-inclusiveness of the theory, at the expense of the clinical realities. As Stolorow (1993) has acknowledged, "In an apparent reversal of my earlier position, I wish to point out a potential pitfall of this emphasis on the newness of the selfobject experiences provided by the analyst's empathic communications: the danger of neglecting the contribution of the *patient's* psychological organization" (p. 36). Needless to say, the extreme positions on either end of this question are subject to the same considerations.

The second point, related to the first, addresses the likelihood that if the "here and now" in the analytic transaction becomes the primary focus of attention—along with an emphasis on empathic failures as the sole source of negative affects—then developmentally earlier phenomena that may conceivably be the source of such experiences are categorically excluded. It is precisely to such earlier phenomena, briefly alluded to by Kohut (1971, 1984) and Bacal and Newman (1990), that the issue of the effects of attachment in the formative period of life to structurally sustaining but negative, "noxious," or distorting selfobjects is relevant. It may not be, in other words, solely an issue of *failures* (on the continuum from traumatic to optimal) that is relevant to assessment of the long-term consequences of selfobject functioning, but also of the structural consequences concerning self-development and character of such negatively charged *attachments* in the early caretaking relationships.

In this sense, "failure" is too narrow a word to describe the developmental dynamic in question, and "deficit" too misleading a characterization of the consequences. Rather, the entirety (or perhaps nearly so) of attachments founded on profound negativism become every bit as developmentally significant as organizers of the psyche as do those attachments founded on more recognizably optimal emotional valences: mother's milk is swallowed and is structurally sustaining regardless of the defects or "distortions" of relating that come with it. (At somewhat later developmental levels, such dynamics may be encompassed under the rubric of "negative identifications" because of their more partial impact on the overall fabric of the self.) Consequently, transferences evolving from such early deformations of self-structure are not likely to reflect "ordinary" developmental fantasies (e.g., the absence of suitable opportunity for idealization). From a technical standpoint, under such circumstances, cohesion-enhancing responsiveness in an analytic environment of empathic attunement in which certain functional opportunities might be provided is not likely to achieve expectable results. In other words, the concept of "failure" as applied to the dynamics of early structure formation is the reflection of a moral position, rather than an observational position focusing on developmental dynamics per se (i.e., what matters is what [for example] the mother [or primary caretaker] *does*, and not what she does *not* do).

The psyche of the developing child (from this perspective) knows only what the mother does; it is only the external observer of the process of development, informed by a theory of caretaking adequacy, who brings into the equation a hierarchy of presumptions about developmental requirements. This is not to say that such requirements may not exist, but only that from within the internal perspective of the organizing self (structure), growth occurs around the environment that is experienced, whatever its qualities may be. This developmental phenomenon may be roughly illustrated by the example of a tree that grows in, around, and through a fence that is placed next to or over it; the trunk and branches may grow to incorporate the fence itself; the fence and tree become as intertwined as two distinct objects can be while each still retains its own existence, although heavily defined by the presence of the other. In an even more extreme version, if the tree is young and the fence is made of new wood, there may come to be actual shared structure. The development of the tree, under such circumstances, is not the result of a "failure," but rather a product of circumstance[1]: certainly the fence-builder might have avoided this development by placing the fence differently. We have tended to view development as defined by its presumed goals, rather than as a process without inherent values; the values that are added are those of culture and society in which particular sorts of characterological outcomes are preferred, or are more or less adaptive (less inconvenient) for the context.

To reiterate: the self is formed around early experience, and the result of this process becomes the "shape of the self" and the template through which the environment is subsequently experienced. This structure is reliably adaptive to the kind of experience that had been predominant during the formative period, and does not go away or fundamentally change due to the subsequent presence of an "empathic" environment. Structure accrues from experience during the formative period regardless of its valence; its substance includes the internalized, subjectively organized early versions of experience that tend to remain relatively constant over time, and subsequently acts as a kind of template through which new experiences are processed. The perspective of object relations theory is useful here, insofar as an important facet of the theory of the negative selfobject is a theory of attachment: the self is formed around attempts to maintain essential relatedness (see Fairbairn, 1952; Guntrip, 1961) to the early object through whatever means are possible. Self-experience is structuralized in this context—that which results from the attempts by the immature self to maintain emotional connectedness at any cost (see Gehrie, in press).

Under these conditions, the emergence of hostility in the transference may not relate to empathic failure in the usual sense; what amounts to an "empathic" response will of necessity be defined by the shape of the self in question (having been defined by the childhood ambience). Whereas for many "expectable" developmental patterns the analyst's "empathic" responsiveness will be recognizable in terms of the selfobject

---

[1] "This should not be confused with the concept of 'optimal failure' in analysis: that the selfobject transference "is disrupted time and again by the analyst's unavoidable, yet only temporary and thus nontraumatic, empathy failures—that is, his 'optimal failures'" (Kohut, 1984, p. 66). This theory of structure formation in analysis may not be completely analogous to structure formation in early life.

transferences that have already been described by Kohut (1971, 1977) and elaborated by many others, self-development that has taken place under more profoundly different circumstances may require empathy of a different sort.

The patient "turns back" (Kohut, 1984) to the archaic selfobject relationships because it is in that context that emotional safety is available and recognizable. The patient turns back when there is some disturbing discontinuity between the environment in the analysis and the structuralized expectations that are a reflection of the early developmental environment. The archaic transferences, therefore, are the reflections of this environment with the early caretakers, and simultaneously define the nature of the adaptive modifications during these earliest years. Empathy—or, more properly speaking, a psychological environment that facilitates the development of the capacity to reflect (Gehrie, 1993b)—must be defined precisely with reference to the specific archaic transference constellations and the character structures that present themselves; this is most challenging to the analyst when the early structuralizations have been organized around experiences that may be characterized as negative or "noxious." Valenstein's (1973) comments "on attachment to painful feelings" are especially relevant to this point: "[since] affects representing object experience could equally much crystallize in the direction of pain (*Unlust* rather than *Lust*), then it follows that the nature of the object tie during the earliest period of life is critical for the qualitative structuralization of affects" (p. 373).

With reference to the third issue raised at the outset, Goldberg (1990) reminds us that "every theory constrains us, and . . . we cannot practice without our guiding theories. But when our constraints seem no longer to reflect or develop our ideas, when we become servant to the procedure, then we must ask if something else is operating, especially if we are impeding the growth and development of our science" (pp. 5–6).

Gedo (1991) stresses the technical implications: "There are no clean vessels in psychoanalysis—our observations are never about the analysand per se; they are at best about the nature of the mutual influence exerted within the analytic dyad" (p. 90).

The across-the-board presumption that empathy is always the same thing—the acceptance of the patient's currently manifest subjective point of view, and always leads to a similar outcome, "the [remobilization of the] originally established selfobject transference" (Kohut, 1984, p. 67)—should be reexamined, especially in instances where there is a question as to whether the existing selfobject transference is the result of an analytically induced regression, or whether a chronic (traumatic) state of disorganization[2] is emerging and being smoothed over by an unceasingly soothing attitude of responsiveness. A key to recognizing such a condition might be the reappearance of such an underlying disturbance whenever such efforts are even temporarily interrupted or suspended. Kohut (1971) also referred to this issue in his discussion of the likelihood of the repetition of past patterns in the context of the breakdown of an idealizing transference. This is not the equivalent of an "empathic break" in which the analyst made a (nontraumatic) "mistake" in understanding, and in which the dynamics of the error are then explored by both analyst and analysand, leading to a healing of the breach and acquisition of "self-esteem regulating psychological structure in the analysand" (Kohut, 1984, p. 67). In the instances to which I refer, the analyst's acknowledgment of the error is not likely to have the effect noted previously; it is more likely to be met with an increasingly strident, anxious, or depressive reaction, indicating the failure of the ability of the analysand to process the dynamics of the experience, and the continuance of the uncontrollable traumatic repetition.

To hold at such moments to a theory which insists that the key to the difficulty must be an (iatrogenic) empathic failure is to limit our understanding of this other possibility, as well as to demand of the analyst that at all costs the patient must be protected from the potential of such a traumatic regression. Such events often take the form of what Gunther (1984) has described as an "archaic transference crisis." Gedo (1979, 1981, 1988) has proposed that such conditions be understood "as the continuous repetition of the experiential patterns that characterized the person's early life, particularly in terms of their affective coloring . . . [and that] a disruption of this 'structure' amounts to an interruption of the automatic repetition of these fundamental patterns" (1988, p. 74). For the purposes of this discussion, such underlying "patterns" form what I have earlier described as a "template" of subjective experience, which becomes an issue for treatment when efforts to maintain such a template result in increasingly costly [mal-]adaptive arrangements.

Such a "template" provides the structural components for what Freud (1920) called the "repetition compulsion," and what Gedo (1991) later described as "automatisms that do not necessarily involve any object relationship" (p. 87). Such "primitive" building blocks of character structure, Gedo continues, "are not pathological; they are woven into the fabric of adaptation seamlessly, as building blocks of the person's individuality, basic components of self-organization that guarantee the continuity of the subjective sense of self (Stern, 1985)" (p. 87).

---

[2] What Gedo and Goldberg (1973) have described as a "structural regression."

Rather, however, than turning toward the "biological bedrock" (Gedo, 1981) for the exploration of such basic underlying patterns of affect, I suggest that there exists an additional layer of the preverbal organization of subjectivity that is not immediately referable to biologically determined sets of programs for motivation, such as those described by Lichtenberg (1989). Although such "programs" do indeed relate to the biologically based propensity to repeat patterned experience, they do not explain the critical affective coloring that each individual's experiential template acquires. As Gedo (1991) notes, "these basic blueprints are accumulated through the mediations of affectivity into a need to repeat a set of concrete experiential states" (p. 40).

Under circumstances of the "optimal" variety, this template of early structure works silently, beneath and within the rest of the personality structure such that its presence is virtually not noticeable, and certainly in most analytic efforts its presence is not an issue in the exploration of either more developed or more archaic transferences. Typically, analytic interventions—whether organized around theoretical paradigms of conflict resolution or the treatment of developmental disturbances ("deficits")—tend to evoke and process transferences that reflect early object (or selfobject) relationships that become manifest in the "here and now" (Gill, 1979, 1982) of the analytic interaction. Meissner (1991) has also questioned whether such "archaic aspects . . . can be adequately regarded simply as transference manifestations or whether something else may not be involved. My own view is that something else may be in play, even when transference derivatives are detectable" (p. 37). For Meissner, the issue comes down to "real aspects of the intersection of their personalities . . . that have nothing to do with transference," and this leads him to "aspects of the therapeutic alliance."

In my own view, the underlying structures at issue form the basis for expressed archaic transferences, but may not be directly accessible for the management of such transferences in the here and now. The expressed transferences are the present-day version of this underlying structure, a kind of secondary-process derivative the engagement of which in terms of present-day interactions is not likely to impact the underlying organization. In many and perhaps most cases that we see in analysis, this does not become a technical difficulty precisely because it is the transferences that *are* the issue; "successful" analyses are those that properly address the range of transference issues on multiple levels; in those analyses the work is not interfered with by overwhelming structural features of a primarily negative sort that essentially limit the transference engagements to relatively superficial processing. Under ordinary circumstances, in other words, the underlying structure is not so profoundly organized around adaptations to negative affects. Negative selfobject relatedness as a bedrock for structure formation is a more perva-sive phenomenon than the analysis of transferences by ordinary means (viz., techniques of ego psychology or self psychology) is able to address; technique must take into account structural conditions of the personality that may preclude the "expectable" effects of such technique, and espe-cially when there is no or virtually no immediate access to some "positive transference" upon which we usually rely so heavily.

TECHNIQUE

Having outlined such a set of conditions, the unavoidable question that follows is, What do you do about it? A friendly colleague with whom I had shared some of these considerations accosted me after a recent pre-sentation about all this and demanded, "So how do you get such patients out of this [archaic] state? Dynamite?" As I have suggested pre-viously (Gehrie, 1993b), the answer is a qualified yes. Once the repeti-tion has been engaged, the old structures must be worked with before there is any opportunity for new development; therefore the technical management of the "here and now" must reflect this. The attempt to supply "optimal functions" in order to restabilize an underlying disequi-librium must be seen as a technique that produces its own effects, and may not on its own be adequate (in instances such as I am describing here) as a foundation for new growth to occur.

An analytic patient with a history of profound early losses complained bitterly and constantly about objectively small occurrences in the pattern of analytic transactions, such as minor (less than 60-second) differences in the analyst's and patient's reckoning of the time, or about how long he had to wait for an elevator in the analyst's building (rarely more than a minute), or whether the analyst could "really" be emotionally present with him because the previous patient was more interesting to the ana-lyst, and so on. No amount of understanding and acceptance of the patient's subjective experience, or interpretation about the meaning of such experience based on his past history, had much of an ameliorative effect. One day, exasperated by the umpteenth repetition of this litany, I exclaimed with some intensity, "Damn it! It seems like you'd rather keep criticizing me for all my 'failures' than to examine why so many things provoke these feelings in you. I do make mistakes! Mostly I don't! Don't you see that your complaints overwhelm everything else that happens here?" The patient started to cry softly, acknowledging, "You must mean so much to me. . . . I always come and you're always here . . . and when you just now were angry, I could feel that you cared about me."

Apparently, the analyst's affect demonstration was able to have an effect on this patient's experience beyond anything that had previously been communicated in more ordinary ways. The usual forms of analytic communication, including the validation of the patient's subjective experience, empathic attunement to the identifiable "failures" of the analyst in the interactive context, and the interpretation of the patient's experience in the transference and within a context of genetic reconstruction, were all of limited utility in establishing meaningful communication. When I finally got angry and permitted its expression (not so much "using" the countertransference as simply expressing it), this patient correctly assessed its meaning and "felt" the underlying affective connection. Certainly it could be argued that I missed the correct interpretive level or content meaning of the patient's experience (an issue that could be addressed only through an extensive case presentation, which is not the point of this chapter), but it is also true that as I became aware of the effects of this level of communication in the analysis, new possibilities did gradually open up, and issues that had been frozen in angry, resentful patterns of interaction began to become accessible. Furthermore, the constant retraumatizations that would occur with more "ordinary" attempts to access his experience began to diminish.

What happened? What was the "dynamite" and why did it work? My hypothesis about this interaction and its consequences (repeated countless times), is that despite the otherwise high-level functioning of this patient and his ability to grasp intellectually the symbolic interpretations that I had been offering, there remained a fundamentally inaccessible core of experience bound up with his early chronic-traumatic attachment to his mother, which my original approaches did not access. It was not that my interpretations were incorrect, but rather that the patient could not utilize them in the form in which I presented them (see Gedo, 1993). It appears as if the only access, at least initially, to such levels of preverbal, presymbolic experience must be constituted by experiences (in the interaction) that to some measure resemble the level on which the core template exists; the patient will "hear" the analyst's emotionality with this preverbal "ear" in a way that no higher-level, symbolically encoded communication alone could accomplish. Even if the content of the interpretation is intellectually unrecognized at this point, the patient's core experience will remain isolated without this quantum of level-appropriate emotionality (which had been the case in the clinical instance cited previously). After repeated "enactments" of this sort, combined with gradually increasing emphasis on verbalization and reflection, there may occur a gradual education of the patient to the *verbalized version* of this (otherwise inchoate) early experience. This constitutes the verbalizable construction of the past—the linguistic, cognitive encoding of early experiential templates through the use of a psychoanalytically informed emotional narrative.

A very high-functioning, professional woman patient with a history of early and chronic sexual abuse by her father began her analysis with a nearly intolerable level of anxiety that had not been apparent in the diagnostic, face-to-face interviews. She seemed especially panicky upon lying down on the couch, and could hardly speak—in marked contrast to her previous sophisticated communications. I immediately addressed this with her, but in order to tolerate talking about her experience it was necessary for me to suggest that she sit up and face me. It became apparent to her that despite her intellectual understanding of the arrangement, she felt as if she were about to be attacked by anal rape, and she was terrified. However, until she could keep her eye on me as we talked, the content of this intense and humiliating fantasy had not been coherently organized; she had not been able to formulate for herself the nature of her fear until the arrangement had been altered. After a few meetings like this, she was able to return to lying on the couch, and the analysis proceeded, incorporating this newly verbalized experience, which subsequently led to other discoveries. In this example, the experience was not accessible to meaningful verbal intervention until an action was instigated that had the effect of reducing overwhelming archaic affect surrounding the core template. Communication took place through postures rather than words.

The technical justification for such interventions is most apparent in instances such as these, but to varying degrees I suggest that virtually every analysis is likely to require some such maneuver if core issues are to be accessed. It is precisely a question of access, and not cure; these technical recommendations are intended to provide a context such that ordinary analytic work may then proceed. In every relationship there are multiple levels of simultaneous experience, of which only a small portion may be considered "manifest" on the most obvious, verbal level of interaction. This is true even if it is emotions that are being discussed. These other levels are not necessarily codified or easily recognizable in a verbalizable way, but are experienced as part of the milieu. Such issues are particularly relevant in the treatment of people for whom the earliest defining features of the "shape of the self" have been negative, and subsequently for whom the analytic relationship is so defined.

This suggests that in order for an analysis to progress, the fundamental organizing underlay of the self must be brought into the process. It is often not enough, however, to simply talk *about* the phenomenon (i.e., to "interpret" the presumed meaning of the patient's experience); this experience must be brought into the interaction and experientially reorganized by means of interventions that engage the underlying affective organization. Only secondarily will interpretation of the usual type have a chance to become relevant to progress in the analysis. Loewald (1981) has discussed an aspect of this phenomenon in his remarks on regression, in which he notes that "the analyst's adequately conveyed responsiveness" is of fundamental significance in the "flowering and course of the transference neurosis" (pp. 25, 26). More specifically, however, he stresses that gaining access to "regressive levels of the patient's mental life" allows them

> to be genuinely re-experienced and self-validated in their own right by virtue of the analyst's recognizing and validating responses that help to free the developmental thrust of those earlier levels as they are less encumbered by inhibiting defenses. I am not speaking of defenses against the "discharge" of impulses and feelings in action, but of defenses against that inner transformative development of impulses by which they can become integral elements of the total ego organization [p. 27].

This "restorative function" of regression relates to what I have described as the creation of a verbalized version of previously verbally unencoded experience. Loewald (1981) stresses that access to such "earlier and deeper levels" are able to be validated by the therapist through "*whatever forms such recognizing validation may have to take with different patients and at different moments during the treatment.* . . . [Such] validation affirms and confirms the dignity, the reality, and the truth of an experience and of its particular mode. It is, one might say, the reality test of inner experience, of psychic reality" (p. 29, italics added). I would add that it also makes such experience organizable and hence integrable with the rest of the psyche for the first time, and as such becomes an essential component of cure.

Turning to the role of the analyst, Loewald (1981) goes on to note that

> in order to be attuned to where the patient is at a given moment in his mental functioning, the therapist must be able to regress, temporarily, to that level ["trial identification"]. . . . This trial identification with the patient involves an identification, so to speak, with one's own (i.e., the therapist's) regressive level of experience; . . . the former does not occur without the latter. . . . An analytic interpretation starts, as it were, at the regressive level shared by the patient and the analyst and from there proceeds to reorganize that experience level within a more complex and more comprehensive context, i.e., on a higher level. The regressive experience is not thereby to be got rid of, excluded, or undone, but is to be encompassed in the novel organizing activity and organizational level as a dynamic element. An important part of working through is the interplay by which regressive and progressive levels of experience enliven and illuminate each other [pp. 34, 35].

Although the clinical example supplied by Loewald to illustrate the "transference-countertransference undercurrents" relates to more organized and developmentally advanced levels of experience, it is clear that the same principles would apply regardless of what underlying issues the patient presented with; that the analyst must find some means by which to access and address core organizing experience. Such goals provide a much more broadly defined set of technical potentials and emphasize product (the maintenance of analytic goals) over technical stricture.

NOTE ON TRANSFERENCE AND INTERPRETATION

Considering the foregoing issues requires the reassessment of the meaning of transference and its interpretation in such circumstances. What we ordinarily identify as "transferences" may be understood as observations of partial phenomena, rooted in the repetition compulsion, but more likely indicative of a more global phenomenon. Concentrating on these "partial phenomena" ("transferences") suffices in most ordinary instances in which the underlying structure of the self has not been massively "deformed" by early negative attachments. In this view, the underlying shape of the self is the source of all transference manifestations, and the motivation for their expression is the attempt to restore an earlier balance reflective, in a subjective sense, of a familiar "matched pattern" (Lichtenberg, 1989), in which some form of basic pleasure is reexperienced. Specific transference manifestations may represent only partial pictures of such attempts. From such a vantage point, the interpretation of any object-related transference constitutes only a portion of the pie and may leave untouched the underlying structural template.

Selfobject transferences may also be seen as representatives of partial phenomena, and although focused on self-experience, are often interpreted as if they were a kind of object transference, and as if the identification of the proper sequence of such transferences (mirror, idealization, twinship) is in itself evidence of the entirety of the relevant experiential domain. The underlying "iceberg" of self-structure—usually visible only through the "tip" which is above the surface, so to speak—may go untouched by the interpretation of select transferences of any type: we may trim the branches of the tree that grow out from the trunk, but if the trunk remains entwined with the fence through which it grew, then the fundamentals remain unchanged (and certainly unseen).

Many authors have acknowledged the indispensable role of the analyst's affect in accessing experience that lies at developmentally earlier levels of organization. Among them, Gedo (1979, 1988) offers an expanded definition of interpretation for communication with, and the teaching of "psychological skills" (including reality testing) that must be present for the processing of experience at these levels. Kohut's contributions have focused more on crucial sectors of self-experience which must be addressed if development is to proceed, and the expression of these sectors in the experiences of basic relatedness in an analysis. Goldberg (1988, 1990) has emphasized the principles of communication that involve the crucial shift from empathic understanding to explanation. Each of these venues, and the work of others, including Winnicott (1972), Leavy (1973), Valenstein (1973), and Modell (1990), have gradually shifted the attention of psychoanalysis toward broader questions of character formation (and deformation) in place of a more limited focus on specific transferences.

This focus has also had the effect of emphasizing that as more fundamental, underlying levels of possibly preverbal and presymbolic experience are addressed, the form of interpretations must more closely "echo the analysand's language" (Gedo, personal communication) rather than some technical presupposition about "neutrality" (Gedo, 1991). It has, however, been extremely difficult to specify the form that such level-appropriate interventions should take; if the "omnipotence of technique" (Gedo and Gehrie, 1993) is to be replaced by customized environments, then certain factors become even more important than before: 1) the correct assessment of the essential underlying level of affective experience in a patient's communication (which may rapidly shift), and 2) the willingness and ability of the analyst to access and reveal similar levels of emotionality in order that contact may be established: this is equivalent to permitting a (partial) dyadic enactment under circumstances in which communication of the more ordinary variety fails to establish such contact. For Gedo (personal communication), this has meant speaking in a "shared language" or with "one voice," so that interventions are not experienced as separate; he suggests that this leads to increased insight because it conveys a "more precise portrait" of the affective state. For Kohut and self psychology, the emphasis has been on empathy as the central means of data acquisition about these levels, and it has been assumed that an attitude of "optimal responsiveness" would overcome the technical difficulties inherent in assessing and responding to the proper levels of the patient's experience.

In my view, the management of enactments constituted by unconscious, nonverbal repetitions from a variety of developmental levels is a major personal and technical challenge, in which the relationship between analyst and analysand becomes a crucial *venue*, but in which the relationship itself does not constitute the treatment. It remains essential that as much of the underlying template as possible be brought into the light of the analytic transaction and subsequently transformed into secondary-process communications so that understanding may occur. The capacity to tolerate this transformation of levels of experience is one central factor in analyzability. Finally, specific transferences are points of entry to the more global characterological picture, and when warranted are used as such. These transferences, and the underlying organization from which they stem, do not become "resolved" through analytic intervention, but rather may become visible to the analytic eye, and hence capable of reprocessing (and ultimate transformation) in the analytic environment.

If a broader picture of underlying self-structure and organization is to be permitted to emerge, then the focus on specific transferences must give way to the elaboration of the more global underlying formations. Precisely because a large part of this template is likely to be organized in preverbal ways, the analyst's affect becomes the primary tool for (at least) the initial point of entry, and most likely will remain an essential medium for maintaining contact with these underlying levels. Under these circumstances, the "re-processing of transference-organized subjective experience" (Gehrie, 1993b) becomes a process goal of analysis, insofar as increased self-reflection may lead to new developmental opportunities.

A very mild-mannered young physician, a hand surgeon, sought analysis for his inability to establish a meaningful relationship with a woman of his own age and social class. He complained that he was "stuck" (for several years) in a relationship with a much older married woman "who is the embodiment of all my sexual fantasies." This woman was available to him "on demand" and seemed to be the perfect sexual "fit" insofar as her sexual desires coincided with what he desired from her. Beyond this aspect, however, he was frustrated and embarrassed with her in social situations, and did not feel that she was a a proper partner. He was terrified of revealing her existence to his family, and was forever trying to explain these things to her and get her to agree that she was not right for him so that she would "let him go." Although he would episodically establish relationships with other women who he felt were more appropriate for him, and whom he could imagine marrying and having a family with, none of them could hold a candle to this other woman's remarkable emotional and sexual availability. He felt like the moth caught circling the flame, mesmerized by it, and drawn ever closer.

The third of four children and the only son, the patient grew up with a hostile ambivalent relationship to his mother, who he felt blamed him for a (then unrecognized) Hirschsprung's disease, in which he suffered an absence of the physiological urge to defecate. He endured massive bowel obstructions, requiring enemas (given by his mother until age 14) followed by explosive, bloody bowel movements that would often occur at unpredictable times. These bowel problems and his attendant sense of dirtiness were the focus of their relationship, and the basis of his mother's (and several psychotherapists') interpretations about his "unwillingness to cooperate." He felt continuously "watched" by her in case he should have an "accident" (i.e., uncontrolled defecation) and felt overwhelmingly humiliated and guilty on such occasions. His attempts to "do whatever he could" to be the good boy and avoid conflict with his mother became a global orientation in his life and took on many displaced forms as he grew older; he would go far out of his way for even casual friends regardless of the personal cost in time, money, or inconvenience, and in general took the role of Good Samaritan to extremes. He would subsequently complain about all this, but felt that he had no choice lest he be open to criticism for not being a "good friend." He felt (and feels) that "everything is connected back to me if it is a problem . . . and if I don't fill the vacuum (of responsibility) I'll be blamed even if it wasn't my problem. So, solving other people's problems gives me relief. I can't stop people from getting mad at me. I can't make any move without causing problems. I wouldn't want to be you (the analyst), having to empathize with all this."

The father was essentially absent from the boy's experience, culminating in a divorce when the patient was eight years old, but was mostly away from home even up to that time. The patient recalls using the same approach to his father, that is, trying to be a "good boy" so that father would spend more time (or money) with him. It was especially devastating to the patient when, in his teens, the father got remarried to a woman with several children of her own, who (it seemed to the patient) were more liked, admired, and tended-to by the father than he was. He felt he had failed to be a "good son." He felt "wrongness in everything I did . . . with no possibility of escaping it." He feels his older sisters were extensions of his mother, always critical and judgmental, and the younger one he felt enslaved to "helping" in the (futile) attempt to gain his mother's approval.

At work in the hospital, although he was recognized as talented for his careful and successful clinical work, his characterological efforts to solve his personal dilemmas often took extreme forms, leading to his being the butt of jokes on the surgical unit: he often worked extra shifts as favors (which he was then reluctant to ask to have returned) and was mocked by the staff. On one such occasion, a young nurse in whom he had shown some romantic interest teased him about why he never emptied the patients' bedpans, who did he think he was, and so on. Feeling terribly accused, he arrived at the hospital earlier than usual the next day, and before scrubbing for surgery emptied all the bedpans on the unit—with the attendant fantasy that the nurse would be pleased and appreciative. She, of course, was flabbergasted and embarrassed and turned away from him, which he experienced as another rejection and criticism.

Needless to say, in the analysis at the outset the relationship to the analyst was filled with anxiety, but with the establishment of an empathic, understanding context in a mirror transference, he calmed down. As the patient came to feel "safer," there emerged a background but powerful idealization that provided the opportunity for a gradual move into an explanatory phase. We talked about his desperate seeking of affirmation in a mirror transference, and his anxiety in a negative mother transference. The effect of this was to lead to the strengthening of the idealizing transference in which the patient experienced the analyst as a "mentor." He seemed, in short, to be getting better, and although there were these profound changes within the analysis, the pattern of his outside life remained largely as it was.

He gradually came to feel that the analyst was not "doing enough" for him, that is, the analyst was focusing on the interaction inside the analysis, which was "well and good," but he felt he needed concrete instruction as to what to do about the problems in his "real life." This took the form of pressing the analyst for direction on problems with colleagues, friends, and his romantic life; he seemed unable to take the experience of the analysis and the understandings that he seemed to have gained into these other areas on his own. At first I found this puzzling, especially since the patient's engagement with the dynamics of the analytic interaction and their interpretation seemed very real and certainly not just an intellectual exercise: his affects were readily available and engaged with the process. He kept saying that he felt much better while he was in the treatment situation, but that somehow it failed to "impact" him enough to make him change his ways. In fact, he began to feel "blamed" in the context of the transference interpretations; the analytic process itself was experienced as a reenactment of the basic issue yet again. It seemed as if the selfobject transferences were significant sources of homeostasis, but that subsequent transference interpretations were understood yet not integrated, and hence of little use, leading only to retraumatization.

This state of affairs went on for a while, until the analyst began to shift the nature and focus of the interventions—less as a consequence of a specific plan to do so, but rather out of a sense that something was not being accessed. On one such occasion, the patient asked for a schedule change for the next day, and the analyst was unable to accommodate. The patient then asked if he would be charged for the missed hour (as per our long-standing agreement), and the analyst indicated that he would. (This response was in contrast to what had often transpired, in which the analyst would be more likely to address the underlying longings that the request seemed to contain). The patient flew into a rage (most unusual for the analysis), got up off the couch, and struck the wall with his fist. "God damn it! I try and try, and still nothing works! I talked with you about it, was reasonable about it and explained the circumstances, and it still made no difference!" He then burst into tears. Whereas at such a juncture I might have addressed his experience of the analyst's empathic "failure" (to understand and respond in a way that might have warded off the rage), and how he experienced the inter-action as he had the relationship with his mother (i.e., being charged for the missed hour would be a kind of punishment), in this instance I said, "You have been enraged your entire life, and you use this 'nice guy' stuff to keep it at bay! Now you want me to participate in this system, and protect you from your outrage about everything!" The patient replied: "I *am* angry about everything . . . and I feel like I have had to solve all of my parents' problems . . . and you're *making* it so I can't!" In the patient's experience, the analyst had finally "done" something ("empathic"), as painful as it was.

This patient's character had been so "distorted" by the nature of his early environment that the development of certain critical faculties, including reality testing and ordinary self-reflection, were significantly impaired. The essential failures of mirroring and idealizing selfobjects did not just leave empty spaces to be filled later, but were developmentally significant in terms of the adaptations that resulted in the establishment of a "structure" of accommodation, heavily reliant on negative identifica-tions with his mother. Everything was subject to intense criticism, and meaningful access to this character organization required an enactment that could then, possibly, be subjected to analysis. The interaction reported previously was no remarkable turning point in the analysis, but only one instance among many that have been repeated countless times, leading to gradual shifts in degrees of awareness. In a manner of speaking, these "crises" serve as functional moments when the patient is able to get a glimpse of the operation of his own character, and provide an essential backdrop for the subsequent interpretation of various spe-cific transferences; in this instance, he began to get some purchase on the negative mother transference (and his masochistic solutions) as he realized his need for the analyst to cooperate in "protecting" him from his rage.

The use of the analyst's affect in such ways may contribute to the development of the capacity of some patients to establish an emotional context for reflection and understanding of transferences that previously had not existed (Gehrie, 1993b). To a certain extent, each of the clinical examples cited here illustrate the re-creation of a piece of the emotional past accessed through an enactment in a new context. I would like to emphasize that this is not the equivalent of the analyst acting as a "new object," and neither is it the case that the patient experiences the analyst as a "new object." Rather, this example illustrates the establishment of a context in which previously split-off states may be brought into the analytic relationship. "Newness" in the relationship is to be had only when the "old" is experienced, understood, and integrated. "Newness" is not achieved through a laminate of relational experience with the analyst as if the old structuralized experience did not exist. When previously warded-off states are accessed, transference interpretations then begin to have a chance to be "heard," whereas previously they had been experienced without a sufficiently differentiated perspective. Given such conditions for the establishment of a perspective on character, early organizations may (to a certain extent) be able to become verbalizable instead of simply repeated. This is crucial for the utilizable recognition of various transference trends, and particularly in the instance of early sources of negativity that may be mistaken for selfobject failures in the present.

In conclusion, it seems useful to consider that the concept of psychological "deficit" does not imply the absence of structure. On the contrary, "deficits" are a kind of structure the true nature of which may be disguised by the availability of symbiotic assistance. The task of analysis is involved precisely with the struggle to provide a context in which these early developmental products (of "failures" in caretaking) may be revealed as the underlayment of character. There appears to be little reason to believe that different experience with the analyst alone— regardless of how salutary or reliable, etc.—will be adequate to influence this underlayment, and even runs the risk of complicating matters by creating an environment unrealistically adjusted to maladaptive structural requirements. In addition, the attempt to focus on specific transferences may, under certain conditions such as those outlined here, have the effect of re-creating the traumatic environment that was one source of the structural "malformation" (Pulver, 1991). This is especially true in instances in which the patient enters analysis already in a chronically regressed (and possibly traumatized) state that may not be fully recognized. Empathy, properly speaking, must include ways of responding to such negatively organized underlayment of character in ways that can be "heard" by the patient and used in the service of new development.

REFERENCES

Bacal, H. & Newman, K. (1990), *Theories of Object Relations: Bridges to Self Psychology.* New York: Columbia University Press.

Brandchaft, B. (1992), Codetermination and change in psychoanalysis. Unpublished manuscript. Presented at the Fifteenth Annual Conference on the Psychology of the Self. Beverly Hills, CA.

Fairbairn, W. R. D. (1952), *Psychoanalytic Studies of the Personality.* New York: Routledge.

Freud, S. (1920), Beyond the pleasure principle. *Standard Edition,* 18:7–64. London: Hogarth Press, 1955.

Gedo, J. (1979), *Beyond Interpretation.* New York: International Universities Press.

—— (1981), *Advances in Clinical Psychoanalysis.* New York: International Universities Press.

—— (1988), *The Mind in Disorder.* Hillsdale, NJ: The Analytic Press.

—— (1991), *The Biology of Clinical Encounters.* Hillsdale, NJ: The Analytic Press.

—— (1993), Psychoanalytische interventionen: Überlegungen zur form. *Psyche.* 47(2):130–147.

—— & Gehrie, M., eds. (1993), *Impasse and Innovation in Psychoanalysis: Clinical Case Seminars.* Hillsdale, NJ: The Analytic Press.

—— & Goldberg, A. (1973), *Models of the Mind.* Chicago: Univ. of Chicago Press.

Gehrie, M. (1993a), Commentary on Marohn's "rage without content" and Ornstein's "chronic rage from underground." In: *The Widening Scope of Self Psychology, Progress in Self Psychology, Vol. 9,* ed. A. Goldberg. Hillsdale, NJ: The Analytic Press, pp. 159–165.

—— (1993b), Psychoanalytic technique and the development of the capacity to reflect. *J. Amer. Psychoanal. Assn.,* 41(4):1083–1111.

—— (in preparation), *Forms of Relatedness.*

Gill, M. (1979), The analysis of the transference. *J. Amer. Psychoanal. Assn.,* 27 (Suppl.):263–288.

—— (1982), *Analysis of Transference.* New York: International Universities Press.

Goldberg, A. (1988), *A Fresh Look at Psychoanalysis.* Hillsdale, NJ: The Analytic Press.

—— (1990), *The Prisonhouse of Psychoanalysis.* Hillsdale, NJ: The Analytic Press.

Gunther, M. (1984), The prototypic archaic transference crisis: Critical encounters of the archaic kind. In: *Psychoanalysis: The Vital Issues, Vol. 2,* ed. G. Pollock & J. Gedo. New York: International Universities Press, pp. 69–96.

Guntrip, H. (1961), The schizoid problem, regression, and the struggle to preserve an ego. In: *Schizoid Phenomena, Object Relations and the Self* (1992, tenth printing). New York: International Universities Press, pp. 49–86.

Kohut, H. (1959), Introspection, empathy, and psychoanalysis. *J. Amer. Psychoanal. Assn.,* 7:459–483.

—— (1966), Forms and transformations of narcissism. *J. Amer. Psychoanal. Assn.,* 14:243–272.

—— (1971), *The Analysis of the Self.* New York: International Universities Press.

—— (1977), *The Restoration of the Self.* New York: International Universities Press.

—— (1980), Summarizing reflections. In: *Advances in Self Psychology,* ed. A. Goldberg. New York: International Universities Press, pp. 473–554.

—— (1982), Introspection, empathy, and the semicircle of mental health. *Internat. J. Psycho-Anal.,* 63:345–407.

—— (1984), *How Does Analysis Cure?* ed. A. Goldberg & P. Stepansky. Chicago: University of Chicago Press.

Leavy, S. (1973), Psychoanalytic interpretation. *The Psychoanalytic Study of the Child*, 28:305–330. New Haven, CT: International Universities Press.

Lichtenberg, J. (1989), *Psychoanalysis and Motivation*. Hillsdale, NJ: The Analytic Press.

Loewald, H. (1981), Regression: Some general considerations. *Psychoanal. Quart.*, 50:22–43.

Meissner, W. (1991), A decade of psychoanalytic praxis. *Psychoanal. Inq.*, 11:30–64.

Modell, A. (1990), *Other Times, Other Realities: Toward a Theory of Psychoanalytic Treatment*. Cambridge: Harvard University Press.

Ornstein, P. (1993), Chronic rage from underground: Reflections on its structure and treatment. In: *The Widening Scope of Self Psychology, Progress in Self Psychology, Vol. 9*, ed. A. Goldberg. Hillsdale, NJ: The Analytic Press, pp. 143–158.

Pulver, S. (1991), Psychoanalytic technique: Progress during the past decade. *Psychoanal. Quart.*, 11:65–87.

Stern, D. (1985), *The Interpersonal World of the Infant*. New York: Basic Books.

Stolorow, R. (1993), Thoughts on the nature and therapeutic action of psychoanalytic interpretation. In: *The Widening Scope of Self Psychology, Progress in Self Psychology, Vol. 9*, ed. A. Goldberg. Hillsdale, NJ: The Analytic Press, pp. 31–44.

Valenstein, A. (1973), On attachment to painful feelings and the negative therapeutic reaction. *The Psychoanalytic Study of the Child*, 28:365–394. New Haven, CT: Yale University Press.

Winnicott, D. (1972), Fragments of an analysis. In: *Tactics and Techniques in Psychoanalytic Therapy*, ed. P. Giovacchini. New York: Science House, pp. 455–693.

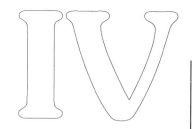

Child
Studies

Chapter 10

A Self-Psychological Approach to Child Therapy: A Case Study

Ruth Banovitz Suth

"I don't know how you did it, but you sure got rid of my fears." Keith, almost 10 years old, said this to me one month before we terminated a biweekly therapy lasting four and a half years. His words illustrate the creative nature of a self-psychological therapy. The purpose of the case material is to illustrate how self psychology as a theory is appropriate as a model of treatment for children. The case presented demonstrates the process of the patient's individual therapy, which utilized play therapy, verbal interactions and interpretations, and shared experiences, along with a combined treatment approach that included collaborative parental involvement.[1] The work with the parents demonstrates the inherent value in mobilizing a different set of responses within the child's environment to facilitate age-appropriate growth and development. The work with the patient was based on an empathic attunement and treatment ambience which allowed for the emergence of fluctuating idealizing, mirroring and alter-ego selfobject transferences and responses. Through transmuting internalization in an optimally responsive environ-

The author wishes to thank Joseph Palombo, M.A., Allen Siegel, M.D., Andrew Suth, M.A., Marian Tolpin, M.D., and Jeffrey Trop, M.D. for their help in editing this paper, as well as for their continued support and encouragement.

[1] This material was presented with the consent of both the patient and his parents. In giving consent, the parents again expressed their pleasure with the outcome of the treatment and said, "We were a great team." Keith was pleased with the possibility of our work being helpful to other "kids" and their families. Although the identity of this family is protected, the material is not disguised.

ment, the patient was able to internalize appropriate selfobject functions, resulting in the reorganization and further development of self-structure. The patient's dreams were a fairly accurate diagnostic tool throughout therapy in that they reflected how the patient experienced himself and the areas in which he was struggling. As such, they were also an indicator of the changes taking place in his self-experience.

CLINICAL MATERIAL

Keith began treatment at the age of five and a half and continued until he was 10. This family was referred by their pediatrician shortly after they moved to a new area because of the father's business. Keith had an older sister, Sarah, age nine, and a younger brother, Kevin, age two. Diagnostic evaluation included a joint session with parents and individual sessions with both Keith and his parents.

The parents were extremely concerned about Keith. They saw him as anxious, depressed, and oppositional. Symptoms had intensified since about age four. At the time of referral, Keith was having nightmares from which he awoke crying and in terror. One or the other of the parents would go into his room to try to soothe him. In spite of his parents' attempts to calm him, Keith often remained very agitated. When he was unable to fall back to sleep, he would often take a blanket and sleep outside his parents' room, or he would sleep in his younger brother's room in order not to be alone. His parents felt there was a correlation between the dreams and the times when Keith was punished. Punishments usually consisted of sitting on the steps, no TV, or no Nintendo. They resulted from Keith's failing to listen, having a tantrum, or being unable to calm himself down. He would also be punished for watching a video that he knew would give him a nightmare. Keith would often shatter when his parents tried to set limits (many times he would be inconsolable for hours), but he would also punish himself by sitting on the steps when he thought he was bad. His parents described him as having "terrible black moods" that were chaotic and unpredictable. He was extremely oppositional; if his parents said the sky was blue, he would say it was raining. The week before they called me, Keith had decided to run away because he was so unhappy and angry with his parents. Keith had wanted to buy a cap gun, claiming he could if he wanted to, even though his parents refused to give permission. He packed his sleeping bag, took his own money, and said he wanted to run away. His mother was frightened and did not want to let him go. His father, however, refused to intervene, and his mother did not interfere with his departure. He left the house and walked several blocks to a relative's home. His parents did not follow him, but the relatives called them when he arrived. He stayed there several hours until he had calmed down; his uncle then brought him home. His parents were extremely upset by his distress and their inability to intervene effectively. This incident was one of the precipitating factors for the referral.

During diagnostic sessions, the parents reported the following dreams Keith told them about. In the first dream, Goofy was the captain of a team on which Keith was playing. Keith told of being unable to catch the "discus" or to participate in any of the sports the team was playing. In reality, the parents described Keith as an excellent athlete, but one who would fall apart if he made a mistake. Keith also had another dream in which a "mummy" came alive and he had to chop off its head. To do so, Keith had to close one of two gates (one was a good gate, the other a bad one). He had to close the bad gate in order to kill the mummy and was unable to do so.

The background history of family is as follows. Both parents are extremely bright and gifted. The father, age 40, is the president of a well-known corporation. His work requires frequent travel and public appearances. The mother is extremely talented and is beginning to be recognized in a creative field that allows her to work at home and still be available for her children. The father describes himself as very intense and goal directed from early childhood. The paternal grandfather was educated and successful, but was physically and emotionally abusive to the father. The paternal grandmother, though sometimes critical, was very involved with the father, but was unable to protect him from the paternal grandfather. Once the father left for college, he never returned home. His academic accomplishments were outstanding and he was soon recognized as an exceptional entrepreneur.

The mother was the oldest of two siblings. The maternal grandmother was reclusive and had difficulty in sustaining relationships with family members and friends. The maternal grandfather was a more gentle man. He had a warm relationship with Keith's mother, but the maternal grandmother was jealous of their closeness. She was often enraged and abusive to the mother.

Keith's parents met during college and married after graduation, despite objections by both sets of parents because they were so young. The father was extremely busy pursuing his career during the mother's first two pregnancies and played a minimal part in caretaking. After Kevin was born, he tried to work more regular hours and be more available to the family. The mother describes her pregnancy and labor with Keith as normal. However, during the pregnancy, the maternal grandmother died suddenly in a car accident. The maternal grandfather died a few years earlier. The maternal grandmother's death devastated the mother, who was extremely depressed during the remainder of the pregnancy and during the first year of Keith's life. However, she was delighted to have a son and remembered Keith as being a "wonderful, warm, affectionate baby."

The mother had few specific memories of his first year except that she nursed him for nine months and carried him around with her constantly. The father remembered Keith as a "sunny" infant who, at 13 months, became "wild, fast, big, and tough." Both parents agreed that at 16 months they felt he became a "terror" and was impossible to handle. He climbed and touched everything; they saw him as destructive and unable or unwilling to accept any limits. Both parents became quite strict in an attempt to contain him, wondering at times if they were too rigid. They felt completely helpless in dealing with him. At age three, Keith went to nursery school and then to Montessori classes, as he expressed a wish to do "real work." The parents saw Keith as extremely bright and talented; they felt he could achieve anything he wanted if he could overcome his emotional problems. They described him as moody, unpredictable, anxious, and sad. A typical conversation could include the following: "Go away, I want to eat, I don't want anything, I hate myself. I don't deserve to eat, I deserve a punishment. I'm stupid." Keith found it very difficult to play by himself. When left alone, he would sit and watch TV for hours, which his parents thought was not productive or desirable.

The older sister had been openly angry about his birth, and the parents felt she played a big role in Keith's problems. Keith constantly sought acceptance and acknowledgment from Sarah, but she would have nothing to do with him. Or she would tease him because he was so fearful or "such a baby." Keith, in turn, was extremely nurturing and protective of Kevin. Parents felt that he was able to compensate for Sarah's abuse and exclusion of him in his closeness with Kevin.

Regarding peer relationships, Keith had only one friend with whom he played. David, also age five, was perceived by his parents as a "neglected" child. Both his parents worked and David frequently played with Keith at their home. Keith's parents saw David as exploitive of Keith; Keith was unable to assert himself or be self-protective with David because he was so fearful of losing his friendship. One incident that particularly upset the parents was when the father found Keith and David playing in the nude, drawing pictures on each other's bodies. David's parents were very distraught and found this behavior to be completely inappropriate. School was Keith's only conflict-free area. He enjoyed the work, performed well, and had no problems with the teacher or with other children. However, he made no attempt to make plans with his classmates outside of school.

Keith's mother brought him to his first appointment. There was something appealing about this little boy, and I immediately felt engaged by him. He separated easily from his mother, and we went upstairs to my office. I suggested he sit on the couch across from my chair and he did so. His manner was compliant; he sat with his hands folded, motionless, looking at me, and waiting. Although he may have been scared, his primary affect seemed to be sadness. Keith appeared cautious, resigned, and inhibited. There was little evidence of vitality and spontaneity. I asked Keith what he knew about coming to see me. He told me he knew his parents had met with me and were concerned about his nightmares. I wondered if he could tell me more about what was bothering him. When he began speaking, he was extremely articulate and capable of relaying feelings and facts. He said that although his worries might sound silly, they were really sort of scary. He had nightmares three nights in a row; once he had three in one night. Many times the nightmares were about Goofy, who was throwing a discus. Sometimes Keith felt he was Goofy, other times he was himself. Then a "mummy" would appear, and Keith, wearing a dagger, had to chop off his head. Sometimes Keith awoke screaming and was afraid to go back to sleep. As we were talking, I asked a few questions about the dreams, primarily about his feelings and associations to the content. As he spoke, I became increasingly aware of his terror and fear of going to sleep. In my responses, I felt that Keith sensed my attunement with him as he continued to share his dreams and thoughts. The image of a discus thrower and his father recurred throughout several dreams. Keith's only association was that a discus thrower was powerful and that his father had more power than the whole family put together. In other dreams, Goofy was a clumsy and ineffectual coach. He was "not real smart" (the same way he was in a favorite video of Keith's). I suggested that Keith sometimes felt like Goofy, clumsy and unable to protect himself from these frightening dreams and feelings.

In our next session, Keith immediately began talking about the dreams. He had them every time he was punished, except that he had three nightmares in one night after he watched the video about Goofy while his parents were out for the evening. While watching the video, he would sometimes get excited or he would feel sad. I wondered if he watched the video to try to stop the sad feelings. Keith thought about what I said, and thought it might be possible. When he felt sad, he also thought about building a tree house. Keith asked if he could draw the tree house for me and proceeded to make several detailed sketches. Mother had promised him one for a long time, but whenever he asked about it, he felt she ignored him. She also ignored him when he wanted to rent or buy new Nintendo games. Although he really wanted a lot of gifts, he felt he didn't deserve them, as he had not done that many things for his mom and dad. His affect was flat and solemn, and he was unable to elaborate on his failures. I said it sounded like he felt he had disappointed them. He agreed. Sometimes he got so angry at himself, he would shut off Nintendo games just when he reached the highest level, thus preventing himself from winning. We both agreed how hard it was for him to hold on to a good feeling about himself.

The diagnostic evaluation consisted of one joint session with the parents, one individual session with each of the parents, and two individual sessions with Keith. The diagnostic formulation was as follows. I felt that Keith did not have the capacity to regulate and soothe himself. He seemed to be overwhelmed by his own feelings and his inability to exert control over himself. Once he was out of control, he would feel terrible about himself, experience himself as bad, and have a need to be punished. I felt he was suffering from a depression that could be reactive or related to his self-deficits that led to his deregulation. One contributing factor to the underlying depression was his inability to idealize his parents and then use them to regulate himself. There may also have been something in his endowment and temperament that made it more difficult for him to use what the parents did have to offer him. His underlying irritability led to the feeling that nothing was right. He was easily frustrated and when he got out of control, he deprived himself of the mirroring he needed to strengthen his vulnerable experience of himself. His primary issues were not around a competitve relationship with his father, but around his self-deficits and his longing for a relationship with the idealized father. I recommended that Keith be seen twice a week in individual therapy and that his parents be seen regularly, together or individually, depending on their needs as parents and on Keith's needs as they emerged in therapy.

The focus with the parents was to help them acquire parenting skills and provide selfobject functions that were age appropriate and developmentally attuned to Keith. While helping them become better selfobjects in the here and now, I was working with Keith in the treatment to fill in the older deficits. Both parents had experienced deficits in their relationships with their own parents and had not acquired the capacity for protective parenting (e.g., the failure to intervene in Keith's running away). Running away appeared to be a desperate attempt to make an impact on his parents (efficacy needs) and to get help with self-regulation (idealizing needs). These very bright and verbal parents seemed to lack the instinct for action that would interfere with potentially destructive behavior. Because of the highly verbal quality of their interactions, the parents were unable to resonate with Keith's needs for active intervention to ward off danger and fragmentation. Both parents were extremely invested in Keith and motivated to help him and improve their relationship with him.

In subsequent contacts, I was struck by the nature of their struggles with Keith. Often they would fight with him as if he were a peer or a sibling, turning to each other for validation. For example, if Keith would defy his father, the father would turn to the mother and say, "Did you see that?" The parents were extremely responsive to my interventions with them and often one or the other would call in between the regularly scheduled appointments. For example, during the first year of treatment, the father called to talk about how impossible it was to set limits with Keith. He told of a situation where he warned Keith several times not to take Kevin's car. Keith did not listen to his father and kept grabbing the car, dropping it behind the couch, and reducing Kevin to tears. Finally, Keith's father exploded and Keith was punished. The father had a hard time grasping any other way of handling the situation.

While understanding how difficult it was for the father to feel so ineffectual, we worked hard on helping him see a way of intervening that would avoid verbal threats and power struggles. I urged the father to interfere before the situation escalated by taking the toy away from Keith, giving it to Kevin, and helping to soothe and calm Keith, thus protecting both of them. Again, the focus was on helping the father provide regulation, with minimal verbal intervention. Keith desperately needed to idealize his father, and by being "bad" he ended up terrorized by a father whom he continued to admire at his own expense. The mother also needed help in regulating Keith's behavior and allowing him to make more autonomous choices without feeling endangered. For example, one morning Keith completely fell apart when she insisted he wear a certain kind of shirt instead of the one he had chosen. Keith was unable to calm himself and cried for three hours, finally going to school two hours late. When his mother became so frustrated with her inability to calm Keith, he and his father would become aligned. After this incident, his mother refused to care for Keith and his father took over the morning and evening care-taking.

In an individual session, the father had complained there was no way but his wife's. She, on the other hand, complained about the father's detachment and impatience. I tried to help the mother give Keith more age-appropriate choices and accept Keith's need for permission to be either dependent or more autonomous, depending on the signals she picked up from him. For example, there was one week when Keith wanted his mother to brush his teeth for him. Although his mother thought this was ridiculous, as he was completely capable of doing so for himself, I urged her to agree because he seemed to be expressing a longing for her to care for him. After about a week, he resumed brushing his own teeth and the situation never came up again. Both parents desperately wanted to be "good" parents; they just needed help in learning there was a wide variety of choices available to them, depending on what would best resonate with their children's needs. Their work with me was primarily related to Keith's therapy. Both parents ultimately sought individual therapy.

The process of my therapy with Keith was as follows. During the first few months, he was extremely verbal and continued to talk about his dreams or make up stories that he dictated to me. He moved into the therapeutic relationship quite easily and was probably using his verbal and imaginative skills with me, much as he did with his parents and other adults. However, there was no sign of the negative and defiant behavior that he demonstrated at home. He was always extremely polite and restrained when I went to get him after his mother or father dropped him off.

I am including a few of the stories he told me to demonstrate the richness of this young boy's fantasy life, his innate talents, and the continuance of themes that were introduced in the diagnostic evaluation. The stories were as follows:

The Genie

Genie was coming home from work and there were some blue jays flying around. An enormous eagle came, and the family used magic dust and a magic rope, but it didn't work. The whole family shot at the eagle with guns and bows and arrows. Then there were three more eagles. They boarded up the house and shot them with cannons. Two other baby eagles came and they were very strong. The family had tiny pins and arrows to shoot the eagles when they got closer to the walls. It didn't work and they finally used a tiny cannon and it did work. They were surprised. The end.

The Dragon Killer

A little boy was walking down a mountain and found a cave and a dragon. The dragon asked the boy if he wanted a picnic and the little boy said no. He went further down the mountain to his castle and got his father, the Dragon Slayer. The little boy and his father walked up the mountain. The dragon asked them if they wanted a picnic. The father started fighting the dragon, but he was just pretending. Then there was a big gust of smoke and they all went down to the castle and had a party. The end.

The Genie Who Was Hero

There were some eagles who were trained to attack other people. The eagles were made out of metal and had computers in their head. The Genie used his magic rope to get off his carpet and save all the people. The Genie was the hero. Keith associated him to his father. Father had more magic than anyone. The end.

The themes in all these stories were expressions of Keith's feelings of helplessness and his longing for the protection of idealized adults, particularly of his father. He was searching for the "magic" that would allow him to feel more empowered, in better control, and less vulnerable or easily injured. He also wished for more shared experiences with his father, which would provide him with a feeling of kinship and mutuality. These longings were interpreted to Keith throughout the treatment, as were his struggles to idealize his own power.

Keith kept relaying nightmares, stories, and illustrations for several months. In addition, he repeated various events or occurrences that happened to him or to his family. When he acted out stories or thought about them in his head, he usually took the role of the good people. One guy kept turning back and forth from good to bad, and Keith tried to save him. Keith explained that in the middle of his brain, there was a good gate and a bad gate. When he had nightmares, the two gates mixed together. Here again is the recurring theme of Keith's difficulty in self-regulation and his fear of being unable to contain his anger. During these early sessions, I continued to acknowledge how scary it must feel to be unable to control how he felt or acted, and how hard that made it for him to feel safe. I also connected to Keith's embarrassment about the nightmares and tantrums, particularly when they made him feel self-conscious in front of his family. I felt that Keith was longing for the acceptance and protection of his idealized father, but saw himself as a disappointment. He also sensed himself as different and was in need of validation from both parents for his own uniqueness and specialness.

Our relationship continued to develop, and I sensed that Keith felt increasingly comfortable and safe with me. He had been playing with Legos at home and wondered if we could build together. He brought in a few models that we completed; we continued working with Legos or other building materials for at least a year. One kit we tried was too hard, and when Keith became frustrated with it, I acknowledged his disappointment at being unsuccessful. I suggested we put the kit away for a while and try it when he was a little older. This intervention helped Keith to deal with his frustration in a way that did not shatter his grandiosity. When Keith got irritated or frustrated with himself, I suggested we stop for a minute or so until he was able to calm down. He responded extremely well to these interventions and became increasingly more capable of regulating himself. First we built together; gradually the process shifted so that I became the facilitator and assistant. I found the parts Keith needed for his constructions, and he built them, with increasing skill and spontaneity. Although still very intense, he was more relaxed and better able to tolerate his mistakes and frustrations. I felt he was able to use me as a source of soothing, regulating, mirroring, and validation for his accomplishments. His increasing ability to regulate himself made it possible for him to tolerate the mirroring and mend his self-esteem.

Our sessions settled into the following pattern. Keith would come into my office, sit down, talk to me for 10 to 15 minutes, and then ask if we could work on a project. When talking, he reviewed the events of his week or spoke specifically about something that was bothering him. When I compared Keith's information with that received from his parents, I found him to be a fairly accurate reporter. He always gave me a good sense of his life outside the office. For the first two years we spoke of his nightmares and fears. During one session (age seven), he told of his discomfort about an impending family vacation. He was scared of going to an unfamiliar place and sleeping in a strange bed. He also did not want to be belittled by his family about his fears. His anxiety about being viewed as a disappointment or as different was a recurring theme, as was his concern about the impact of his anxiety on the family. He did not want to hold them back, but couldn't help being scared. We talked about how ashamed he felt because of his fears and his feeling different from other people. I encouraged him to talk to me about the fears and in doing so, hoped that by my continued acknowledgment of his feelings, he would be better able to tolerate and accept his feeling states without shame. Keith thought it might help if he could imagine the vacation in detail and we did so, talking about the imagined surroundings and the feelings he might have. For example, we discussed how one might feel uncomfortable in a strange room until it felt more familiar. Parents were also very aware of Keith's feelings, and we had a session before their vacation to help them in being supportive and protective of him.

After two years, the nightmares and tantrums diminished, as did the punishments. He still had a particularly hard time when one or both parents were gone. As we began our third year of treatment, I took a vacation for 17 days. It was the longest trip I had taken since Keith began his therapy. We made a calendar showing when I would be gone, something we had also done with parents' trips in order to help Keith feel more in charge and less disoriented by their absences. When I returned, Keith resumed his therapy. A few weeks later, he told his mother he wanted to take a "vacation" from therapy, just for a few times. His mother said it would be okay, but he had to call me himself. When he did, he was unable to give a reason for the request, he just wanted to. I said it would be fine and we would resume at the end of two sessions, which we did.

When Keith returned from his "vacation," we talked about how important it was for him to be able to leave and not be the only one left behind. Keith had often said, "When my parents are away, it doesn't feel the same to me as when my parents take care of me." He missed both his parents, particularly his father, who traveled frequently. He reported the following dream during one of his father's trips. In the dream, a little boy, dressed in his father's clothes, was seated at the dining room table; he had to take care of the family while his father was away. After his return, I suggested, it didn't feel the same when I was gone, and he must have felt the same way he did in his dream about wearing his father's clothes. He gave me a little half-smile and said he didn't like it when I took such a long vacation. I smiled and said, "So you wanted to show me how you felt. You took a vacation too." He smiled and said, "You always seem to know what I'm thinking, even when I don't say it." The vacation had been experienced by Keith as a rupture. He expressed his anger in his decision to take his own vacation. This is an example of the disruption-restoration process in treatment. His behavior might also be seen as his fulfilling efficacy and adversarial needs. He wanted to make an impact on me and protest my absence. My responses showed him he could be heard and be assertive without injuring me and threatening the relationship, that is, he could have a separate center of initiative without being endangered.

During the next two years, Keith made many changes. He began to participate in a team sport that gave him a sense of kinship with his peers. Both his coaches and his teammates admired his athletic prowess. One day he called me up to ask if I could come to a game on a Saturday afternoon. I decided to attend the game as an enactment of my validation of him. This decision was consistent with my conviction regarding the importance of a child sometimes needing more than a verbal interpretation of his longings for a selfobject experience with the therapist. His parents were there, and his father was videotaping the game. The entire family was supportive of Keith's participation and attended out-of-town games when he was on the all-star team. During our sessions, Keith was able to talk about how good it felt to be admired by his family, as opposed to all those times he felt they experienced him as "weird." At the same time, Keith was becoming an outstanding and disciplined student. He read voraciously for pleasure. His friendships expanded to several boys and even "a very good pal who was a girl." He began to accompany his father on some business trips and shared other mutual experiences with his father such as hiking, camping, and skiing.

He moved out of his brother's room into his own, which he and his mother redecorated together. At his insistence, he went to overnight camp for two weeks during the summer after third grade (age nine). He took an active part in choosing the program with the help of a camp counselor and his parents. The camp experience was extremely successful and Keith was proud of himself. The following summer he once again took an active part in planning his activities. He took two summer school courses and explored the neighborhood on his new bike. He was insistent about his wish for autonomy and independence and ably demonstrated his initiative and responsibility.

After the summer, at the beginning of our fourth year, Keith reported the following dream. He was on a mountain for his first day of skiing. He was trying to remember how to make turns. He kept falling, but he would get back up and do it again until he was finally able to go down the hill twice. When he finished, he walked through a door at the bottom of the hill and his father was waiting to pick him up in the car. As Keith associated to the dream, he recalled a time in Colorado when he lost control, flew through the air, and hit the ground. His father had to rescue him. He felt very good in this dream because he was able to help himself. I wondered about the door and his father picking him up. Keith thought a moment, smiled, and said it was kind of like leaving my house and having his father pick him up, as he often did. Keith said, "I guess I'm learning how to take better care of myself, and somehow you're teaching me." This was a lovely moment of mutuality and alignment with each other.

During the spring of the last year of treatment, Keith became very interested in making models, particularly rockets. We began building them together, but clearly Keith was the expert and my role was peripheral. Although his standards were very high, he was able to tolerate mistakes or imperfections. In fact, he assured me we did not have to worry if there were slight deviations. He worked confidently and competently, clearly enjoying the task and his expertise. During the summer, he took a course in rocketry and launched several rockets he had built. We had been working on the rockets for about five months and Keith wondered if we could launch them in the fall. I thought about it carefully, and again I thought the shared experience would be more valuable than a verbal interpretation. We decided to launch the rockets while his parents were away on vacation.

Throughout that summer, I felt that Keith was ready to consider termination. In August, he came in, sat down, and began looking at my bookshelves and the titles of some of the books. He noticed several on child and adolescent psychology. He knew they were all different, as they had different colored covers. But they were all about psychology. He wondered if I had read them all. I said I had read many of them and parts of almost all of them. Why was he asking? He wondered what psychology really was and how it worked. In other words, "What do you guys really do?" I wondered what he thought we did. He knew we helped people with their worries and that it worked because he was a lot happier. His nightmares had disappeared, and he recently had a really great dream. He dreamed he could fly. He could really feel it. Then Kogi and Dick (cartoon characters) popped into his dream. When he tried to fly again, he seemed to have forgotten how. Keith kept trying and all of a sudden it worked. He felt great. I felt this dream was evidence of a healthy exhibitionism as seen in his elation from the experience of successfully mastering the ability to fly. We talked about how good it was to feel his own power.

At our next session, he came in looking rather serious and anxious, which was now unusual for him. I said it looked like he had something on his mind. This was hard to say, but even though he really liked coming to see me, he didn't think he needed to come anymore. I knew how hard it was for him to tell me this, but I wanted him to know how glad I was that he could do so. Keith had really been worried; he didn't want me to be upset or angry with him. Again, I reiterated how pleased I was that he could tell me how he felt, and I agreed we should think about ending our sessions. But my feelings weren't hurt; in fact, although I would miss him, I was pleased for him that he felt happier inside and more confident about himself. I wanted to discuss his worry about my being angry and that this must be a feeling he has with other people as well. Keith said that sometimes he worries that people will be upset with him if he says how he feels or what he wants. But he really tries to stand up for himself and not be afraid, the way he used to be. As we talked, he seemed to enjoy comparing his past and present feelings. Thinking about termination, Keith suggested that he could stop for a while and then come back. I said he could always come back if he wanted to—I would be here—but I then explained a little more about what stopping meant. We decided to terminate six weeks later, around the time of his 10th birthday. He entered the date into his digital watch, making it a reality for both of us.

During the next six weeks, we spent more time thinking about what had happened in our work together, and the difference in how Keith felt. A lot of time was spent talking about how angry Keith used to get. He said he was very "bad" when he first came here; he would have tantrums and break things whenever he got upset. Now it's different—even if he's upset, he can walk away and not hit people. I said it was as if we had put a thermostat in him. He loved that metaphor. Keith recalled playing tennis with his father, making one bad serve, and then quitting. Now he continued playing, even if he wasn't happy with his game. In many situations, he used to get so angry at himself that it ruined the rest of the day. Now if he got angry, only five minutes was ruined. If he was still upset, he tried to do something that helped him feel better. Keith really enjoyed defining the areas where he had been scared or worried and describing the differences in how he felt now. Even if he was scared, he tried new things, just as he had tried overnight camp. When other people got angry, sometimes it was better to leave them alone until they got over it. For example, his father used to get angry more easily, but now he has "mellowed out" a lot. He only gets mad for about a minute and it isn't as frightening to Keith. He doesn't know why, but he and his mother rarely fight anymore. His mother used to keep her anger inside. If she let it out, she could explode. Now, his mother doesn't seem as angry, and they share many special times together. Keith kept looking at himself in relation to his parents and his siblings, and it was clear that he saw them as more human and saw himself as more like them and as an integral part of the family. It was also evident he was aware of the changes he had made, both in his behavior and in his experience of himself. He knew his therapy had resulted in these changes but, like many children and even some adults, he could not describe the process of his therapy or recall many specific insights or interpretations that had resulted in his improved subjective experience of himself and his improved capacity to function.

Treatment was culminated with Keith and I going to the park and shooting off his rockets. In so doing, we were symbolically "launching" both Keith and his rockets. This event was an enactment of an alter-ego selfobject experience. It was an exciting and memorable shared experience. I interpreted that just as we had built Keith's rockets, so had we built his sense of himself, a sense of self that was stronger, happier, and more capable than before. Keith said, "You mean that now I feel like those rockets look. We really did it, didn't we?"

DISCUSSION

There is a wide spectrum of opinion regarding the role of interpretation and understanding to achieve conscious insights. This case presentation represents one point of view in which the treatment is seen as a vehicle for the analytic process, and for the continuation of the developmental process. The goal of the therapist was to provide the patient with an affective experience in a therapy that provided a "background of safety" (Sandler and Freud, 1985, p. 375). This "background of safety" was built up through the continuity and depth of the emotional experience in the treatment, and it was in this environment that the patient's experience of himself was altered.

Self psychology focuses on the patient's experience of himself and the acquisition of an improved sense of well-being and resiliency (Wolf,

1988). The therapeutic work was based on a self-psychological appraisal of what this boy needed as his fluctuating selfobject transferences emerged. By the living through and interpretation of the integrative transference, the patient was able to emerge at the end of treatment with a newly acquired sense of internal strength. This newly developed self-structure was not merely the result of the patient entering latency. Without his developing capacities for self-regulation, he would have found the tasks of this stage much more difficult. My work with the parents helped them to become better selfobjects to Keith in the here and now, and my work with Keith helped to fill in the older deficits so that he was better able to continue his developmental process and utilize his peers, parents, and other adults for the acquisition of skills and the provision of experiences of likeness and belonging.

Although current thinking in self psychology circles is divided as to whether a valid distinction can be made between analysis and psychotherapy, the therapist clearly felt psychotherapy was the treatment of choice. In analysis, we are theoretically dealing primarily with transference interpretations. For Keith, the issue was not simply to deal with the transference distortions of and defenses against selfobject needs, but to deal with the absence of a selfobject experience that could have provided those needs. His primary issue was not anxiety around a competitive relationship with his father, but instead around his longing for a structure-building relationship with his idealized father. The central theme in Keith's therapy is the unfolding of an idealizing transference and its resolution. In other words, Keith needed to acquire the capacity for self-regulation through the idealization of the therapist. The nature of his deficits indicated he needed more than an interpretative approach. He needed an experience with a selfobject that would fill in those deficits and then provide him with an understanding of what those deficits were.

Throughout the treatment, the therapist had to decide how best to accomplish the goals of the therapy, by verbal interpretations or by mutually shared experiences. In applying self psychology to this child, both techniques were used. The therapist made many decisions that extended the boundaries of the therapy to a shared experience, both inside and outside of the office (e.g., attending a sports event or deciding to actually launch a rocket we had built together). These decisions reflected the therapist's belief that there is a significant difference, particularly for a child, between sharing an experience and interpreting the longing for or meaning of a shared experience. Erikson (1962) distinguishes between reality and actuality as follows: "*Reality* then is the world of phenomenal experience, perceived with a minimum of idiosyncratic distortion and a maximum of joint validation; while *actuality* is the world of participation, shared with a minimum of defensive maneuvers and a maximum of mutual activation" (p. 463). Erikson is arguing for the therapist to understand the patient's need for an actuality consistent with his inner and outer reality and with his developmental needs. For Keith, a shared participation in his launching of the rockets we had built was an insistence on the importance of the therapist recognizing his need for a mutual participation that would not be satisfied by a verbal interpretation.

SUMMARY

This is a clinical presentation of the therapy of a five-year-old boy, lasting four and a half years. The patient entered treatment because of recurrent nightmares, severe anxiety, and depression. He shattered easily and would cry for hours without being able to accept soothing or to calm himself down. The treatment plan was for the patient to be seen twice a week and for the parents to be seen collaboratively, both on a regular and an as-needed basis. The patient's therapy was based on an empathic attunement and treatment ambience that allowed for the emergence of fluctuating idealizing, mirroring, and alter-ego transferences and responses. The primary tools of therapy were play, verbalizations, dreams, and fantasy. Verbal interpretations were made in all these areas, in an atmosphere of shared mutuality. This material demonstrates treatment with a child from the vantage point of self psychology. It illustrates how it was necessary to engage in a therapy mindful of the need for verbal interpretation, but also reliant on shared subjective and empathic experiences to build self structure. Changes in Keith were contingent not only on therapeutic intervention, but on changes in the responses from his environment as well. A combined treatment approach that included collaborative parental involvement was therefore employed, resulting in a different set of interactions within the child's environment to facilitate age-appropriate growth and development. He indicated a lessening of narcissistic vulnerability and greater insight into his capabilities. By the end of treatment, Keith acquired the kind of functional change in himself we are looking for, the kind of change that is necessary for the patient to be able to experience an improved sense of well-being, vitality, and resiliency.

REFERENCES

Erikson, E. (1962), Reality and actuality. *J. Amer. Psychoanal. Assn.,* 10:451–474.

Sandler, J. & Freud, A. (1985), *The Analysis of Defense: The Ego and Mechanisms of Defense Revisited*. New York: International Universities Press.

Wolf, E. (1988), *Treating the Self: Elements of Clinical Self Psychology*. New York: Guilford.

Chapter 11

Discussion of "A Self-Psychological Approach to Child Therapy: A Case Study"

Morton Shane

Ruth Suth has presented us with a wonderful description of an extremely effective child therapy organized, understood, and effected in a self-psychological framework. We are indeed fortunate to have such a child case study because there are, as yet, precious few of them in print, and the value of work such as hers will surely be to encourage others along this same line. She herself contrasts her work with that done in accordance with classical theory, using a distinction pointed out by Ernest Wolf for that purpose, and it seems to me that in my discussion it may be useful to expand upon Suth's presentation from this perspective, comparing and contrasting her work with the classical child analytic model. You may remember that the principal distinction between self psychology and classical analysis identified by Wolf (1988), and referred to here by Suth, is that those analyzed in a classical way gain knowledge of themselves, as contrasted with those analyzed in a self-psychological way, who gain an improved sense of the subjective experience of them-selves—in other words, consistent with the patient's own goals on entering treatment, the patient comes to feel better, and the why and hows seem only secondary. Keith's end of treatment observation, "I don't know how you did it, but you sure got rid of my fears," would seem pertinent here, with Suth's chapter being an answer to Keith's query. For my own part, I'm not sure this particular distinction holds, particularly for children who notoriously forget a large amount of their psychotherapeutic experience, regardless of the theoretical orientation of the therapy, but there are other distinctions that seem more persuasive, at least to me.

Suth has a particular approach to this case that, although encompassing the format of child analysis, incorporates significant differences, attributable, I believe, to the self-psychological theoretical stance. As to format, the work she does is neither family therapy, nor does it leave out the family. That is, Ruth centers her work on Keith, but in so doing, she does not neglect the power and continuing influence on the child of his mother and father in the here and now. This important stance vis-à-vis the parental surround is in clear contrast to the more classical child analytic approach, which, although always sensitive to parental influence, is by theory committed to a model of internalized conflict. In a classical model, then, the child's pathology is conceptualized as stemming from the past, as being unconscious, and now more or less impervious to current parental influence, putting the parents and their contemporary impact somewhat in the background. The analytic process itself in classical child work centers around the nodal transferences, or the transference neurosis, as it unfolds in relation to the analyst, requiring elucidation and interpretation within the therapeutic hours in order for the child to experience real and effective change. Of course, as in adult analysis, one interpretation alone is not expected to do the job of uncovering the unconscious contributants to the internalized, unconscious conflict; rather, an extensive period of working through is required. The ongoing developmental experiences with the analyst (i.e., the new object relationship) is viewed in classical analysis as secondary, if it is acknowledged at all.

You can hear how this approach to child work is in marked contrast to Suth's presentation. It is not that Suth was unaware of the traumatic history regarding her patient's life with his parents, their insensitivity to his needs, their unfortunate handling of his powerful anxieties, and their inability to respond appropriately to his requirement for soothing and containment. Suth, too, most likely conceptualizes these experiences as having created in her patient intrapsychic conflicts and developmental difficulties. But she apparently views the conflicts not as sequestered and circumscribed within the child, but, more importantly, as ongoing and interactive with the significant people in Keith's intimate family environment. That is, the unconscious conflicts resulting from past traumatic experience are viewed as open to day-to-day current interactions. Therefore, a different strategy of treatment is employed. You will note that interpretation is not central to Suth's work; rather, a sensitive attunement to Keith's self-states is in the foreground. Moreover, because she conceptualizes the trauma as ongoing rather than in the past, she met regularly with the parents in an effort to effect change in their general parenting style. This is not to say she was not interested in Keith's past, or unknowledgeable about the impact on Keith's development of Keith's parents' fantasies, both conscious and unconscious. For example, Suth notes that his father viewed Keith at the young age of 13 months as "wild, fast, big, and tough." She notes also that both parents saw Keith as destructive and unwilling to accept limits, viewing him as autonomous and independent beyond his years, as exemplified by the father's apparent lack of concern when Keith actually ran away from home at the age of five.

She is also very sensitive to the formative experience of Keith's parents, demonstrating to us how each parent had been abused in their own childhoods and were consequently impaired in their ability to parent Keith smoothly and effectively. When Suth reports, then, that Keith says, "I hate myself and I deserve punishment and I am stupid," she is cognizant that something important has been internalized, built into his character, and influences his interactions and his sense of self-worth. And she is also aware of "conflict-free" areas in Keith's life, operating when he is away from home, at school. Nevertheless, Suth's approach is to deal with the here and now. She is not so interested in going back into his brief history, when Kevin was born, for example, or in dwelling on possible unconscious sexual fantasies that might be present, buried somewhere (maybe buried in the theory). Rather, she sees in relation to Keith the kind of transference experiences that have been described in the self-psychological literature, as we have heard: the mirroring, idealizing, alter-ego, adversarial, and efficacy selfobject experiences. These transference manifestations are not interpreted, not worked through in the way familiar to classical analysis, but are, rather, as I have written about elsewhere, *lived through* in the current new object–selfobject relationship. This is, incidently, how I understand Kohut's original use of the term "transferencelike" relationships, rather than "transference" per se, when he first (1971) described his salient selfobject transference contributions.

Let me illustrate these differences in technique I am drawing between the classical approach to the child and Suth's self-psychological approach with some clinical episodes taken from Suth's chapter that highlight the distinction between a classical child analytic approach and a self-psychological one. (I feel especially qualified to comment on this distinction, having made a transition from the classical child analytic approach I learned in my training, and taught for many years, to a self-psychological–developmental approach, which I now use clinically and in my teaching and supervision.)

The first example occurs early in the treatment when Suth notes that there was no sign in the treatment with her of the negative and defiant behavior Keith had exhibited so often with his parents at home. A classical analyst would be suspicious that such defiance and negativity would need to emerge in the transference, as the conflict that produced this behavior was internalized and could only be resolved through interpretation in the analytic relationship. If this behavior failed to emerge, as with Keith and his therapist, the friendly relationship would be conceptualized as a defense against its expression, and the analyst might say to Keith that he seems to need to be nice and agreeable because he is afraid to show other feelings that he does express at home. But Suth apparently did not view the absence of negative and defiant behavior as defensive; rather, she saw Keith's cooperative and friendly responses to her as resulting from new selfobject experiences that were in themselves developmentally meliorative. She did not postulate, therefore, that the aggression stemming from past relationships *had* to emerge and be expressed with her.

When Keith did defy her later on in the treatment, by taking his own two-week vacation from therapy, she understood this behavior as a clear response to her own vacation, conceptualizing even this rather mild defiance on his part as structure building through fulfillment of his current efficacy and adversarial selfobject needs. When she interpreted that he wanted to show her how he felt when she left him, Keith did confirm clearly the correct fit of her comments with his own experience. He said, "You always seem to know what I'm thinking even when I don't say it." It seems important to note that this expression of the idealizing selfobject transference is not interpreted by Suth, as it might be in a classical analysis where idealization is most often seen as a defense against destructive aggression, and in any case, a gratification for the patient that proper technique dictates should be frustrated so that the underlying unconscious fantasy can be uncovered and tamed. Obviously Suth views it differently, the idealization evident in his praise of her being development enhancing and confirmatory of his sense of being understood by her.

As I review this clinical work, I am reminded of Wolf's (1988) understanding of countertransference in the self-psychological model, that is, that the analyst inevitably needs the patient to fulfill his or her selfobject needs, mature or otherwise, in order to gain a sense of competence and effectuality as an analyst. I don't know what Keith does for Suth, but I know what such a patient would do for me in this regard; Keith confirms so beautifully his therapist's understanding of him.

The next clinical example, the dream of flying, inevitably evokes in all analysts more speculative and fanciful musings. Here the dream illustrates the many options that child therapists have for understanding specific and isolated material in their work with patients. Irrespective of context, a dream of flying (if such a thing were possible) in classical work is most often seen in males as some kind of erection experience. In Kleinian analysis it is seen as an expression of grandiosity. In self psychology, too, grandiosity is posited, without the defensive cast inherent in the Kleinian model. I was surprised to hear from a self-psychological colleague who knew Kohut well that Kohut believed in the universality of fantasies of flying. I am unaware of any studies that would verify this belief. It is my conviction that any fantasy or dream can only be understood in its idiosyncratic personal meaning and context. So it is pleasurable to note that in this case presentation, the dream of flying is viewed in the context of the specific, ongoing therapeutic work; Keith is understood through the dream to feel powerful, strong, and effective, reflective of the progress he already had made in his therapy. However, I cannot imagine a classical analyst refraining from making a connection between the cartoon character of Dick popping up in the dream, to paraphrase Keith himself, as a very specific reference to the child's erect penis. In this same interpretation, the rockets fired off by Keith at the end of treatment, with Suth looking on in admiration, would inevitably be seen by this same classical analyst as a *phallic* exhibitionistic achievement, perhaps saying to Keith, "Shooting off the rocket means to you that someday you, too, will have a penis as large and powerful and impressive as your father's, a penis that will impress everyone, including me." This is, after all, the central configuration in the classical approach, postulated as a universal phase of libidinal development. I wonder, would Keith have responded to that interpretation in the same way he did to the one that Suth gave?

Suth told Keith, "Just as we have built your rockets, so we have built your sense of self, a sense of self that is stronger, happier, and more capable than before." And Keith replied, "You mean that now I feel like those rockets look? We really did it, didn't we?" Hypothetically, were Keith to respond to the oedipal interpretation with the same words he used in response to Suth's self-psychological interpretation, no doubt the classical analyst might have counted it as confirmation of the correctness of *his* formulation, just as I am sure Suth experienced Keith's response as confirmation of *her* approach. Confirmation in child work is even more difficult than in adult work, because children (though not Keith, at least here) tend to be more cryptic and more tangential than grown-ups, heightening our awareness of how much analytic work with both children and adults relies, for better or worse, on the theory we hold. In this pluralistic world, we cannot prove our theories, and our patients cannot prove them for us.

Be that as it may, because I do believe that the analyst who speaks to the whole child—to the child's conscious sense of power, competence, and progress in growing up—forms a different, more sturdy, more genuine and authentic relationship with the child than the analyst who speaks to the child in parts, in terms of specific defenses and, especially, specific libidinal phases of development, I'm convinced that Keith couldn't have been in better hands. Child therapy such as that reported here prepares one to accept the insights of self psychology.

I will close with a remark about optimal responsiveness. Suth says that through transmuting internalization in an optimally frustrating environment, the patient was able to internalize appropriate selfobject responses, resulting in the reorganization and further development of self-structure. Many still hold strongly to construct, so central to Kohut's formulation of the therapeutic action of clinical work. But my own contention is that the ongoingness of a well-functioning therapeutic relationship is of more significance in effecting therapeutic change, including transmuting internalization, than is the frustration, optimal or otherwise, so inevitable in our clinical work. In fact, this beautiful clinical presentation demonstrates to me how little this effective work has been characterized by frustration and repair. I don't mean to suggest that disruption and repair are not important, as when Keith responded the way he did to Suth's vacation, but I am convinced it was the pleasure of being understood by Suth, even in this context, that was the salient feature in his improvement.

One last thought: At ICP in Los Angeles we are in the process of developing a contemporary child analytic curriculum. This case we will use, with Suth's permission, as one of our models of how child analytic work should be conceptualized in the contemporary world. I close by thanking Suth for the privilege of discussing her clinical chapter.

REFERENCES

Kohut, H. (1971), *The Analysis of the Self*. New York: International Universities Press.
Wolf, E. (1988), *Treating the Self*. New York: Guilford.

Chapter 12

Flight from the Subjectivity of the Other: Pathological Adaptation to Childhood Parent Loss

George Hagman

Frequently psychoanalysts and other psychotherapists encounter patients who suffered parent loss during childhood. Over time a small but significant literature has developed that focuses on the special clinical problems of this population (Freud, 1927; Lewin, 1937; Deutsch, 1937; Fleming and Altschul, 1962; Jacobson, 1965; Altschul, 1968; Fleming, 1972, 1974; Stolorow and Lachmann, 1975; Blum, 1980, 1983, 1984; Shane and Shane, 1990a,b). A frequent observation of these analysts has been that many analysands who have experienced parent loss avoid engagement in and experience of the transference, and it has been agreed that the analyst's ability to understand and analyze this complex transference response is essential to successful treatment outcome. To this end, I intend to explore a key motivation of the transference in these patients.

My observation has been that a certain group of these patients withdraw psychologically and emotionally from others as a result of the childhood loss of a sustaining intersubjective context of mutual relatedness that was lost with the death of a parent. More specifically, the resistance to the experience of the transference and the engagement in a

The author wishes to thank Peter Zimmerman, Ph.D. and Alan Roland, Ph.D. for their assistance in the writing of this article.

"new relationship" with the analyst arises from anxieties regarding the recognition of the analyst's subjectivity (the experience of his or her "otherness" [Shane and Shane, 1990b]), which is associated by the patient with vulnerability to traumatic loss. Because of this the patient resists, often for some time, the experience of the analyst as a separate and distinct other, thus turning the analytic situation into a one-person process with the primary, dynamic tie being to the internal representation of the lost parent. This state of flight from the other's subjectivity results in chronic pathology of the self. An associated finding is that the recognition of otherness (the *experience* of intersubjectivity [Benjamin, 1991]) is essential to good enough, mature self–selfobject relationships and thus the full vitality and cohesion of the self.

I will begin with a brief review of the parent loss literature that highlights the clinical observations and theoretical formulations regarding the transference resistance of these patients. I will also discuss recent concepts from self psychology, intersubjectivity theory, and developmental psychology. I will then reinterpret the transference resistance in light of my notion of a flight from the subjectivity of the other. A case illustration will follow, and the chapter will close with a discussion.

A REVIEW OF PARENT LOSS LITERATURE

In this section I will briefly highlight several major findings in the parent loss literature. I will break down the discussion into three areas: 1) the unconscious attachment to the lost parent, 2) issues of defense and deficit, and 3) the problem of the transference.

The unconscious attachment to the lost parent

Freud (1927) observed that some patients who had suffered the death of a parent in childhood continued to deny the reality of the loss into adulthood. In the cases he discussed he noted a "split" in the patient's mental life: one current fitting in with reality, the other current continuing to deny the fact of the parent's death. This early observation of Freud's has been validated time and again by subsequent analysts (Lewin, 1937; Deutsch, 1937; Fleming and Altschul, 1962; Jacobson, 1965; Blum, 1984). These authors found that though the clinical manifestations of the "split" between acceptance and denial can take many forms, all of their patients remained attached to the memory of the lost parent.

Defense and deficit

Freud (1927) asserted that the motivation for the "split" was to defend against the recognition of a traumatic and unacceptable reality. Trauma arises owing to the immaturity of the child at the time of the loss; children in this situation are incapable of realistic understanding and are victimized by their own primitive fantasy life and cognitive limitations. Virtually all the parent loss authors agree that the defenses erected in response to loss can interfere with the developmental process, and that some level of arrest is common. Hence, the adult patient may show a range of problems involving deficits and conflicts. Most of the parent loss analysts make note of the obvious psychological immaturity of their patients, who continue to struggle with early developmental challenges well into adulthood.

Transference issues

Fleming and Altschul (1962) were the first to emphasize the importance of transference resistance in these patients. Most of the other authors agree that there is a defense against regression and fears regarding attachment to the analyst as a "new object." Belief in the dead parent's survival may remain the central organizing principle in the patient's life, and the patient will resist anyone or anything that might threaten recognition of the loss. These patients seek treatment during periods when this fantasy attachment is threatened by current separations, transitions, or actual losses. Therefore, there is a window of opportunity in which the analyst is able to analyze the core issues of the patient's conflict. The resulting emotional investment in the analyst, combined with his or her survival and continuing availability, provide the security necessary to complete the work of mourning.

In summary the classical literature of parent loss stresses several points: 1) these patients remain preoccupied with the internal attachment to the dead parent, 2) they attempt to reenact the relationship with the lost parent in the transference, 3) they fear the experience of the analysis as a "new relationship," 4) to a greater or lesser degree they suffer from developmental arrest, and 5) they resist engagement in the work of mourning.

The impact of parent loss is influenced by many variables, most importantly the developmental level at which the loss occurred and the presence or absence of preexistent psychopathology. In the specific instances that we will be discussing the loss of the parent occurred late in a relatively healthy childhood after the consolidation of the self, but before full maturity. Typically development had been arrested at the level concurrent with the parent's death. As an adult, the patient remains tied to an unconscious fantasy of the lost parent that continues to serve selfobject functions. The analyst as a potential source of new selfobject experiences is feared, both in terms of the threat of the loss of a new object and the even more fearful loss of the tie to the inner representation of the dead parent. In support of my thesis I will briefly discuss the problem of recognition of the other, selfobject functions, intersubjectivity, and loss.

THE OTHERNESS OF THE SELFOBJECT

A number of analysts (Winnicott, 1965, 1971; Modell, 1984; Stern, 1985; Benjamin, 1988, 1991; Stolorow and Atwood, 1992) have argued that the experience of the self is inseparable from intersubjective relatedness. Stolorow and Atwood (1992) in particular believe that the "myth" of the isolated, intrapsychic mind does not accurately portray the reality of human psychological experience, which is profoundly interrelational and intersubjective. They state: "The concept of an intersubjective system brings into focus *both* the individual's world of inner experience *and* its embeddedness with such worlds in a continual flow of reciprocal mutual influence. In this vision, the gap between the intrapsychic and interpersonal realms is closed, and, indeed, the old dichotomy between them is rendered obsolete" (p. 18). However, the fact that persons are indissolubly linked does not tell us about how intersubjectivity is experienced by the coparticipants; most importantly, by emphasizing intersubjectivity in a *general* sense (i.e., as an essential dimension of all levels of human relatedness) Stolorow and Atwood do not consider the specific area of *recognition* of the other by one or both subjects (intersubjectivity in the *specific* sense), which I believe comprises the dynamic tension of the interpersonal field.

Jessica Benjamin (1991), in agreement with Stolorow and Atwood, stated: "The human mind is interactive rather than monadic, that the psychoanalytic process should be understood as occurring between subjects rather than within the individual" (p. 43). However, she continued: "A theory in which the individual subject no longer reigns absolute must confront the difficulty that each subject has in recognizing the other as an equivalent center of experience" (p. 43). It is the vicissitudes of recognition of subjectivity that Benjamin placed at the center of her developmental model: "The other must be recognized as another subject in order for the self to fully experience his or her subjectivity in the other's presence. This means, first, that we have a need for recognition and second, a capacity to recognize others in return, mutual recognition. But recognition is a capacity of individual development that is only unevenly realized" (p. 45). Utilizing Winnicott's theory of the use of the object, Benjamin described a dialectical process of negation and recognition through which the developing child finds pleasure in the experience of the mother as a subject. Benjamin stated: "The capacity to recognize the mother as a subject is an important part of early development" (p. 46).

Daniel Stern's research (1985) confirmed the fact that by the ninth month infants exhibit a capacity to recognize the mother as a subject distinct from themselves. Stern stated: "Infants gradually come upon the momentous realization that inner subjective experiences, the 'subject matter' of the mind, are potentially sharable with someone else" (p. 124). From that point a central feature of the infant's reality is the perception of the mother as *subject*. In fact Stern described how the recognition of *inter*subjectivity develops along with the awareness of the self's own subjectivity. For Stern the pleasure of intersubjectivity unfolds spontaneously as an inherent part of the infant's experience of the world. Affective attunement and empathy are other forms of intersubjective sharing—the core experiences that contribute to the crystallization of a cohesive self, an earlier form being "core relatedness" and a later form being "verbal relatedness" (Stern, 1985).

Although an archaic experience of "being-at-one-with" an idealized or mirroring other has been found to be essential to the establishment of a cohesive and vital self, the creative elaboration of mature selfhood throughout the lifespan depends on the capacity to recognize the *inter*subjectivity of the selfobject bond; it is through this creative *tension* (Benjamin, 1988) between recognizing the other and asserting the self that self-experience is elaborated and continually renewed. Kohut (1984) distinguishes the undifferentiated nature of archaic selfobjects from the recognition of separateness that characterizes *mature* self–selfobject relations. See also Ornstein (1991) for a discussion of the "intertwining" of selfobject and object experiences in maturity. In the absence of these renewing experiences development ceases, resulting in arrest, fixation, and stasis.

Winnicott (1971) argues powerfully that the recognition of otherness is essential for useful engagement in the social world (which includes psychoanalysis). He writes: "A world of shared reality is created which the subject can use and which can feed back other-than-me substances into the subject" (p. 94). It is through this process, according to Benjamin, that the ability to love, empathize, and be an other to the other arises (see also Shane and Shane, 1990, on the capacity to be an "other"). These forms of subjective-selfobject relating, felt to be simultaneously part of and separate from the self, are essentially mature self-object experiences; they reflect a developmental advance beyond the self-consolidating experiences of archaic merger toward a lifelong elaboration of the vital and creative self (Kohut, 1984).

But the recognition of the other and the experience of that other's unique subjectivity leaves one vulnerable to irreplaceable loss. Benjamin

(1988) considered this possibility: "When the other does not survive . . . it becomes almost exclusively intrapsychic." A defensive process of internalization takes place when "mutual recognition is not restored, when shared reality does not survive destruction, complementary structures and 'relating' to the inner object predominates" (p. 54). Stern (1985) described a similar process in the child's response to the massive misattunement of the parent: the infant learns that there is a "danger in permitting the intersubjective sharing of experience, namely that intersubjective sharing can result in loss" (p. 214). (This process must be distinguished from transmuting internalization, which occurs in the context of the survival or restoration of the selfobject tie.) In other words, when the subjective other is traumatically lost (as in death and bereavement, or more commonly in empathic failure) there may as a result be a flight from other-recognition and subjective relating, and a defensive retreat into an inner fantasy life.

FLIGHT FROM THE SUBJECTIVITY OF THE OTHER

The loss through death of a parent whom one has experienced as a distinct, delimited center of subjectivity and with whom one has shared a crucial, mutually regulating selfobject bond is traumatic. The self has developed, has been sustained, and has continued to be elaborated with the support of the unique selfobject functions provided by the essential other—the parent. The child experiences the core danger as follows: "I have invested my self innocently in the unique, irreplaceable existence of another, my own subjectivity has been inextricably bound to their special nature, and now they are gone from me forever. How can I possibly give them up; and how can I dare to risk another such loss." In response to this experience of danger to the self the child seeks refuge by means of a retreat to forms of schizoid relating; this primarily takes the form of the reactivation of the selfobject functions of the internal fantasy tie to the lost parent accompanied by a flight from the recognition of others. Lacking the vital, protean nature of "a true other," the memory of the parent joins the traumatized self in a frozen state of internal exile. The bereaved's connection to vibrant, unpredictable, and ultimately creative involvement with other persons becomes attenuated, or perhaps even severed.

Essentially, I am describing a process similar to that identified by Kohut (1984) as the reactivation of archaic selfobject relating in reaction to the loss of more mature selfobject experience. More specifically in the cases we are discussing, the patient retreats from involvement with significant objects and reactivates the archaic, fantasy selfobject tie with the memory of the dead parent; hence, these patients fear and avoid the experience of the transference. Therefore, as we will see later, it is important for the analyst not to simply facilitate the spontaneous unfolding of the selfobject transference (the development of which the patient *resists*), but more importantly, to do so through the interpretation of defenses *against* selfobject relating in the treatment relationship.

Clinically, we observe this conflict most clearly during the first weeks of treatment when the patient's reliance on long-term, defensive strategies are threatened or fail in their functions in sustaining self-experience (owing to transition, new losses, increased intimacy, etc.) and the person enters a state of self-crisis that may be manifested by acute anxiety, depression, work inhibitions, and most commonly, complex difficulties experienced in engaging in and sustaining intimate relationships. Characteristically with this patient, the most striking feature of the beginning phase of treatment (often continuing to some degree into the middle phase) is an avoidant, even evasive, attitude toward the analyst. In severe cases it is as if the patient is alone in the room engaged in a self-analysis.

This flight from recognition of the subjectivity of the analyst results in one of the most characteristic features of the treatment relationship during its early phases. That feature is the absence of a feeling of mutual responsiveness and affective interplay between the analyst and patient—a lack of *the empathic resonance*, which Kohut (1984) identified as the hallmark of mature selfobject relating. This leads to a quality of emotional deadening, and experiences of isolation and self-attenuation in the analyst. It is this sense of affective estrangement that I will describe in the following case.

PATRICIA

Patricia, a 24-year-old woman, had lost her father when she was 14 years old. She had moved to the city 6 months before entering treatment to pursue a career in publishing. She complained of depression and loneliness, and was preoccupied with her involvement in an emotionally highly wrought, sexually charged "platonic" relationship with her male roommate. Intense unconscious longings for him, coupled by conscious denial of her sexual needs, made their friendship stormy at best. Patricia claimed to be desperate.

She was white, middle class, and from a large rural town. She did not describe significant early pathology in herself or her family, until her father's death. As she reported it, she had been arguing with her father, refusing to help him shovel the snow from the front walk. He had gone out to do the job himself while she remained in the house with her brother. Sometime later, they found their father lying unconscious on the snow. They were unable to revive him and he was dead upon arrival at the hospital.

Patricia did not remember grieving. She vividly recalled her mother's subsequent depression. Withdrawing to her bed, the mother became physically and emotionally incapacitated. By Patricia's account, the social context that might have supported her involvement in mourning collapsed. Her relationship with her mother became strained and later, after the mother recovered, they fought frequently and for a time were estranged. Patricia's adolescent character was one of self-sufficiency, coupled with care-taking for others. She did well in college, after which (as noted previously) she left her hometown to pursue a new life in the city.

Patricia dominated our sessions with her frantic, rapid-fire speech and relentless, fruitless groping for the "answers" to her problems. She was preoccupied with trying to control the convoluted and conflicted nature of her relationship with her roommate. She was afraid of being left alone, unable to return home and incapable of finding a place for herself in the city.

My initial assessment was that Patricia might have been suffering from a severe character disorder; however, the lack of childhood family pathology and the evidence that she presently functioned at a high level, handled complex interpersonal work situations well, and had maintained healthy long-term relationships with childhood friends seemed to counterindicate a diagnosis of severe psychopathology.

Over the first three months I went from being an eager and curious "potential" analyst to a frustrated and ineffectual witness to her solitary search for answers. It was as if there was a one-way mirror between us—I felt blocked, anonymous, and unrecognized. This feeling persisted for the first 6 months of treatment.

Nevertheless, the treatment appeared to be helpful to Patricia, lending her support as her troubled friendship "self-destructed" several months later. Subsequently she became more relaxed in session, more reflective. Given this, 3 months into the treatment, I proposed analysis. "Funny," she noted in response, "I haven't even noticed the couch until now." It was as if entire aspects of the treatment situation had gone unrecognized by her—the large blue couch . . . myself.

She said that she feared the return of memories of her father. In fact, soon after the beginning of the analysis she shared dreams of his return, as if from a trip, healthy and intact, his disappearance unexplained. The first analytic month coincided with the anniversary of her father's death. That day she spent alone waiting for a call from her family that never came. "There is a wall," she said. "I am on one side, everyone else is on the other. I have been behind the wall for years. But I sense it most now. They don't feel anything. Do they even remember my father?"

Despite Patricia's increasing openness about her isolation the wall loomed large in sessions. But what I came to experience most acutely was the absence of physical interaction. Most of my patients respond to me physically as they enter the room, as they settle in, and even while they lie on the couch. It was this subtle, usually subliminal, "background" quality to the interaction that I experienced as absent with Patricia. She would pass me on the way to the couch with little or no acknowledgment of my presence. It wasn't that she ignored me, in fact I spoke often to her and she responded, often thoughtfully, to my interventions. However, I felt unrecognized as a distinct person, as someone physically, emotionally, and psychologically relating to her, person to person. I felt like a shadow, a ghost.

But it is not as simple as saying she related to me as if I were her dead father. More to the point, it was her fear of my "coming to life" for her, that she might become involved with a "flesh and blood" *other* who might draw her out of her self-sufficient, mournful inner world of memory and self-protection. Nevertheless, she reported a dream with a new figure, "the man of my dreams," she noted, who would take her away and care for her.

However, for a time, even my queries about the meanings of her often dramatic and emotionally vivid dreams met with shrugs and denials of meaning—"just silly and useless," she would say of them, as if to suggest that hidden meaning would court discovery and disaster.

I began to interpret to her my experience of her fear of me, of her need to protect her self-sufficiency, her fears of revealing the unresolved grief and feelings of abandonment and loss. For a while there seemed to be no effect. She would be silent. I would continue to feel as if I were talking to myself.

But during the next summer, after I returned from a short vacation, she reluctantly admitted that she missed me. "I don't feel comfortable with that . . . missing you. I don't want to feel this way. What if you leave, or something else."

"What if I died."

"Yeah. Died or left the city, or something. You can't say . . . I can't control you, or what might happen."

"As you couldn't when your father died . . . and then you were alone with nobody."

"Nobody . . . Even my mother was no good for me. I took care of her, and then when I still needed her she threw me out. I'm better if I take care of things alone."

It was after this that I felt a change in my experience of Patricia. One day I went out to the waiting room to invite her into a session. She walked toward me down the narrow hallway, and I felt a sudden attraction to her, not powerful or compelling by any means, but a sexual response that was quite unusual. Thinking about it later, I realized that she had subtly responded to me as she approached, glancing at me and reacting to my welcome with a slight nod and shrug. She responded to me as she hadn't before—not seductively (or rather, not purely so), so much as a normal, expectable relating. Soon after that she called me for the first time by name. These developments by no means led to a flowering of the transference, but I had a growing, cumulative experience of being recognized by her. This feeling deepened over time as the analysis ventured into unresolved areas of her bereavement and current struggles around her work ambitions, self-image, and sexuality. But the primary feeling I had was of eventually being related to as a subjectively recognized other with whom she was willing to engage in a mutual process of exploration and change.

DISCUSSION

This short case report is not intended to convey the full complexity of Patricia's five-year treatment. Rather, what I have tried to do is sketch the development of a type of transference encountered in work with some adults who suffered parent loss in later childhood. The following is a summary of the analysis of Patricia's flight from recognition of *my* subjectivity.

The experience of her father's death was sudden and traumatic. The additional loss of her mother to depression and the eventual collapse of their relationship, and thus the last vestiges of parental support, led to the crystallization of Patricia's pseudoindividuation and defensive self-sufficiency. Unconsciously she remained preoccupied with her father and nurtured a continuing fantasy attachment to him. Countertransferentially this was reflected in my sensation of "being like" the dead father. But more important, on a deeper level, she feared recognizing me as "someone new" with my own unique identity, sense of self, and distinct perspective on life. To risk recognizing me would mean moving away from her father toward an "other" man and engagement in a new relationship that could be lost just as suddenly, and perhaps irrevocably, as was her father. Patricia's flight from relating to others resulted in a broad developmental arrest in midadolescence and a retreat from the work of mourning.

This became evident to me through my understanding of the estrangement that dominated my experience of our relationship. This lack of relatedness is consistent with Benjamin's viewpoint referred to previously: flight from the subjectivity of the other means a retreat to more schizoid forms of relating, often with adaptive results; however, reliance on internal "objects" (as opposed to subjectively experienced others) impacts negatively on the person's capacity for mutual recognition, psychological development, and self-elaboration. The parent loss analysts noted the clinical manifestations of this retreat from other-relating in their patient's transference resistances, states of developmental arrest, and obsessive engagement in repetitive and generally self-defeating relationships. Optimally the development of the self involves a movement over time from the need for self-consolidating, repairing, and self-sustaining merger experiences toward more differentiated, creative, and mature ones (Kohut, 1984). Flight from the subjectivity of the other is a retreat from these developmentally advanced selfobject experiences. In the best of cases, such as with Patricia, the person attempts to maintain, through the continuing fantasy tie to the lost parent, a cohesive and vital sense of self. However, it is eventually revealed that engagement in new forms of truly creative and mature forms of relating has been defensively foreclosed. To that end, what I have encountered in cases such as Patricia's is a retreat from engagement with subjectively recognized others as mature selfobjects in favor of a reliance on a moribund selfobject tie lacking in the perishable qualities of subjectivity.

Technically the treatment of Patricia illustrates a three-step sequence involved in the resolution of the transference resistance frequently encountered in parent loss cases: 1) the facilitation of the emergence of defenses against selfobject relating in the treatment situation, 2) the exploration of the function of the inner tie to the lost parent, and 3) the interpretation of defenses and underlying anxieties related to engaging in developmentally more advanced levels of self-experience involving recognition of the selfobject's perishability. With the provision of continuity, security, and the growing experience of empathic resonance in the analytic situation Patricia began to risk the recognition of, and engagement with, me as an other. It was through this process that a mature selfobject tie was restored and the previously arrested self-elaboration processes resumed. Over time, I found myself experiencing a growing excitement and investment in the treatment. The transference grew richer and more varied. She accepted my interpretations and valued them for their freshness, their potential for surprise and usefulness. Patricia and I shared the experience of a working alliance. It was during that period of the analysis when the full creative capacities of the treatment were realized.

CONCLUSION

The idea of a flight from subjectivity in response to the experience of selfobject failure has potentially broad applications. This chapter focuses on childhood bereavement, but loss later in life may result in similar reactions. Winnicott's (1971) notion of the use of the object involved not just the recognition of the existence of the other as outside the range of one's omnipotence, but extended the idea to explain broad areas of culture and creativity. In 1984, Model saw the retreat from relating to and communicating with others as one of the fundamental defenses of the narcissistic disorders. Stern (1985) believed that a typical response of children to empathic failure and misattunement is withdrawal from involvement with the subjectivity of the other. Benjamin (1988) argued powerfully that the failure to recognize the subjectivity of the mother, and women in general, is the basis of male sexual tyranny in western culture. Given this, the fate of our capacities to recognize *other* selves as distinct and unique while at the same time similar to ourselves may be a core issue in human relatedness in general and psychopathology in particular. This viewpoint may broaden the traditional concepts of the object and selfobject to include areas of human relating that have so far remained undeveloped.

REFERENCES

Altschul, S. (1968), Denial and ego arrest. *J. Amer. Psychoanal. Assn.*, 16:301–318.

Benjamin, J. (1988), *The Bonds of Love*. New York: Pantheon Books.

────── (1991), Recognition and destruction: An outline of intersubjectivity. In: *Relational Perspectives in Psychoanalysis*, ed. N. Skolnick & S. Warshaw. Hillsdale, NJ: The Analytic Press, pp. 43–60.

Blum, H. (1980), The value of reconstruction in adult psychoanalysis. *Internat. J. Psycho-Anal.*, 61:39–52.

────── (1983), The psychoanalytic process and analytic inference: A clinical study of a lie and loss. *Internat. J. Psycho-Anal.*, 64:17–33.

────── (1984), Splitting of the ego and its relation to parent loss. In: *Defense and Resistance: Historical Perspectives and Current Concepts*, ed. H. Blum. New York: International Universities Press, pp. 301–324.

Deutsch, H. (1937), Absence of grief. *Psychoanal. Quart.*, 6:12–22.

Fleming, J. (1972), Early object deprivation and transference phenomena: The working alliance. *Psychoanal. Quart.*, 41:23–49.

────── (1974), The problem of diagnosis in parent loss cases. *Contemp. Psychoanal.*, 10:439–451.

────── & Altschul, S. (1962), Activation of mourning and growth by psychoanalysis. In: *Childhood Bereavement and Its Aftermath*. Madison, CT: International Universities Press, 1988, pp. 277–307.

Freud, S. (1927), Fetishism. *Standard Edition*, 21:235–239. London: Hogarth Press, 1961.

Furman, E. (1974), *A Child's Parent Dies: Studies in Childhood Bereavement*. New Haven, CT: Yale University Press.

Jacobson, E. (1965), The return of the lost parent. In: *Drive, Affects, Behavior, Vol. 2*, ed. M. Shur, New York: International Universities Press.

Kohut, H. (1984), *How Does Analysis Cure?* ed. A. Goldberg & P. Stepansky. Chicago: University of Chicago Press.

Lewin, B. (1937), A type of neurotic hypomanic reaction. *Arch. Neurol. & Psychiat.*, 37:868–873.

Modell, A. (1984), *Psychoanalysis in a New Context*. New York: International Universities Press.

Ornstein, P. (1991), Why self psychology is not an object relations theory: Clinical and theoretical considerations. In: *The Evolution of Self Psychology Progress in Self Psychology, Vol. 7*, ed. A. Goldberg. Hillsdale, NJ: The Analytic Press, pp. 17–30.

Shane, E. & Shane, M. (1990a), Object loss and selfobject loss: A consideration of self psychology's contribution to understanding mourning and the failure to mourn. *The Annual of Psychoanalysis*, 18:115–131. Hillsdale, NJ: The Analytic Press.

Shane, M. & Shane, E. (1990b), The struggle for otherhood: Implications for development in adulthood of the capacity to be a good-enough object for another. In: *New Developments in Adult Development*, ed. R. Nemiroff & C. Colorosso. New York: Basic Books, pp. 487–498.

Stern, D. (1985), *The Interpersonal World of the Infant*. New York: Basic Books.

Stolorow, R. & Atwood, G. (1992), *Contexts of Being: The Intersubjective Foundations of Psychological Life*. Hillsdale, NJ: The Analytic Press.

—— & Lachmann, F. (1975), Early object loss and denial: Developmental considerations. *Psychoanal. Quart.*, 44:596–611.

Winnicott, D. W. (1965), *The Maturational Processes and the Facilitating Environment*. New York: International Universities Press.

—— (1971), The use of an object and relating through identifications. In: *Playing and Reality*. London: Tavistock, pp. 86–94.

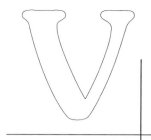

Applied

A Self-Psychological Approach to Attention Deficit/ Hyperactivity Disorder in Adults: A Paradigm to Integrate the Biopsychosocial Model of Psychiatric Illness

Howard S. Baker

Margaret N. Baker

Attention deficit/hyperactivity disorder (AD/HD) is a serious illness that probably afflicts at least 2% of adults (Wender, 1995). It often goes unrecognized. When it is not properly treated, it creates great suffering, and it may account for a significant number of psychotherapeutic treatment failures.

The purpose of this discussion is twofold. We will present clinical material about AD/HD, particularly as it involves adult patients. We also intend to show how the principles of self psychology can integrate the elements of the biopsychosocial model (Engel, 1977) of psychiatry. AD/HD offers a clear example of how biological, intrapsychic, and social factors can be synthesized into a coherent etiologic explanation and comprehensive treatment plan.

We will have only minimal comments regarding the diagnosis, etiology, and pharmacological treatment of AD/HD, since they are readily discussed elsewhere (Barkley, 1990; Silver, 1992; Weiss and Hechtman, 1993; Wender, 1995). Instead, using clinical examples, we will concentrate on the ways that the attentional symptoms disrupt the efforts of AD/HD patients to find sufficient selfobject experiences throughout the life cycle. Because of this, there often are intrapsychic deficits and intensified conflicts that yield a weakened self-structure. This in turn leaves these people in particular need of selfobject experiences, and the symptoms continue to interfere with their ability to generate these experiences or process them when they are present.

Most leaders in the behavioral sciences pay consistent lip service to the importance of the biopsychosocial model. In reality, it has been neglected every bit as regularly as it has been acknowledged. One reason for this is that, without a self psychological perspective, the model is difficult to consolidate. This creates a major impediment to pragmatic clinical application. In the present medical and economic climate, with its pressure for cheap, quick-fix treatments, the biopsychosocial perspective is especially likely to be disregarded. We believe, therefore, that it is particularly crucial to find a way to clarify this model.

We hope, then, to describe an important diagnostic entity from the perspective of self psychology and offer a comprehensible way to integrate and use the biopsychosocial model of etiology and treatment.

A HISTORICAL PERSPECTIVE ON AD/HD

Attention-deficit hyperactivity disorder is a pervasive developmental disorder that afflicts between 6% and 10% of children (Wender, 1995), although some popular literature places the incidence as high as 25%. AD/HD was recognized as a diagnosable illness 50 years ago; it has had an interesting history, being called "minimal brain damage," "hyperactive child syndrome," and attention deficit hyperactivity disorder in *DSM-III-R*. The *DSM IV* terminology is attention deficit/hyperactivity disorder, the slash added to recognize three subtypes: Combined, Predominantly Inattentive, and Predominantly Hyperactive-Impulsive.

Initially, it was assumed that AD/HD was more common in boys and usually was outgrown by the end of adolescence. It seemed clear that there was a biologically based difficulty sustaining attention. Ritalin and other stimulants improved attention and, "paradoxically," diminished hyperactivity. Stimulant use was discontinued in adolescence when it was believed that the medication would no longer provide the paradoxical calming, and when the stimulants supposedly would create a potential for addiction. Use of the medication caught the attention of the

Church of Scientology and others, and they led a campaign to discredit its use. Although their claims were unfounded, the Church of Scientology did succeed in seriously stigmatizing the diagnosis and its medical treatment.

Published follow-up of children diagnosed as having AD/HD date back to a 1976 effort by Menkes, Rowe, and Menkes (1967). This was followed by the improved work of Weiss and her colleagues, who began to publish their data in 1971. Papers by her group and by others began to show that there were significant long-term sequelae, including reduced academic and job success, increased contact with the law, higher levels of substance abuse, and troubled interpersonal relationships. Initially, it was assumed that any long-term problems were a secondary result of the now-outgrown biological elements of the illness. This belief persisted until the last decade, when a series of publications (Cantwell, 1985; Wender et al., 1985; Thorley, 1988) finally began to alter professional opinion.

Recent work by Zametkin et al. (1992) provides compelling evidence that supports Cantwell, Wender, and Thorley's hypotheses that there are biological differences between adults with AD/HD and normal controls. Using PET scans, they found that the AD/HD sample had reduced global glucose metabolism and that there were larger reductions in the premotor and superior prefrontal cortex. Those areas have been "shown to be involved in the control of attention and motor activity" (p. 1361). The specific neurochemical explanation for these findings is not established conclusively, but the catacholamine neurotransmitters dopamine and norepinephrine (Silver, 1992) and serotonin (Desch, 1991) have been implicated.

Although psychological testing is often used in establishing a diagnosis of AD/HD, there are no definitive diagnostic tests that robustly establish the diagnosis. Although Holdnack et al. (in press) have shown significant problems in memory processing in a controlled sample of AD/HD adults, standard neuropsychological testing scores are not abnormal in as many as half of patients who appropriately carry the diagnosis (Golinkoff, personal communication).

A series of clinical interviews (which may include the patient's family members, close friends, and even work peers) is the most valid and reliable way to make the diagnosis. The diagnostic criteria are summarized in the DSM IV (1994). It is necessary to show a childhood history consistent with the diagnosis. This may be difficult, especially when the symptoms were primarily attentional. Particularly if the patient is bright, they may have done passable work that merely was not up to their potential; they may have avoided teacher criticism because they developed ingratiating defenses pleasing to teachers. Still, they often will recall clearly how they always were concentrating on several things simultaneously or that their minds were "out the window more than in the classroom." Over the course of several appointments, a characteristic cognitive pattern usually emerges. In general, AD/HD patients hop from one subject to another in an apparently unrelated fashion. Unlike people who use this primarily as a defensive maneuver, these patients eventually and happily return to the original subject, surprised that they have been confusing and able to make their circuitous thinking clear. The typical response engendered in others by this cognitive scatter is for the listener to want to control and organize. People often feel frustrated that these patients are not getting to or sticking to the point, or that they are not developing a coherent emotional theme. This clinical picture is described more fully in the following section.

There is thus an emerging professional consensus that AD/HD's biological elements persist and cause continuing impulsivity and barriers to sustaining attention. As a result, adults have been treated effectively with stimulants. Nevertheless, *The American Medical Association's Drug Evaluations Annual 1994* only minimally addresses the use of medication in adult patients. Clear recognition of AD/HD's biological elements persisting into adulthood has yet to be achieved.

We believe that about half of children diagnosed with AD/HD will not have entirely normal brain function in adulthood. This results in difficulty sustaining appropriate levels of and direction to attention. In addition, either because of the altered brain function itself or as a secondary consequence of the attentional difficulties, these patients show varying degrees of impulsiveness and hyperactivity. Moreover, there are frequent secondary problems with self-esteem and affect regulation.

PHENOMENOLOGY OF ADULT AD/HD

The literature on children with AD/HD focuses on three basic difficulties: impulsiveness, hyperactivity, and attentional problems. We think that the difficulty establishing and sustaining appropriate levels of attention may be the most fundamental element in adults, and we suspect that this may create or at least intensify hyperactivity (which in adults may be expressed as hyperverbalization) and impulsiveness.

There are two opposite difficulties with attention: (1) sudden shifts of focus dart to all sorts of relevant or entirely irrelevant subjects, and (2) attention hyperfocuses so completely that the person is almost inaccessible. Since the onset of the illness is during childhood, the symptoms pervade and shape most areas of development. It also contrasts with many psychiatric disorders since there is no symptom-free reference state, as there would be in episodic depression. The "blinks" (Reisinger, 1993) in attention may seem normal.

The shifts in attention occur on the basis of independent, essentially random, biological events; they are not motivated in the usual sense of the word. Clinicians and patients have consistently noted that physical exhaustion, illness, and the boredom or affective turmoil that accompanies loss of self-cohesion will increase the intensity, duration, and frequency of the symptoms. Patients may discover that "tuning out" can be used to meet defensive ends. Failure to distinguish "blinks" from defenses will result in empathic failures that will increase symptom intensity. Neither those around them nor the patients themselves know where their thoughts and feelings will be next—and the reasons for these disruptive and aggravating shifts often are obscure and misunderstood by both the patient and other people.

Clinicians, let alone family members, find it difficult to explain "blinks." For example, a patient we'll call Tom was literally in the process of particularly enjoyable sexual foreplay when he began unfolding his fingers one by one. His surprised wife asked, "What are you doing?" "Counting how many hours of sleep I had last night," he replied. Startled, her organization of the event was narcissistic injury; she became furious and stopped the sexual interaction. From his perspective, the thought entered his mind and he became as captured by it as with sex. For him his irrelevant thought and sex could coexist. For his wife it signaled emotional withdrawl. He hoped to find comfort and self-restoration in sex. His wife's rage not only deprived him of a needed selfobject experience, it was a self-disruptive interaction, particularly since he was feeling loving toward her—not the insult she rather naturally experienced. It is this irrelevant, biological, inattentive event that must be distinguished from similar behavior that actually is motivated and intended to protect the self or hurt the other.

The "blinks" that disrupt attention break up normal thought processes and interfere with the integration of cognitions and affects. At times, they create almost continuous background noise, so that the person may be humming a tune mentally while talking seriously to a friend or thinking about a problem. In Tom's case, his sexual enjoyment was accompanied by something unnecessary and irrelevant; this led to an interaction that diminished his capacity to use sex for appropriate self-consolidation and self-enhancement. It is not only sexuality that becomes muddled. All cognitive and affective organizing, reorganizing, and processing can be disrupted by these disjointed cognitive patterns.

AD/HD patients usually do not know when they will be out of contact with their internal or external environment. They randomly respond to any variety of irrelevant internal or external cues. They also get locked into their own thoughts in a way that makes them completely unaware of what others are saying or doing. People will speak to them and get no answer. Repeating the comment may not help, and family members often resort to comments like, "Earth to Mars." They may try to cover for lapsed attention during a conversation; having missed crucial details, however, their responses may appear inappropriate.

Popper (1988) has compared the internal affective and cognitive experiences of the AD/HD child to life "under a light strobe. Sudden attentional shifts and brief flashes of experience lead to a constantly changing view of the world: disconnected appearances impair the ability to form complex cognitions, respond emotionally, and learn social norms. The attention-shifting complicates learning about human emotions and complex thinking" (p. 653).

This combination of scattered and overfocusing often results in communication patterns that seem extremely convoluted or impulsive. Both factors increase the likelihood that they will interject ideas into conversations that are related to their unique attentional patterns rather than to the flow of the conversation. For example, during an initial evaluation, a man we'll call Mario was asked, "What did your father do for a living?" He replied, "He's retired. Well actually, he and a partner have a part-time business in which they install valves in sewage systems for industry. If the sewage comes back into the plant, this can mess up the manufacturing process. You would be amazed at the problems that it can create, and these companies really need Dad's product. But before he retired, he was an engineer for Kodak. He worked on their instant camera. You know, there really wasn't a patent infringement with Polaroid. The processes are really different, but Polaroid sued anyway, and they got a big judgment."

Scattered or overfocused attention can lead to behaviors and communications that most people find confusing, impulsive, and often aggravating. Tom's wife did not find his counting to be an aphrodisiac. Their lovemaking shifted to an argument, depriving both of them of libidinal gratification and an interaction that could have been self-consolidating. Mario recently reported that his wife feels at "the end of her rope. We love each other, but she just can't stand never knowing what I'll talk about or do next. I never know either, so I forget things that are important. In the 10 years of our marriage, I always remember her birthday a week in advance; but then I think about other things, and when the day comes, I've forgotten to get a gift." On careful examination, there was sometimes a dynamic issue that explained the behavior, but often none could be found.

Other people may try to engage these patients, pulling them back into reasonable contact. However, from the perspective of the person who has AD/HD, these efforts may feel like efforts to control him or her. In fact, Tallmadge and Barkley (1983) observed that parents tended to be more controlling, directive, limit-setting, and negative toward their AD/HD children. Clinically, these parents seemed anxious and intrusive, reinforcing the child's symptomatic behavior. However, following stimulant treatment, there often was an immediate reduction in the parents' controlling and negative behavior (Popper, 1988).

AD/HD shapes the interactions that these children create with their caretaking surround. Most parents and teachers will find them difficult, and some will respond in ways that generate negative interactions—unless the biological elements are ameliorated. As a result, it is likely that many of them will formulate organizing principles that a) others are critical and controlling rather than supportive and caring, and b) they themselves are failures and a source of disappointment rather than pleasure. These attitudes structure interactions that often have a pernicious trajectory throughout life.

To further add to an already grim sounding picture, the ability to internalize events and store them in memory is compromised in AD/HD (Holdnack et al., in press). Immediate, present experience must be attended to for it to have salience and enter long-term memory. Since frequent attentional shifts occur, this process is disrupted; data often are gone and forgotten or never became actual input. Others usually are unaware of the lapses and operate as if interactions were taken in. When they are not, misunderstandings are frequent. It is not surprising that afflicted adults often have checkered job histories and a higher divorce rate.

Few adults are very hyperactive. Instead, they may merely shift in their seats frequently or quietly drum out rhythms with their fingers. Those rhythms are also going on in their heads, perhaps as a part of a song that is in the back of their minds while they are listening to a conversation. There is often a feeling of internal restlessness or drivenness. It is possible that, for some patients, the hyperactivity is simply a consequence of the difficulty with attention.

Although there is substantial variability in those with AD/HD, there are two basic clusters of behavior and related organizing principles: a) overt rebelliousness, reflecting a struggle to maintain a sense of independence and an expectation that others will be critical and intrusive; and b) excessive compliance, reflecting an expectation that they will regularly disappoint others. Any patient may fall primarily into one category or the other, but most will shift back and forth when interactions with others appear either intrusive or abandoning.

Although we have focused on negative aspects of AD/HD, there are some positive elements. Because attention is so prone to shift, these people will often make connections that others do not. This may result in a heightened sense of humor or significant creativity. Those who have struggled with feelings of being a disappointment may also be very astute at empathic understanding. The problem often comes when follow-through is necessary, so there is often a trail of innovative, incomplete projects and intense, disrupted relationships.

SELF PSYCHOLOGY AND THE BIOPSYCHOSOCIAL MODEL

Kohut focused primarily on temperamental mismatch and emotional limitations in the caregivers as the most salient causes of developmental failures. He reasoned that these factors were the most common causes of empathic ruptures, and that excessive relational disruptions prevented the child's finding the sort of selfobject experiences that are vital for self-delineation and structure building. He was also convinced that biological limitations could interfere with this process, but he didn't devote much of his thinking to describing how this worked. Kohut appreciated that the clinical outcomes of normal conflicts and traumatic events is not determined merely by their intensity. Whether caretakers offer empathic, partially empathic, or nonempathic responses is crucial. He also insisted that selfobject needs persist throughout the life cycle, even for those with a resilient self-structure; however, people with vulnerable selves are in particular need of ongoing selfobject experiences to help them maintain self-cohesion.

Our ongoing level of self-consolidation is determined at the interface of (1) the current level of stress we endure; (2) the strength, flexibility, and resilience of our intrapsychic self-structure (or, if one chooses, the effectiveness of the schemas, model scenes, and organizing principles that structure the nature of our experience); and (3) the empathic quality of our current object relationships that offer or refuse the opportunity to generate selfobject experiences. Any biological factor can intensify or diminish stress, facilitate or impede development, and impact the generation of selfobject experiences. Like a variety of other biological factors, attention deficit/hyperactivity disorder has a variable but usually pervasive impact on each of the following elements.

1. Stress: AD/HD patients have an unpredictable and multishifting internal world, a considerable part of which is created by biological factors. This increases stress in and of itself. This happens because affects, cognitions, and relationships are not properly integrated. AD/HD also leads to impulsiveness, forgetfulness, and procrastination that increase stress in a direct fashion.

2. Intrapsychic structure: The biological factors make building self-structure, resolving conflicts, and establishing self-delineation even more

difficult than they are for most people. This happens both directly and indirectly. The shifting and overly focused attention directly interferes with necessary processing and integrating cognitions, affects, and relationships. Because AD/HD symptoms are annoying to others, and because they directly muddle interactions, they impede developmentally necessary object relationships. This, in turn, has made it more difficult for the child to generate—and to use—selfobject experiences crucial to normal self-development. Conflicts are often intensified, important organizing principles are distorted, and needed self-consolidating capabilities may be weak or missing (or, as many would say, there are deficits). Moreover, many people with AD/HD also have at least one parent with the affliction. This may complicate the difficult job of being a good parent and disrupt the marital alliance.

3. Meeting ongoing selfobject needs: Since AD/HD is a lifetime condition, object relationships are affected throughout the life cycle. Relational difficulties disrupt the ability of afflicted individuals to generate normal, healthy, and necessary selfobject experiences. There is a reduced capacity to find in relationships with others selfobject experiences that can maintain, restore, or transform the self. When there are weaknesses in self-structure, selfobjects are especially necessary, but AD/HD also interferes with meeting this ongoing need. The result is that many of these people are prone to loss of self-consolidation and are forced to generate selfobject experiences in symptomatic ways.

From a self-psychological perspective, the biological aspects of AD/HD impose (1) intrapsychic problems integrating current affects and cognitions every day throughout the life cycle, (2) problems in object relationships, (3) problems in generating selfobject experiences, (4) problems integrating available selfobject experiences, and (5) developmental problems resulting in weakened self-structure that is deficit and conflict ridden. A vicious circle ensues, with distorted and arrested development that both increases the need for and disrupts the empathic responsiveness necessary to maintain self-cohesion.

The result is that these people are prone to experiences of self-fragmentation, with its terrible anxiety and rage, and to states of depletion and depression. Clinicians and patients consistently observe that these affects will intensify the biological elements of AD/HD, increasing attentional difficulties and further complicating the ongoing task of maintaining a healthy self. Although there are not research data on AD/HD adults to support this observation, abundant research on state-dependent learning demonstrates that affect states alter cognitive capacities.

AD/HD impacts all aspects of the biopsychosocial model. The *bio*logical hyperactivity, impulsiveness, and attentional problems increase stress. It also complicates *psycho*logical development, leaving a weakened self-structure that requires increased needs for *social* interactions that could be used to generate essential selfobject experiences—but at the same time disrupts necessary empathic interchanges. There is an endless loop, and it is not realistic to sequester any aspect of the biopsychosocial model from any other aspect. AD/HD can increase stress, weaken self-structure, and block the generation of selfobject experiences. That is to say, it increases the potential for loss of self-cohesion—and any reduction of self-cohesion seems to increase the frequency and intensity of the "biological" AD/HD symptoms.

Figure 1 indicates the interactive nature of forces that complicate the development and maintenance of a consolidated self. It is our hope that it points out an essential *interactive* aspect of the biopsychosocial model. Although there is a biological pathophysiology, it cannot sensibly be separated from the psychosocial factors, and cannot be considered *the* etiology.

Figure 1
A Self Psychology/Biopsychosocial Schema

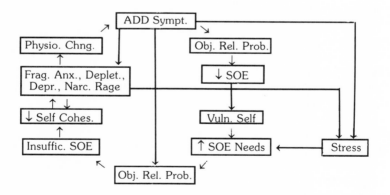

Abbreviations: SOE = selfobject experiences; Obj. Rel. Prob. = object relations problems; Vuln. Self = vulnerable self prone to loss of self-cohesion; Frag. Anx., Deplet., Depr., Narc. Rage = fragmentation anxiety, depletion, depression, narcissistic rage

We believe that this model may be helpful in understanding the interactive contributions of biological, psychological, and social elements of several psychiatric illnesses. For example, depression interferes with the generation of selfobject experiences. In *Listening to Prozac*, Kramer (1993) notes that patients may show rather dramatic alterations in their entire personality structure when they take Prozac. It is our experience that a biological shift out of depression, such as occurs with Prozac, makes the generation of selfobject experiences much more possible. Not only is biology changed, the entire available selfobject milieu is altered. This leads to far more consistently available opportunities to use interpersonal interactions and life events in ways that maintain, restore, and even transform self-organization. The patient will pass through this window because biological bars have been removed. However, when well-established intrapsychic organizing principles continue to complicate the generation of selfobject experiences, a biological shift will not be sufficient. Some gains may occur, but a window of opportunity may be lost without the addition of psychotherapy (whether individual, group, or family).

The recovery from biological barriers does not ensure that all patients will be able to use available environmental selfobject experiences, nor does it guarantee that such possibilities will realistically be available. Their illness may have yielded object relationships that actually do limit opportunities to find selfobject experiences. There is, in other words, a substantial percentage of people who will require a psychotherapeutic relationship to reinstitute growth even though biological barriers have been medically remedied. On one hand, if the need for psychotherapy is ignored, these people will only gain superficial symptom reduction; many will be prone to relapse. On the other hand, without removing the biological barriers, the psychotherapeutic work may be impossible or at least much more difficult, and perhaps less successful.

CLINICAL ILLUSTRATION

Many AD/HD adults need psychotherapy, but because of problems sustaining attention, they have particular difficulties in developing useful selfobject transferences and reorganizing intrapsychic structures. Minimally productive therapeutic relationships are common. With the addition of medication, however, therapy can take a new turn that is often dramatic. The biological symptoms diminish, making more effective work with internal experience possible. Likewise, relying on medication as if it were the treatment may be insufficient. The following case material illustrates why we recommend a comprehensive, biopsychosocial treatment for these patients.

Beth sought treatment with one of us (MNB) because she was having difficulty with Max, her boyfriend of several years. She wanted to get married. He was afraid of making the commitment even though he said he loved her. She had a long history of attracting men who loved her but who had one foot out the door.

Beth is the oldest of three children, with a younger brother and sister. Her father is a highly successful, driven businessman. She experienced her mother as very caring, but somewhat distant and very bound by the rules of traditional decorum. Her parents are invested in the perfection of their family at the expense of emotional honesty. They regarded negative affects as threats to the "happy family" posture, and they discouraged complaints with comments like, "Oh, don't worry. . . . You'll get over it. . . . You'll grow out of it. . . . Think how lucky you are to have all that you have."

Although bright, Beth was put in the lower-level classes during elementary school. In first grade she became an entertaining storyteller. To avoid doing homework, she would throw all her school papers in the bushes as she got off the school bus. When her mother discovered this, she felt humiliated by Beth's behavior, and scolded and humiliated her daughter. Her father engaged in "Beth battles" by forcefully helping her with homework. During these nightmarish sessions, he got angry at her inattention and "stubbornness," often adding "lazy" and "dumb" to a chain of invectives.

In third grade, Beth often arrived at school very unkempt. The youngest girl in the neighborhood, she so hungered for inclusion and attention that she invited teasing by the older girls. Beth's primary experience of her elementary school years was one of frustration, humiliation, and intense attention seeking. She even created a fictional brother who supposedly returned from Vietnam hooked on drugs. Although her actual report cards present a picture of a happy, outgoing, cooperative child, she had academic difficulties, failing to follow through on assignments and struggling with reading, spelling, and math. A quote from her fifth-grade teacher is the only indication in her report cards that she was struggling: "She has made quite a bit of progress. She knows what the problem is and that she is capable of doing better work than she has shown in the past. It takes lots of effort and completion of all assignments in order to achieve. I believe that she is learning the fact that one can't get along on personality alone. Her self image as far as work is concerned is improving." Beth's parents were upset that she wouldn't conform to school expectations, but because she was a girl, they did not expect her to be a high achiever.

She was clearly her father's favorite, and her brother was the mother's special child. Whenever Beth talked about her father in therapy, she would say that she would get overwhelmed by his desire to "know every little thing about her." When she was not forthcoming, he would feel hurt and rejected. He could not hear what was important to her; this would often evoke an intense fear that she found crushing, like an internal whirlwind that would swoop her up and hurl her into an ocean of suffocating terror.

In my initial formulation of Beth, I thought that she was caught in oedipal and mirroring attachments to her idealized father. These attachments were intensified by her mother's aloofness, conventionality, and overindulgence of Beth's younger brother. She desperately craved both typical and compensatory attention from her father, but she felt buffeted about by his demanding nature, intensity, and lack of boundaries. Beth struggled to be entirely independent, competent, and "in control," but this often gave way to the other extreme of being compliant and, at times, merged with her boyfriends. She would swing unexpectedly and rather dramatically between these two poles. When frustrated that she wasn't getting enough attention, or when "the other" in her life felt drowned by her needs for reassurance, attention, and sex, Beth would catapult herself into a defensive independent posture, declaring that she would take care of herself—forget them!

The pattern of organizing her self-esteem around the amount of attention she could get from men (women didn't count) became a focus in therapy. She would understand what she did and why she did it, and she would leave most sessions convinced she could maintain her self-esteem independently. She would often return feeling both ashamed that she had failed to meet this goal and relieved that she had gotten needed attention, no matter what the cost. When I tried to focus on what might be going on between us in the therapy, Beth said she experienced me as understanding and supportive. It was hard for her to experience disruptions with me. Although increasingly dependent on me, she did not talk about her experience of the relationship, except to say that there was a deep level of hunger that she was afraid of. When I asked more about it or suggested that it had its origins in her relationship with her mother, she would shake her head in agreement and continue to talk about her boyfriend.

Beth soon broke up with Max and got involved with someone at work. Joel was 15 years older and the divorced father of two teenaged children; he had just broken up with his steady girlfriend of three years. Beth knew it would be complicated to get involved with him, but she just couldn't say no. Much of our work centered on understanding her experience with him. But as with Max, before she knew it, her longing for mirroring by an idealized man led her to merge with him and do his biddings—as long as she got her ration of attention.

When she related her experiences, I would feel drowned in her words and intensity. At times, I had strong impulses to take control and organize her. At other times, I felt I was comprehending her words while my mind wandered elsewhere. No matter what we accomplished in the session, it would dissolve away by next session; we would be again at square one.

I was concerned that our relationship lacked the depth that is generally present when a good selfobject transference has developed. She said she liked her sessions and the way I responded to her, but she didn't feel close to me, nor did she feel that what I said to her ever really "got inside." Beth wanted the closeness, but when it was there, she couldn't really take it in.

During Beth's therapy, I developed a professional interest in adult AD/HD. I began to think back to the difficulty she had in school and her description of her mother's lack of physical closeness and playfulness when she was very young. Was the problem just that some primary archaic selfobject experiences were lacking, was it related to oedipal conflicts, or was her physical craving also an attempt to calm the physiological turmoil of AD/HD? How might these aspects have interacted?

I asked her for old school records and found that although bright, she was in the middle or lower group in reading and math. The report cards talk about her overly social nature and her not living up to her potential. When Beth talked about her early school years, the unhappy picture described earlier emerged. Because I now looked from a different perspective, it was obvious that she met *DSM-III-R* criteria for attention deficit disorder. Although there are impulsive criteria, she has a relative paucity of hyperactive symptoms, so current nomenclature places her in the Predominantly Inattentive Type (*DSM-IV*, 314.0). It is common for females to cluster in that category rather than the Predominantly Hyperactive-Impulsive or Combined Types (both 314.01). Since it is usually the hyperactivity and impulsivity that lead to intervention and diagnosis, it is common for adults with the Predominantly Inattentive Type not to have been diagnosed in childhood. Psychiatric referral confirmed the diagnosis, and she began a regimen 10 mg of Ritalin three times daily.

Within a week Beth noticed a difference. The "white noise, or whirring" that was a constant internal companion abated. Her intensity was replaced by a sense of inner calm she had never before experienced. When doing a solitary activity, like making up her teaching lesson plans, instead of looking at the clock every five minutes, she would be totally absorbed and would not notice the time for an hour. When interacting with her friends, Beth was better able to listen without blurting out what she was thinking. She became less focused on her boyfriend and was able to better organize herself at work and during recreational activitie. She felt she had begun to process all aspects of her life better— including therapy.

Beth had always rigidly insisted on doing things her way. It often seemed to others that she was "just stubborn." To Beth, it was a means of internally organizing herself. Without doing this she would feel chaotic: the constant whirlwind inside sucked her attention away and produced "static." With proper medication and an understanding of the consequences of having AD/HD, Beth has calmed much of her internal chaos and her defensive "stubbornness" has diminished.

Fortunately, when medication better controlled her scattered thinking, we gained greater access to her psychodynamic issues. Containing her biological distractibility and limiting the turmoil that it often engendered were additional factors that led to her intense, ambivalent efforts to merge with an idealized man.

For Beth, AD/HD was a complicating factor that interacted with other developmental issues. By itself, its only significance is that it causes shifting attentional focus and some impulsiveness; any psychodynamic picture can evolve. In Beth's case, her struggle was with both oedipal and preoedipal issues.

AD/HD seemed to have placed a greater barrier between Beth and her unattuned mother, who, for reasons of her own personality structure, found Beth's impulsiveness, high level of activity, and distractibility particularly difficult. It is impossible to know if the two of them would have connected under any circumstances, but Beth's AD/HD certainly seemed to have made adequate attachment even more difficult. She turned to her father, where she was able to find more opportunities for interactions that she could use to meet selfobject needs. He also was more accepting of her overtures, finding in his daughter an enjoyable liveliness. Throughout her schooling, this bright woman was unable to achieve fully. All of these factors combined to leave her with low self-esteem, which she had learned to repair through admiring and sexual responses from men. But she often chose narcissistic, ambivalently attached men. She impulsively mistook their responsiveness as genuine interest in her, when it was often only an aspect of their enticing her into mirroring them. These interactions left her wounded, frustrated, and determined to get them to pay attention to her.

During the early part of her therapy, she gained a superficial understanding of all of this. It was as though she could repeat exactly what she was doing, but it meant little to her, and it certainly did not help her to make better object choices or form a more internally based sense of self-esteem.

I often found myself feeling disappointed with her inability to make better use of treatment, and I thought this must have recapitulated what her mother had regularly felt toward her. I was also frequently lost in her scattered associations. Beth's general thought processes would meander through a rabbit's warren of seemingly unrelated ideas, leaving me by turns confused, bored, or fascinated with her insights. As a consequence, I found it more difficult than usual to maintain an empathic bond to her; when I would feel that I had succeeded, Beth would feel our bond one moment and then lose it the next. The net result was that, during the initial phase of treatment, her useful selfobject transference would taper off with each succeeding hour away from the office, finally disappearing altogether. Like someone moving before an irregular strobe light, her self-regulatory capacities would suddenly disappear and reappear. When they were unavailable, she would experience the painful affects associated with moderate loss of self-cohesion. She would then resort to symptomatic object choices in an effort to generate selfobject experiences, but she would be shocked at her behavior as she reconstituted.

With the addition of Ritalin, her thinking became more focused, making it easier for her to connect elements of what she was thinking and feeling. It also made it easier for me to remain in good empathic contact with her. As a result, she has begun to make real progress in therapy. There remain, however, a number of areas in which she has not developed self-regulatory techniques. For a considerable time, her judgment remained poor. For example, she might go out with a new date fully deciding to get to know him as a person before allowing sexual contact. But she would skip a dose of Ritalin and find herself in bed with the man. Eventually, she began to see this pattern and take her medication before going out.

Over the last six months, Beth's developmental gains have focused around her involvement with a man she plans to marry. Unlike previous object choices, her fiancé is able to respond to her needs and enjoys doing so. She has introduced him to her family and gotten their approval. Planning for the wedding has reignited her difficulties with her parents. As Beth deals with their controlling and intrusive maneuvers, she has been able to stand her ground and set her own boundaries. A recent telephone conversation with her mother and father sums up her latest developmental achievements: "I was 34 at the start of the conversation, was reduced to 6 in the middle of it and came back up to 29 at the end."

GENERAL TREATMENT CONSIDERATIONS

As we have tried to show throughout the chapter, the difficulties imposed by AD/HD do not explain the clinical picture by themselves. Instead, they perniciously alter many aspects of living. They can be a barrier to the development of needed selfobject transferences for two reasons: they disrupt the intrapsychic processing of a successfully formed therapeutic relationship, and they provoke countertransference problems. Medication has a powerful salutary effect in both the transference and the countertransference.

Particularly when the patient is properly medicated, psychotherapy is often more helpful. We basically adhere to standard self-psychological treatment principles. Within the context of a functional selfobject transference, we examine in detail the disruptions and repairs in relationships, their selfobject implications, and any symptomatic consequences. Attention is paid to relationships both inside and outside the treatment situation.

Because the symptoms are difficult for other people to tolerate, couples and family therapy may be useful. Self-help groups, such as Children and Adults with Attention Deficit Disorders, play an important role. Ch.A.D.D. chapters generally meet one to two times monthly, have formal informational presentations about AD/HD, and offer general support. We have also found group therapy to be a particularly effective adjunct to individual therapy. As in other self-psychologically run groups (Baker and Baker, 1993; Baker, 1993), patients use other group members to generate selfobject experiences, provide insight through understanding the feelings and behavior of others, and discover new experiences that can provide the basis for development of healthier intrapsychic structures and organizing principles. In addition, members teach one another new coping strategies.

Specific behavior patterns that are a part of AD/HD may need to be addressed through cognitive-behavioral techniques in individual therapy as well. These may include having the patients (and perhaps their families) read popular books, like *Attention Deficit Disorder in Adults* (Weiss, 1991) or *Driven to Distraction* (Hallowell and Ratey, 1994). Virtually everyone writing about treatment today finds that such extra-analytic techniques are generally useful because they help patients and families better understand the nature of the handicaps that AD/HD creates.

Since we are convinced that the development of self-structure and the reconfiguration of organizing principles is accomplished best in the sustaining therapeutic atmosphere of a functioning selfobject transference, we believe that any adjunctive approaches must be considered in light of its impact on these transferences. They may facilitate necessary transferences, but they may occasionally disrupt them in nontherapeutic ways, so caution and care are essential.

CONCLUSION

We have described the clinical picture, etiology, and treatment of attention deficit/hyperactivity disorder in adults. Our purpose was not merely to offer a clinically useful perspective on this troublesome common illness. We also used AD/HD as a paradigm to integrate the biopsychosocial model of psychiatric illness from a self-psychological perspective. We believe that this theory provides an inclusive, comprehensive, and parsimonious way to synthesize the model so that it can be put to pragmatic use in treating people with a wide variety of diagnoses.

Biology can never be isolated as a unitary cause of anything. We all bring our biology and our unique, historically formed psychology into a relational matrix. Behavior is developed through the interaction of each of these factors. AD/HD alone does not cause anything other than some difficulties in sustaining appropriate levels of attention, and perhaps hyperactivity and impulsiveness. This particular biology, however, almost always complicates interaction between people—but the specific consequences are necessarily codetermined by all participants. Some AD/HD children will find empathic responsiveness that makes it possible to generate selfobject experiences they can use in the process of creating a healthy self-structure. Others routinely will be unable to find selfobject experiences in their relationships with others.

Whatever the specific interactions are, the developing child must struggle to understand them. Like everyone else, AD/HD children must begin to create self-regulatory capacities and formulate a history, creating organizing principles and model scenes that will constitute their intrapsychic structure. The specific nature of that structure must always result from the interplay of biology, ongoing interactions, and the psychic structure that previously existed. Each of these three elements will both shape and be shaped by the other elements. Thus, a new psyche is constantly being assembled in a biopsychosocial context, and it will be a determinant of future interactions. This three-part matrix will facilitate or inhibit the person's efforts to develop and strengthen specific capabilities to regulate self-esteem and affects, resolve conflicts, form useful defenses, and reintegrate intrapsychic organizing principles and model scenes. In other words, the self cannot emerge independently from a biopsychosocial process.

AD/HD usually complicates this process to some greater or lesser degree because it often disrupts interpersonal interactions. AD/HD always complicates this process because it disrupts the capacity for sustained attention. As a result, the task of creating a cohesive, resilient self will be confounded to some greater or lesser degree. Again, the extent of this tangle depends on whether the child finds empathic, partially empathic, or nonempathic responsiveness from his or her selfobjects.

When one tries to understand people from a biopsychosocial perspective, self psychology offers a theory that can encompass the interaction between biology, psychology, and social interactions. Since the principal motivation of human behavior is to maintain the self and give expression to its nuclear program, and since this program is created by each individual at the interface between his or her unique biology, psychological structure, and ongoing selfobject milieu, all elements of the biopsychosocial model are integrated in a manner that is inclusive, comprehensive, and useful in guiding clinical interventions.

REFERENCES

American Medical Association (1993), *Drug Evaluations Annual 1994.* Chicago: American Medical Association.

Baker, M. & Baker, H. (1993), Self-psychological contributions to the theory and practice of group psychotherapy. In: *Group Therapy in Clinical Practice,* ed. A. Alonzo & H. I. Swiller. Washington, DC: American Psychiatric Press, pp. 49–68.

—— (1993), Self psychology and group psychotherapy. In: *Comprehensive Group Psychotherapy,* ed. H. I. Kaplan & B. J. Sadock. Baltimore: Williams & Wilkins, pp. 176–185.

Barkley, R. A. (1990), *Attention-Deficit Hyperactivity Disorder: A Handbook for Diagnosis and Treatment.* New York: Guilford.

Cantwell, D. P. (1985), Pharmacotherapy of AD/HD in adolescents: What do we know, where should we go, how should we do it? *Psychopharmacol. Bull.,* 21:251–257.

Desch, L. W. (1991), Neurochemical aspects of attention deficit hyperactivity disorder. In: *Attention Deficit Disorders and Hyperactivity in Children,* ed. J. P. Accord, A. T. Blondes & B. Y. Whitman. New York: Marble Decker, pp. 57–84.

Diagnostic and Statistical Manual for Mental Disorders, Fourth Edition (1994), Washington, DC: American Psychiatric Press.

Engel, G. (1977), The need for a new medical model: A challenge for biomedicine. *Science,* 196:129–136.

Hallowell, E. M. & Ratey, J. J. (1994), *Driven to Distraction.* New York: Pantheon.

Holdnack, J. A., Moberg, P. J., Arnold, S. A., Gur, R. C. & Gur, R. E. (in press), Speed of processing and verbal learning deficits in adults diagnosed with attention deficit disorder.

Kramer, P. (1993), *Listening to Prozac.* New York: Viking.

Menkes, M. M., Rowe, J. S. & Menkes, J. H. (1967), A twenty-five-year follow-up study on the hyperkinetic child with minimal brain dysfunction. *Pediatrics,* 39:393–399.

Popper, C. W. (1988), Disorders usually first evident in infancy, childhood, or adolescence: Attention-deficit hyperactivity disorder. In: *The American Psychiatric Press Textbook of Psychiatry,* ed. J. A. Talbot, R. E. Hales & S.C. Yudofsky. Washington, DC: American Psychiatric Press, pp. 651–664.

Reisinger, J. (1993), Blinks: A phenomenon of distractibility in attention-deficit disorder (ADD). Privately circulated, copyrighted manuscript.

Silver, L. B. (1992), *Attention-deficit Hyperactivity Disorder.* Washington, DC: American Psychiatric Press.

Tallmadge, J. & Barkley, R. A. (1983), The interactions of hyperactive and normal boys with their fathers and mothers. *J. Abn. Child Psychol.*, 11:565–579.

Thorley, G. (1988), Adolescent outcome for hyperactive children. *Arch. Diseases Children,* 63:1181–1183.

Weiss, G. & Hechtman, L. T. (1993), *Hyperactive Children Grown Up.* New York: Guilford.

Weiss, L. (1991), *Attention Deficit Disorder in Adults.* Dallas: Taylor.

Wender, P. H. (1985), Pharmacological treatment of attention deficit disorder, residual type (AD/HD, RT, "minimal brain dysfunction, hyperactivity") in adults. *Psychopharmacol. Bull.*, 21:222–231.

—— (1987), *The Hyperactive Child, Adolescent and Adult: Attention Deficit Disorder Through the Life Span.* New York: Oxford University Press.

Zaemetkin, A. J., Nordahl, T. E., Gross, M. et al. (1992), Cerebral glucose metabolism in adults with hyperactivity of childhood onset. *New England J. Med.,* 323:1361–1366.

Chapter 14

Discussion of "A Self-Psychological Approach to Attention Deficit/ Hyperactivity Disorder in Adults: A Paradigm to Integrate the Biopsychosocial Model of Psychiatric Illness"

Joseph Palombo

We owe a debt of gratitude to Howard Baker and Margaret Baker for bringing to our attention an important but neglected area of theory in self psychology. To my knowledge, this is the first time a paper that deals with issues of biological endowment has been presented in a self psychology conference. In many of my published papers I have attempted to conceptualize a framework for the integration of biological and self psychological concepts (Palombo, 1979, 1985, 1987, 1991, 1993a,b, 1994, 1995; Palombo and Feigon, 1984). However, these efforts have largely gone unnoticed in self psychology circles. I therefore find it gratifying to participate in a discussion about this important contribution.

I believe the Bakers are correct when they state that Kohut focused on the mismatch between the child's temperament and the caregivers' limitations as the salient cause of developmental failures. But he did not devote much thinking to the biological components that contribute to this failure. To my knowledge, the only reference Kohut made regarding the contributions of biological factors to the development of the self and disorders of the self is found in the Introduction to *The Analysis of the Self* (1971). In that introduction, in speaking of borderline and psychotic disorders, he states: "From the genetic point of view one is led to assume that in the psychoses the personality of the parents (and a number of other environmental circumstances) collaborated with inherited factors to prevent the formation of a nuclear cohesive self" (p. 11). Later on he adds: "The second elaboration of the dynamic-genetic proposition . . . concerns the role of innate, inherited factors in producing the propensity toward the fragmentation of the self encountered in the psychoses and in producing the propensity toward the maintenance of a cohesive self which exists in the narcissistic personality disturbances" (p. 14).

He cautions against attempts to analyze these disorders. In his view, the vulnerability of the self in these patients is such as to make any but the most supportive measures inappropriate.

On the other hand, concerning patients with narcissistic personality disorders, he finds that "the conclusion seems at times inescapable that the patient should be more severely disturbed than he, in fact, is. . . . [O]ne is led in such instances to the assumption of the existence of innate factors which maintain the cohesiveness of the archaic grandiose self and the idealized parent imago despite catastrophic traumas to which the child was exposed during crucial phases of early development" (p. 14).

The current focus in psychiatry on the biological contributors to psychopathology has not led to a parallel interest in psychoanalytic circles. The contributions of Levin in *Mapping the Mind* (1991), Hadley's chapter in Lichtenberg's *Motivation and Psychoanalysis* (1989), and, more recently, Schore's monumental work *Affect Regulation and the Origin of the Self* (1994) attempt to correlate brain function with the major constructs of self psychology. These efforts are broad based but have little applicability to the clinical situation. Their value lies in the contribution they make toward the goal of mapping psychological constructs onto brain systems. However, at this point in the state of our knowledge, a bridge between neurobiology and behavior can best be built by using a different strategy, that of relating specific neurobiological deficits to specific behaviors. It is more fruitful to begin with specific identifiable deficits and work back to the affected psychological structures. The Bakers use such a strategy by focusing on the neuroregulatory dysfunctions that in patients with AD/HD represent a component of frontal lobe executive functions. In addition to the impulsivity and attentional problems seen in AD/HD patients, these dysfunctions often produce more general executive function difficulties in setting goals and in planning, organizing, and implementing strategies to attain their goals. These in turn create conditions in which the capacities for self-regulation and self-soothing are deficient. It is therefore refreshing to see a contribution that attempts to relate directly these specific types of brain dysfunction and their clinical manifestations to a self-psychological framework.

The Bakers' thesis is that it is possible for the principles of self psychology to integrate the elements of the biopsychosocial model of psychiatry. They attempt to synthesize into a coherent etiological explanation the contributions of the biological and social factors to the pathological outcome. In their biopsychosocial framework the Bakers describe the disruptions AD/HD creates in the patient's capacity to avail himself or herself of the selfobject functions caregivers are prepared to provide. They illustrate through their case examples the disorders these produce in patients' functioning, the resulting disruptions in the developmental dialogue into adulthood, and some of the issues that arise in their treatment.

I would summarize their contribution as follows: Each patient's experience is filtered through the patient's endowment. The aspect of endowment involved in AD/HD is the neuroregulatory control system. Because of the neuroregulatory deficits the patient cannot adequately regulate thought processes, affect states, and behaviors. The patient responds to events based on his or her experience, but the responses are not congruent with the expectations of those in the context. Efforts by both the patient and others to continue the dialogue lead to confusion and a derailment of the dialogue. The consequence is that the patient cannot avail himself or herself of the obtainable selfobject functions. Others, in the patient's context, misinterpret the motives behind the patient's responses and perceive the behavior to be defiant, oppositional, or negativistic. A set of patterns of interactions is established in which the patient expects to be misunderstood and is made anxious because of his or her failure to understand. The patient's frustration increases and eventually leads to enraged responses or to withdrawal. Overlaid over this set of patterns are the selfobject deficits that result from the primary neuroregulatory deficit. The outcome manifests in the familiar narcissistic personality disorders described by Kohut.

In the clinical setting, patients present the embodiment of their current level of integration. To the extent that they are cohesive they demonstrate healthy competencies and a sense of cohesion, that is, they can give a coherent account of themselves. To the extent that they are troubled, they lack cohesion. They fail in the attempt to create a coherent narrative of their lives. Their distress arises from the fact that they are unable to make meaningful what has happened to them. Experiences of fragmentation are experiences of the lack of order or the loss of meaning. The deficits of the patient with AD/HD are evident in the way the patient presents, in the story the patient tells, and in the transference the patient forms. The specific selfobject functions affected may be the idealizing function, with its correlated experience of self-regulation; the mirroring function, with its correlated experience of feeling worthwhile; and the alter-ego function, with the feeling of difference as negative. One or more of these selfobject functions may be deficient in patients with AD/HD.

The concept of complementarity is useful in understanding the complex types of transferences these patients form. At its simplest level the concept of a selfobject provides a model for understanding the types of complementarity I wish to discuss. The concept of "selfobject" delineates the ways in which others provide psychological functions necessary for a person's self-cohesion (Kohut, 1971, 1977). In other words, the context in which the person lives becomes a part of that person's sense of self. Most often these functions operate silently and outside the person's awareness, although they are provided by another person. The experience of the subject is that their location is within and part of the sense of self.

Another group of phenomena operates similarly but must be thought of differently. This group I designate with the term *complementary functions.* In our relationships with people we make use of others as means to ends we wish to attain. We use secretaries, bus drivers, policemen, waiters, and so on. We also use a variety of objects that our culture has created to extend our limited human capacities. It is possible to conceptualize these as prosthetic devices that enable us to do more than we could do alone, but do not necessarily serve selfobject functions. These objects, although self-sustaining, can hardly be said to provide selfobject functions. We can say that all selfobject functions provide complementarity, but not all complementary functions are selfobject functions. In the caregiving relationship, complementary functions that parents perform for the child dominate the relationship. The caregiver is also a selfobject for the infant. Children with neurobehavioral deficits tend to draw from caregivers functions that serve to complement their immature or deficient psyches and their incomplete neurological systems.

In short, we can distinguish two types of complementarity that patients evoke in their therapists, and that therapists are drawn to provide to their neurobehaviorally impaired patients with. One type of complementarity provides the neuroregulatory functions the patient is missing; the other type of provides selfobject functions. In the former case the patient uses the therapist as a tool that serves a specific purpose, usually that of performing a task the patient is unable to perform. This type of complementarity produces in the patient a dependence on the tool, although the provider is interchangeable with others who can perform the same function. In the case of AD/HD patients, as the Bakers' case examples illustrate, the therapist is called upon to provide complementary functions in the areas of regulation, attention, focus, and organization.

In the case of the selfobject function the situation is different. The complementarity is to the patient's sense of self. The patient experiences the function as part of his or her self. This function is not as easily interchangeable as are the prosthetic functions. Selfobject functions are performed in the psychological area and consist of the regulation of affect states, the sharing of emotional experiences, and the affirmation of the patient's sense of self.

Whether both types of complementarity constitute transferences is subject to debate. However, unless therapists are clear about this distinction, their interventions are likely to result in confusion. Patients must be helped to differentiate between their selfobject deficits and their neurobehavioral deficits. In the case of patients with AD/HD, the neuroregulatory deficits often can only be dealt with through medication. Some patients may develop compensatory stratagems or may use others in their contexts to help regulate them. The point is that improvement cannot occur in these deficits through interpretation of their meanings. Behaviors that result from selfobject deficits are motivated behaviors. However, behaviors produced by neuroregulatory deficits are not part of the patient's motivational system any more than the stroke patient's aphasia can be said to be motivated. The fact that these behaviors have a meaning to the patient, and that they enter into the patient's narrative, does not mean that they can be eliminated through interpretation and understanding of their meaning. Although it may be possible to heal the patient's self-deficits that are due to selfobject deficits, helping the patient with the other deficits is much more complex. Some patients could probably compensate for their neurobiological deficits; while others may find more reliable means through which to complement their deficits. As the Bakers' case demonstrates, distinguishing between the two types of deficits is essential if the treatment is not to end in stalemate or failure.

REFERENCES

Hadley, J. L. (1989), The neurobiology of motivational systems. In: *Psychoanalysis and Motivation,* ed. J. D. Lichtenberg. Hillsdale, NJ: The Analytic Press, Chapter 11.

Kohut, H. (1971), *The Analysis of the Self.* New York: International Universities Press.

—— (1977), *The Restoration of the Self.* New York: International Universities Press.

Levin, F. M. (1991), *Mapping the Mind.* Hillsdale, NJ: The Analytic Press.

Lichtenberg, J. D. (1989), *Psychoanalysis and Motivation.* Hillsdale, NJ: The Analytic Press.

Palombo, J. (1979), Perceptual deficits and self-esteem in adolescence. *Clin. Soc. Work J.,* 7:34–61.

—— (1985), The treatment of borderline neurocognitively impaired children: A perspective from self psychology. *Clin. Soc. Work J.,* 13:117–128.

—— (1987), Selfobject transferences in the treatment of borderline neurocognitively impaired children. In: *The Borderline Patient: Emerging Concepts in Diagnosis, Psychodynamics and Treatment,* ed. J. S. Grotstein, M. Solomon & J. A. Lang. Hillsdale, NJ: The Analytic Press, pp. 317–345.

—— (1991), Neurocognitive differences, self-cohesion, and incoherent self-narratives. *Child & Adol. Soc. Work J.,* 8:449–472.

—— (1993a), Neurocognitive differences, developmental distortions, and incoherent narratives. *Psychoanal. Inq.,* 3:63–84.

—— (1993b), Learning disabilities in children: Developmental, diagnostic and treatment considerations. *Proceeding: National Academies of Practice, Fourth National Health Policy Forum, Healthy Children 2000: Obstacles and Opportunities,* April 24–25.

—— (1994), Incoherent self-narratives and disorders of the self in children with learning disabilities. *Smith College Stud. Soc. Work,* 64:129–152.

—— (1995), Psychodynamic and relational problems of children with nonverbal learning disabilities. In: *The Handbook of Infant and Adolescent Psychotherapy: A Guide to Diagnosis and Treatment,* ed. J. A. Incorvia & B. Mark. Northvale, NJ: Aronson, pp. 147–178.

—— & Feigon, J. (1984), Borderline personality in childhood and its relationship to neurocognitive deficits. *Child & Adol. Soc. Work J.,* 1:18–33.

Schore, A. N. (1994), *Affect Regulation and the Origin of the Self: The Neurobiology of Emotional Development.* Hillsdale, NJ: Lawrence Erlbaum Associates.

Chapter 15

The Function of Early Selfobject Experiences in Gendered Representations of God

Lallene J. Rector

As though the world had not riddles enough, we are set the new problem of understanding how these other people [religious believers] have been able to acquire their belief in the Divine Being [Freud, 1939].

Since the beginning of psychoanalysis, various attempts have been made to explain the predilection of many persons to seek meaning, consolation, and inspiration in religion. Of historical *and* contemporary interest has been the experience of an individual's relationship to the sacred, or to a Divine Other. Who and what is God to the individual? What does one believe and feel about God? More importantly, what does God feel about him or her? How are these beliefs formed and what changes them?

This chapter addresses a particular aspect of the subjective experience of an anthropomorphized god-image, that is, the significance of gendered representations of God and the role of early selfobject experiences in an individual's preference for a masculine or feminine god-image. Though there are many implications for clinical practice, a variety of philosophical and theological perspectives that could be engaged, and multicultural dialogue with other world religions, this exploration is delimited to include a theoretical consideration of self psychology as an organizing explanatory schema for this phenomenon in Western experience of the Judeo-Christian tradition.

The argument is offered that a complex web of interrelation exists among the self's experience of gender, the psychology of an individual's psychic representation of God, and the role of early selfobject experience in both. More specifically, it is argued, based on Lang's (1984) work, that the subjective sense of gender identity may be mediated through the selfobject functions provided by early caregivers and that the ways in which femininity and masculinity are valued (i.e., idealized and mirrored) by the child's selfobjects also interact with cultural perspectives on gender (Lang, 1984). These experiences and the various internal and external meanings attributed to gender have implications for the psychological function of gender choice in an anthropomorphic god-image. It is suggested that a shift in gender of the god-image may be precipitated by experiences (both psychotherapeutic and extratherapeutic) that stimulate a reemergence or reconfiguration of certain selfobject needs.

In clinical practice, a variety of religious beliefs and experiences may emerge during the course of an analytic or psychotherapeutic treatment. If the clinician is curious and the patient is so inclined, implicit and explicit descriptions of god-images may be explored. Following are some examples:

A thirty-five-year-old woman from a Catholic family sends "Father God" on a sabbatical. As a Catholic sister returning from seven years of missionary work in South America, she has just begun to recover memories of sexual abuse by both parents. The ideas of "Jesus inside me" and "Jesus in my heart" have become frightening intrusions. While devoted to her religious vocation, she has lost a sense of who God is, but knows somehow that while God was on sabbatical, *He* became *She*, a feminine image. Eventually, the patient decides she no longer believes in God at all.

A man in his early thirties is raised in a home by parents who were both traumatized by conservative religious practices and who have taken an understandably negative view toward religion. The patient converts to a fairly conservative Christian group in his adolescence and becomes a faithful but quiet adherent. As we explore his own childhood, what emerges is an experience of a depressed and emotionally unavailable mother, and a critical, workaholic father who can never be pleased and who is also unavailable. God is distant and critical and the patient weeps over the dilemma he feels between the prospect of hell should he alter his beliefs, or the prospect of eternity with a critical "heavenly father."

A young clergywoman and mother falls in love with her best female friend. The consequences have a devastating effect on the lives of all those involved and result in rejection by friends and family. Her mother had been a beauty pageant winner and wanted this daughter to follow suit, at least in appearance. The patient had always wondered if she was feminine enough and her homoerotic desires now heightened these worries. Her choice of profession was linked to a wish to be closer to her father—to be the son he wanted. Feeling abandoned even by God, she says, "God has turned His back on me. And God is a *Him*; otherwise *She* wouldn't have abandoned me."

A *middle-aged professional woman*, raised in a liberal, mainstream Protestant family, describes God as a wise, old, and distant figure. She consciously recognizes the resemblance to her idealized father. He had provided a refuge from a depressed, obese mother who created a chaotic environment, not only in the home, but also in the psyches of her children. She depreciated any attempt by women to enhance their appearance. "One should be clean and nice." Anything else indicated a woman whose values were misplaced, implying questionable character and probable sexual promiscuity. While the patient held a fairly traditional view of God as "the wise, old grandfather in the sky," during the treatment, she reported actually praying to Mother Nature. "Mother nature is close to us and she understands our difficulties."

Each of these reports would justify an in-depth case study, but even as brief vignettes, they are illustrative of the variety of patients' descriptions in relation to their subjective experiences of God. These reports stimulate inquiry about why some persons transform the gender of God (typically from masculine to feminine imagery) when their needs are not being met by the masculine figure, whereas others seem stuck with their experiences of an oppressive male deity. Still others regard a "heavenly father" as an idealized version of an earthly disappointment and have no interest in or need for a feminine image of the Divine. Why do some continue to believe and others abandon their beliefs? Notable is the complex interaction of early unempathic selfobjects, the interplay of attitudes about femininity and masculinity, trauma, and a variety of meanings in religious experience and god-image.

AN OVERVIEW OF GOD-IMAGE RESEARCH

In reviewing a number of empirical studies, Beit-Hallahmi and Argyle (1975) conclude there is support for psychoanalytic notions that early object relations have an impact on religious ideas and feelings and that there is evidence of similarity between parental images and deity images. Rizzuto (1979) notes:

A statement, for example, that "the findings of a relationship between the image of God and the image of the opposite-sex or preferred parent lend support to the notion that the deity is a projected love-object" may be statistically correct, but it does not do justice to large numbers of patients who have very complex and painful relations with their Gods. For the psychoanalyst the facts about a person's God need to be personalized and specific to be understood at all [p. 5].

Part of the specificity Rizzuto calls for may be found in a self-psychological understanding. The nature of selfobject functions and self–selfobject transferences delineated in Kohut's corpus (1971, 1977, 1984) with the notions of lifelong idealization, mirroring, and alter-ego needs are pertinent to understanding psychological meanings and functions of god-images. For example, Kohut (1984) writes: "When we feel uplifted by our admiration for a great cultural ideal, for example, the old uplifting experience of being picked up by our strong and admired mother and having been allowed to merge with her greatness, calmness, and security it may be said to form the unconscious undertones of the joy we are experiencing as adults" (p. 50).

Formal attempts at psychological understandings of god-images began with Freud in the first half of the century and have been continued by the more recent work of Rizzuto (1979) and Vergote and Tamayo (1981). Although there were many different research efforts in the early twentieth century focusing on conversion experiences and other mystical experiences (see the work of Coe, 1916, 1922; Starbuck, 1899; Leuba, 1912, 1925; and James, 1902), Freud was really the first to give sustained theoretical attention to the psychological derivatives of the concept of a father God—and for Freud, it was an exclusively male image of God. Freud concluded that religion is primarily a form of paternal transference with negative and positive aspects, a neurotic replay of childhood, motivated by fear and unresolved oedipal conflicts (1913, 1927, 1930, 1939).

Freud's perspective was not entirely new. Feuerbach (1841), whom Freud greatly admired, had already explicated the notion of God as a human projection of the self, that is, theology is essentially an expression of anthropology. What has proven to be significant is Freud's suggestion that the understanding and psychological experience of God is directly related to early childhood experiences with parental figures. Religion was primarily motivated by a longing for the father. There are many criticisms of Freud's perspective, most notably his restricted view of religion as neurotic, his failure to deal with differences between believers and nonbelievers, his failure to deal with the mother's role in later religious experience, and his failure to deal with religion in women. Given even these limitations, however, Freud has at least pointed us in the direction of a deeper psychological understanding of the relationship of parental experience to the formation of god-images.

Rizzuto became convinced that if Freud's theory of God as an exaltation of the parental imago was correct, at least psychologically speaking, then psychiatry had been missing very important information about patients' developmental histories. One of the primary concepts in her research is that of "mental representation," including its dynamic nature, and the ways in which mental representations (or, in this case, god-images) are reworked and reinterpreted as a result of life experiences and therapeutic treatment. Rizzuto suggests that the way in which individuals come to terms with God at various points in their lives (childhood, adolescence, young adulthood, marriage, career/vocation, and death) affects the meaningfulness or affective obsolescence of the god-image. She concludes that an image or mental representation of God is constituted in the interaction of the parental god-image, images based on the real-life parent, the wished-for parent, the feared parent of the imagination, and the image that official religion offers. These images do not go away, she claims, but are repressed, transformed, or used.

Rizzuto does not concur with Freud's notion that images of God are simply expressions of the oedipal conflict writ large; rather, she believes that these images derive from the nature of the individual's object relations. Therefore, in assessing a person's image of God, Rizzuto finds it important to consider the following dimensions:

1. whose God is represented
2. the nature of the individual's object relations
3. the nature of the experience of the self, and
4. the specific moment or period of life in question

The nature of the self-experience is especially relevant to our interests. Rizzuto *does* concur with recent empirical research that there is a consistent link between how one feels about oneself and one's particular god-image.

In summary, the research literature is largely in agreement theoretically, and is confirmed empirically, about two points. First, images of God, feelings about God, and the needs brought to God are closely connected with early childhood experiences of primary caretakers, or for our purposes, selfobjects. Second, these images of God are intimately connected with thoughts and feelings about oneself.

SELF PSYCHOLOGY AND THE PSYCHOLOGY OF RELIGION

Kohut allows for the possibility that religious experience need not be regarded primarily as a pathological development. Instead, it may serve selfobject functions of enhancing self-esteem and self-cohesion, and may even be expressive of the transformations of narcissism into wisdom, empathy, and creativity. Mirroring, alter-ego, and idealizing selfobject needs may all be experienced in relation to a psychic representation of God. A review of Kohut's treatment of religion indicates that he maintained a critical perspective, in the best sense of "critical," and that his views contained both positive assessments of the function of religion, and a discriminating view toward the regressive and defensive dimensions of religious experience. In a moment, I will trace Kohut's view: more systematically in terms of the developmental trajectories of selfobject needs, from archaic ones to the more mature transformations of narcissism.

In contrast to Freud's views about religion, Kohut argued that the Oedipus complex can be used to indict neither religion nor antireligious attitudes. A further departure from Freud is seen in Volume 2 of *The Search for the Self* (1978):

> The recognition, for example, that the self arises in a matrix of empathy, and that it strives to live within a modicum of empathic responses in order to maintain itself, explains certain needs of man and illuminates the function of certain aspects of institutionalized religion, thus allowing us to appreciate certain dimensions of the culture-supportive aspects of religion and making it less necessary for us to see religion only as an illusion. . . .
> The insights of the psychology of the self enable us to shed our intolerant attitude toward religion [p. 752].

In *How Does Analysis Cure?* (1984), Kohut discusses the results of a successful analysis and notes that the former reliance on security provided by archaic merger states gives way to a security provided by empathic resonances that the patient can now elicit from his or her environment. Sometimes this involves the capacity to utilize substitute selfobjects through visual imagery. He notes in particular the "hallucinatory conjuring of the presence of the idealized Godhead which enables certain individuals to carry out acts of supreme courage. . . . It leads in addition, to a nonapologetically positive assessment of the role and significance of art and religion which differs from the assessment of classical analysis" (p. 76).

However, Kohut also saw the less positive ways in which religion might function intrapsychically. In particular, he (1994) observes that the Judeo-Christian value system of altruistic object love has led to the disregard of the "potentialities of narcissism" (pp. 145–146). Although Christianity leaves open narcissistic fulfillment in the realm of merger with the idealized, omnipotent selfobject, it attempts to curb manifestations of the grandiose self (1978).

For Kohut, this was seen most clearly in the distinction between "Guilty Man" and "Tragic Man." The guilty human being is associated with the primacy of guilt over pleasure; the tragic human being experiences the frustration of a blocked path to realization of the self. Kohut (1978, p. 754) viewed Christianity (and classical psychoanalytic perspectives, as well) as addressing conflict and not the more fundamental issue of the self's development. In the essay "On Leadership" (1969–1970, in Ornstein, 1990) he offers the following scathing observation:

> The psychological demands which Christian ethics have made upon Western man [and woman] may very well be considered as excessive, or at least as traumatically premature. In essence, Christian ethics are not satisfied with the ego's domination over the grandiose self and with the integration of its demands with the interest and goals of the ego; Christianity insists on the complete neutralization of the grandiose self and of the egotistical purposes of the personality. "If you love only those who love you," Jesus preaches in the Sermon on the Mount (Luke 6, NEB, 1961), "what credit is that to you? . . . if you do good only to those who do good to you, what credit is that to you?" [pp. 124–125].

It is clear that Kohut viewed such ethical demands as inhibiting any expression of the grandiose self, archaic or mature.

Although Kohut deals more extensively with the idealizing selfobject need and its expression in religion, he does give attention to the mirroring and alterego selfobject functions. In *The Kohut Seminars* (1987), he captures very succinctly the subjectively experienced dimension of the mirroring need. When the child realizes that the original narcissistic equilibrium has a perfection for which there is no adult replica, the child tries to save this "narcissistic paradise" in one of two ways. First, the child adopts this stance: "I am all good, but everything else is bad. I am all great, but there is some badness outside that doesn't belong" (Kohut, 1987, p. 78). The solution is to have others confirm how great one is, to find a mirroring selfobject experience. In the archaic version of this need, a merger state is sought. Kohut (1971) speculated that when the transference equilibrium is disturbed in a reactivated grandiose self, there may be a regression to archaic forms of idealization and the expression of ecstatic, trancelike religious feelings.[1]

---

[1] See the case of Mr. X in *The Restoration of the Self* (1977) for a clinical treatment of entering ministry as a "carrier of consciously entertained grandiose ideas (identification with Christ)" (pp. 200, 218).

Beyond Kohut's elaborations, I would suggest a further archaic expression, in religion, of the grandiose-exhibitionistic self, that is, the appeal to God in the claim that one "is a child of God," is "chosen," or in the hope that God recognizes one's specialness. Perhaps a more mature expression of the need to be known and recognized is seen in the opening verses of Psalm 139 (RSV): "O Lord, thou hast searched me and known me! Thou knowest when I sit down and when I rise up; thou discernest my thoughts from afar. Thou searchest out my path and my lying down, and art acquainted with all my ways." This passage suggests the sense that an individual knows oneself as he or she is known. However, an element of merger is still present, and as William James noted in his classic, *The Varieties of Religious Experience* (1902), union is a characteristic feature of mystical experience.

The alterego solution of expanding into others who are acceptable because they are like the self is another approach to saving the grandiose self of the early "narcissistic paradise." Kohut says little about this selfobject need and its relation to religion, but he (1990, Vol. 3) does imply an alter-ego dimension in observing the tragic figure's "incarnations in the myths of organized religion" (p. 214) and in the reference made previously (1984) to consequences of a successful analysis, that is, the capacity of a "broadened sense of being in tune with the preoccupations of a group" to which the patient belongs (p. 76).

The twinship or alter-ego needs do appear to be seen most commonly in various understandings and expectations of an incarnational God become human, or in spiritual leaders. Part of the emotional appeal to many people of "Jesus/Son of God" is the fact that God is seen as human, like us. The recognition of a spiritual dimension to human nature, expressed in Genesis as the *imago dei*, or the concept of being "created in the image of God," is expressive of desires to be like God, belong to God, and return to God at death. It could be argued that an even closer alterego appropriation of a god-image would include a gendered image of God matching that of the believer. Paradoxically, the tradition teaches that human beings are not God (though they seem to struggle through life with the wish to be God), and at the same time they are created in the image of God.

The second solution to saving the "narcissistic paradise" of early childhood is to adopt the following position: "I am nothing, but at least there is something great and perfect outside myself that is the carrier of what I formerly experienced. All I can do now is to try to attach myself to it . . . and then I will become as great as it is" (Kohut, 1987, p. 79). In his discussion over the years of the idealizing selfobject need, Kohut offers a more fully developed set of observations regarding this function of religion. In the archaic state, mystical mergers are not unusual. Kohut

(1971) characterizes these "vague religious preoccupations" as a "fuzzy idealism" that no longer emanates from a clearly delimited admired figure (p. 85). The loss of an idealized figure in early life "not infrequently" leads to a kind of nature religion or philosophy (e.g., Thoreau) (Kohut, 1987, p. 289). In *The Analysis of the Self*, Kohut (1971) describes the prestages of an idealizing transference that may carry seemingly abstract preoccupations with philosophical and religious questions about existence, life, and death. It seems that in both these cases of fuzzy idealism that the patient fears loss of self in the deep wish to merge with an idealizing selfobject, or retraumatization of the early loss of the idealized selfobject. Idealization also raises the question about what is deemed idealizable and what kind of impact this may have on the preferred gender of an individual's god-image in our culture.

The nature of God indicated in more recent theological developments parallels both archaic and mature expressions of idealization. Liberation theologies of the third world, with their notions that God is primarily for the oppressed and poor, and not for the affluent oppressors, might be viewed as a more archaic attempt to align with perfection outside of oneself. The story of the Exodus could be considered a prototype. The theologies following World War II and the Holocaust (i.e., the "Death of God" theologies) may represent a traumatic deidealization of the omnipotent god-image. These theodicy issues challenge what Kohut called an archaic form of idealization. Process theology, however, with its idea of God as limited by human freedom and the notion of human beings as "cocreators" with God, might represent a less traumatic deidealization. Finally, we might understand the experience of Job's arguing with God as the expression of both the adversarial and efficacy selfobject functions that Wolf has delineated in *Treating the Self* (1988).

God-image research and the psychology of the self have important points of intersection for understanding more about how early childhood experiences of parents and the developmental fate of the narcissistic needs for mirroring, alter-ego belonging, and idealizing have impact upon religious commitments and experiences of God. Psychoanalytic perspectives underscore the necessary recognition that the beliefs and feelings toward God that are psychologically, and perhaps unconsciously, operative in one's experience may be radically different from what is cognitively adhered to and consciously articulated (Jordan, 1986).

GENDER IDENTITY AND DISTURBANCE IN SELF PSYCHOLOGY

How an individual comes to know there are two genders, how one settles in on some certainty about which gender he or she is, and how one feels about it have important implications for gender differences in religious experience and for attractions to and repulsions from gendered images of God. Gender identity—that socially and culturally defined sense of being a boy or a girl and what it subjectively means to be masculine or feminine, female or male—has been the focus of numerous investigations (Freud, 1925, 1931, 1933; Stoller, 1990; Fast, 1984).

Rehearsing Freud's views here is not necessary, but generally speaking, he based much of his theorizing about sexuality on the assumption that boys and girls initially regard all persons as male. In his treatment of the clitoris as the female version of the penis, Freud (1931) postulated that girls are originally "masculine" and have to accept and develop into a feminine identity. Hence, there is no primary femininity. In addition to this perspective, Freud has been criticized for failing to deal adequately with a major preoedipal developmental factor for both boys and girls (i.e., identification with the mother). In contrast, self psychology (along with the object relations school) has addressed the significance of this earlier period for the development of the self.

Kohut did not systematically address questions of how the self acquires a sense of gender identity, nor did he address the related issue of how gender difference might affect the individual's experience of selfobject functions. Instead, he tends to appeal to the overarching importance of the empathic matrix. In *The Kohut Seminars* (1987), he discusses the issue of women with careers and says, "I think the crucial issue is not the difference between the sexes. The crucial issue is the specific individual's history" (p. 234).

In the essay "The Self in History" (1978, Vol. 2), Kohut is asked to explain why so few women have been idealized figures in society. He replies that he does not know and cites the classical perspective that penis envy is a severe injury to the little girl's self-esteem. However, he observes, the little boy also suffers an equal injury with reference to his small penis. (Parenthetically, it is interesting to note the misstep in Kohut's logic, that is, what about the experience of womb-envy in little boys?) He concludes again: "I believe however that a child is much more significantly influenced by the empathic attitude of the grownups around him or her than by the givens of organic equipment. . . . The importance of the matrix of empathy in which we grow up cannot be overestimated" (pp. 776–77). In *How Does Analysis Cure?* Kohut (1984) continues: "I do not believe, in other words, that a child's low self-esteem, in general, and low body-self-esteem, in particular, are in essence gender-related. For the little boy no less than for the little girl, such disturbed self-esteem is a pathological state with genetic roots in the flawed mirroring responses of the selfobjects" (p. 214).

It is suggested that self-esteem disturbances are not primarily gender related, but are more fundamentally related to "flawed mirroring responses." However, as Lang (1984) argues, whereas the self's needs for mirroring, idealizing, and belonging may in the abstract be androgynous, the content of some selfobject experiences is directly related to gender. Kohut (1984) seems to observe this when he says:

> The girl's rejection of femininity, her feeling of being castrated and inferior, and her intense wish for a penis arise not because the male sex organs are psychobiologically more desirable than the female ones, but because the little girl's selfobjects failed to respond to her with appropriate mirroring, since either no idealizable female parental imago was available to her, or that no alter ego gave her support during the childhood years when a proud feminine self should have established itself [p. 21].

Beyond Kohut's thoughts, there seems to be some agreement that core gender identity, that is, the sense that one is male or female, is established in the first few years of life (Stoller, 1990; Fast, 1984). Lothstein (1988) explored the relationship between selfobject failures and gender-identity disorders. Lothstein observes that gender-identity pathology can be manifested before the consolidation of the nuclear self, which leads to a hypothesis that the early organization of self-experience must involve a male or female imprint. In other words, the primary caretaker's self-images of the baby become the baby's self-images, and thus Lothstein agrees with Lang that "an awareness of one's gender [ought to] occupy a central place in one's sense of self." We might even raise the question as to whether there is, at least subjectively speaking, a "genderless" sense of the self. The point is that an experience of gender is in the mix *before* the consolidation of a nuclear self.

It is important to note that gender identity entails at least two dimensions: 1) the sociocultural role definitions and valuations of gender, and 2) the subjective meaning of gender to the self. Lang challenges the assumption that gender roles are so compatible with inner (psychobiological) agendas that parental and cultural transmission will not constitute empathic failures. Here, Kohut (1987) tends to minimize the influence of culture: "In the use of the body, there is no question that the coquettishness of the late oedipal girl is very different from the attitude of the boy. I doubt very much indeed that these are simply reflections of the predominant parental expectations because of the cultural dominance of such expectations" (p. 150).

Lang, however, insists that gender theory must include an account of how sociocultural role definitions get transmitted into psychic structures. [2] In spite of these debates, Lang's argument poses significant implications of self psychology for the development of a feminine or a masculine self. She inquires, "Are there gender-specific differences in the kinds or qualities of selfobject relationships experienced by children?" Specifically, Lang avers that the self is influenced by which qualities are mirrored and which attributes are considered appropriate for idealization. Referring to the conditions for transmuting internalizations, she (1984) makes the following observations:

1. the infant is mirrored according to rules and categories fitting the selfobject's notion of what is gender-appropriate
2. gender-stereotyped external agendas will come from both parents because they are culturally prescribed
3. worthy attributes presented to the child are classified by gender [p. 60].

Self psychology needs a more systematic theoretical development regarding the acquisition of gender, gender differences in the experience of empathic selfobjects, and the role of culture in determining the content of selfobject functions (i.e., what will be mirrored? what is idealizable? and what gender-based qualities must one assume in order to experience belonging?). At this point, however, we might agree with Kohut about the significance of the empathic matrix *and* with Lang about gender-related experiencing of selfobject function.

THE INTERSECTION OF GENDER THEORY AND GOD-IMAGE RESEARCH

If we take seriously the findings of god-image research, and we recognize that religion functions, in part, as an expression of lifelong selfobject needs, then how might we understand the prevalence of male imagery for God in our culture and a generalized resistance to feminine images of the Divine? Lang outlines a powerful sequence of relationships that she claims evolve in typical Western family life—a sequence that has profound implications for the predominantly masculine images of God that

---

[2] The recent discussions (Ornstein, 1991; Fosshage, 1992; Stolorow and Atwood, 1992; Bacal and Newman, 1990) of one-person versus two-person psychologies, and the understandings of the term "selfobject" being restricted only to the experience of a selfobject function or to the actuality of the person or thing providing the experienced function, is especially relevant when Lang suggests "the selfobject relationship is the crucial mediator between external and psychic reality." Whether this appeal to culture steps outside the clinical purview of intrapsychically focused psychoanalysis is debatable and beyond the scope of this chapter.

have been transmitted by official religion and for how men and women have appropriated or rejected these images. Lang's (1984) sequence is as follows:

> *First*, we recognize that the mother (or a female substitute) has been almost exclusively responsible for child care; thus it is she who primarily provides the early mirroring and who serves as the earliest omnipotently idealized figure. She is the all-powerful provider of care, protection, and nourishment.
>
> *Second*, and correspondingly, it is also the mother who is inevitably experienced as the all-powerful destroyer/frustrator of the child's selfobject needs. [Note that Chodorow (1978) postulates that this early experience of helpless dependence on an omnipotent female figure who can "give or take away" underlies a defensive posture, in this society, in which women become devalued, and thus their "omnipotent power" is diminished.]
>
> *Third*, when the father becomes more prominent in the child's selfobject experiences, the child realizes that it is the father who turns out to possess what "society defines as really admirable and powerful." It is of further interest to note that Kohut (1971, 1977, 1984) regularly, though not exclusively, tends to describe disappointment in the adequacy of the mother's mirroring and a turn to the father as the provider of idealizing selfobject needs.
>
> *Fourth*, a young girl quickly learns that certain characteristics (particularly the expression of anger, assertiveness, and competitiveness) are regarded as unfeminine—but that these are the very traits society most values and consistently rewards. The feminine characteristics left to her (e.g., to care for relationships, to be emotionally expressive, to support others) are devalued by society and regarded as indications of weakness, dependence, and immaturity.[3]
>
> *Finally*, both boys and girls must undergo what Lang calls a "rather drastic revision of their former omnipotent idealization of the mother" [p. 66].

This "massive disillusionment" in the mother has serious implications for the subjective meaning of gender and for an individual's subsequent attitudes about masculinity and femininity—and, I propose, about God. Given the basic human need to idealize, and an understanding of god-images providing selfobject functions and being intimately connected with early parental experiences, the resistance to feminine images of

---

[3] Chodorow (1978) addresses the consequences of this gender valuing of certain attributes in her observation that boys will have specific difficulties related to their own desires for intimacy and the social constrictions about expressing those needs in primarily sexual ways.

God in men *and* women may, in part, be due to feelings that the feminine in much human experience is simply not idealizable. Masculine
images seem to be more easily idealized and therefore godlike. This
becomes even more striking when one considers that the act of giving
birth seems perhaps the most godlike and literally creative of human
capacities. From a psychological perspective then, the account in Genesis, roughly speaking, of man giving birth to woman becomes an even
greater curiosity. A defense against a feared merger, engulfment, or loss
of self with the omnipotent mother may be operative for both genders.

To return to the literature of the psychology of religion for a moment,
Vergote and Tamayo (1979) added a further explanation to the prevalence of masculine images of God in their research on the relation
between symbolic parental representations and god-images. After
reviewing a list of maternal and paternal characteristics and the ways in
which they are most typically attributed to God, they concluded that
North American culture has a predominantly paternal view of God. Vergote and Tamayo explain that although persons attributed a variety of
both maternal characteristics (like nurturance and availability) and paternal characteristics (like law and authority) to God, the symbolic representation of God as paternal more easily incorporates the maternal characteristics than vice versa. In other words, it is easier to appropriate a
father-image of God with the characteristics of being nurturant and
available than it is to appropriate a maternal image of God that carries
law and authority. (It is important to note how these paternal and
maternal characteristics may be configured differently in other cultures.)

The disturbance of early selfobject functions in the traumatic loss of a
father or mother, whether through emotional unavailability, divorce, or
death, or through negative selfobject experiences (Gehrie, this volume),
may lead to the need for specific gender preferences in the god-image.
In addition, the tenacity with which these gendered dimensions of God
are held could be understood in terms of the particular selfobject needs
of a feminine or masculine self. For example, does a man need to maintain an idealizable masculine figure in God in order to strengthen and
reassure his own masculine self? Or might the gender of the god-image
serve a certain kind of early mirroring need that was not sufficiently satisfied, leaving self-esteem problems with one's gender? For some, perhaps a same-sex–gendered God is simply more emotionally appealing
on the basis of a particular alter-ego need.

Conversely, how might we understand the preference for an
opposite-sex–gendered image of God? It seems rare that men will
exchange a male god-image for a female image, though some men will
include feminine god-images in a broader understanding of God. It has
already been suggested that the prevalence of masculine images may be

due to a difficulty at both cultural and intrapsychic levels of idealizing the feminine, or a fear of merger. Failed early selfobject experiences with female caretakers could also lead to a compensatory appeal for another chance with a divine female selfobject, or to a more hidden appeal for the maternal dimension in a masculine god-image.

In the case of early disappointing selfobject experiences with male caretakers, women do articulate several reasons for rejecting a masculine god-image: 1) traumatic experiences with men, 2) the need for an idealizable feminine presence, or 3) a compensatory need to redeem a failed selfobject experience with the maternal figure. Why, given these variety of choices, an individual develops a particular preference is the more difficult question.

Of therapeutic interest is the likelihood that shifts in the gender of a patient's god-image may be particularly illustrative of a shift in selfobject needs and the archaic or more developed expressions of these needs, as well as increases or decreases in self-esteem. Some of these shifts may be precipitated indirectly through a psychotherapeutic or psychoanalytic process in which selfobject needs become more directly engaged in the transference and take on a new developmental trajectory.

CONCLUSION

In conclusion, let us return to one of the vignettes at the beginning of the chapter and briefly sketch a few ways in which we might understand the patient's experience of God in terms of gender-related selfobject needs. "Ms. M," who prays to Mother Nature, offers an interesting attempt to meet certain selfobject needs and at the same time protect herself from the emotional pain of other recognitions.

Though she prays to Mother Nature, Ms. M believes in a masculine image of God, a wise, old, distant figure, and consciously recognizes the resemblance to her idealized father. Her father was a quiet man who retreated to his bedroom every night after dinner to listen to classical music and read (he read the Bible regularly). Ms. M experienced his room as a refuge from the otherwise chaotic environment of the home. Though Ms. M understood an open invitation from her father to visit him upstairs, it was always she who took the initiative.

Ms. M regarded her father as an emotional lifeline and thought herself to be his favorite because they seemed to share a similar emotional temperament: quiet, shy, and calm. Given the fact that her mother and father had slept in different bedrooms since the patient was seven, and Ms. M's perception that the marriage was a miserable experience for her father, she developed a sense that it was *her* duty to keep her father happy, so that he would return home from work each night. Calling it an "oedipal victory," as the patient did, we also understood the patient's favored position with the father and the mother's distance as very stimulating to the patient's grandiose self. An intensive therapeutic process uncovered deeper feelings of the father's betrayal in his refusal or inability to protect Ms. M from the mother's emotional abandonment and chaos.

Ms. M's mother was a professional woman who was successful enough in her field, but who was clearly depressed and obese. Ms. M reports the horror and disgust of being exposed to her mother's naked body during her childhood. Her mother depreciated any attempt by women to enhance their appearance and suggested moral failings as a result of such efforts. The mother regarded herself as the superior intelligence in the home and never expected anything but an average performance from Ms. M, explaining that she would grow up, get married, and have babies. The mother allowed only a very narrow range of affective expression and required Ms. M to behave in certain ways so that the mother could prove she was being a good mother. For example, during a bedtime story, she would say, "Shut up, don't interrupt me with questions. I'm being a good mother by reading you a story."

The treatment was intense and lengthy, and dealt with numerous issues including the patient's notion of an oedipal victory with her father, her recognition of disappointment with her father, her continued attempts in adult life to win the oedipal object (fantasied affairs, an actual affair, and marriage to an older man), serious self-esteem disturbances, weight gain and loss, and the development of her own professional competence.

Transference issues focused on Ms. M's experience of me as a good mother, an idealized selfobject who appeared to be a self-possessed, feminine professional. There were also twinship dimensions of a selfobject transference. Ms. M observed similar interests, values, and interpersonal styles between us. Earlier in the treatment, there was a period of time in which she took on a style of dress similar to mine. At times, I was a bad maternal figure, a negative selfobject around whom she had to accommodate herself in order to stay connected. She felt this required maintaining control of her own self-esteem and consequent rage at being "kept down" and unrecognized. Did I believe she could be successful and pretty? Did I hold the secrets to these things, and if so, why would I withhold them? Would I be jealous if she was really competent and attractive? Would I abandon her if she began to feel happier? Did she have to stay overweight in order to be connected? Could she bear the guilt of a more significant separation from her depressed mother?

Mirroring selfobject functions were sought in the celebration of her attempts to define her own feminine style and pursue the deeper wishes of a repressed grandiose self to be regarded as an attractive woman. It was interesting to note that Ms. M responded most intensely to the attention of men in her life and found it difficult to fully utilize the mirroring she felt I offered.

A fuller treatment is not possible in this chapter, but the case does suggest a few thoughts for consideration. Ms. M resolved her need for a feminine figure to idealize by creating a split in the deity, hence her appeal to Mother Nature—perhaps an expression of Kohut's notion of "fuzzy idealism" in the choice of a nature-oriented, less clearly delimited idealized figure as an attempt to deal with the fear of retraumatization. It is clear from her personal history that Ms. M suffered significant disappointments in all three selfobject arenas with her mother. The mother mirrored only what she could tolerate in her daughter and failed to recognize Ms. M's intellectual capacities. Mother forbade expression of sexuality and squelched any attempt on Ms. M's part to dress attractively, failing again to recognize a natural feminine attractiveness in her daughter. Given her attitudes and own physical appearance, the mother could not represent an idealizable female.

The male part of God, for Ms. M, carried wisdom, law, and authority. This was in part an expression of the idealization of the father, who more positively mirrored Ms. M's femininity. The distance she felt in this god-image was a reproduction of the deeper, less obvious failing of the father to rescue Ms. M from her mother and the deeper wish for a feminine figure to serve all three selfobject functions. Mother Nature carried the empathic affective connection and the possibility of feeling good about herself as a woman. It is interesting to note that for Ms. M, women were not quite fully idealizable in that they did not seem easily able to carry the characteristic of wisdom. Perhaps her mother's psychotic dimension precluded a more unified sense of a god-image within one or the other gender. As the treatment progressed, Ms. M continued to feel increasing self-esteem, discovered her own feminine style, and enjoyed a significant level of professional achievement.

Finally, it is not possible to do explanatory justice here to the complexity of the issues raised, the relevance of compensatory structures, or the variety of experienced selfobject needs. Further questions about why some images of God are genderless and nonanthropomorphic, or why god-images may have little significance in some persons' lives must continue to be explored. A recent conversation with a colleague suggests that the emotional appeal of God to some may really be a matter of finally finding a selfobject that can be regulated by the self in terms of need, proximity, and protection against retraumatization.

Only preliminary speculations are offered as to the effects of early selfobject experience on gender identity and the relation of this to the preference for a particular gendered representation of God. However, the theoretical convergences of early selfobject experience on subjective meanings of masculinity and femininity, and on the selfobject functions sought in relation to a god-image, hold promising possibilities for empathic engagement with and understanding of human religious experiences. In *The Restoration of the Self*, Kohut (1977) offered the following observation:

> And nowhere in art have I encountered a more accurately pointed description of man's yearning to achieve the restoration of his self than that contained in three terse sentences in O'Neill's play *The Great God Brown*. These are Brown's words close to the end of his long day's journey into night, after a life torn by uncertainty about the substance of his self: "Man is born broken. He lives by mending. The grace of God is glue" [p. 287].

In our patients' experiences of religion, we often see a struggle of the tragic self to deal with brokenness and the attempt to find ways of mending through grace—whether we define brokenness, mending, and grace religiously or psychologically. In either case, Kohut recognized a fundamental human need to be met graciously and to be known empathically. It therefore behooves those of us with therapeutic ambitions to take seriously the role of inevitably gendered experience and its relation to the variety of selfobject functions that religion provides for some patients in their search for "the glue."

REFERENCES

Bacal, H. & Newman, K. (1990), *Theories of Object Relations*. New York: Columbia University Press.

Chodorow, N. (1978), *The Reproduction of Mothering: Psychoanalysis and the Sociology of Gender*. Berkeley: University of California Press.

Coe, G. A. (1916), *The Psychology of Religion*. Chicago: University of Chicago Press.

—— (1922), *The Spiritual Life*. New York: Abingdon.

Fast, I. (1984), *Gender Identity: A Differential Model*. Hillsdale, NJ: The Analytic Press.

Feuerbach, L. (1841), *The Essence of Christianity*, trans. G. Eliot. New York: Harper, 1957.

Fosshage, J. L. (1991), The selfobject concept: A further discussion of three authors. In: *New Therapeutic Visions: Progress in Self Psychology, Vol. 8*, ed. A. Goldberg. Hillsdale, NJ: The Analytic Press, pp. 229–239.

Freud, S. (1913), Totem and taboo: Some points of agreement between the mental lives of savages and neurotics. *Standard Edition*, 13:1–161. London: Hogarth Press, 1955.

—— (1925), Some psychical consequences of the anatomical distinction between the sexes. *Standard Edition*, 19:243–258. London: Hogarth Press, 1961.

—— (1927), The future of an illusion. *Standard Edition*, 21:1–56. London: Hogarth Press, 1961.

—— (1930), Civilization and its discontents. *Standard Edition*, 21:57–145. London: Hogarth Press, 1961.

—— (1931), Female sexuality. *Standard Edition*, 21:223–243. London: Hogarth Press, 1961.

—— (1933), Femininity. *Standard Edition*, 22:112–135. London: Hogarth Press, 1964.

—— (1939), Moses and monotheism. *Standard Edition*, 23:7–137. London: Hogarth Press, 1964.

James, W. (1902), *The Varieties of Religious Experience*. New York: Longmans, Green.

Jordan, M. (1986), *Taking on the Gods: The Task of the Pastoral Counselor*. Nashville, TN: Abingdon Press.

Kohut, H. (1971), *The Analysis of the Self*. New York: International Universities Press.

—— (1977), *The Restoration of the Self*. New York: International Universities Press.

—— (1978), *The Search for the Self*, Vols. *1 & 2*, ed. P. H. Ornstein. Madison, CT: International Universities Press.

—— (1984), *How Does Analysis Cure?* ed. A. Goldberg & P. Stepansky. Chicago: The University of Chicago Press.

—— (1987), *The Kohut Seminars on Self Psychology and Psychotherapy with Adolescents and Young Adults*, ed. M. Elson. New York: Norton.

—— (1990), *The Search for the Self*, Vols. *3 & 4*, ed. P. H. Ornstein. Madison, CT: International Universities Press.

—— (1994), *The Curve of Life: Correspondence of Heinz Kohut (1923–1981)*, ed. G. Cocks. Chicago: The University of Chicago Press.

Lang, J. (1984), Notes toward a psychology of the feminine self. In: *Kohut's Legacy: Contributions to Self Psychology*, ed. P. E. Stepansky & A. Goldberg. Hillsdale, NJ: The Analytic Press, pp. 51–70.

Leuba, J. H. (1912), *A Psychological Study of Religion*. New York: Macmillan.

—— (1925), *The Psychology of Religious Mysticism*. New York: Harcourt Brace.

Lothstein, L. (1988), Selfobject failure and gender identity. In: *Frontiers in Self Psychology: Progress in Self Psychology*, Vol. 3, ed. A. Goldberg. Hillsdale, NJ: The Analytic Press, pp. 213–236.

Ornstein, P. H. (1978), *The Search for the Self, Vols. 1 & 2*. Madison, CT: International Universities Press.

—— (1990), *The Search for the Self, Vols. 3 & 4*. Madison, CT: International Universities Press.

—— (1991), Why self psychology is not an object relations theory: Clinical and theoretical considerations. In: *The Evolution of Self Psychology: Progress in Self Psychology, Vol. 7*, ed. A. Goldberg. Hillsdale, NJ: The Analytic Press, pp. 17–29.

Rizzuto, A-M. (1979), *The Birth of the Living God: A Psychoanalytic Study*. Chicago: The University of Chicago Press.

Starbuck, E. D. (1899), *The Psychology of Religion*. New York: Scribner's.

Stolorow, R. D. & Atwood, G. E. (1992), *Contexts of Being: The Intersubjective Foundations of Psychological Life*. Hillsdale, NJ: The Analytic Press.

Vergote, A. & Tamayo, A. (1981), *The Parental Figures and the Representation of God: A Psychological and Cross-Cultural Study.* New York: Mouton.
Wolf, E. S. (1988), *Treating the Self: Elements of Clinical Self Psychology.* New York: Guilford.

Chapter 16

The Severed Self: Gender as Trauma

Janice Crawford

Brew us a magic in which all limits dissolve

. . . .

Dissolve with a few drops whatever excludes in the limit
of the ages, which makes our past wisdom a fraud;

. . . .

Don't rest until the boundary that keeps the sexes
in meaningless conflict has disappeared.

> Rainer Maria Rilke
> *The Sonnets to Orpheus*

We see the pain caused by this "meaningless conflict" day after day. Sadly, we are often trained to see this particular pain as either idiosyncratic or somehow inevitable. But we know from our own lives and our own struggles that neither of those approaches reflects the whole truth. Thus we continue to attempt to understand more deeply the "boundary" of which Rilke speaks.

This chapter seeks to question whether in fact the gender system as we have come to construct and maintain it is itself a major source of conflict between the biological sexes and within the self. Does this gender system ultimately obstruct rather than contribute to, at the very least, cohesive self-experience and, at most, aspects of the numinous self-experience Kohut (1966) referred to as "cosmic narcissism"?

Further, is the "magic" we need to brew a magic that allows us the courage and clarity to continually examine our convictions or beliefs about the rightness of the gender ascription system?

Although sex in the biological sense of being male or female is acknowledged, this chapter implicitly questions the meanings and impact of biology on destiny. We do know, for example, that males and females use the brain differently in some functioning, that males are generally physically stronger, and that we are bathed in different hormones. The prevailing school of thought assumes that these and other biological differences are the cause of conflict between the sexes.

This paper assumes that these differences do not in themselves inevitably result in conflict. The use of the word *gender* here acknowledges biologic sex differences but focuses on the sense of gender referred to much as Stoller (1985) defines it, "a psychologic state—masculinity or femininity" (p. 6) and as "a belief—more precisely a dense mass of beliefs, an algebraic sum of ifs, buts and ands—not an incontrovertible fact" (p. 11). Further refining this definition, Butler (1990) suggests that gender is "the cultural meanings that the sexed body assumes" (p. 6). I propose that it is these beliefs and cultural meanings that create most of the conflict. We can begin to understand these beliefs and meanings as conscious and unconscious fantasies of the sexed body derived from complex self—selfobject experience.

As Palombo proposed at the 1993 Self Psychology Conference, owing to "the ferment of the feminist movement," these gender beliefs or, as he calls them, narratives, are beginning to be more carefully examined. Radical critiques of gender, however, often call forth a deep fear of living with less certainty or a fear of loss of privilege, perhaps even a fear of fragmentation. Kaplan (1989) poetically and, I believe, accurately describes this fear as follows:

> The primitive ideals of gender have been with us for so long that we still think of them, even now, as human destiny, as god-given, as nature's way. Some of us are convinced that any challenge to these ideals will offend the Gods, causing earthquakes and tidal waves that will scatter and overrun the planet, destroying every sacred boundary between above and below, good and evil, clean and dirty, male and female (p. 487).

Perhaps offending the gods, and in all probability psychoanalysis, this chapter questions the supposition that the self is naturally gendered, and the concept of "core gender identity" in particular. Although I do not question that a person identifies as "I am girl" or "I am boy," I do question that depth and centrality of the fact of biological sex difference as a major foundational predictor or determinator of human characteristics and behaviors. Here I draw on Kohut (1969), who believed that the concept of identity itself was not a depth-psychology concept and was more related to one's "role and personality" (p. 579).

Although aligned with Stoller in many respects, I believe the self fantasy that results from reinforcement of "core gender identity," and to a large degree "gender identity," mandates what I call the severed self. The severed self is created by rigid enforcement of what is acceptably masculine or feminine. I contend that this leads to an inevitable sense of inadequacy, incompleteness, and basic lack of trust in the self and others. One mistrusts the self because one can never fulfill the pure requirements of what is expected of one in terms of cultural gender expectations and because one is always aware of gender dystonic qualities. It also leads to distrust of the other, partly due to the fact that the other must then be relied upon to supply "complementary" qualities that in fact the other may not either possess or wish to supply. Struggling blindly or in "meaningless conflict" for an experience of wholeness through the other, these gender-traumatized selves may manifest their confusion and pain in expressions of self-hatred, violence, psychic numbness, or rage at the "other" in everyday acts of relational avoidance, resentment, negligence, or overdependence. This conflict is sometimes expressed on a global scale and manifests itself in crimes like female slavery, female genital mutilation, and battery.

Paradoxically, my approach toward healing the gender-severed self involves deepening and extending the notion of gender. It also involves understanding how gendered and hence truncated self fantasies may be functioning in both patient and analyst. Ultimately the effect of applying this understanding of gender reconstructs it in such a way that radically dichotomized fantasies of gender are dissolved. Then aspects of the self less encumbered by gender expectations are permitted to develop.

I will now return to a discussion of what gender is believed to be. The following table lists well-known ideals of masculinity and femininity usually viewed as naturally occurring and immutable:

MASCULINITY	FEMININITY
Active	Passive
Idealizable	Mirroring
Rational	Emotional
Serious	Sweet[1]
Ruled by the mind	Ruled by nature

---

[1]Kohut (1974b) suggested that girls be mirrored for "sweetness, in their bearing of children, in whatever potential of her femininity she displays" (p. 777).

MASCULINITY	FEMININITY
God or Jesus as masculine ideal	Mary as feminine ideal
Penetrating	Receptive
Protective and courageous	In need of protection
Physically strong	Weak or less strong
Dreams of mastery or humiliation	Dreams of danger or rescue
Silent and self-contained	Communicative
Sense of entitlement	Need for approval by the entitled other
Possessor of will/agency	Dependent
Longing for autonomy	Longing for connection
Dominant	Submissive
Sure/Confident	Attractively insecure

These notions of gender imply a radical dichotomy between the masculine and feminine core selves. As becomes apparent from reviewing the preceding ascribed qualities of masculinity and femininity, adult masculinity is significantly defined by what self psychologists might describe as traits consistent with the left side of the vertical split (i.e., archaic or untransformed grandiosity). Kohut (1974b) laid the groundwork for this thesis when he said that "the recognition of the possession of a penis by the little boy will tend to reinforce (and lend a specific content to) the propensity for grandiosity which is also present in every human being, male and female, and will leave a distinctive imprint on the personality of men" (p. 784). Such a view of masculinity mandates a repudiation of feminine-ascribed traits.

Femininity is significantly defined more in terms of qualities described on the right side of the vertical split (i.e., the deflated self). In order to establish self-cohesion the feminine self must merge with a grandiose figure. She does this by providing mirroring functions to male grandiosity.

Further, because of this bifurcation of human qualities males must project the capacity and responsibility for relatedness onto females, and females must project the capacity and responsibility for agency, competency, and protection onto males. Both must then trust in "the other" to provide lost functions (see Brothers, 1995).

It must be noted, of course, that the feminine self or self fantasy also includes dimensions of archaic grandiosity, particularly as manifest in the powerful though sexless "phallic" mother or in the woman who is seen as highly sexual though not motherly. Unlike the masculine-assigned attributes, the archaic grandiosity associated with femininity is based on qualities that are more dependent on approval or appreciation by the idealized male. Thus they are more tentative and easily devalued qualities (e.g., the ability to be a nurturant and self-sacrificing mother, the ability to possess and maintain a perfect, youthful feminine body, and the unlimited capacity to endure pain for love).

It is important to clarify that not only are the qualities listed above not necessarily gender specific but also to clarify that the qualities Kohut described as reflecting "joyful self-realization" are not gender specific. Those qualities are the capacity for humor, the ability to love and work successfully, a sense of continuity of self, the ability to face transience, a firmly cathected system of values, a well-integrated set of ambitions, and a wisdom that includes the capacity for creative expansion beyond old ideals.

Regrettably, in the current binary gender system there is great potential for both males and females to feel a sense of betrayal by the other because of the lack of mirroring of many of these gender-ascribed qualities. Thus one might say there are two gender traumas: first, the trauma of being ascribed only one sector of human capacities, and second, the inevitable betrayal or inadequacy of continuous mirroring from "the opposite" gender. The first of these forms of gender trauma, I contend, is maintained through gender-stereotypical psychological developmental theories and also by unreflective psychoanalytic theory and treatment.

However, despite such acceptance, and even creation, of reified gender ascriptions by psychoanalysis, Kohut laid the foundation for a fuller exploration of the impact of gender on development and on the psychoanalytic dyad. He did this by focusing more on the selfobject function rather than the sex of the early caregiver or analyst who is providing those functions. This occurred despite the fact that Kohut himself was guilty of adhering to and reinforcing stereotypical gender characteristics.[2]

GENDER AS TRAUMA

Ulman and Brothers's (1988) work on fantasy and trauma can contribute to a clearer understanding of gender. It proposes that we see self-experience as structured by unconscious fantasies consisting of affect-laden images of self in relation to selfobjects. These self–selfobject fantasies constitute the basic psychic structure that "forms the subjective frame of reference from which we must understand and interpret the unconscious meaning of all personal experience and conduct" (Ulman, 1988, p. 6). Gender, I believe, is an important dimension of the self—

---

[2]Kegan-Gardiner (1987) suggests that Kohut was "oblivious to gender issues" and "that this may devolve from his association with Freud's views on women, his special sympathies for men and general cultural prejudice" (p. 766).

selfobject fantasies that constitute the self. I conceive of gender as an aspect of self-experience that crystallizes in the self–selfobject matrix of intersubjective experience.

Lang (1984) paved the way for understanding the traumatic nature of these gender fantasies when she stated:

> The empathic failures caused by imposing gender stereotyped external agendas on the child's own are not limited to idiosyncratic response dictated by one parental personality, but—being culturally prescribed—will be more or less consistently presented by both parents and most selfobjects the child encounters. Thus the *traumatic* [emphasis mine] self constrictions must be experienced by the child as a "signal" rather than as incidental trappings [p. 60].

The process by which these stereotypical external gender agendas are internalized also may meet Ulman and Brothers's (1988) criteria of trauma because gender socialization or ascription constitutes "a real occurrence the unconscious meaning of which so shatters central organizing fantasies of self (selfobject fantasies) that self-restitution is impossible" (p. 3). Using some of the most obvious examples, we know for example that expression of sensitive emotionality in young boys is usually met with peer group humiliation, while the expression of a sense of athletic or scholarly competency in girls is often met with humiliation or discouragement.

Further, masculinity, when understood as constructed by untransformed grandiose fantasies, may itself represent a defensive attempt to restore early grandiose fantasies that have been traumatically shattered. Concerning the false or defensively sustained self, Tolpin (1985) reminds us that Kohut believed all unconscious mental activity must be understood as "the self attempting by any and all means to remain as cohesive, as solid, and as far away from disintegration-depletion experiences as possible" (p. 87). As Benjamin's (1988, 1995) work points out, for the male child these disintegration-depletion experiences threaten the self even further because they combine with the patriarchal command that he renounce, create himself as profoundly different from, and ultimately devalue the mother and all things feminine ascribed.[3]

Benjamin (1995) suggests, "The problem . . . then, is not simply that male children disidentify with and then repudiate the mother. It is also

---

[3]Although to my knowledge no self psychologists have proposed anything approaching the general thesis of this chapter, numerous object relationists have begun to analyze gender, critically (for example, Benjamin, 1988, 1993; Harris, 1991; Dimen, 1991; Shapiro, 1993; and Goldner, 1991). Goldner has in fact proposed a gender paradigm in which "normative masculinity with its repudiation of femininity would be viewed as psychically problematic if not eventually diagnosed" (p. 270).

that this repudiation involves the psyche in those projective processes—she is . . .—that intensify the fear of the other's omnipotence as well as the need to retaliate by asserting one's own omnipotence" (p. 86). Benjamin also proposes that the mother has been socialized to be the object of desire versus the subject of her own desire. Therefore, the male child must disassociate from the devalued mother and move toward the valued other.

The male's need for an archaic grandiose fantasy of self is often further intensified by the fact that many fathers are absent, physically or emotionally, and thus unavailable for merger needs. Kaftal (1991) proposes in this regard that because of the "culturally prevalent absence" of solid identificatory ties to adult males, males must "turn inward to find what is missing . . . thus, fantasies of manhood come to be told in the grammar of the heroic" (p. 309).

In terms of the vertical split, femininity is proposed as significantly constructed by adult males as their projected deflated passive self.[4] This thesis does not suggest, however, that females are simply passive victims of male archaic grandiosity. It does imply, however, that there are often violent cultural consequences for females from males' attempts to maintain their fragile omnipotent self—fantasy. Crimes like rape and domestic violence may very well involve males' attempts at defensive self-restoration. I believe that in order to attempt not to succumb to these attempts females must often exert painful, unnecessarily conflictual, and sometimes physically dangerous efforts that are sometimes beyond their ability and resources particularly owing to their training to be mirrors to male grandiosity. More than any other factor, the impact of males' efforts at self-restoration at the expense of women's sense of self may in fact partly define "tragic woman."

MULTIPLE DIMENSIONS OF GENDER FANTASY

Despite these and other threats to true self-cohesion and full self-expression, we know that the human spirit is strong and that the defective self "will mobilize its striving to complete its development" (Kohut, 1984, p. 4). This self emerges if there is a sufficiently supportive selfobject milieu. I have defined three dimensions of gender fantasy that I believe have clinical relevance and illustrate how this yearning for wholeness attempts to manifest itself in the therapeutic dyad.

---

[4]Reich (1973) has described these fantasies as "phallic narcissism" in her paper "Pathological Forms of Self Esteem." She sees this as a pathology specific to men. I view the same phenomenon as defining of masculinity.

The first dimension of gender fantasy I refer to as the *performance dimension*.[5] This most manifest level addresses social behaviors like mannerisms, speech, dress, language, posture, style, and courting behaviors (although not necessarily true sexual object choice). Gender performance may or may not be consistent with one's biological sex, but in most cases is relatively consistent with cultural expectations for that sex. In this sense the person is attempting to receive approval and appreciation from the culture as a whole (as serving mirroring selfobject functions.)

The second dimension, which I call the *selfobject dimension* and which I believe to be the most determinative dimension of actual self-experience, is usually unconscious or semiconscious. It is at this level that we find gendered psychological characteristics, some of which are referred to in our list. It is the dimensions within which the child identifies with parent who provides the most reliable mirroring, idealizing, and/or twinship selfobject experience. The child may become like that parent or be compliant with what that parent needs. This parent may or may not be the idealized parent, who may be too distant or forbidding to identify with. The gender identification of this parent, which is not necessarily the biological sex of the parent, then becomes determinitive of the masculine- or feminine-ascribed qualities and gender fantasies adopted by the child. In other words, gender identification is more related to who attends to the child best and fulfills his or her needs than to biological determination.

This dimension most reflects Atwood and Stolorow's (1984) prereflective unconscious. Here personal reality is shaped by unconscious "invariant organizing principles." According to them, it is possible, through careful analytic investigation, for these "structural invariants" to be transformed. The identification at this level may or may not be consistent with one's biological sex or with the parent of the same sex.

The third dimension of gender fantasy is the compensatory *restorative dimension*, which might also be seen as the realm of the unexpressed self and the location of the individual's efforts to transcend the confinements of binary gender. "Compensatory" here refers to Kohut's (1977) concept of structures that "compensate for the defect . . . bringing about a functional rehabilitation of the self by making up for the weakness in one pole of the self through the strengthening of the other pole" (p. 3). In this dimension gender fantasies contain qualities in opposition to those ascribed in the second dimension. These are the qualities that, when adequate mirroring and idealization have occurred, can be

---

[5]I am indebted to Butler for her analysis of performative gender. My analysis differs in that Butler focuses significantly less on the identificatory implications of gender.

transmuted and can move one toward greater integration. When expression of this third dimension is blocked or unmirrored, more defensive aspects of the selfobject dimension of gender are rigidified.

It is very important to note here that these dimensions are not absolute or mutually exclusive. Moreover, even though this is a complex system, actual self-experience is even more complex and multidetermined. For example, there may be selfobject functions served by one parent in one area of behavior or experience and other selfobject functions served by the other parent. One may also be influenced by a combination of parental influences. However, I believe there are important overarching tendencies and areas of influence that these dimensions of gender fantasy begin to describe. Recognition of the particularity of these fantasies in each patient, the resulting different selfobject transferences, and the gender agendas of the analyst and analysand, whether complementary and compensatory or conflictual, become valuable clinical tools in working through intersubjective gender-agenda conjunctions or disjunctions. Disjunctions involve situations in which both the analyst and patient have defensive gender agendas wherein the analyst may be unconsciously reluctant to recognize what needs to be analyzed, or may be reluctant or unable to the serve the selfobject functions required by the analysand because they threaten the analyst's own agenda.

TREATMENT OF GENDER

Gender considerations are among the most significant determinants of which selfobject transferences will develop and how they will unfold. Therefore a deeper understanding of these complex phenomena is essential for treatment. The analyst's gender agenda (conscious or unconscious) for the patient creates a selective empathic response that profoundly influences the outcome of each case.

An understanding of gender fantasies gives us a new way of listening, a greater clarity about the intersubjective field and the selfobject functions we are serving, and a new way of understanding inevitable gender-related derailments of treatment. What, for example, is the patient's gender fantasy configuration in terms of the dimensions described? What are the meanings of those fantasies to the patient?[6] How does the patient experience the analyst's gender in all those dimensions? How does the analyst experience his or her own gender fantasies? What is the analyst's gender agenda for herself or himself and for her or his

---

[6]Ulman and Brothers would urge the analyst to reconstruct and work through the unconscious meanings of the psychic trauma (read gender fantasies) to restore central organizing fantasies. I would add that expanded central organizing fantasies would then be consolidated.

patient? Are analysands complying on any of these dimensions? Are gender-agenda conflicts a significant dimension of the transference/countertransference neurosis (Ulman and Stolorow, 1985)? Finally, are psychoanalysts serving the culture-maintaining function of consciously or unconsciously programming what "natural gender laws" will be transmuted by the patient?

Because of socialization it would appear obvious that most feminine-identified analysts need to work toward examining and more consciously expanding their own gender fantasies to include therapeutically useful aspects of traditionally masculine-ascribed qualities. By doing so they can work against foreclosing the possibility of potentially serving more traditionally idealizable "masculine" functions and more traditionally "feminine" mirroring functions. The reverse is of course true for masculine-identified analysts. In other words, whatever the analyst's identification on the second dimension of gender fantasy, the analyst may need to work on expanding his or her own unexplored gender-based limitations in terms of the selfobject functions she or he is likely to elicit from or hold out to the patient.

In the following case I have focused on some of the gender issues discussed previously in order to illuminate some of the questions posed in this chapter.

CASE VIGNETTE

Brigitte is a 54-year-old heterosexual woman with red hair and an artsy style. She had just divorced for a second time when she entered treatment six years ago. Her presenting problems were agoraphobia and severe hypochondriasis, one symptom of which was that she was in constant terror of having a heart attack.

Brigitte is traditionally feminine in appearance; that is to say, on the performance dimension of gender fantasy she is feminine identified. Because of her appearance, mannerisms, and style it took several years to understand that on the selfobject dimension Brigitte is identified with her primarily masculine-identified father. Her restorative dimension of gender fantasy therefore contains primarily feminine-ascribed qualities.

This configuration of gender fantasies resulted from many factors. In her Irish American family her father was idealized despite his obvious alcoholism, womanizing, physical abuse of her mother, and eventual career failure. In Brigitte's early childhood he was still considered glamorous in their working-class neighborhood and could function with some success in the world outside the home.

Brigitte's mother, who was seen as a very strong woman in Brigitte's early years, became more and more a victim of her own childhood history of abuse and her husband's physical abuse and pathology. She became agoraphobic by the time Brigitte was six.

Brigitte learned early in life of the dangers of feminine identification and of being female. She was molested by her beloved Uncle Freddie at 6 and by a grocery store clerk at 11. She was also very aware of her father's dangerous incestuous interest in her older sister. Brigitte became the responsible and caretaking child in the sense of playing the role of the husband to her mother (i.e., negotiating the world for her). Eventually she would employ her whole family in her business.

In terms of financial success in the world, twinship with the archaic grandiosity of her father tended to serve her well. However, in terms of overall happiness and health, this identification has been a source of severe emotional pain and deep confusion.

Like the six men Kohut described when he illustrated archaic grandiosity, Brigitte was desperately dependent on mirroring to sustain her hollow, defensively maintained, haughty grandiose fantasies. Her husband had been a more feminine-identified man who was rejected when he began to step outside his primary function as mirror of her archaic grandiosity. Masculine identification severely interfered with her capacity for relatedness in every area of her life. She used her "feminine charms" (performance dimension of gender) to engage men but in no way was she capable of or attracted to some of the more potentially satisfying, traditionally feminine-ascribed qualities like nurturance or focus on relatedness.

With a great deal of pain she said several times, "I was never a mother to my daughter." When we began to explore gender issues, it became evident that Brigitte was semiconsciously aware of her masculine identification. After exploring her fantasies of greatness and brilliance more deeply, she tearfully concluded, "The tragedy of my father's and my life has been that we could never really deeply care about another person."

In terms of my own gender issues, during the earlier years of Brigitte's analysis, both my performance and selfobject dimensions of gender fantasy were more predominantly feminine identified. Therefore, for the first three years of therapy I primarily functioned with relative ease in a traditionally feminine mirroring selfobject role to both Brigitte's compensatory and defensive mirroring selfobject needs. During that time Brigitte says she experienced me as a "good nun."

As some of the earlier nondefensive mirroring needs were met, Brigitte became more strengthened and soothed. Her agoraphobia and hypochondriasis gradually subsided. Through my own growth and as a result of supervision, I began to expand or step outside of my primary role as mirror. No matter how gentle or subtle my efforts, on those occasions Brigitte would become enraged and threaten to leave analysis. At those points the passive aspects of my feminine socialization would reemerge, and I would subtly return to serving mirroring functions to her defensive archaic grandiosity. It became increasingly clear that we were at the risk of being locked in a gender-agenda conflict as part of the countertransference/transference neurosis.

In order for Brigitte to begin to develop what Benjamin calls the "capacity for mutual recognition," I needed to analyze and interpret Brigitte's archaic grandiose self and transference fantasies and reconstruct the meanings of the traumas of gender she had experienced (i.e., feminine role assignment itself, molestations, the threat of incest by virtue of observing her father's sexual attentions to her sister, and her father's physical abuse of her mother). In addition, I also needed to further develop and more fully express my own restorative gender qualities concerning some of the more salutary attributes of the traditional masculine fantasy (e.g., sense of sureness; confidence; and an increased ability to invite, withstand, and, when appropriate, delight in the patient's anger). It was in this way that the stage was set for the more idealizing aspects of selfobject transference to develop. The hope was that this possibility of increased idealization would break the deadlock and ultimately provide Brigitte the safety to begin to further explore her split-off feminine-ascribed potentials.

Despite many disjunctions in which Brigitte, in a rage, experienced me as "too present" (i.e., not mirroring her enough), this transferential shift did occur. More oedipal issues involving competition began to emerge. Additionally during this period, however, Brigitte said that she was more and more coming to experience me as a teacher. She appeared to begin to experience me more as a person with a separate subjectivity.

Brigitte's relationship with her daughter became less characterized by her control and dominance, and a greater mutuality developed between them. She became less subject to narcissistic injury and attack and became increasingly able to tolerate disagreement and criticism in her life outside analysis. She began to entertain the hope that before she died she might be able to experience relationships in which "I don't have to be right, and I can rest back and just be."

The primary selfobject transference (i.e., the demand for mirroring of her defensive grandiosity), occurred at the selfobject dimension of gender fantasy. This eventually gave rise to a deadlock. Had I not become aware of this the treatment might have been seriously compromised.

Also important in this case was the fact that I was not attempting to solidify Brigitte's "feminine core gender identity." Brigitte and I were both attempting to complete and consolidate our self-fantasies to include all potential attributes. In Brigitte's case these happened to be feminine-ascribed qualities. I believe that, in some very complex ways, my shift allowed Brigitte's. The proposal here is that the gender fantasy of the analyst has some significant affect on how the analyst is experienced in gender terms and affects the degree to which the analyst can be experienced as functioning in ways that help the analysand complete her (usually semiconscious or unconscious) compensatory goals.

CONCLUSION

This chapter is an attempt to approach gender assumptions with a faith in the vastness of the possibilities of gender multiplicity and a belief in the transcendence of gender as a singularly determinative aspect of self-experience. It represents an attempt to gain distance from the culture's profound overdetermination of gendered behavior.[7] It proposes, as does Aron (1993), that we do not just "need access to both masculine and feminine qualities . . . but rather we must throw open to question what we might ever mean by either masculine or feminine" (p. 233). Perhaps it will be concluded that we will always need some form of gender identity or identification. However, until we come to understand what is irreducible about being male and female, we must treat the traumas of gender and keep going deeper into our raw human experience.

Kohut (1974a) believed "tragic man" or the man "who is blocked in his attempt to achieve self-realization" (p. 754) was rendered tragic because of the "flawed personalities of selfobjects who were unable to respond to the needs of his self in statu nascendi" (p. 789). However, it may be that "tragic males" and "tragic females" may not be tragic because of the flawed personalities of those serving selfobject functions. The culturally prescribed grandiose and deflated fantasies of masculinity and femininity may interfere with one's capacity to "realize the program laid down in one's depth" (Kohut, 1981, p. 3) rather than facilitate that possibility. This also renders one's capacity to serve as a trustworthy selfobject inevitably and predictably flawed.

The multidimensional model of gender fantasy helps us understand and treat these current configurations of masculinity and femininity. In so doing, the proposed self-psychological treatment of traditional gender fantasies implies an ultimate move toward recognition of the desire for wholeness and of the elements of essential sameness. Perhaps one day

---

[7]Shapiro (1993) states, "Too often I think psychoanalysts' insistence on aiding the culture in maintaining its dichotomous view of gender limits our understanding of our patient's reality. We collude in gender splitting at our own and our patient's peril" (p. 376).

unique qualities of heart will become more important and interesting than assumed implications of sexual difference.

REFERENCES

Aron, L. (1993), *The internalized primal scene. Psychoanal. Dial.*, 5:195–238.
Atwood, G. & Stolorow, R. (1984), *Structures of Subjectivity.* Hillsdale, NJ: The Analytic Press.
Benjamin, J. (1988), *Bonds of Love.* New York: Pantheon Books.
—— (1995), The omnipotent mother: A psychoanalytic study of fantasy and reality. In: *Like Subjects, Love Objects.* New Haven, CT: Yale University Press, pp. 81–113.
Brothers, D. (1995), *Falling Backwards.* New York: Norton.
Butler, J. (1990), *Gender Trouble.* New York: Routledge.
Dimen, M. (1991), Reconstructing difference: Gender splitting and transitional space. *Psychoanal. Dial.*, 1:335–352.
Goldner, V. (1991), Toward a critical relational theory of gender. *Psychoanal. Dial.*, 1:249–272.
Harris, A. (1991), Gender as contradiction. *Psychoanal. Dial.*, 1:197–224.
Kaftal, E. (1991), On intimacy between men. *Psychoanal. Dial.*, 1:305–329.
Kaplan, L. (1989), *Feminine Perversions.* New York: Doubleday.
Kegan-Gardiner, J. (1987), Self psychology as feminist theory. *Signs*, 12:721–780.
Kohut, H. (1966), Forms and transformations of narcissism. In: *The Search for the Self, Vol. 2,* ed. P. Ornstein. New York: International Universities Press, 1978, pp. 427–460.
—— (1969), Discussion: Levin. In: *The Search for the Self, Vol. 2,* ed. P. Ornstein. New York: International Universities Press, 1978, pp. 577–588.
—— (1974a), Formation of the self. In: *The Search for the Self, Vol. 2,* ed. P. Ornstein. New York: International Universities Press, 1978, pp. 737–770.
—— (1974b), The self in history. In: *The Search for the Self, Vol. 2,* ed. P. Ornstein. New York: International Universities Press, 1978, pp. 771–782.
—— (1975), On female sexuality. In: *The Search for the Self, Vol. 2,* ed. P. Ornstein. New York: International Universities Press, 1978, pp. 783–792.
—— (1977), *The Restoration of the Self.* New York: International Universities Press.
—— (1984), *How Does Analysis Cure?* ed. A. Goldberg & P. Stepansky. Chicago: University of Chicago Press.
Lang, J. (1984), Notes toward a psychology of women. In: *Kohut's Legacy,* ed. P. Stepansky. Hillsdale, NJ: The Analytic Press.
Palombo, J. (1993), Comments on a self-psychological view of gender. Paper presented at the 16th Annual Self Psychology Conference, Toronto, October 30.
Reich, A. (1973), Pathological forms of self-esteem regulation. In: *Psychoanalytic Contributions.* New York: International Universities Press, pp. 215–232.
Rilke, R. M., *The Sonnets of Orpheus.* Boston, MA: Shambhala, 1993.
Shapiro, S. (1993), Gender-role stereotypes and clinical process: Commentary on papers by Gruenthal and Hirsch. *Psychoanal. Dial.*, 3:371–378.
Stoller, R. (1985), *Presentations of Gender.* New Haven, CT: Yale University Press.
Stolorow, R. Brandchaft, B. & Atwood, G. (1987), *Psychoanalytic Treatment: An Intersubjective Approach.* Hillsdale, NJ: The Analytic Press.

Tolpin, P. (1985), The primacy of the preservation of self. In: *Progress in Self Psychology, Vol. 1,* ed. A. Goldberg. New York: Guilford, pp. 83–87.

Ulman, R. (1988), The Achilles complex: A self-psychological analysis of the warrior hero fantasy. Unpublished paper presented at the SASP/TRISP Annual Conference, New York, May 21.

—— & Brothers, D. (1988), *The Shattered Self.* Hillsdale, NJ: The Analytic Press.

—— & Stolorow, R. D. (1985), The transference-countertransference neurosis in psychoanalysis: An intersubjective viewpoint. *Bull. Menn. Clin.,* 49:37–51.

Chapter 17

Self Psychology:
A Feminist
Re-Visioning

Susann Pangerl

From an ego-psychological perspective it can be seen how women will form their personal identities from the same identity mechanisms as those of men but by interacting with a cultural environment which denies them, as women, the imaginary models that nurture competence, genius, and transcendence.

—Marissa Zavalloni

A FEMINIST PRELUDE

How to speak of developmental and relational processes in ways that privilege women's experiences is central in feminist writings. Lacking in most of this literature is a dynamic psychological language capable of sharpening the critical edge of the feminist analyses of women's subjectivities and relational experiences. Furthermore, many feminist authors are highly suspicious of the constructive potential of psychoanalytic theory and practice.

Self psychology weathers the feminist critique of psychoanalysis. It offers the weight of an experientially based theory in which to situate the feminist concerns of conceptualizing subjectivity as gendered. Self psychology contains the expansive possibilities of articulating aspects of feminist theory in a language that can be gender sensitive. Self psychology, in collaboration with intersubjectivity theory, has the potential to reclaim the complex and lifelong significance of female relationships without invoking the reductionist fallacy of construing them as narrowly genital or regressive. Notions of self–selfobject relations, intersubjective field, and self needs lend a psychological depth to feminist portrayals of such relations in both their private and public forms. Self psychology, in tandem with intersubjectivity theory, undermines the false dichotomy of the intrapsychic versus the cultural. Together, they provide a conceptual bridge between the cultural-intrapsychic divide, without resorting to some form of reductionism. The collaborative use of self-psychological and intersubjectivity theory presents the possibility of holding in creative tension cultural and intrapsychic realities with a sense of "both/and," rather than requiring a stance of "either/or." The phenomenon of gender is one location in which this conceptual divide can be bridged.[1]

This chapter looks at the gender-related aspects of self psychology specific to females. The conceptualization of the developmental sequence, the consolidation of the self, and the significance of the self-object's gender are of special interest. The major focus will be on disentangling from Kohut's writings those extraneous, patriarchal remnants in order to appreciate more fully the potential contributions of self psychology to the psychological and cultural concerns of feminism.

CULTURAL MYTHOS AS DEVELOPMENTAL MODEL

Kohut's metaphor of Tragic Man mirrors his reliance on certain culturally normative assumptions in the unfolding of a meaningful life. It is the figure of the tragic hero (Shakespeare's Hamlet or the Judeo-Christian story of Jesus), that epitomizes, in mythic form, the realization of the pattern of the nuclear self.

> Both heroes are idealistic and beloved adolescents, . . . *both turn away from their mothers* although their mothers never cease to admire them. . . . [T]heir death coincides with the fulfillment of the deepest pattern of their nuclear selves . . . in both instances seeming defeat is actually a narcissistic triumph. . . . The resurrection and ascension, symbolizing *the full merger with the father ideal*, is the glorified narcissistic triumph which permanently transforms the humiliated, suffering seeker into the God [Strozier, 1985, p. 44; italics added].

This western image of the hero is paradigmatic for Kohut.[2] It is around such a figure that the destiny of a people coalesces, especially in times of crisis. Kohut's (1977) interpretation of the life course of Jesus reflects the general developmental outline of what he presumed as normative: the movement is from selfobject relations of mirroring to those

---

[1] I am indebted to Mark Gehrie and Susan Lazar for their thorough and thoughtful responses to the initial presentation of this paper in 1993. Their insights were most helpful specifically in this volatile area where clinical theory, politics, and values overlap.

[2] Kohut's paradigm of the western hero contrasts with the warrior hero of the epic tradition.

of idealization (pp. 185–186). The selfobject function of mirroring is carried by the mother, whereas the function of idealization is carried by the father, or God as his symbolic substitute. Developmentally, it is a movement out of the mirroring selfobject relation with the mother, a turning away in spite of her continued admiration, into an idealizing selfobject relation with the father. Relocated from the global level of myth into the technical level of clinical theory, the expectable developmental sequence is linked to a differential functioning of the early, caretaking selfobjects in which the maternal figure is linked with early mirroring and merging experiences of the child. The mirroring function is consistently associated with the maternal function as the sequentially prior developmental stage. Kohut does not argue for the necessarily differential functioning of early selfobject relations. Rather, he presumes this as a given. The connection between the gender of the caretakers and the provision of selfobject functions is an ever-present, but largely invisible theoretical assumption (Kohut, 1977, pp. 185–186).[3]

The development of a stable, well-differentiated psychic structure in which the internalization of adequate values and ideals has taken place is not contingent upon the presence or absence of certain parental actions. The healthy outcome of this process is deeply dependent on the personalities of the parents in their capacity to respond to the developing needs of the child. Within Kohut's writings, there are two versions of the father's role. One version suggests that in the maturation of the self there are two chances. In other words, "A failure experienced at the first way station can be remedied by a success at the second" (Kohut, 1977, p. 186). The selfobject response of one parent can offset the dysfunctional response or personality of the other. In the second version, the father's function is analogous to that described in classical theory. He serves to rescue the son (or daughter) from enmeshment with the mother: "If he is able to let himself be idealized by the child . . . then the child may turn toward his wholesome influence, form a team with him against the mother, and escape relatively unscathed" (Kohut, 1971, p. 66). In this second version, the personality of the mother bears a particular burden when the genetic locus of psychopathology is discussed.

Kohut's references to the maternal and the mother fall into two categories. They reflect, on one hand, the maternal as the biological mother or her female substitute. On the other hand, they signify an intrapsychic focus, the functional essence implied within the term of mothering. In this broader definition, it is the psychological substance, the complexity of the experience of receiving mothering that is of concern: the

---

[3] For other references to this sequential move from mirroring (mother) to idealizing (father), see Kohut, 1971, pp. 186, 248.

empathic responsive matrix. This second understanding suggests Kohut's emphasis on psychic function without its conflation with gender or biology. Although the vignettes used by Kohut inadvertently reenforce the cultural link between women and caretaking, he sought to demonstrate the substitutability of selfobjects and to underline his point that he was not talking about biological mothers per se (Kohut, 1985b, p. 167).

Ideals, especially as they are publicly imagined, are construed in culturally masculine terms (Goldberg, 1988, pp. 195–209). The paternal figure is the carrier of the culturally valued ideals, the selfobject link between the dyadic world of mother–child and the larger world (see, for example, Kohut, 1978b, p. 484). Kohut does not argue for a necessary link between ideals, the paternal, and culture. He continues certain assumptions that link things "masculine" as embodying that which is idealizable within the public dimensions of culture.[4] This bias privileges the values of work as primarily the domain of men in western, late twentieth century technological society. The psychic function of the father is as ideal, and that of being available for idealization. In the normative developmental sequence presented, it is a conceptual rarity that the mother might serve this function. Whereas Kohut notes the significance for the child's developing self of the mother's failure to idealize the father, the failure of the reverse is not discussed.[5]

Kohut (1977) was guarded concerning the question of the lack of idealized women within the public sphere of culture (pp. 224–231). He eschewed the biological explanation of Freud, alluding to the impact of selfobject relations that are inadequately responsive to the developing female child. His brief discussion links the content of the idealization of the female to her potential reproductive and mothering capacities. This conceptual collapsing of what it is to be a woman with the potential to be a mother conflates one description of a specific content of feminine identity with a presumption of it as culturally normative.[6] The aspirations of women to participate in the public arena are not elaborated. Motherhood as *the* content of feminine identity is an overly narrow and constricted understanding of women's psychological reality; it is the historical remnant of another time.

---

[4] The phenomenon of "professional women" in the public sphere remains a theoretical anomaly not easily contained within the existing theoretical structures of self psychology.

[5] See Kohut 1984, p. 151, for a discussion of the recovery of the *need* for the idealizable father. See also Kohut 1977, p. 6.

[6] See Gaines 1982 for an analysis of the ironic constriction of female subjectivity to the readiness for motherhood even as it is forsaken.

ANDROGYNOUS SELF: GENDERED OR GENERIC?

Initially, the structure of the nuclear self is construed as androgynous, and the developmental process for male and female children is construed as symmetrical (Kohut, 1977, pp. 224–231). Kohut maintained that the outlines of the self and its developmental needs were, in theory, without gender distinction. It is as content of the self that these qualifiers of self-experience (e.g., gender identity and sexual identity) become relevant. In Kohut, the contents of the self are presented as secondary phenomena. Whether such contents of the self are so inextricably interwoven into the formative coalescing of the nuclear self that to speak of the self as abstract and neutral is *only conceptually* possible and not a factual reality remains undecided. In other words, are the contours of a gendered-self and a nuclear self conceptual distinctions not possible to maintain in the lives of actual human beings?

What Kohut argued was that a gender-neutral or generic model of the self was, in fact, premised on a gendered version of the self.[7] Lang (1984, pp. 51–69) and Lachmann (1988, pp. 195–209) convincingly argue that remnants of a masculine model underlie this ostensibly androgynous self. The need to address the gender-specific aspects of development lead away from an androgynous model. Kohut's evolving view of the female child's negotiation of the oedipal phase initiates this revision. While continuing to emphasize the symmetry of selfobject developmental needs, he postulated that, for the female child, the sequential needs of mirroring and idealization are directed toward the same-sex parent. This reformulation stands in striking contrast to his earlier understanding, which assumed a shift from female to male parent in the developmental movement from mirroring to idealization needs. Herewith the differential need of the female child toward the female parent is introduced into the theory. This developmental difference in the consolidation of a girl's sense of self places enormous significance on the mother-daughter relationship, the full complexity of which has not yet been articulated. It is not just the preoedipal period in which the mother is of importance for the girl's sense of self as gendered. In her responsiveness to the girl's selfobject needs rests the potential of being *like,* and being valued as like, the mother. For the female child, the same-sex parent is crucial in the developmental consolidation of the young girl's feminine self. To experience oneself as female and feminine is to experience oneself in meaningful continuity with the mother, as

---

[7] Kohut tacitly acknowledged the underlying masculine model in his discussion of the shift in the content of ideals and values in the female self in a less patriarchal culture (see Kohut, 1977, p. 232).

subject, in her self-expressive functions. This understanding of self is deeply rooted in the experience of connection through similarity.[8]

The cultural absence of idealizable women ceases to be a question of abstract historical significance. It becomes an issue of clinical significance in the evolution of a healthy female self. The lens of gender focuses the question of what kind of relational responsiveness is required to sustain one's emotional life. The possibility of the emergence of a healthy sense of the feminine self, inclusive of imaginary models which nurture competence, genius and transcendence, seems greatly diminished without the availability of women to be idealized. The idealization under discussion is one disentangled from the normative presumption of motherhood as the primary self expressive form. The phenomenon of a girl's rejection of femininity is attributed to the failure of appropriate mirroring, since either no idealizable female parental imago was available . . . or that no later ego . . . gave her support (Kohut, 1984, p. 21). Elsewhere Kohut suggests that the narcissistic injuries specific to women grow upon a soil of broader and deeper narcissistic deprivation (Kohut, 1978a, p. 791). This soil seemingly alludes to the cultural and societal factors that contribute to the diminished cultural valuing of women as subjects. The specific ways in which cultural factors such as language and the gendered power dynamics of relationships reenforce the devaluing of women, and things associated with women, remains for contemporary self psychologists to elucidate.

THE GENDER-SELF SYSTEM

The reintroduction of questions of gender and sexuality in the formation of the self test the boundaries and assumptions of self psychology. The developmental aspect of the acquisition of a sense of oneself as masculine or feminine is of particular interest within the simultaneous process of the consolidation of the nuclear self. Lang (1984) summarizes Kohut's position: "[A] properly empathic selfobject milieu will facilitate the unfolding of nature's blueprints, and boys will become masculine and girls feminine without anyone needing to pay specific attention to the matter—beyond . . . the healthy mirroring of parental joy in these developments, and the healthy acceptance of sex-role-related idealizations" (p. 52). The process by which one's sexual orientation is acquired is not a primary focus. Kohut reformulates the classical interpretation of penis envy and the core dynamic of the Oedipus complex. The realization of

---

[8] Arnold Goldberg's discussion of idealization and what is internalized as meaningful illumines aspects of the phenomenon of the cultural devaluing and deidealization of women, specifically as women themselves participate in this process (see Goldberg 1988).

sexual difference is recast in terms of the adequacy of the responsive selfobject milieu. It is the manner in which the parental figures, as self-objects, engage the child through this developmental phase. Sexual difference is not inherently tied to the cultural valuing of the male over the female, although it may be and historically has been. This developmental theory relies on both a naturally unfolding process rooted in biology *and* the interaction with the personalities of the parental figures (whether homogenital or heterogenital). The significance of the oedipal phase is the consolidation of a specific sexual orientation. The interruption of this biologically unfolding process is assumed to be rooted in disturbed self-selfobject relations. In question are the selfobject functions of relationships in their sexual and nonsexual forms.

Certain vulnerable assumptions underlie this formulation of the oedipal phase. First, it relies on the confluence of the biological category of female, the sociocultural category of gender, and the psychological category of feminine. The assumed convergence of some notion of a biological blueprint and the cultural and social prescriptions about gender is continued.[9] Not developed is how the gendered selfobject responses impact the child's internalization of what is experienced as self. Second, Kohut's assumptions about the content of the self for female children, in continuing the western cultural notions of femininity, as grounded in mothering and childbearing unnecessarily constrict the richness of a feminine identity. The wish for a child is understood as rooted in the core ambitions and ideals of the girl's nuclear self as the high point of a development that has its beginnings in the archaic self's urge toward self-expression (Kohut, 1978a, p. 785). The import of this cultural context is ever present as the broader matrix in which the parent–child relationships unfold.

Third, although he acknowledged the social content of gender categories, Kohut continued to assume that these socially defined gender expectations were naturally compatible with the child's inner agenda. For instance, he assumed that the parental and cultural selfobject responses, structured largely according to the gender expectations of the culture, would not be empathically dissonant or distorting for the child. The assumption of a harmonious resonance between the inner agenda of the child and the adequate parental and cultural selfobjects is dubious if the parental figures assume, as congruent for their child, externally determined forms irrespective of that child's self-expressive needs.

Fourth, the tacit content of masculinity and femininity are defined by a heterosexual orientation; the core of femininity proper is linked to a

---

[9] For example, he links the attribute of passivity with femininity and that of activity with masculinity (see Kohut, 1978, p. 785).

heterosexual orientation (Kohut, 1985a, p. 10).[10] One's sense of gender is presumed to lean on sexual orientation. This collapsing of sexual orientation and gender conflates two distinct aspects of self-experience. For Kohut, the pressing question was not that of sexuality as the gateway to maturity, but rather that of what is experienced as having significance and containing the possibilities of meaningful fulfillment. Kohut's refocusing on the mother as crucial in her daughter's developmental consolidation of her femininity is suggestive of an evolving sense of gender that does not lean exclusively on sexual orientation. As self psychology has loosened its ties to the biological determinism of Freud, it is embracing new conceptual territory that allows for the disentangling of aspects of self-identity, such as gender, sexual orientation, and biological anatomy. Possible is a more complex understanding of the selfobject meaning for the individual, in her or his experience of gender and sexuality. Kohut's assessment of health from the perspective of structure and function versus the attainment of a particular stage of sexual organization cautions us to be wary of the implicit cultural biases invoked in the operative criteria of health. Health is pragmatically and experientially assessed rather than abstractly and externally applied. A more expansive understanding of sexual identity, which may require new or redefined terminology, would allow for discreet distinctions between sexual orientation and identity expressed through gender.

INTERSUBJECTIVE ROOTS OF GENDER

If one assumes as discredited the basis of gender difference as innately given to be discredited, the question becomes one of what is the socioculturally and psychobiologically patterned subjective world (Lang, 1984, p. 54) in which women must search for adequate selfobject relations in order to sustain their sense of self, and in which, the consolidation of their nuclear self takes place developmentally. The complexity of gender expectations[11] and the subtle intricacy needed to understand the interface between the acquisition of sexual identity and gender identity[12] become the touchstones from which to analyze the significance of gender. Gender as a static form, conveying an essentialist understanding of personhood, is obsolete. Gender ceases to mean an inherent or

---

[10] Lang (1984) continues this presumption of femininity as defined by heterosexuality, distinguishing a feminine gender identity from that of a lesbian identity.

[11] Included within the complexities surrounding gender expectations is the potential for distortion and empathic failure, due not to gross pathology, but to the devaluing of women in a patriarchal society.

[12] The working assumption is that the structuralization of the nuclear self, inclusive of sexual and gender identity, is mediated through selfobject relations.

inevitable polarity or dichotomy.[13] It is more aptly pursued as the internalization of complex relational realities, in which dichotomy is one possibility. If one takes seriously the structuring potential of self–selfobject relations, gender develops through a complex matrix of primary relational realities. As a social construct, it is open-ended; its meaning is relational and evolving.

The ways in which gender-related attributes have a bearing on the structuralization of the self gains clarity through the constructs of selfobject and intersubjective field. The responses of early selfobjects guide the child's ability to differentiate, modulate, interpret, and give expression to the meaning of its affective experiences. Lothstein links together these affectively tinged, early bodily experiences as the precursors of gender identity and the experience of self-cohesion. Lothstein (1988) extends the selfobject functions of caretakers to the development of one's genital schematization, affect and sense of self" (p. 228). Potentially affected are a range of human experiences, such as feeling states, bodily anatomy (especially the genitals), and other cognitive-affective self-states. One outcome may be that what is unresponded to remains insufficiently developed in the child's emerging self. What is unmirrored in the child remains unavailable, or unreliably available, in the self-structure. What is unmirrored fails to be integrated into the positively toned functions and structure of the self.

Lothstein (1988), following Kohut's developmental schema of the movement from the maternal mirroring function to the paternal availability for idealization, locates the burden for the consolidation of self and the coalescing of gender identity squarely with the personality of the mother, in that the child's early gender images and early gender-self expressions are the creations of the mother-figure (p. 229). Lothstein (1988) places this maternal selfobject empathic failure within the larger construct of parental transferences: "[T]he parental wishes and transferences concerning the sex of the child and the family's expectations and goals for the newborn gender-self structure" (p. 239) are foundational in the structuring of self-experiences.

Lothstein's construct of parental transferences bears a strong resemblance to the construct of intersubjective field (see Atwood and Stolorow, 1984), which provides a more inclusive framework from which to conceptualize a reality as complex as a gender-self system. Rather than limiting the focus to the mother–child dyad, intersubjective field expands the conceptual horizon to include the range of parenting others in their reciprocal, interactive influence upon each other and the child. The use

---

[13] For a detailed discussion, from an object relations perspective, of gender as dichotomous see Benjamin (1988).

of intersubjective field enables the active inclusion of the sociocultural dimension in the psychological process of internalization and the formation of the self. An adequate formulation of the earliest relational beginnings of the self requires an articulation of the reciprocal and interactive relationships in which the child is situated—a context that is minimally a tripartite set of relationships.[14] The developing structure of the female self is given form by its immersion in the complex relational dynamics of its parenting figures. What is experienced as meaningful, as holding the possibility of idealization, must be interpreted through the interactive web of these early relational experiences. What is often, in a patriarchal culture, experienced as available for idealization, and therefore experienced as meaningful, is linked to the masculine gender.

The functional significance of the selfobject relations to maintain the structural cohesion, temporal stability, and positive affective coloring of the self (Stolorow and Lachmann, 1980, p. 10) is the motivational force behind the maintenance of self–selfobject relations. In a still largely patriarchal society, the factor of sexual difference, whether a child is responded to as a boy or girl,[15] increases the likelihood of empathic distortions in the self–selfobject relations. Lang suggests that the effects of such empathic distortions can be predictably identified in terms of the conscious and unconscious gender-based constrictions of the mirroring and idealizing selfobjects. The constrictions alluded to are both those external expressions resident within the cultural milieu *and* the internalized versions we each carry as part and parcel of our self-structure: attitudes and ways of experiencing so much a part of our sinew as not to be a focus of critical reflection.

Within the contemporary context, sexual difference influences the structuralization of the self and shapes the content of the self. It is not sexual difference as innate, but its significance in structuring the responsivity of the caregivers that is influential. The consequences of such empathic failures eventuate in the consolidation of the core self, particularly in terms of unresponded to and disavowed parts of the nuclear self and its inner agenda (Lang, 1984, p. 60). In other words, the self remains insufficiently structured, and therefore heavily dependent on the presence of archaic selfobjects for the maintenance of stability and cohesion.

The empathic failure of self-selfobject relations is equivalent to the premature separation of the emerging self of the child from the life-sus-

---

[14] This construction assumes some version of the nuclear family.

[15] This extends from before birth (the use of current medical technology to abort female fetuses, the clothing of newborns in gender-specific colors, or the culturally condoned killing of female newborns in China) until the end of life.

taining selfobjects, whether this separation is physical or psychological. The danger to the insufficiently structured self is the threat of disintegration, of ceasing to be. The risk is posed by the violation of the established and selfobject-sanctioned boundaries of the incomplete structure, with its necessary enmeshment with archaic selfobjects (Lang, 1984, p. 61). To experience attributes culturally defined as not feminine (e.g., sexually or physically aggressive, competitive, or intellectual) is to experience the threat of disintegration. Such attributes need to be disowned in order to maintain one's necessary archaic self-selfobject relations. To experience such an attribute is to risk endangering your self, repudiating some idealized selfobjects, and risking the loss of other mirroring selfobject relationships" (Lang, 1984, p. 62). The selfobject functions in this formulation are needs of the developing self.

In a society in which gender differentiation is premised on a model of dichotomy, in which there continues to be the cultural valuing of things masculine over things feminine, and in which certain social roles and realities are defined by gender, the specifics of this process can be expected to vary in gender-consistent ways. Elaborating on the normative developmental sequence implied for females, given this context, Lang (1984) suggests that women should be able to more easily retain the "*undisturbed and secure sense of having a feminine self*, but the development of that pole of her nuclear self which is organized around ideals and values may be severely derailed, even arrested, or at least disavowed" (p. 67; italics added).

This version of a feminine self is what radical feminists refer to as man-made femininity. The conflictual nature of this version of femininity as developed within parental relationships unempathic to the developing child's assertiveness *belies* Lang's claim of this being an undisturbed and secure sense of self. First, there is the potential for profound tension in the mother–daughter relationship precisely around the conflicted notions of what feminine is. This tension is glaringly reflected in the generational polemics between traditional women (feminine as epitomized in the classical analytic description) and feminist claims for a "feminist identity." [16] Such polemics highlight the tensive, potentially conflictual connections between one's sense of self and the normative role of social and cultural definitions. Second, Kohut's reformulation of the developmental process for girls, as needing the mother, both in her function of mirroring and as available for idealization, taken in conjunction with Lang's formulation of the propensity for the nonrealized self of female children to continue

---

[16] Recall the positioning of the wives of the presidential candidates in the 1992 American presidential campaign.

disavowal of nonself attributes, underscores the heightened potential empathic distortion in parental selfobject functions.

For the girl, a developmental phase of hostility toward the mother, conceptually coinciding with the developmental move from mother to father, is presumed. Chodorow (1978) understands this as a defensive move; hence the separation can be considered premature, rather than a naturally unfolding developmental process. The selfobject significance of this hostility is equivalent to the traumatic disillusionment in the idealization of the maternal figure. An interpretation as to why this occurs requires the inclusion of the broader cultural context replicated consciously and unconsciously within the intersubjective fields of the parental selfobjects, namely, the child's growing realization of the father figure as possessing what is socially defined as desirable and powerful. For the girl, these attributes are linked with a gender that is not hers; left to her are the gender attributes not culturally valued (see Schulz, 1975, pp. 64–75). One thinks of the phrase women's work as something eschewed by men and women. The early idealization of the mother (understood in the context of mother as sole caretaker) is subject to traumatic disappointment, thus hampering the process of transmuting internalization.

At issue is the disruption of the idealization of the mother as archaic selfobject; although her function as a soure of mirroring may still be available, her availability for idealization (of what is culturally valued) is disrupted. Raymond (1986), a feminist ethicist, describes the young girl's acquisition of femininity, within a patriarchal context, as the acquisition of a false self. It is the development of a self-identity rooted in a sense of inferiority and self-contempt. This construction of femininity is marked by the turning away from her own sex, in the person of the mother, obscuring the deep connection between them. Thus the acquisition of femininity, in classical terms, is a process of psychic dislocation; the creation of a sense of self as male-centered. It is a sense of self premised on hostility and the absence of positive relationships with other women—of which the mother-daughter relationship is paradigmatic. The feminine (as traditionally defined) woman's self-esteem is conditioned by this sense of isolation and hostility toward the other most like herself. Raymond describes one cultural variation of the distortions of mother–daughter relationships as resulting in unmentored daughters. Self-psychologically speaking, these are mother–daughter relationships that are prematurely ruptured.[17] One recalls the Greek myth of Demeter and Persephone, a myth often used to illustrate the normative move of the

---

[17] Raymond's analysis of the external and internalized cultural dynamics that contort mother-daughter relationships defies easy summation.

young girl from mother to father/male. Another reading suggests the experience of forced or premature disruption. The crucial loss is of the bond between mothers and daughters. In feminist literature, this bond is experienced as the wellspring of self-acceptance and the ability to tolerate the solitude of creativity. The essence of this bonding eventuates in mutual recognition, the seeing clearly and holding well the uniqueness of each other.

Basch (1988) describes, in more psychologically precise language, the experiential consequences of such disruptions in the development of the female child: "[There is] a warding off of memories that rightfully involved the self through the creation of an affective blockade in response to a selfobject failure of traumatic intensity; that makes mobilization of affect appear potentially disorganizing or even fragmenting. Kohut called this the vertical split, the patient presenting a false self to consciousness and to the world, always vulnerable and in danger of having the earlier self and its affective needs intruding and disturbing the pathological balance that had been achieved" (p. 148). The denial of memory is the denial of needs unmet. At first glance, the construal of a false self seems to imply stasis, as if there is some separate entity called a true self buried within or behind the defensive facade of the false self. It is more accurate to think of the false self as a dynamic process by which the unmet needs, are experienced as dangerous. These unmet needs are kept at bay—out of awareness.[18]

The self-psychological contention that premature separation is the causative factor in the incomplete structuring of the self gives one pause when one reflects on contemporary American culture, in which relationships among women are often denied and discouraged. Furthermore, the constrictiveness of our conceptual language fails to adequately describe the richness of these relationships. Intersubjective and self-psychological languages detail and nuance with greater precision the contours of subjectivity as deeply relational. This relationality conceptually includes not only the immediate context of family, but the cultural reflections of what counts as male and female, feminine and masculine, within a particular historical era. If we choose to see and hear, our conceptual language can hold as well the echoes and reflections of the cultural and historical locations in which human subjectivity responsively evolves. Still awaiting our descriptions are the multitudinous variations in the relationships between and among women.

---

[18] This traumatic disruption, the massive deidealization of the mother, has differential consequences for the male and female child. The exploration of this phenomenon exceeds the limits of this chapter.

REFERENCES

Atwood, G. E. & Stolorow, R. D. (1984), *Structures of Subjectivity: Explorations in Psychoanalytic Phenomenology*. Hillsdale, NJ: The Analytic Press.

Basch, M. F. (1988), Reflections on self psychology and the psychoses. In: *Frontiers in Self Psychology: Progress in Self Psychology, Vol. 3*, ed. A. Goldberg. Hillsdale, NJ: The Analytic Press.

Benjamin, J. (1988), *The Bonds of Love*. New York: Pantheon Books.

Chodorow, N. (1978), *The Reproduction of Mothering*. Berkeley: University of California Press.

Gaines, A. (1982), *Apples and Ashes*. Missoula: Scholars Press.

Goldberg, A. (1988), *A Fresh Look at Psychoanalysis: The View from Self Psychology*. Hillsdale, NJ: The Analytic Press.

Kohut, H. (1971), *The Analysis of the Self*. New York: International Universities Press.

—— (1977), *The Restoration of the Self*. New York: International Universities Press.

—— (1978a), A note on female sexuality. In: *The Search for the Self: Selected Writings of Heinz Kohut: 1950–1978, Vol. 2*, ed. P. H. Ornstein. New York: International Universities Press, pp. 783–792.

—— (1978b), The psychoanalytic treatment of narcissistic personality disorders: Outline of a systematic approach. In: *The Search for the Self: Selected Writings of Heinz Kohut: 1950–1978, Vol. 1*, ed. P. H. Ornstein. New York: International Universities Press, pp. 477–509.

—— (1984), *How Does Analysis Cure?* ed. A. Goldberg & P. Stepansky. Chicago: University of Chicago Press.

—— (1985a), On courage. In: *Self Psychology and the Humanities*, ed. C. B. Strozier. New York: Norton, pp. 5–50.

—— (1985b), The self in history. In: *Self Psychology and the Humanities*, ed. C. B. Strozier. New York: Norton, pp. 161–170.

Lachmann, F. M. (1988), On ambition and hubris: A case study. In: *Frontiers in Self Psychology: Progress in Self Psychology, Vol. 3*, ed. A. Goldberg. Hillsdale, NJ: The Analytic Press, pp. 195–209.

Lang, J. (1984), Notes toward a psychology of the feminine self. In: *Kohut's Legacy: Contributions to Self Psychology*, ed. P. Stepansky & A. Goldberg. Hillsdale, NJ: The Analytic Press, pp. 51–69.

Lothstein, L. (1988), Selfobject failure and gender identity. In: *Frontiers in Self Psychology: Progress in Self Psychology, Vol. 3*, ed. A. Goldberg. Hillsdale, NJ: The Analytic Press, pp. 213–235.

Raymond, J. (1986), *A Passion For Friends*. Boston: Beacon Press.

Schulz, M. (1975), The semantic derogation of women. In: *Language and Sex*, ed. B. Thorne & N. Henley. Rowley, MA: Newbury Press, pp. 64–75.

Stolorow, R. D. & Lachmann, F. M. (1980), *Psychoanalysis of Developmental Arrests*. New York: International Universities Press.

Strozier, C. B., ed. (1985), *Self Psychology and the Humanities*. New York: Norton.

Author Index

Subject Index

A

Abstinence. *See under* technique
Adversarial selfobject needs, xv
Affect attunement/differentiation disorders, 50
Affect regulation disorders, 50
Affirmation, needs for, 111
Ally–antagonist selfobject needs, xv
Analysts. *See* therapists
Analyzability, therapist–patient match and, 61
Androgynous self, 289
Assertive-exploratory mode, 48
Attention-deficit hyperactivity disorder, 223–248
  medication and, 239
  psychodynamic effects of, 230–232, 240, 245
Autonomy, impossibility of complete, 81

B

Bipolar self. *See* self, bipolar
Borderline patients, treatment of, 15
  optimal frustration in, 6–14
  shift to narcissistic personality, 15

C

Case material
  affective estrangement, 213–217
  attention-deficit hyperactivity disorder, 233–238
  borderline patient, 6–14
  child therapy, 183–206
  emotional deadening, 213–217
  empathic focus in face of rage, 6–13
  gender issues, 278–281
  intersubjective disjunction, 141–157
  masculine *vs.* feminine God-images, 263–265
  optimal frustration, 6–13
  parental loss in childhood, 213–217
  pathological self-regulation, 126–138
  self- and mutual regulation in establishing selfobject relation, 126–138
  technique and therapeutic processes, 167–169
  therapeutic role of relatedness, 45
  therapists
    difficulty facing shame, 28–29
    need to supply care, 25–26
    self-awareness, 141–157

Feminism, and self psychology, 285–
286, 291
Feminist theories of self, Kohut and, 80
Frustration, optimal. *See* optimal frustration; therapeutic factors,
frustration

G

Gender
deconstruction and reconstruction of,
270–271, 292–297
ideals of, 271–272
intersubjective roots of, 292–297
Gender attitudes, 273n, 286–289
and idealizable women, 290
cruelty toward women, 271
male self-restoration and, 275
developmental basis of, 261
idealization *vs.* devaluation of women
infantile roots of, 261
Gender fantasy
and countertransference, 277
clinical use of, 277
performance dimension of, 276
restorative dimension of, 276–277
selfobject dimension of, 276
Gender identity, 257–260. *See also*
self, androgynous
development of, 289
God-image research and, 260–263
rigid reinforcement of
and betrayal, 273
and empathic failures, 274
and mistrust of self and other, 271
and severed self, 271
Gender trauma, 271–274
Giving, as most deep and vitalizing
need, 20–21
God-images
determinants of, 253
gender of, 250–251, 260-266
alter-ego/twinship needs and, 256
disillusionment in mother and,
261, 265
resistance to feminine God-image,
261–262
selfobject needs and, 262–263,
265

women's rejection of masculine
God, 263
paternal *vs.* maternal qualities, 262
research on, 251–253
gender identity and, 260–263
Grandiose pole of self, philosophers on,
68–76
Grandiose self, inhibited by moral
demands, 255
Grandiose *vs.* idealized poles. *See*
under self, bipolar

H

Hegel, G. W. F., 74–76
Homophobia. *See* femininity, devaluation of; gender identity, rigid
reinforcement of
Homosexuality. *See* sexual orientation

I

Idealized pole of self, philosophers on,
71–76
Idealized *vs.* grandiose poles. *See under*
self, bipolar
Ideals, 71–73
as masculine, 288
vs. superego, 71
Independence, impossibility of complete,
81
Innate knowledge, 115n
Internalization, without frustration, 5–6
Intersubjective disjunctions
and transference-countertransference
impasse, 141, 156–157
and use of enactments, 142
Intersubjective relatedness, 44, 59
Intersubjectivity, 87–88, 91
empathy and, 93–94
gender and, 292–297
imposition of therapist's reality on
patient and, 101, 109n
patient's *vs.* therapist's view of reality and, 101, 109n
psychotic delusions and, 110
therapeutic use of, 112
vs. therapist's need for affirmation,
111

Religious beliefs. *See* God-images
Repetition, as basis of structure, 41

S

Sartre, J-P., 76
Schizoid regression, 217
Self
  androgynous, 289
  defects in. *See* deficits
  developmental components of, 259
Self psychology. *See also* Kohut, H.
  reformulations of, xiii–xiv
  vs. object relations theory, 77
Self, bipolar (nuclear), 67
  dialectic of grandiose *vs.* idealized
    poles, 67–80
  philosophers on, 68–76
Self- and mutual regulation, 124–126,
    136–138
  pathological, 136
Selfobject countertransference, 18, 20
Selfobject loss. *See* parental loss in
    childhood
Selfobject needs. *See also* male–female
    relations; therapists, selfobject
    needs
  adversarial, xv
  affirmation, 111
  ally–antagonist, xv
  giving as most deep and vitalizing of,
    20–21
Selfobject relations, moribund
    unperishable
  parental loss in childhood and
    regression to, 217
Selfobject relationships
  developmental line of, 260–261
Selfobject transference. *See* transference
Selfobject *vs.* self-other relatedness, 44,
    59
Selfobjects, death of. *See* parental loss
    in childhood
Sexual orientation, and gender identity,
    291–292
Signal disruption in therapist, 21
Socrates, on idealized pole, 68–69, 71–
    73

Sophists, 72, 73
  and grandiose pole, 68–69
Structure
  building of, 163
  empathy *vs.* frustration as basis of,
    38, 40
  from frustration, 57
  repetition as basis of, 41
  role of selfobject transference in,
    42
  satisfaction opens new pathways,
    40
  without frustration, 5–6
  dialogue of construction as, 41
Subjectivity, existential
  evolutionary perspective on, 99–106
  limits of, 97–99
  psychoanalysis and stance of, 108–
    115
  vs. objectivity, 85–90, 94–97
Superego. *See also* moral demands
  as inhibiting grandiosity, 255
  vs. ideals, 71
Supervision groups, and selfobject
    needs, 31
Supervision, from one's training analyst,
    30

T

Technique, 38–43, 47, 58, 177, 217.
    See also therapeutic factors
  abstinence, 42
  criticism of, 42
  vs. optimal restraint, 43, 57
  confrontation *vs.* affirmation, 110–
    111
  empathic focus *vs.* responsiveness,
    92–93
  as self psychological *vs.* object rela-
    tional, 14
  in face of rage, 6
  selfobject transference facilitated
    by, 6
  enactments, responses to, 142
  intersubjectivity and, 112
  motivational systems as guide to, 47
  patient as guide to, 14, 42
  reaching inaccessible patients, 126